THE CITIES BOOK

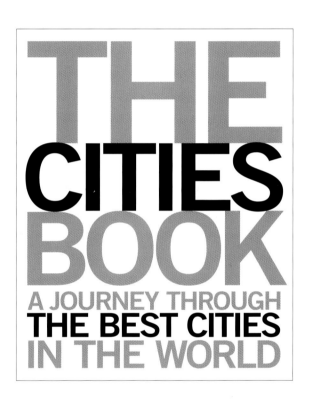

THE CITIES BOOK

A JOURNEY THROUGH THE BEST CITIES IN THE WORLD

MELBOURNE · OAKLAND · LONDON

Best Cities 01-10

001 **Paris** 304

002 **New York City** 296

003 **Sydney** 372

004 **Barcelona** 68

005 **London** 232

006 **Rome** 326

007 **San Francisco** 334

008 **Bangkok** 66

009 **Cape Town** 108

010 **Istanbul** 188

The heart of this book was set beating by our travellers who provided us with the list of 200 cities for inclusion in the book, via a survey we ran on www.lonelyplanet.com asking travellers (and our staff) to nominate their favourite cities.

The top five held no major surprises – Paris, New York, Sydney, Barcelona and London – although a quick glance at the top 25 cities certainly speaks to the adventurous spirit of our travellers. In the top 10 we have Cape Town and Bangkok, and the top 25 features Kathmandu, Buenos Aires and Jerusalem. In the 200 cities selected, we were able to display the great diversity of city life as it is experienced all over the globe: in the classic Western European cities such as Paris; ancient South American cities such as La Paz and Quito; island cities such as Apia in Samoa; trading centres such as Nairobi, hi-tech/futuristic cities such as Hong Kong and Tokyo; and those iconic cities like London, Florence or Rome, where time appears to stand still and accelerate in the same moment. The incredible diversity of day-to-day life explored through these pages challenges our very notion of a consistent 'city lifestyle', and yet something about the energy, pace and commonality of experiences connects these cities.

We don't set too much store by the 'rating' of these cities, but it was interesting to see just how the city standard is set by Paris. There are several other cities in this book that claim the reputation by association: Budapest, as the Paris of Eastern Europe; Beirut, as the Paris of the Middle East; Buenos Aires, as the Paris of the South; and Melbourne, as the Paris of the southern hemisphere!

TITLE PAGE
CITY LIGHTS
Photographer: Brian Stablyk / Getty Images

RIGHT
GRAND BASSIN IN JARDIN DU LUXEMBOURG
Photographer: Bruce Bi / LPI

PAGE 11
A STANDOUT PARTY ANIMAL REVELS IN THE MASSES AT BERLIN'S LOVE PARADE
Photographer: Guy Moberly / LPI

PAGE 23
THE HELIPAD OF THE EXTRAVAGANT BURJ AL ARAB HOTEL, DUBAI
Photographer: David Cannon / Getty Images

Best Cities 011-200

Page

011	Melbourne	262
012	Hong Kong	184
013	Kathmandu	204
014	Prague	310
015	Vancouver	398
016	Buenos Aires	102
017	Rio de Janeiro	324
018	Berlin	84
019	Jerusalem	194
020	Montréal	280
021	Edinburgh	148
022	Venice	402
023	Hanoi	168
024	Amsterdam	38
025	Singapore	362
026	Tokyo	386
027	Florence	156
028	Dublin	144
029	Mexico City	268
030	Kraków	210
031	Toronto	388
032	Cairo	106
033	Budapest	100
034	Chicago	122
035	Havana	170
036	Madrid	246
037	Munich	286
038	Athens	56
039	New Orleans	294
040	Vienna	404
041	Ho Chi Minh City	178
042	Marrakesh	256

043	Sarajevo	348
044	Seville	356
045	Kyoto	216
046	Las Vegas	222
047	Perth	306
048	Shanghai	358
049	Los Angeles	234
050	Lisbon	226
051	Stockholm	368
052	Kuala Lumpur	212
053	Damascus	134
054	Luang Prabang	236
055	Seattle	352
056	Phnom Penh	308
057	St Petersburg	366
058	Cuzco	130
059	Dubrovnik	146
060	Delhi	138
061	Moscow	282
062	Salvador da Bahia	330
063	Beijing	72
064	Helsinki	174
065	Kolkata	208
066	Santiago de Chile	344
067	Fès	154
068	Auckland	58
069	Manila	252
070	Puerto Vallarta	312
071	Chiang Mai	120
072	Varanasi	400
073	Cartagena	116
074	Zanzibar Town	422

075	Innsbruck	186
076	York	418
077	Mumbai	284
078	Hamburg	166
079	Oaxaca City	300
080	Galway	158
081	Siena	360
082	Esfahan	150
083	Wellington	410
084	Ljubljana	230
085	Seoul	354
086	San Cristóbal de las Casas	332
087	Taipei	374
088	Tallinn	376
089	Lhasa	224
090	Bled	88
091	Hobart	180
092	Jaipur	190
093	Brussels	96
094	La Paz	218
095	Québec City	316
096	Valparaíso	396
097	Naples	292
098	Memphis	264
099	Heidelberg	172
100	Dhaka	140
101	Amman	36
102	Monaco	276
103	Washington DC	408
104	Quito	318
105	Christchurch	124

106	Glasgow	162	138	Montevideo	278	170	San Salvador	338
107	Muscat	288	139	Yangon	412	171	Cardiff	114
108	Panama City	302	140	Arequipa	48	172	Minsk	272
109	Dakar	132	141	Bucharest	98	173	Thimphu	382
110	Bratislava	92	142	Apia	46	174	Khartoum	206
111	San Sebastián	340	143	Belgrade	80	175	Anchorage	40
112	Bern	86	144	Dar es Salaam	136	176	Mecca	260
113	San Juan	336	145	Kyiv	214	177	Aswan	54
114	Aleppo (Halab)	30	146	Bukhara	104	178	Yerevan	414
115	Dubai	142	147	Male'	248	179	Luxembourg City	240
116	Rīga	322	148	Caracas	110	180	Georgetown	160
117	Asmara	52	149	Tirana	384	181	Maputo	254
118	Kabul	198	150	Suva	370	182	Baku	62
119	Bath	70	151	Tbilisi	378	183	Belize City	82
120	Copenhagen	128	152	Agadez	28	184	Essaouira	152
121	Macau	242	153	Ushuaia	392	185	Santo Domingo	346
122	Sofia	364	154	Kampala	202	186	Addis Ababa	26
123	Hoi An	182	155	Bogotá	90	187	Pyongyang	314
124	Marseille	258	156	Bridgetown	94	188	Lahore	220
125	Zagreb	420	157	Ulaanbaatar	390	189	Cayenne	118
126	Manchester	250	158	Abuja	24	190	Almaty	34
127	Antigua	44	159	Christiansted	126	191	Mombasa	274
128	Reykjavík	320	160	San'a	342	192	Valletta	394
129	Yogyakarta	416	161	Livingstone	228	193	Antananarivo	42
130	Carcassonne	112	162	Alexandria	32	194	Miami	270
131	Lübeck	238	163	Belfast	78	195	Bamako	64
132	Tel Aviv	380	164	Savannah	350	196	Saint-Denis	328
133	Hiroshima	176	165	Nuuk	298	197	Granada	164
134	Mendoza	266	166	Jeddah	192	198	Beira	74
135	Nairobi	290	167	Johannesburg	196	199	Madang	244
136	Beirut	76	168	Kairouan	200	200	Ashgabat	50
137	Vilnius	406	169	Austin	60			

Tony's Best
10 Additional Cities

Detroit

VITAL STATISTICS

NAME: DETROIT

NICKNAME: MOTOR CITY

DATE OF BIRTH: 24 JULY 1701; WHEN FRENCH EXPLORER ANTOINE DE LA MOTHE CADILLAC SET UP A FUR-TRADING POST ON THE DETROIT RIVER

HEIGHT: 177M

SIZE: 219 SQ KM

ADDRESS: USA (MAP 1, L9)

POPULATION: 951,000

Detroit is the Motor City, Tamla Motown and home to Henry Ford's Greenfield Village, but it's also the doughnut city, a symbol of urban decay whose centre was abandoned as people moved out to a fringe of rich, thriving suburbs, trying to turn their collective backs on a core that might as well have been nuked. As a child I spent four great years there, back when what must have been half the world's chromium production was rolling down GM, Ford and Chrysler assembly lines, car fins were flying high, and the Detroit Tigers were the hottest baseball team around. It's never going to recover those glory days, but Detroit is still worth a look and Greenfield Village remains a truly fantastic museum, incorporating not only the laboratory where Thomas Edison conducted his pioneering work on electric lighting but also the bicycle shop where the Wright brothers built their first aircraft, quite apart from all the Model T stuff.

Jakarta

VITAL STATISTICS

NAME: JAKARTA

NICKNAME: BIG VILLAGE

DATE OF BIRTH: 22 JUNE 1527; WHEN IT WAS NAMED JAYAKARTA (CITY OF GREAT VICTORY) BY FATAHILLAH, A LEADER FROM A NEIGHBOURING SULTANATE

HEIGHT: 1M

SIZE: 661 SQ KM

ADDRESS: INDONESIA (MAP 1, HH16)

POPULATION: 9.3 MILLION

Indonesia's sprawling capital is yet another city considerably overshadowed, in the popularity stakes, by a smaller and more glamorous sister city, in this case tourist favourite and cultural capital Yogyakarta. Nevertheless, Jakarta is, in its own fashion, a mega-city that works from its teeming freeways to its old Dutch colonial capital, the one-time Batavia now known simply as Kota ('city' in Indonesian). No visit to Jakarta is complete without a stroll past the incredible line-up of brightly painted Makassar schooners (pinisi) in the old port district of Sunda Kelapa, living proof that the age of sail is definitely not finished. The city is also home to an impressive collection of imposing Stalinist-style socialist-era monuments, including the towering column in the centre of Merdeka (Freedom) Sq, popularly known as 'Soekarno's last erection'.

Karachi

VITAL STATISTICS

NAME: KARACHI

NICKNAME: CITY OF LIGHTS

DATE OF BIRTH: 1795; WHEN THE MIRS OF TALPUR CONSTRUCTED A MUD FORT AT MANORA

HEIGHT: 4M

SIZE: 1994 SQ KM

ADDRESS: PAKISTAN (MAP 1, CC12)

POPULATION: 9.3 MILLION

From my first birthday to my fifth this was home and, like any childhood memories, my pictures of Pakistan's troubled port city are rose-tinted: a melange of camels, sailboats, sandy beaches and exotic colours. Way back then Karachi was going through wrenching changes as India and Pakistan tore themselves apart and floods of refugees propelled the city's rocketing growth. To my pleasant surprise, when I returned to Karachi after an absence of 40 years, the city still had some of the charm I remembered. I could still hire a sailing boat and crew, drift out on the harbour and dangle a line over the side to pull up crabs to be cooked on the deck, just as I had done with my father all those years ago.

Mandalay

VITAL STATISTICS

NAME: MANDALAY

NICKNAME: CITY OF GEMS

DATE OF BIRTH: 1857; WHEN IT WAS ESTABLISHED AS A NEW CENTRE FOR THE TEACHING OF BUDDHISM

HEIGHT: 74M

ADDRESS: MYANMAR (MAP 5, J5)

POPULATION: 801,000

Kipling never actually took the 'Road to Mandalay'; the road to Mandalay is really a river, the mighty Ayeyarwady, but this is still the heart and soul of Myanmar. Quite apart from the huge Mandalay Fort (gutted during the closing phases of WWII), there's a host of temples and assorted Buddhist sites around the city. Plus it's the home of street theatre (pwe), and no visit to Mandalay is complete until you've caught a performance by the subversive Moustache Brothers. Nevertheless, it's outside Mandalay where the real surprises lie: the abandoned royal capitals of Inwa (Ava), Amarapura and Sagaing, and the massive Mingun Paya (pagoda), all a short boat ride north up the Ayeyarwady. Further afield there's the British colonial-era hill station of Pyin U Lwin (formerly Maymyo), or you can jump aboard a river ferry and head downriver all the way to the amazing ancient city of Bagan.

Oslo

VITAL STATISTICS

NAME: OSLO

NICKNAME: TIGER CITY

DATE OF BIRTH: AD 1048 (ACCORDING TO THE NORSE SAGAS); HOWEVER, ARCHAEOLOGICAL RESEARCH HAS UNCOVERED CHRISTIAN BURIALS DATING FROM BEFORE AD 1000

HEIGHT: 629M

SIZE: 454 SQ KM

ADDRESS: NORWAY (MAP 3, J2)

POPULATION: 529,000

Cold, conservative and mouth-droppingly expensive, it's hardly surprising that Norway's capital and largest city doesn't feature on the city hit parade. Choose a sunny summer day, however, and Oslo can still charm you with leafy parks, busy cafés and restaurants, plenty of outdoor sculpture (Gustav Vigeland is the big name) and a simply dazzling collection of museums and art galleries. The Viking Ship Museum with its collection of longboats is my favourite, but ship lovers can also visit the Kon-Tiki Museum with Thor Heyerdahl's balsa raft and the polarship Fram, which carried Roald Amundsen down to Antarctica for his epic journey to the South Pole in 1911. Of course, walking out of an Oslo art gallery with a Munch masterpiece under your arm seems to have become a Norwegian tradition.

MOTOR CITY TEST DUMMIES LINE UP FOR THEIR LAST DAY ON THE JOB.
Photographer: Louie Psihoyos / Corbis

BOATS DOCKED AT SUNDA KELAPA, JAKARTA'S PORT.
Photographer: Glenn Beanland / LPI

SELLING CAKES TO KARACHI'S HUNGRY PORT WORKERS.
Photographer: Martin Puddy / Getty

DELICIOUS STEAMED BUNS AWAIT IMMEDIATE CONSUMPTION.
Photographer: Jerry Alexander / LPI

HOLMENKOLLEN, SITE OF THE WORLD'S OLDEST SKI JUMP.
Photographer: Galen Rowell / Corbis

It's easy to love cities like Paris and San Francisco – I've lived for a year in each of them, written guidebooks to them and am a total enthusiast – but there are lots of things to like about cities that don't pop up on anybody's favourites list. Here are 10 cities, in alphabetical order, that didn't make the cut but where I've still managed to leave a piece of my heart.

Tony Wheeler
Cofounder, Lonely Planet

Papeete

VITAL STATISTICS

NAME: PAPEETE

DATE OF BIRTH: 1824; WHEN THE LONDON MISSIONARY SOCIETY (LMS) SETTLED HERE

HEIGHT: 2M

ADDRESS: TAHITI (MAP 1, D18)

POPULATION: 26,000

The capital of Tahiti and French Polynesia has a reputation as an overpriced, shonky Pacific disaster zone, a mere jumping-off point to the much more beautiful (though equally overpriced) attractions of neighbouring islands such as Bora Bora. Yeah, sure, but this is still a great place to buy a baguette, sip a glass of wine, sit by the harbour and watch the pirogues (six-man outrigger canoes) charge across the harbour. Meanwhile those dramatic green-draped mountains rise up right behind you, cruising yachts drift in from all over the world, catamaran ferries surge out to nearby Moorea, cargo ships steam out towards the exotic Marquesas (Gauguin's final retreat), the *roulottes* (vans) set up to turn out bargain-priced food beside the docks in the evening, the towering *mahu* (Polynesian cross-dressers) totter off in their high heels and it's all done with a certain French style. What's not to like?

Stanley

VITAL STATISTICS

NAME: STANLEY

NICKNAME: CAPITAL OF 'THE CAMP' (FALKLAND ISLANDS)

DATE OF BIRTH: 1843; WHEN THE BRITISH ABANDONED PUERTO DE LA SOLEDAD AND ESTABLISHED STANLEY AS THE CAPITAL

HEIGHT: 135M

ADDRESS: FALKLAND ISLANDS (MAP 1, O23)

POPULATION: 2100

Some of my neglected favourites are those mega-cities few people can warm to, but Stanley is the polar opposite (and not that far from the South Pole). The capital 'city' of the Falkland Islands may be home to 75% of the 'kelpers' (as outsiders sometimes call the islanders), but that still means it can barely scrape together 2000 people. Despite this small population base, colourful Stanley (the islanders love decorating their houses with a technicolour paintbox) has plenty to see. There's a church fronted by a whalebone arch, a line-up of wrecked or dumped ship hulks along the shoreline, several noisy pubs, an iconic hotel (the Upland Goose), and a world-class garden-gnome collection in one front garden.

Tehran

VITAL STATISTICS

NAME: TEHRAN

NICKNAME: CITY OF 72 NATIONS

DATE OF BIRTH: 1553; WHEN RAMPARTS WERE CONSTRUCTED AROUND THE VILLAGE OF TEHRAN

HEIGHT: 1200M

SIZE: 1500 SQ KM

ADDRESS: IRAN (MAP 3, BB17)

POPULATION: 12 MILLION

The Islamic Republic of Iran has a long list of cities that score more highly than its chaotic capital. Sophisticated Shiraz has culture, and gave its name to one of the world's great wine varieties. Nearby lie the ruins of mighty Persepolis (whisper it). Mashhad and Qom far outscore Tehran when it comes to religious piety, Yazd and Kashan are way ahead when it comes to beautiful old traditional buildings and, of course, Esfahan is everybody's favourite and truly one of the world's most stunning cities. But there's no denying Tehran's energy and enthusiasm, from trendy shopping centres where teenagers raise a tentative finger to the fundamentalist mullahs, to madhouse traffic where women at the wheel give no quarter as they fight it out with their male counterparts, and all the time the magnificent Alborz Mountains (if you can see them through the pollution) rise up like a lodestone to the north – a clear reminder that the ski slopes on Mt Damavand are only a couple of hours away.

Tunis

VITAL STATISTICS

NAME: TUNIS

DATE OF BIRTH: 814 BC; FOUNDED BY PHOENICIAN SETTLERS

HEIGHT: 4M

SIZE: 346 SQ KM

ADDRESS: TUNISIA (MAP 3, J16)

POPULATION: 985,000

The sprawling Mediterranean capital of Tunisia is not going to win any beauty contests – although there's a fine World Heritage–listed medina (the ancient walled city) and some great restaurants. But Tunis also has one attraction that alone makes the trip across the Mediterranean from Europe worth the fare: the Bardo Museum. Even if you've never had an enthusiasm for Roman mosaics you will be a convert after you've wandered this treasure house. The Romans left mosaic treasures everywhere they built, from the frigid north of England to the warm Turkish coast, but it was in Tunisia where the art reached its apogee. The glowing artwork, which studs the Bardo's walls, underlines the fact that the colony's rich Roman settlers clearly knew how to build with style.

Warsaw

VITAL STATISTICS

NAME: WARSAW

NICKNAME: BIG POTATO

DATE OF BIRTH: 13TH CENTURY; IN 1413 IT BECAME CAPITAL OF THE DUCHY OF MAZOVIA AND, IN 1596, CAPITAL OF POLAND

HEIGHT: 106M

SIZE: 512 SQ KM

ADDRESS: POLAND (MAP 3, O7)

POPULATION: 1.69 MILLION

Poland's capital city, the 'Big Potato', ranks nowhere in the country's glamour stakes – as a tourist attraction Kraków gets all the votes. In fact, this is a city that has clearly gone through hell, and come out the other side throwing high-fives. The Old Town Sq was totally destroyed by Hitler's storm troopers during the closing days of WWII and so flawlessly rebuilt you'd have trouble telling where medieval Europe segues into the reconstruction of the 1970s and '80s. Weep at the poignant reminders of the Warsaw Ghetto; rage at the incredible story of the Warsaw Uprising, meticulously detailed in the Museum of the Warsaw Uprising; laugh at the 'Elephant in Lacy Underwear', the USSR's unwanted gift and for years the tallest building in Europe outside Moscow. And then hit the city's clubs and bars, where the Poles party as though they've got 50 depressing years to make up for.

LOCAL MUSICIANS TAKE SOME OF THE HEAT OFF A LONG BUS RIDE.
Photographer: Barry Lewis / Alamy

CUNNING GARDEN GNOMES PLOT A TAKEOVER OF THE FALKLAND ISLANDS.
Photographer: Tony Wheeler / LPI

BEND IT LIKE BRANKO: HALFTIME AT A WOMEN'S FOOTBALL MATCH.
Photographer: Caroline Penn / Panos

ROMAN MOSAICS ADORN THE PALAIS D'ORIENT'S TERRACE.
Photographer: Charles Bowman / LPI

CANDLES BURN FOR THE FALLEN SOLDIERS OF THE WARSAW UPRISING.
Photographer: Krzysztof Dydynski / LPI

Cities

When you look at a city, it's like reading the hopes, aspirations and pride of everyone who built it. – Hugh Newell Jacobsen

The Cities Book is a celebration. Of the physical form, in stone, glass, metal and wood, that is taken by these remarkable spiritual, cultural, political and technological bastions. Of the people whose energy spills out into the city, transforming itself into music, art and culture. Of the myriad sights, smells, sounds and other temptations awaiting travellers at the end of a plane, train or boat journey. By celebrating the majesty of cities on every continent we are pausing to marvel at the contribution they have made to the collective richness of humankind over more than six millennia.

Hence it made sense to us to begin this book with a look at the evolution of the city – the roots of cities in the first civilisations, the characteristics that we associate with the great cities of today, and the possible directions that they will take in the future.

Like so many other things, cities come to us as a gift from the ancients. Although capable of great foresight, our urban ancestors could not possibly have predicted the way in which cities were to change the world we live in. According to the UN, the urban populace is increasing by 60 million people per year, about three times the increase in the rural population. To get a sense of the impact that cities have made, try picturing the world without them. Imagine fashion without Milan, theatre without London's West End, hip-hop without New York, classical music without Vienna, or technology without Tokyo.

UN Secretary-General Kofi Annan summed it up best when he said: 'We have entered the urban millennium. At their best, cities are engines of growth and incubators of civilization. They are crossroads of ideas, places of great intellectual ferment and innovation…cities can also be places of exploitation, disease, violent crime, unemployment, and extreme poverty…we must do more to make our cities safe and livable places for all.'

Past
Present
Future

Past

The story of how cities evolved is the story of civilisation. The link is encoded in the words themselves: 'civilisation' comes from the Latin *civitas*, meaning 'city'. We can catch a glimpse of the past in the preserved walls of castles, palaces and places of worship that have survived, albeit haphazardly, for centuries, and which influence the colour and flavour of our present-day cities. Cuzco in Peru is the perfect example. The city's strongest walls remain those constructed by the Inca who, unfathomably, erected enormous stone monoliths carved by hand and laid the blocks so precisely, without mortar, that it is impossible to slide paper between them. Following the Spanish conquest, the ancient Inca stones were used to build palaces and cathedrals, but the stones were so mighty that many could not be brought down and so continue to make up the streets and foundations of newer buildings to this day.

Paradoxically, with the advent of the first sedentary settlements, where people flocked together to settle in large groups instead of roaming the countryside as small bands of hunter-gatherers, came the advent of inter-city travel. Initially people travelled (as they still do) for trade and business, war, or religious pilgrimages, but eventually cities gave birth to the leisured classes who could travel for curiosity and pleasure. Even in ancient times there were hoteliers who ran a roaring trade for prototypal backpackers and travel writers and historians who made their livings from the fantastical tales of their wanderings.

Sumerian Cities

Divine Nature gave the fields, human art built the cities.
– Marcus Terentius Varro

Current archaeological records indicate that the oldest cities are those found scattered along the banks of the Tigris and Euphrates Rivers in Mesopotamia, modern Iraq.

Five thousand years ago merchants travelling upriver from Egypt would have entered the great Sumerian capital of Uruk by boat, sailing swiftly past the fertile shores lined with irrigation ditches that had been dug centuries before. These ditches, filled with water from the Euphrates River, had allowed the Sumerians to begin farming the land, producing surpluses of food that were used to feed an army of construction workers, possibly slaves, to raise the first cities the world had ever seen. The most ancient of these was Uruk and with its construction the door was firmly closed on the prehistoric epoch.

The city of Uruk was famous for its giant defensive walls, luscious gardens and the sophistication of its ruling elite, chief among them the god-king Gilgamesh, who became the subject for the world's oldest epic, the *Song of Gilgamesh*, which is still in print today. Excavation of the vast site where the city once stood, an area covering 450 hectares, has yielded astonishing finds. In the 1900s a cuneiform tablet found at Uruk happened to contain what is regarded as the best and most accurate description of the legendary Tower of Babel, an architectural feat referred to in the Bible.

But the real fascination is with the form of the city itself. In 2003 Jorg Fassbinder, part of a German-led archaeological team conducting excavations at the site, said that in its heyday Uruk must have been 'like Venice in the desert'. The dig covered more than 100 hectares, uncovering extensive gardens as well as an extremely sophisticated network of canals by which the Sumerians swanned around their idyllic city in absolute luxury.

It is incredible to think that after more than 5000 years the legacy of Sumerian culture could still remain potent. Not only did they invent the wheel and come up with the world's first written language (Sumerian cuneiform script, which emerged around 3500 BC), but they also dreamt up the sexagesimal number system, which we still use to measure time. Every time you count down the minutes to an event, you have the Sumerians to thank.

What we know of ancient Sumer has been deduced through careful analysis and interpretation of the discoveries made by archaeologists. These include stone tablets inscribed with ancient stories (the first ever recorded); gold necklaces inlaid with lapis lazuli that were once worn by Sumer's elite; weathered fragments of beautiful vases depicting the conquest and subjugation of rival cities; and the broken outlines of once-feared cities that stretched for kilometres. Interpreting these finds with a little imagination only whets our appetite and makes us want to learn more about these strange worlds that have been lost in time.

Rome – Antiquity's Great Melting Pot

A great city, whose image dwells in the memory of man, is the type of some great idea. Rome represents conquest; Faith hovers over the towers of Jerusalem; and Athens embodies the pre-eminent quality of the antique world, Art. – Benjamin Disraeli

Sicilian writer Vincenzo Salerno said that despite everything that came after it, the blueprint for Western civilisation was the society of ancient Rome. The Romans gave us our alphabet (minus *u* and *w*), and many of the words we still use are derived from ancient Latin. They gave us the 12-month lunar calendar; the rudiments of classical architecture; the pope; straight roads; a system of government; literature; public-ablution facilities; and endless subject matter for Shakespearian plays and even movies, such as *Gladiator* and *I, Claudius*. The Romans came, saw and conquered, and left enough behind that they would never be forgotten. And at the heart of the mighty empire was the imperial capital, a monolith of power carved in brilliant marble, home of the Senate and generations of megalomaniac emperors. Ancient Rome's former pagan glory is still visible if you take a stroll around the modern city, notably the remains of the Roman Forum, the Pantheon and the Colosseum.

Quite clearly, the Romans were a pretty remarkable bunch. But they were not the first people to become civilised, and nor did they develop in a vacuum. They were great assimilators, subsuming the skills, knowledge, literary conventions and even deities from neighbouring or past civilisations – a process hastened through conquest. From afar Rome admired in particular the Greek and Egyptian civilisations, centred on the capitals of Athens and Alexandria, which were already melting pots of ideas, racial groups and culture.

Alexandria the Great

It was in Alexandria, during the six hundred years beginning around 300 BC, that human beings, in an important sense, began the intellectual adventure.
– Carl Sagan

In 332 BC Alexander the Great thrashed the Persians and then conquered Egypt for the Greeks. The following year, after being crowned pharaoh, he ordered the construction of a fortified port which he named, in a moment of egotism, Alexandria. The city was to replace Memphis as the capital of ancient Egypt and, had Alexander not died of fever during the conquest of Babylon, would have become the capital of his enormous empire. As it happened, the empire was carved up by Alexander's generals following his death and Ptolemy Soter took over as pharaoh and king of Alexandria.

During antiquity the Egyptian capital was famous for its wonderful papyrus and had a reputation for producing great medicines, perfume, jewellery and gold work. But most of all, the city was, and still is, legendary for the Pharos Lighthouse, one of the Seven Wonders of the Ancient World, and for its library, established under Ptolemy III. It is alleged that he composed a letter 'to all sovereigns on earth, requesting them to send him works by every kind of author, including poets and prose-writers, rhetoricians and sophists, doctors and soothsayers, historians and all the others too'. Such was his zealousness in collecting knowledge that he gave orders for any books on board ships calling at Alexandria to be copied, and only the copies were returned to the owners. As a secure port city, an industrial and manufacturing base, and a hub of knowledge, Alexandria had a celebrated liberal system of governance that championed diversity.

Less than 500 years after Ptolemy Soter had ascended the throne, Alexandria was reduced to smouldering rubble, destroyed through a combination of Caesar's aggression, petty-minded Christian rebels, earthquake and flood. The coastal Egyptian city we know today as Alexandria bears almost no trace of its amazing history. But through the advanced system of trade and communications that existed throughout antiquity, at least some of the knowledge contained in the library (such as details of the Archimedes screw, a pump that Archimedes invented while staying at the Mouseion, the city university), was not completely lost. Then as now, the great powers adopted and adapted the successful tricks and strategies of their contemporaries and in so doing ensured that the legacies of civilisations dating back countless millennia would be recorded.

Lost Cities – Atlantis to Great Zimbabwe

Towered cities please us then,
And the busy hum of men.
– John Milton

For thousands of years fabled lost cities have had a vicelike grip on our imagination. Even such a wise philosopher as Plato would get excited thinking about how these advanced civilisations could just be mysteriously wiped out. His fascination with lost cities has trickled down hundreds of generations and given us the most tantalising and well-known mysterious lost city of all, Atlantis.

The legend of the lost city of Atlantis has captivated scholarly and public imagination since it was first recorded over two millennia ago. The source of the great legend stems from an account written by Plato (427–347 BC) in *Critias* and *Timaeus*. Plato's account was originally derived from Solon (640–560 BC), the great lawmaker of Athens. It is alleged that Solon was told of the disappearance of a vast and worldly island civilisation by Egyptian priests while he was visiting the Nile delta. This story was told to Plato by Critias (a poet, philosopher and controversial political figure), via his great-grandfather, who had learned the story with Solon. In *Timaeus*, Plato quotes Critias' account of the legend:

> Now in this island of Atlantis there was a great and wonderful empire
> which had ruled over the whole island and several others, and over parts
> of the continent… But, there occurred violent earthquakes and floods,
> and in a single day and night of misfortune…the island of Atlantis…
> disappeared in the depths of the sea.

Right now there are still people out there trying to find the site of this ancient Utopia. Based on the scant detail in Plato's account, it is highly unlikely we could identify Atlantis even if it were to be discovered. But there has been no shortage of possible candidates. Over the past few years a spate of potential Atlantises have been found in waters off India, Cuba and Japan.

In May 2001 underwater archaeologists at India's National Institute of Ocean Technology detected signs of an ancient submerged settlement in the Gulf of Cambay, off Gujarat. Acoustic-imaging analysis identified a 9km-long stretch of what had once been a river now lying 40m beneath the waves. Evidence retrieved from the site, including pottery, beads, broken sculpture, wood and human teeth, has been carbon dated, and a conservative estimate of the age of the site puts it at around 7500 BC. It is not clear whether the Cambay site represents a city or a smaller type of settlement. If it is a city, then the belief that the Sumerians built the first city would be proved wrong, and the whole theory of the origin and spread of ancient civilisations would need to be revised.

But wait, it gets better. In December 2001 another lost city was discovered, this time off the west coast of Cuba in the Yucatán Channel by scientists innocently engaged in sonar imaging for a Canadian company that was hoping to discover sunken ships laden with Spanish treasure. The fact that some of the buildings alleged to be part of the city appear to be shaped like pyramids got dozens of internet Atlantean hopefuls extremely fired up.

Although the jury is still out on whether this Cuban discovery is a lost city or just an anomaly that showed up on the radar, there is no doubt that a strange megalithic structure discovered in Japanese waters off the island of Yonaguni is genuinely man-made. The huge stone structure, which is over 100m long, was discovered by a diver in 1985. By itself the megalith isn't enough to signify the existence of a whole civilisation or even a city, but the estimated age of the structure, put minimally at 6000 years, represents another spanner in the works for those attempting to piece together the chronology of ancient human civilisation.

Each new archaeological find is a puzzle, and as much likely to inspire fear and prejudice as it is joy. Nowhere is this tenet illustrated more plainly than at the site of one of Africa's great lost cities, Great Zimbabwe. The first rumours of a magnificent lost city began circulating around the Portuguese colony of Mozambique during the 16th century. However, the spectacular ruins, with their massive curved walls raised without mortar, were not discovered by Europeans until nearly the end of the 19th century, when a young German explorer named Carl Mauch was directed to the site by a German trader who told him of some large ruins 'that could never have been built by blacks'.

It was almost another 20 years before a full exploration of the site was conducted by J Theodore Bent, an amateur archaeologist at best, bankrolled by British imperialist Cecil Rhodes, a notorious racist and diamond entrepreneur. Despite unearthing masses of evidence that pointed to the indigenous origins of Great Zimbabwe, Bent concluded that the impressive curved-walled enclosures, which stretched over 40.5 hectares and were over 9.1m high, were the work either of Phoenicians or Egyptians who had travelled down from North Africa.

The inability of conquering civilisations to appreciate the achievements of those whom they have conquered has added significantly to the numbers of lost cities and ruined sites on all continents save Antarctica. The ruins of the World Heritage–listed site at Machu Picchu, picturesquely perched among the clouds high in the mountains of Peru, were once the spiritual capital of the Incan population that was decimated by the Spanish conquistadors, and are now an enigma. With the Inca gone and their knowledge lost, the ruins they left behind can never be interpreted with any certainty. But perhaps that only adds to the allure of the lost city. And the dim, irrational thought that perhaps, upon spending time wandering the ruins with the ghosts of our spiritual ancestors, it is possible to catch a glimmer of understanding in these sacred places.

Present

In the days of the European Grand Tour of the 19th century, it was fashionable for young aristocrats to complete their education by travelling to the great cities of the Continent to study their history and art. These 'tourists' are the origin of our modern word. But travel was still time-consuming, difficult and expensive and therefore only really available to the privileged classes. Today, modern transport means that we can travel between cities in hours, not days. The world is becoming smaller while correspondingly people's interests are becoming broader, thanks to our greater access to the world through the media. Recent travel trends show that short-break city trips are one of the most popular kinds of travel, and that the main motivators are education and exploring other cultures, escaping the stresses of everyday life for a while, and a sense of adventure. Travellers claim that travel has had a considerable impact on their lives, helping define a social conscience and positively impacting personal goals and values. Today, the most difficult part of city travel is deciding which city to visit next.

Stormy Weather

Not houses finely roofed or the stones of walls well builded, nay nor canals and dockyards make the city, but men able to use their opportunity. – Alcaeus

In 2004 the reality of a disaster such as that which may have destroyed Alexandria and Atlantis was brought home, literally, when it was beamed into TV sets around the world. The devastating tsunami that struck in December that year, causing widespread coastal damage, affecting 12 countries and causing the loss of hundreds of thousands of lives, was followed by two further brutal natural disasters in the form of Hurricanes Katrina and Rita in 2005.

When Katrina lashed into New Orleans at the end of August, it was confirmation, if such was needed, that in the future even cities with significant defences could not take their safety for granted.

New Orleans lies below sea level in a wide, shallow bowl on delicate marshlands, with the Mississippi River running through the centre. It is situated under the lip of a vast lake more than twice its size, while to the south and east lies the Gulf of Mexico, one of the world's most fertile hurricane zones. Following the devastation that occurred when the Mississippi burst its banks in 1927, engineers designed and built a complex system of flood defences, enough to protect it from a Category 5 storm. Even though New Orleans did not take the full brunt of the storm in 2005, the historic city lost a large number of its priceless old buildings, became engulfed by toxic waters, and many inhabitants suffered significant physical and psychological damage. Many people feel that to avoid a rebuilding process that will benefit property developers rather than those made homeless by the disaster, the authorities should entrust the power and responsibility of reconstructing the old jazz capital to its former citizens.

One thing is certain: however much equity goes into the reconstruction, the next system of levees will have to be a vast improvement on the ones that broke under the weight of Katrina. If New Orleans needs help choosing its future direction, the city's mayor could do a lot worse than turn to the example set by the world's most livable city, Vancouver.

Plan for Living

The chief function of the city is to convert power into form, energy into culture, dead matter into the living symbols of art, biological reproduction into social creativity. – Lewis Mumford

If anyone was surprised that Vancouver emerged as the world's most livable city in 2005, as nominated by William M Mercer quality-of-life survey and the *Economist*, then it certainly wasn't the city's planners or its residents. Over more than three decades the idyllic Canadian city has earned this accolade through the introduction of a simple yet revolutionary approach to city planning and design.

In 1972 the city's planning office took a bold step often feared by public servants scared of opening a Pandora's box. They decided to look beyond the computer models, livability indicators and programme plans they had created and ask the public what they thought would make the city most livable. The more they tried to answer the question 'what is livability?', the more they realised they didn't have the answer. So they decided to phone a friend – millions of friends.

Another instance where Vancouver looked to the needs of its citizens was the Art Underfoot initiative, a competition in which members of the public came up with the best designs for the city's manhole covers. The idea was to help make city infrastructure more visible to the public. How much more a part of the city would you feel if you had a chance to design illustrations that would appear on manhole covers everywhere?

The city's public discourse about livability eventually led to a plan that recognised the city as an organic entity in itself. A discussion paper on Vancouver prepared by the Vancouver-based International Centre for Sustainable Cities stated:

The brain and nervous system of a livable city refers to participatory processes by which a city develops visions and plans, monitors the implementation of its plans and adjusts to changing circumstances. The heart is the common values and public space of a city that define its essential identity. The neighborhoods, industrial clusters, downtown, parks and other hubs form the organs of a city. Similar to the circulatory system and neural networks that weave connections within a living organism, transportation routes, infrastructure, waste disposal, communication lines, water flows, and green space connect these nodes.

The essence of livability was found to be about quality of life, which is tied to the ability of citizens to access food; clean air; affordable housing; infrastructure (transportation, communication, water and sanitation); meaningful employment; and green parks and spaces, and is also determined by the access that its residents have to participate in decision-making to meet their needs.

The *Economist* survey, published in October 2005, assesses living conditions in 127 cities around the world by looking at these factors. Vancouver is the highest ranked city, but a further two Canadian cities (Montréal and Toronto) feature in the top five. Alongside Canada, Australia has some of the most livable places in the world, with Melbourne ranked joint second overall. Perth, Adelaide and Sydney join Zürich, Toronto and Calgary in joint fifth place. Not far behind is Brisbane in joint 11th place.

Elsewhere in the Asian region, cities in Japan, New Zealand, Hong Kong, South Korea, Singapore and Taiwan all offer a good standard of living, and it is only a humid climate that brings scores down slightly. The influx of investment in China alongside the increased availability of goods has helped all six Chinese cities surveyed perform relatively well, along with other emerging business centres such as Bangkok and Kuala Lumpur.

Although higher crime rates and a greater threat of terror put US cities below those of Canada, US cities are still among the world's most livable. Cleveland and Pittsburgh are the joint best scoring cities in the US, in joint 26th place in the global ranking. Although no Latin American city surveyed manages to present ideal living conditions, neither do any fall into the category where extreme difficulties are faced. Montevideo (Uruguay), Santiago (Chile) and Buenos Aires (Argentina), which share joint 64th place, offer the best living conditions in Latin America.

Africa and the Middle East fare the worst of any region. Instability, the threat of terror and many cultural restrictions bring the ratings down, although strong anticrime measures in many Arab states are a stabilising factor, and in Israel the negatives are offset by a generally high level of development that makes Tel Aviv the best destination surveyed there.

Rapt in Wander

We all become great explorers during our first few days in a new city,
or a new love affair. – Mignon McLaughlin

Cities are places to wander, without a map, relishing the freedom that comes of being lost in a strange new world. Whether you're taking a leisurely stroll along the wide, cobblestone pathways of Antigua or letting a doe-eyed dog lead you aimlessly round the busy streets of Bangkok, exploring on foot can easily be the highlight of any trip around a city.

The best thing about walking is that you have control. Whenever you come across something interesting you can stop and check it out, take your time and really savour the experience. Often the most ancient cities are the most rewarding ones to walk through. Perhaps it's because they were built for walking, in a time before cars were invented and carriages and horses were reserved for a small elite. Small cities also lend themselves to walking, as it is easy to learn your way around and to get a feel for their human scale. The slow pace of walking allows us to meditate and absorb the ambiance of a place, particularly in holy cities.

Passing along the decorated walls of the streets of Varanasi in India, winding through the hustle and bustle, can be a dreamlike experience. The myriad temples and sumptious buildings of the place nicknamed 'the eternal city' may help you to understand the Hindu belief that anyone who dies and is cremated in the city automatically ends the cycle of death and reincarnation and ascends immediately to nirvana. Lost in thought, wandering slowly, meandering like the Ganges as it flows through the centre of the city, you might feel as if your sins have been washed away and your mind made clear.

In Mecca, a city where you are required to walk, the sense of renewal and rejuvenation comes from the river of humanity you will find yourself caught up in in the haj pilgrimage. Every year well over two million Muslims perform the sacred pilgrimage, forming a human mass that has to be seen to be comprehended. The focal point of Mecca is the Kaaba, the 'House of God', believed by Muslims to have been built by Abraham (peace be upon him) and his son Ishmael (peace be upon him), and which is covered in a large black-and gold-embroidered cloth. The pilgrims who have made the journey to Islam's holiest city wait patiently to circle the Kaaba seven times before they try to touch or kiss its cornerstone, the Black Stone, which is believed to be a meteorite. The process can take several hours simply due to the unbelievable numbers of pilgrims. This is one walk you won't forget in a hurry.

Tasty Travel

To be tempted and indulged by the city's most brilliant chefs.
It's the dream of every one of us in love with food. – Gael Greene

Food is the foundation of city and human life and a trip to any city would be much the worse for not savouring the flavours favoured by the locals. The quality of a city's restaurants can reveal much about its inhabitants – the importance of their traditions and their openness to new ideas.

Cities around the world, and many in this book, would all claim to be top or near the top of the epicure food chain. New York, Paris, London, Toronto, Melbourne, Montréal would certainly stake a fierce claim, as would San Francisco. Some cities have nice weather, others have nice beaches, but San Francisco has both (most of the time) and great food to boot. Whether you're sampling the city's best seafood with the leather-clad crowd in the Castro, chewing on dim sum (yum cha) in one of the world's biggest Chinatowns, going Mexican in the Mission District or dining sophisto in California's oldest restaurant, Tadich Grill, this is one city that demands you eat, and eat well.

But of course sampling a city's cuisine isn't always about eating the very best. The locals in any city have their own peculiar favourites, often in marked contrast to all the grand fare served up by gastronomic wizards in the finest restaurants at the fashionable end of town. As a general rule Londoners like nothing better than a serving of fish and chips or a juicy kebab of an evening, while the *porteños* of Buenos Aires prefer snacking on *empanadas* (turnovers) and *lomitos* (steak sandwiches). Sometimes it's all about discovering the local secrets, trying something a little different that you wouldn't find at home.

When you're in Minsk and need something to help keep your strength up against the Belarusian wind, make sure you gobble down a couple of fish in jelly. They're a lot tastier than you might think.

In Lahore it pays to explore the full range of Pakistani delicacies and there is no better place to achieve this goal than at the conveniently dubbed 'Gawalmandi food street'. The whole street is cordoned off to traffic, and from where you sit you can order whatever appeals from any of the stalls. Balti and tandoori dishes are most popular, but the more adventurous can tuck into *karai kaleji* (chicken livers), *gurda* (kidneys), *kapureh* (testicles) and *magaz* or *bheja* (brains).

Cro-Magnon men everywhere should make their way immediately to Nairobi to sample the ultimate meat-lover's fantasy at the Carnivore restaurant, on the outskirts of town. As the name of the place suggests, this is one hard-core serving of animal flesh. Dinner or lunch provides the opportunity to get stuck into zebra, giraffe, impala, wildebeest, crocodile and other game meats. Waiters will bring the skewers straight from the fire to the table, and no-one will object if you wolf it down.

In Celebration of Diversity

This is the most happening place in the city, and it happens to be gay. I don't think it's a coincidence. – Paul Colombo

There's something about the Berlin Love Parade, Sydney's Mardi Gras and Rio's Carnaval that makes it hard to picture them taking place in a tiny, sleepy country village with a population of 50 where everyone knows your name and if you go back far enough the inhabitants are all blood related.

One of the great opportunities cities offer new residents is the chance for people to be themselves. Sharing a living space with millions of others is often regarded as a profoundly liberating experience. Anonymity allows for freedom and the chance to become the person you want to be.

Cities have a long history of attracting people who are seeking a fresh start or need to outrun the demons of prejudice and intolerance more common in villages and rural areas. During medieval times throughout Europe, peasants, not to mention thieves and vagabonds, would escape the attentions of despotic landlords by fleeing to the cities, hence the old expression 'city air is free air'. In 19th-century England, following the abolition of slavery in the British Empire, slave ships bound for the Caribbean continued to dock in port cities such as Liverpool. Occasionally slaves would be helped to escape and would hide among the throng of the busy city before eventually being integrated into society. Cities are also centres of migration, from rural areas and from abroad. The relative peace and stability that is enjoyed by people of different races, sexual orientation, cultural backgrounds and political views, who live together side by side in thousands of cities worldwide, is a wonderful advertisement for urbanisation.

The residents of Tbilisi in Georgia take pride in their city's reputation for multiculturalism. It is home to more than 100 ethnic groups, including Georgians, Russians, Armenians, Azeris, Ossetians, Abkhazians, Ukranians, Greeks, Jews, Estonians, Germans and Kurds. On the other side of the world in Puerto Vallarta (Mexico), locals celebrate the city's rich cultural diversity by eating out at the famous mix of restaurants.

Meanwhile, in the 'gayborhoods' of San Francisco, Sydney, Paris, New York and London, predominantly gay, lesbian, bisexual and transgender trendsetters continue to make a vital contribution to their city's economy by attracting curious tourists keen to hang out in a cool part of town. The Chueca barrio in Madrid is one of the city's best-known gay areas, with a totally chilled atmosphere where gay and straight people intermingle, and same-sex kissing and hand-holding is commonplace.

Tolerance and acceptance subsequently gives rise to amazing public spectacles that succeed in uniting everyone in a celebration of diversity. Take the Berlin Love Parade, first held in 1989 on a whim by a German DJ, Dr Motte, who thought it would be cool to hold a free, mobile acid-house street party. The first Love Parade attracted 150 revellers, who followed two cars with cassette recorders along the Kurfürstendamm. Ten years later 1.4 million people were jiving after 51 floats past Germany's most important landmarks in a beautifully outrageous celebration of 'Love, Freedom and Techno'.

Endless Nights

Cities, like cats, will reveal themselves at night. – Rupert Brooke

No matter how many natural, cultural or culinary charms a city may have, it is often judged by the quality of its nightlife. And having explored the delights of your chosen city by day, it's only natural that you should want to check out what happens between dusk and dawn, just to make sure you haven't missed anything.

Often the best nights out are those that are unplanned. Similarly, some of the best nightlife can be found in the cities where you'd least expect to find it.

Take Belgrade for example. Along the Danube you will find dozens of *splavovi* (floating raft clubs) blaring out funky, folksy Balkan beats as they slide out of view. In contrast, you expect New York to deliver – and it does. Whenever, wherever, whatever, however you want it, the world's most extravagant city has it all, 24/7. To maintain its pole position, the city has even spawned the New York Nightlife Association (NYNA), an orderly gang of owners, managers and staff from many of the city's top establishments, who in their own words believe New York City is the nightlife capital of the world and want to keep it that way.

Future

Having lured us out of the wild and into homes that for many are packed with creature comforts, fridges, running hot water, electricity, heating, ADSL connections, telephones and the rest, what more does the city have up its sleeve? One thing is certain and that is that there will be change.

The challenges for the future faced by cities mainly revolve around sustainability and managing growing populations. Among the UN's Millennium Development Goals is a target to 'significantly improve' the lives of at least 100 million people living in urban slums by the year 2020. At the same time, cities must also plan to be less enviromentally damaging. Economic factors and the desire for unparallelled luxury are also motivators for city planners of the future. Technology moves ahead in leaps and bounds, and ultimately the only thing that can limit a city is the imaginations of the people who are building it. And today, perhaps more than at any time in history, ordinary people are nearer to turning their own city daydreams into something real.

New Real Estate

In a real estate man's eye, the most expensive part of the city is where he has a house to sell. – Will Rogers

In an essay entitled 'The Rise of the Ephemeral City' published in *Metropolis Magazine*, Joel Kotkin has suggested that we are witnessing the emergence of a new urban environment populated by 'non-families' and the nomadic rich whose needs are attended to by a subservient service class. He calls it the ephemeral city and suggests that it prospers merely through its ability to provide an 'alternative' – and one suspects extravagantly decadent – lifestyle for the wealthy few who can afford it. Even though Kotkin wasn't referring to the city of Dubai, he might well have been describing the glittering, paradisal playground for the rich, famous and, especially, the nouveau riche.

Often the difference between the possible and the impossible is someone brave enough to have a vision. In the coastal city of Dubai, part of the United Arab Emirates, Sheikh Mohammed bin Rashid Al Maktoum is such a man.

In 2001 he ordered construction work to begin on two palm tree–shaped artificial islands. According to the European Space Agency, whose satellite has been monitoring the construction, the islands comprise approximately 100 million cubic metres of rock and sand and are set to increase Dubai's shoreline by 120km.

When complete, the Palm Islands will support over 60 luxury hotels, 5000 residential villas, 5000 apartments, marinas, water theme parks, restaurants, shopping malls, sports facilities, health spas, cinemas and numerous dive sites. It is hoped the development, dubbed by proud locals as the Eighth Wonder of the World, will further secure the city's reputation as a top tourist destination and fantasy playground for the fabulously wealthy. Football ace David Beckham is rumoured to have purchased an apartment.

To prove that less is not more, the sheikh announced in 2004 that a third and even grander Palm island, the Deira Palm, was to begin construction. This palm tree–shaped island will become the largest artificial island in the world, with an area of 80 sq km, and will consist of a trunk, a crown with 41 fronds and a surrounding crescent island that acts as a breaker. The residential area, located on the fronds, will consist of 8000 two-storey town houses.

And just in case there was any shadow cast over Dubai's ambition to remain completely over the top, the sheikh has also commissioned the erection of the enormous Burj Dubai, which will be the world's tallest tower when completed. In keeping with the plant theme, the tower's triple-lobed design is based, according to the press release, 'on an abstracted version of a desert flower, while the silhouette of the lobes resonate the onion-dome constructions of an Islamic culture'.

Another epic urban-development project, considered to be the largest private commercial real-estate development in the world, is underway in South Korea. At an initial cost of US$15 billion, New Songdo City is under construction on a 556-hectare landfill connected to mainland Seoul by bridge. When complete it is planned to be home to almost half a million people and an economic hub to rival Hong Kong. The picturesque, high-density city aims to attract multinational corporations wishing to set up new headquarters for their Northeast Asian operations. Developers have declared New Songdo will be a free economic zone, with tax incentives and low-interest loans. It will feature international schools, hospitals and pharmacies, canals, a water shuttle, a golf course and a 'green lung' modelled on New York's Central Park. The city will also become a test-bed for new technology.

Seoul residents have already shown tremendous interest in the project and New Songdo apartments are rumoured to be selling fast. In the past

real estate developers would build houses, office and apartment blocks, it seems that the 21st century has ushered in a new era of real estate where developers construct entire cities.

Raising the Dream

The city is a fact in nature, like a cave, a run of mackerel or an ant-heap. But it is also a conscious work of art, and it holds within its communal framework many simpler and more personal forms of art. Mind takes form in the city; and in turn, urban forms condition mind. – Lewis Mumford

Some city planners have a vastly different vision from the property developers, some would say less mercenary and certainly more environmentally sustainable. In the Arizona desert, north of Phoenix, a revolutionary city has been under construction since 1970. Its founder, Italian architect Paolo Soleri, hopes Arcosanti will inspire a change in the prevailing culture. Arcosanti is said to resemble the modernist urban Utopian designs of Le Corbusier and Sant'Elia. However, the principles of design are based on Soleri's concept of 'arcology' (a fusion of architecture and ecology). His vision is for an organic sustainable city that fits into the ecological system rather than imposing itself upon it. For example, greenhouses beneath residential buildings generate solar energy for heating, as well as producing food. Soleri insists that when people come to Arcosanti they will be inspired and that when they leave they will begin to insist that genuinely sustainable principles start being applied to the development of their own cities.

With an average of only 50 permanent residents who also work to construct the city, Arcosanti is on too small a scale to provide the technical solutions for the challenges that face the world's major urban centres. However, in terms of the principles he has applied to his design, Soleri fulfils the role of a visionary, in that he believes that cities must become confluent with the example set by nature if they are not to be destroyed by the same forces that give them life. He writes:

In nature, as an organism evolves it increases in complexity and it also becomes a more compact or miniaturized system. Similarly a city should function as a living system… The city is the necessary instrument for the evolution of humankind.

Citizen City

I have an affection for a great city. I feel safe in the neighbourhood of man, and enjoy the sweet security of the streets. – Henry Wadsworth Longfellow

While old-school realists take a deep breath and get on with it, dreamers continue to dream. Anyone who has played Sim City knows the allure of being able to construct your own metropolis. Deciding whether the citizens have a greater need for a new university or a high-security prison can be fun, but for an increasing number of ordinary folk the fun is turning into reality.

Constructing cities started off as the sole preserve of warrior god-kings, then it passed into the hands of elected politicians, and now it seems anyone with enough passion, perseverance and financial backing can give it a go.

In the USA the Laurent Company, in rural South Dakota, is trying to recruit a vice president of construction to help it build 'the world's first fully integrated signing community'. The plan is to build a city that centres on the needs of hearing-impaired people who use sign as their first language; The built environment will be constructed to take into account the special needs of its proposed citizenry, expected to number between 1250 and 4000.

The company says homes and businesses will encourage easy visibility for signing across wide distances through the use of glass and open spaces. Fire and police services will be designed with more lights and fewer sirens. High-speed internet connections will be made available throughout, as the internet and video relay service have become vital modes of communication for deaf people. Some critics have warned that the proposed city is segregation, albeit voluntary, and argue that there would be widespread moral outrage had the criteria for entry been factors such as ethnicity or gender (such as at a monastery). Still, the city seems likely to be raised and with the full support of signers, who are already signing up to buy property.

For Florida-based Freedom Ship International (FSI), getting its city off the ground and into the ocean has been far from smooth sailing. FSI has plans to construct a 1371m-long, 228m-wide, 106m-tall, ocean-going vessel known as the *Freedom Ship*. The structure is billed as 'an international, cosmopolitan, full-spectrum, residential, commercial, and resort city that circles the globe once every three years'. If the project ever finds serious investors, the mobile modern city with its 518,160-sq-metre floor-space will have 18,000 living units costing from US$180,000 to US$44 million; 3000 commercial units; 2400 time-share units; 10,000 hotel units; a casino; world-class medical facilities; schools; an international trade centre; and more than 40 hectares of outdoor park, recreation and community space for residents to enjoy when they are not flying to the mainland in the ship's aircraft.

So far Norman Nixon, FSI's CEO, has reported the project has been inundated with offers of finance from bogus investors. But he hasn't given up hope of finding someone real who can turn the dream into reality. If only he could team up with Dubai's Sheikh Mohammed bin Rashid Al Maktoum, perhaps it would be full steam ahead for the world's first mobile floating city.

Clearly if you're looking to set up your own city it would be helpful to have loads of money. Then you could just buy a ready-made city like the one in Wiltshire being sold off by Britain's Ministry of Defence. With an asking price of only UK£5 million, 'Burlington', with its 97 hectares, 100 miles of roads, private railway station and even its own pub, the Rose and Crown, sounds like a snip. The catch is that the Cold War relic, built during the 1950s to house the government, British Royal family and 4000 civil servants in the event of a Soviet nuclear attack, is located underground on the site of a disused and rather dangerous stone mine. However, as an added incentive to prospective buyers, the city will come fully furnished with government-issue ashtrays, lavatory brushes, tea sets and office chairs unpacked from 1959.

Paying Your Part

Man's course begins in a garden, but it ends in a city. – Alexander MacLaren

As the evidence about the impact of climate change mounts there is a growing awareness among city-dwellers that something needs to be done.

The British Council estimates that over 75% of energy consumption is directly related to cities and that in many cases cities are highly vulnerable to the effects of climate change. At the same time, it says that cities have a great potential to 'instigate innovative solutions to the impacts of climate change'. Feeling guilty? Try this then.

The UK's Climate Care Trust offers organisations and individuals a way to live guilt-free in the city by simultaneously selling carbon offsets while funding and managing projects that help to reduce further emissions elsewhere. How does it work? Simple. Using the trust's Car & Home Calculator, you can work out the amount of carbon dioxide emissions (which cause the negative effects referred to as climate change) for which you are responsible by entering how much electricity, petrol, gas and oil you use per annum. The calculator then works out how much carbon dioxide was ejected into the atmosphere as a result of the energy consumption you've admitted to, revealing a total in pounds that the environmentally conscious are then morally obliged to pay in the form of carbon offsets.

According to the nifty Car & Home Calculator, an average one-car household uses about 9.5 tonnes of carbon dioxide, which would cost around £60 to offset. That £60 would in turn go towards funding worthy conservation projects such as disseminating efficient cooking stoves in Honduras or providing finance for renewable-energy cooking stoves in schools in India.

But the Climate Care Trust doesn't just work out your household and car emissions. To ensure guilt-free travel between cities, they have developed the Air Travel calculator that tells you how much carbon dioxide you are responsible for if you take a flight from, say, Boston to Delhi. Such a journey would emit 3.21 tonnes of carbon dioxide and would cost you £20.87 to offset. It may sound like a bit of a scam and critics often ask why the organisation isn't run as a charity. The trust responds with this message: 'The answer is simple: we do not believe that it should be left to the charitable

sector to clear up pollution.' Whether or not you advocate the approach taken by the trust, the message that we have a responsibility to behave in a sustainable fashion to preserve the built heritage for future generations is one that is worth taking seriously.

In 2005 London mayor Ken Livingstone hosted a meeting of leaders from 20 cities in order to exchange ideas on ways to combat the effects of climate change. Representatives from cities including Beijing, São Paulo, Delhi, Stockholm and Kingston attended the World Cities Leadership Climate Change Summit and cited some examples where cities had been successful in finding ways to reduce emissions. In Berlin nearly all new buildings must include solar panels in their design; in Toronto, cold water pumped from the depths of Lake Ontario is circulated around the city as part of the Deep Lake Water Cooling Project to keep buildings cool, rather than using conventional air conditioners; in Mexico City, which suffers from the worst air pollution of any city, they have vowed to replace 80,000 taxis with low-emissions vehicles by 2006; and in Chicago, the government is trying to find new ways to encourage the use of rooftop gardens in order to keep buildings cool.

Overall, delegates who attended the meeting said the event was a success and that they would take back valuable lessons to their home cities. Let's hope they all paid Climate Care Trust to offset the emissions generated by what must have amounted to thousands of air miles.

Fly Me to the Moon

In Rome you long for the country; in the country – oh inconstant! – you praise the distant city to the stars. – Horace

Sometimes the only way is up. And when it comes to building the cities of the future, Professor Ouyang Ziyuan, author and member of the Chinese Academy of Sciences, couldn't agree more. He reckons that within our lifetime work will already be seriously underway to construct a lunar city, and it won't be made out of cheese.

Ouyang outlined his vision for a moon city in *Academicians Envisioning the 21st Century*, a book published in 2000 to encourage children to get interested in science. He predicted that by 2005 astronauts would have begun turning the moon into a 'natural space station' that would have pressurised modules, electricity-generating facilities and groovy roving vehicles. By 2010 the completed and fully equipped station would allow human explorers to stay up there for weeks and in 2015, a small-scale but permanent moon base would appear. Humans living in the base would then start to build experimental factories and farms, gradually developing a fully fledged moon city before realising the dream of a self-sufficient 'earth village' by 2020.

Ouyang's predictions may have been a bit premature, as, in spite of claims by conspiracy theorists that NASA has already established colonies on the moon and Mars, there doesn't appear to have been much work in establishing a lunar base as yet. But those who can predict the future often seem to have a problem with dates – Nostradamus springs to mind – so perhaps we should wait a bit longer before giving the Chinese scholar's ideas the brush-off. After all, with China now spending well over US$1.2 billion on its space programme, maybe it won't be too long before Ouyang is proved correct. And we should hope so, because he also predicts that the moon city will feature a network of mining operations using solar power that will be able to generate enough surplus energy for it to be transmitted back to earth as a long-term, stable energy supply. Now that's got to be better than burning all that coal.

No two cities are the same. Some have great food, others great nightlife, some stunning architecture, some are rich with history and others have an eye on the future. Cities are individuals. Like a human being, a city is a mass of genes, chosen at random by forces beyond our control, fused together in a secret furnace, acted on by nature, reared through infinite probabilities of nurture before finally growing up and trying to make its own way in the world. Only by taking an interest in someone, spending time with them, observing their mannerisms, conversing with them, engaging with their likes and dislikes, strengths and weaknesses, learning their idiosyncrasies and funny habits, listening to them sing in the shower and snore at night, only by walking the path with them and imagining what it would be like if you were wearing their shoes, can you begin to realise how special someone is. And the city is the same, except maybe a little bit bigger.

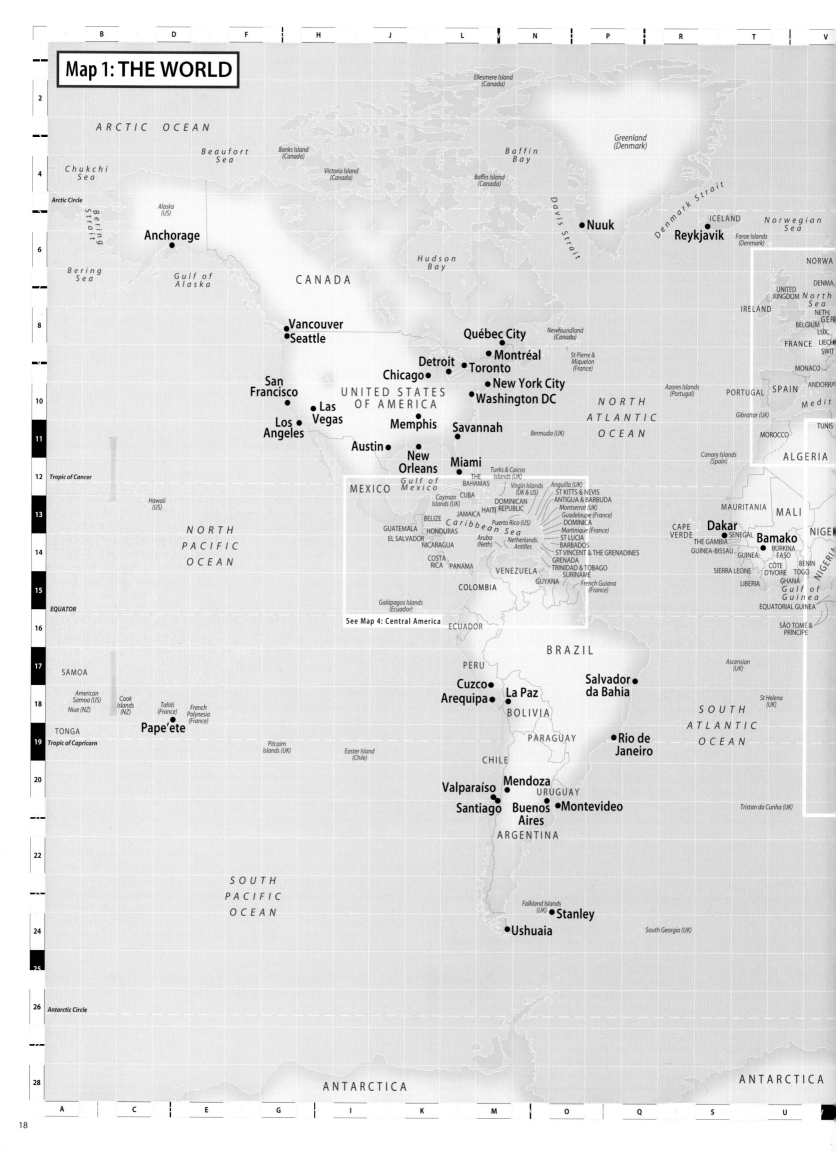

Map 1: THE WORLD

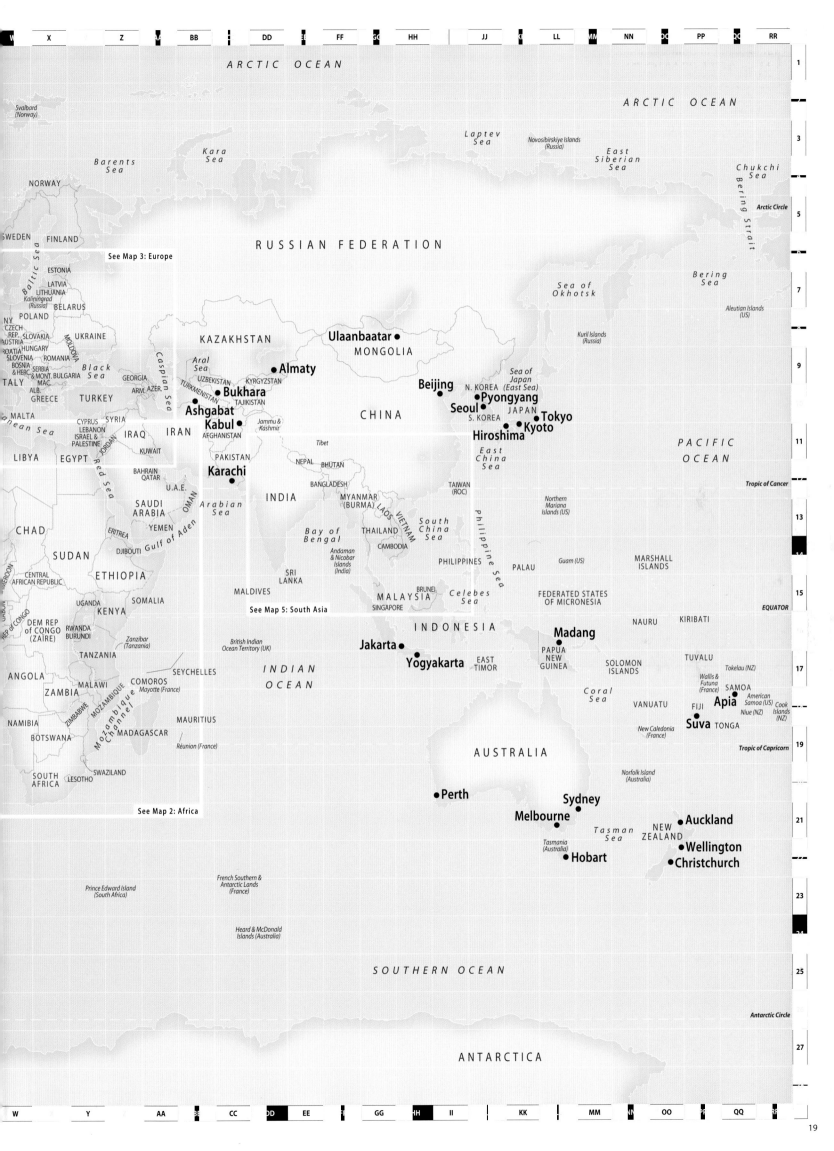

ARCTIC OCEAN

ARCTIC OCEAN

Svalbard (Norway)

NORWAY

Barents Sea

Kara Sea

Laptev Sea

Novosibirskiye Islands (Russia)

East Siberian Sea

Chukchi Sea

Bering Strait

Arctic Circle

SWEDEN   FINLAND

RUSSIAN FEDERATION

Bering Sea

Aleutian Islands (US)

Baltic Sea

ESTONIA

See Map 3: Europe

LATVIA

LITHUANIA

Kaliningrad (Russia)   BELARUS

NY POLAND

CZECH REP.   SLOVAKIA   UKRAINE

AUSTRIA   HUNGARY

CROATIA   MOLDOVA

SLOVENIA   ROMANIA

BOSNIA & HERC   SERBIA & MONT.   BULGARIA

ITALY   MAC.   ALB.   GREECE   TURKEY

Black Sea

GEORGIA   ARM. AZER.

Caspian Sea

KAZAKHSTAN

Aral Sea

UZBEKISTAN   KYRGYZSTAN

Ulaanbaatar •

MONGOLIA

Sea of Okhotsk

Kuril Islands (Russia)

Sea of Japan (East Sea)

• Almaty

TURKMENISTAN   TAJIKISTAN

• Bukhara

Beijing •

N. KOREA

• Pyongyang

CHINA   Seoul •   S. KOREA   JAPAN   • Tokyo

MALTA   CYPRUS   SYRIA

Mediterranean Sea   LEBANON   ISRAEL & PALESTINE   JORDAN   IRAQ   IRAN

• Ashgabat

• Kabul

AFGHANISTAN

Jammu & Kashmir

Tibet

Hiroshima •   • Kyoto

KUWAIT

PAKISTAN

NEPAL   BHUTAN

East China Sea

PACIFIC OCEAN

LIBYA   EGYPT

Red Sea

• Karachi

BAHRAIN   QATAR

U.A.E.

Arabian Sea

INDIA

BANGLADESH

MYANMAR (BURMA)   LAOS

TAIWAN (ROC)

Tropic of Cancer

SAUDI ARABIA   OMAN

YEMEN

Bay of Bengal

THAILAND   VIETNAM

South China Sea

Northern Mariana Islands (US)

CHAD

SUDAN

ERITREA

DJIBOUTI

Gulf of Aden

CAMBODIA

Andaman & Nicobar Islands (India)

PHILIPPINES

Philippine Sea

PALAU

Guam (US)

MARSHALL ISLANDS

CENTRAL AFRICAN REPUBLIC

ETHIOPIA

SRI LANKA

CAMEROON   UGANDA   SOMALIA

KENYA

MALDIVES

See Map 5: South Asia

BRUNEI

MALAYSIA

SINGAPORE

Celebes Sea

FEDERATED STATES OF MICRONESIA

EQUATOR

DEM REP of CONGO (ZAIRE)   RWANDA   BURUNDI

TANZANIA

Zanzibar (Tanzania)

British Indian Ocean Territory (UK)

INDONESIA

NAURU   KIRIBATI

Madang •

SEYCHELLES

• Jakarta

PAPUA NEW GUINEA

SOLOMON ISLANDS

TUVALU

ANGOLA

MALAWI

COMOROS   Mayotte (France)

INDIAN OCEAN

• Yogyakarta

EAST TIMOR

Tokelau (NZ)

Wallis & Futuna (France)   SAMOA

ZAMBIA   MOZAMBIQUE

Coral Sea

VANUATU

FIJI   • Apia   American Samoa (US)   Niue (NZ)   Cook Islands (NZ)

ZIMBABWE

MAURITIUS

New Caledonia (France)

• Suva   TONGA

NAMIBIA   Mozambique Channel   MADAGASCAR

Réunion (France)

AUSTRALIA

Tropic of Capricorn

BOTSWANA

Norfolk Island (Australia)

SOUTH AFRICA   SWAZILAND   LESOTHO

• Perth

Sydney •

• Auckland

See Map 2: Africa

• Melbourne

Tasman Sea

NEW ZEALAND

Tasmania (Australia)

• Hobart

• Wellington

• Christchurch

Prince Edward Island (South Africa)

French Southern & Antarctic Lands (France)

Heard & McDonald Islands (Australia)

SOUTHERN OCEAN

Antarctic Circle

ANTARCTICA

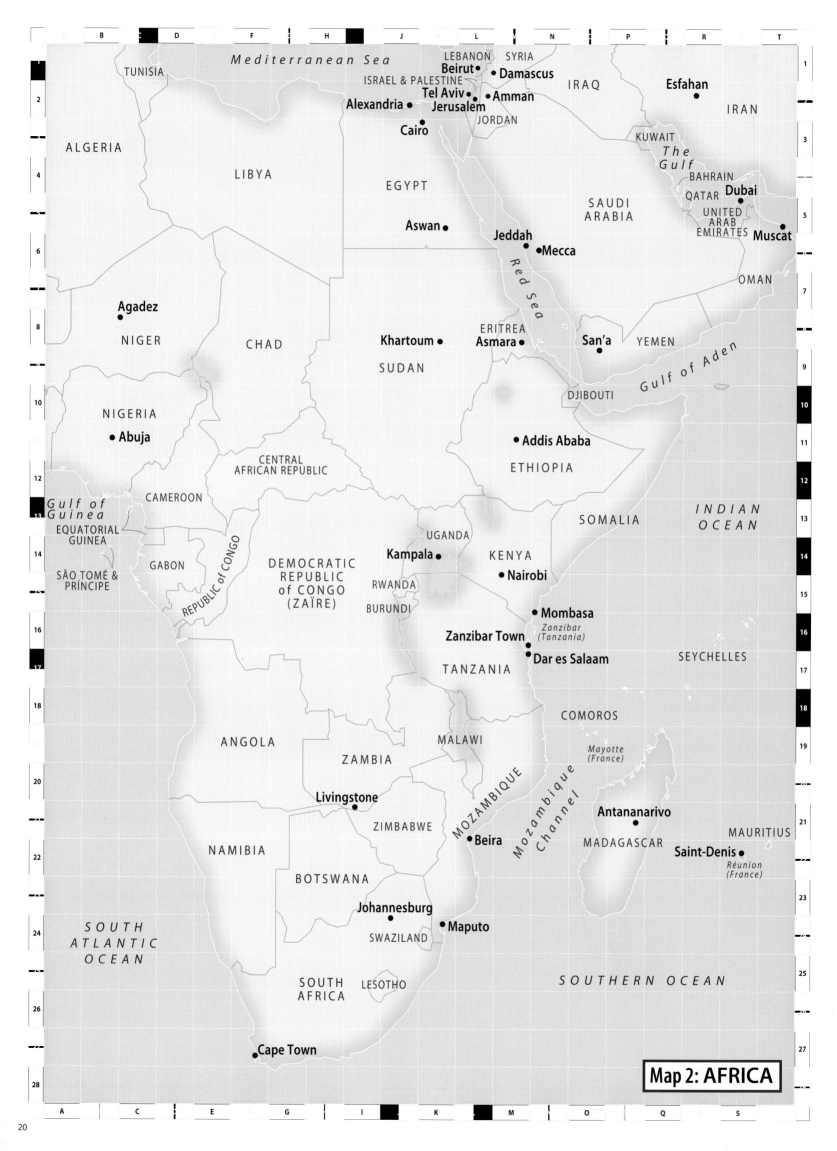

Map 2: AFRICA

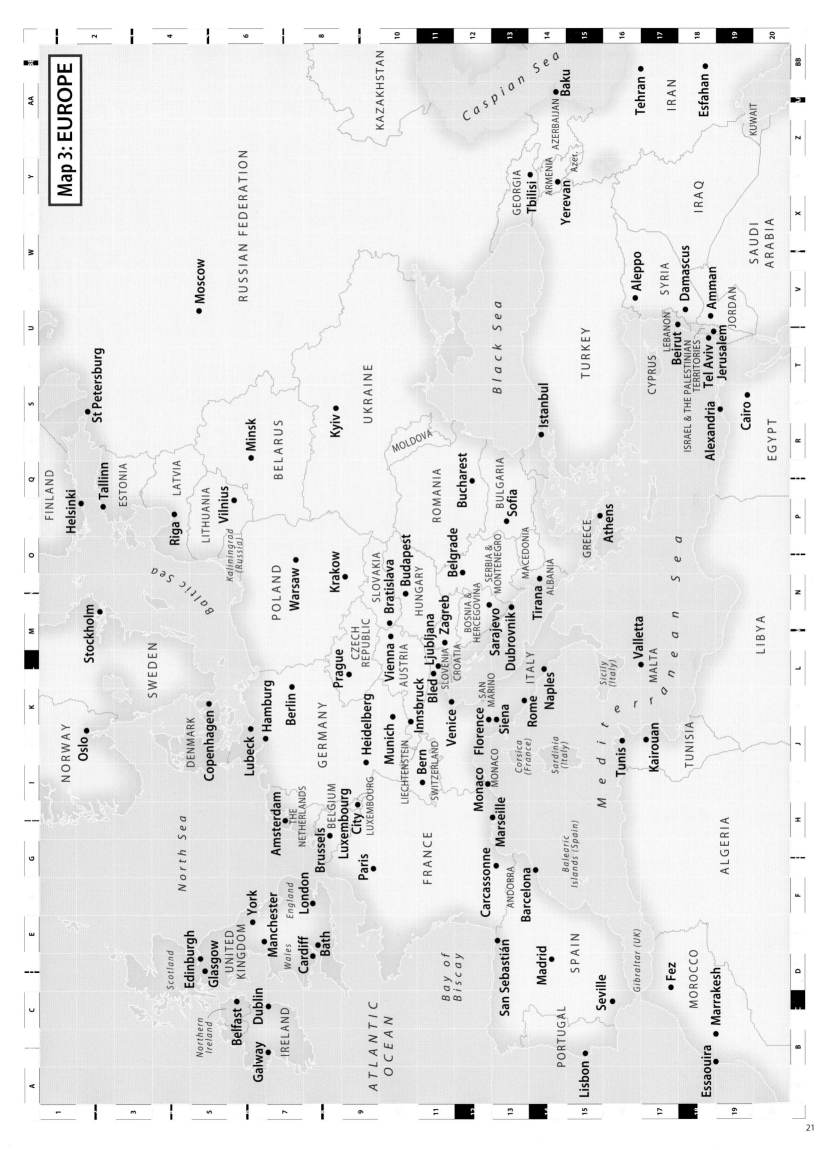

Map 3: EUROPE

21

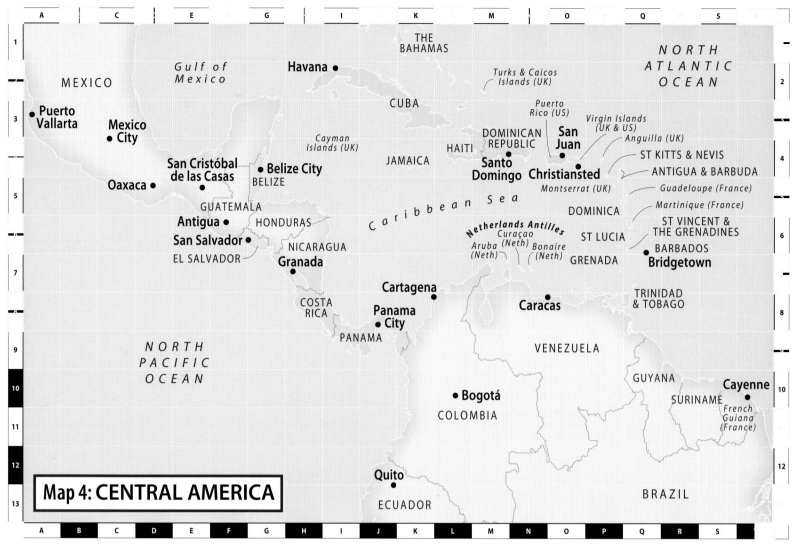

Map 4: CENTRAL AMERICA

MEXICO
Gulf of Mexico
THE BAHAMAS
NORTH ATLANTIC OCEAN

• Puerto Vallarta
• Mexico City
Oaxaca •
San Cristóbal de las Casas •
• Belize City
BELIZE
• Havana
CUBA
Cayman Islands (UK)
JAMAICA
HAITI
DOMINICAN REPUBLIC
Turks & Caicos Islands (UK)
Puerto Rico (US)
• San Juan
Virgin Islands (UK & US)
Anguilla (UK)
ST KITTS & NEVIS
ANTIGUA & BARBUDA

Antigua •
San Salvador •
GUATEMALA
HONDURAS
EL SALVADOR
• Granada
NICARAGUA
• Santo Domingo
• Christiansted
Montserrat (UK)
Netherlands Antilles
Curaçao (Neth)
Aruba (Neth)
Bonaire (Neth)
Caribbean Sea
DOMINICA
ST LUCIA
GRENADA
Guadeloupe (France)
Martinique (France)
ST VINCENT & THE GRENADINES
• BARBADOS
Bridgetown

• Cartagena
• Panama City
PANAMA
COSTA RICA
• Caracas
TRINIDAD & TOBAGO

NORTH PACIFIC OCEAN
VENEZUELA
• Bogotá
COLOMBIA
GUYANA
SURINAME
• Cayenne
French Guiana (France)

Quito •
ECUADOR
BRAZIL

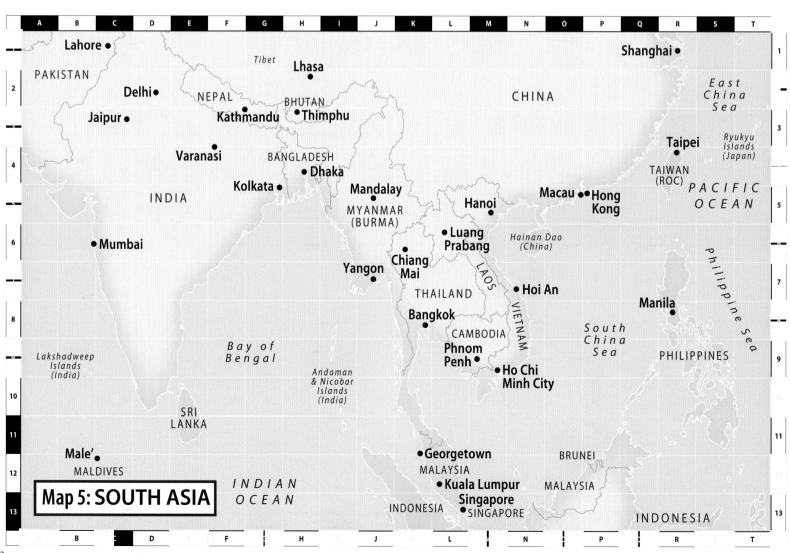

Map 5: SOUTH ASIA

Lahore •
PAKISTAN
Delhi •
Jaipur •
Tibet
• Lhasa
NEPAL
BHUTAN
Kathmandu •
• Thimphu
CHINA
Shanghai •
East China Sea

Varanasi •
BANGLADESH
• Dhaka
Kolkata •
INDIA
Mandalay •
MYANMAR (BURMA)
Hanoi •
Macau • • Hong Kong
Taipei •
TAIWAN (ROC)
Ryukyu Islands (Japan)
PACIFIC OCEAN

• Mumbai
• Luang Prabang
Chiang Mai •
Yangon •
THAILAND
LAOS
Hainan Dao (China)
• Hoi An
VIETNAM
South China Sea
Manila •
Philippine Sea

Bay of Bengal
Bangkok •
CAMBODIA
Phnom Penh •
• Ho Chi Minh City
PHILIPPINES

Lakshadweep Islands (India)
SRI LANKA
Andaman & Nicobar Islands (India)
INDIAN OCEAN

Male' •
MALDIVES
• Georgetown
MALAYSIA
• Kuala Lumpur
Singapore
SINGAPORE
INDONESIA
BRUNEI
MALAYSIA
INDONESIA

One of the newest cities on the planet, Abuja was imagined in the 1970s on the back of oil revenues, and building began in the 1980s at the geographical centre of Nigeria.

ANATOMY

The very character of this purpose-built city has been shaped by the two renowned rock formations around it – Zuma Rock, the 'Gateway to Abuja', and Aso Rock, located at the head of Abuja, with the city extending southwards from the rock. The rolling landscape is dotted with hills and plains, canopied with scenic greenery and virgin forests. As a new city it is serviced by a very good road system, but it's too new to have a bus system; numerous cheap taxis and vans are the main method of getting around and the adventurous take *okada* (bike taxis).

PEOPLE

Several indigenous groups live in Abuja, the largest among them are the Gbabyi (also known as the Gwari) and the Koro. Several smaller indigenous groups are the Gade, Egbura, Gwandara, Bassa and the Gana gana.

TYPICAL ABUJAN

A civil servant, a politician, a diplomat, or a member of the domestic staff of the aforementioned.

DEFINING EXPERIENCE

Meeting early at the International Conference Centre, going hiking in the hills around the city, playing a round of golf in the afternoon, then finding one of the local botanic garden–styled drinking spots in town and sampling some local fare before a spot of dinner at an international hotel.

Abuja

VITAL STATISTICS

NAME: ABUJA

DATE OF BIRTH: 1976; WHEN THE NIGERIAN GOVERNMENT KICKED OUT THE LOCAL GWARI INHABITANTS AND DECIDED TO UP-AND-MOVE THE CAPITAL FROM LAGOS TO ABUJA

ADDRESS: NIGERIA (MAP 2, B11)

HEIGHT: 360M

SIZE: 250 SQ KM

POPULATION: 779,000

LONELY PLANET RANKING: 158

TRADITIONAL TRANSPORT CLASHES WITH THE ULTRAMODERN ARCHITECTURE OF ABUJA.
Photographer: Pascal Maitre / Cosmos // Aurora

STRENGTHS

- Wide-open streets
- Few cars
- A good golf course
- The imposing Zuma Rock
- Aso Rock, the largest rock formation, nearly 400m above sea level
- The Dutse hill range, a sanctuary for baboons and other forms of wildlife

WEAKNESSES

- Its comparative emptiness
- Few people
- Domestic flights are unscheduled, as they are mainly charter flights, even to Lagos

GOLD STAR

Aso Rock, the city's spine, a granite monolith that towers over the gleaming green dome of Nigeria's new National Assembly building.

STARRING ROLE IN...

- The plans of international architecture practices!

IMPORT

- Architects
- Town planners
- Builders
- Tradespeople
- Road builders
- Civil servants
- Bureaucrats
- Politicians
- Diplomats
- Oil companies
- Lobby groups
- Non-governmental organisations (NGOs)

EXPORT

- Conference agreements – Abuja is the site of several international conferences, for example for Unicef and the Commonwealth, on HIV/AIDS in Africa and debt relief

SEE the flowering bougainvillea and other exotic greenery that conceal the high walls and razor wire protecting the office towers, apartment buildings and villas dotting the landscape.

EAT *edikang ikong*, a rich, leafy delicacy from the southeast; probably Nigeria's most famous and most cosmopolitan meal, it's served in many restaurants and the biggest hotels.

DRINK the popular traditional brew *brukutu* – a chocolate-coloured, faintly sour fermented drink made from sorghum.

DO attend Asofest in November, an annual festival of traditional arts and culture.

WATCH baboons in the nearby Dutse hill range.

BUY music by Fela Kuti or King Sunny Ade – leaders of the West African music scene.

AFTER DARK have a drink at Elephant Bar or Dazzles in the Sheraton.

URBAN MYTH

Nigerian internet scams aren't really from Nigeria. Although commonly referred to as 'Nigerian', the various international financial scams that first appeared in 1989 don't necessarily originate here. Many scams originate in other countries including Angola, Sierra Leone, the Congo, South Africa, Mauritius, the Philippines, Zimbabwe and Azerbaijan.

FILING OUT OF THE NATIONAL MOSQUE FOLLOWING FRIDAY PRAYERS.
Photographer: Jacob Silberberg / Panos Pictures

CHECKING OUT THE GOODS: A CATTLE MARKET ON THE CITY'S OUTSKIRTS.
Photographer: Jacob Silberberg / Panos Pictures

TAKING A QUICK BREAK IN THE FIELDS.
Photographer: Chris Illemassene / Expuesto / Alamy

Addis Ababa

VITAL STATISTICS

NAME: ADDIS ABABA

NICKNAME: ADDIS ABABA MEANS 'NEW FLOWER' IN AMHARIC

DATE OF BIRTH: 1886; FOUNDED BY EMPEROR MENELIK ON LAND CHOSEN BY HIS EMPRESS, TAYTU, FOR ITS PLEASANT CLIMATE IN THE FOOTHILLS OF THE ENTOTO MOUNTAINS

ADDRESS: ETHIOPIA (MAP 2, M11)

HEIGHT: 2450M

SIZE: 250 SQ KM

POPULATION: 2.7 MILLION

LONELY PLANET RANKING: 186

Ethiopia has been called the 'cradle of civilisation': one of the few countries on the continent never to be colonised, its unique culture is vibrantly expressed in its teeming capital, which is one of Africa's largest cities.

ANATOMY

Addis lies over a series of folds in the hills, but these have little effect on its sprawling mass, clustered round the Piazza to the north and Meskel Sq to the south. High-rise blocks stand next to fields of thatched, wattle-and-daub huts, air-conditioned taxis ferry businesspeople and bureaucrats while the rest of the population crowds into the fleet of tiny minibuses.

PEOPLE

Addis' population speaks 80 languages: Galla from the south comprise about 40% of the total population, Amhara are the second-largest group at around 30%, and others include Tigrayans, the Somali, Gurage, Borana, Awi, Afar, Wolayta, Sadama and the Beja.

TYPICAL ADDIS ABABAN

Like the city itself, Addis' citizens are a strange mix of the ancient and modern: priests in medieval robes bearing ceremonial umbrellas mingle with diplomats from across Africa visiting the African Union; street kids in filthy football shirts play among Oromo warriors attending tribal conferences, their elaborate hairpieces representing their prowess as hunters.

DEFINING EXPERIENCE

Joining in the week-long celebrations of the Feast of the True Cross in September, when huge bonfires are lit in Meskel Sq, topped by crosses made of flowers, and the singing and dancing goes on long into the night.

STRENGTHS

- Warm, temperate climate
- One of the safest cities in Africa
- Friendly locals

WEAKNESSES

- Extreme poverty
- Corruption
- The lack of education, employment, decent housing…

GOLD STAR

Ethiopians really are among the most welcoming people around: sit down for a natter and a strong, sweet coffee in one of the numerous cafés around the Piazza and just try and get away in a hurry.

STARRING ROLE IN…

- *Shaft in Africa* (1973)
- *500 Years Later* (2005)

IMPORT

- Jazz – while the '50s to the '70s were the foremost years of the Ethio-jazz movement, a love of brass and swing still persists in Addis' nightclubs.

EXPORT

- Coffee – Ethiopia claims to have discovered it, and buyers come to Addis from all over the world to procure the best.
- Hides and skins
- Handicrafts
- Gold
- Oil seeds
- Pulses and spices

SEE the rest of Ethiopia while you're there: from the Great Rift Valley to the Central Highlands, and the 1700-year-old obelisks of Axum to the rock churches of Lalibela, Ethiopia is one of the most fascinating and least visited countries on earth.

EAT Ethiopia's delicious national staple of *wot* (a spicy stew) and *injera* (a soft, spongy bread) at the Addis Ababa Restaurant, housed in a former *Ras* (duke's) residence.

DRINK a flask of *tej*, the powerful local mead brewed from honey, in one of the numerous *tej beats* (Ethiopian pubs).

DO visit one of our oldest ancestors in the National Museum: 'Lucy', an almost complete hominid, was discovered in northeast Ethiopia in 1974, and she's at least 3.2 million years old.

WATCH a football match at Addis San Giorgis stadium in the centre of town, complete with barefoot players, live animal mascots, fire-breathing spectators and lashings of St George beer.

BUY anything you like at the sprawling, open-air Merkato, the largest market in East Africa, from Kalashnikovs to camels and spices.

AFTER DARK head to the bars on the Bole Rd for music and dancing in all styles – everything from *azmaris* (traditional Addis tunes) to international stars such as the adored Gigi Shibabaw.

URBAN MYTH

It may be cruel, but Ethiopian Airlines, one of Africa's most successful national carriers, still fields queries from potential passengers who are worried that they won't get anything to eat on the flight. In fact, both the airline and the city feature some of the finest cooking in Africa.

MAKING ENDS MEET ON THE STREETS OF ADDIS ABABA.
Photographer: Dave Bartruff / Photolibrary

FOOD FOR THE MASSES – THE UNIQUE FLAVOURS OF ETHIOPIA.
Photographer: Frances Linzee Gordon / LPI

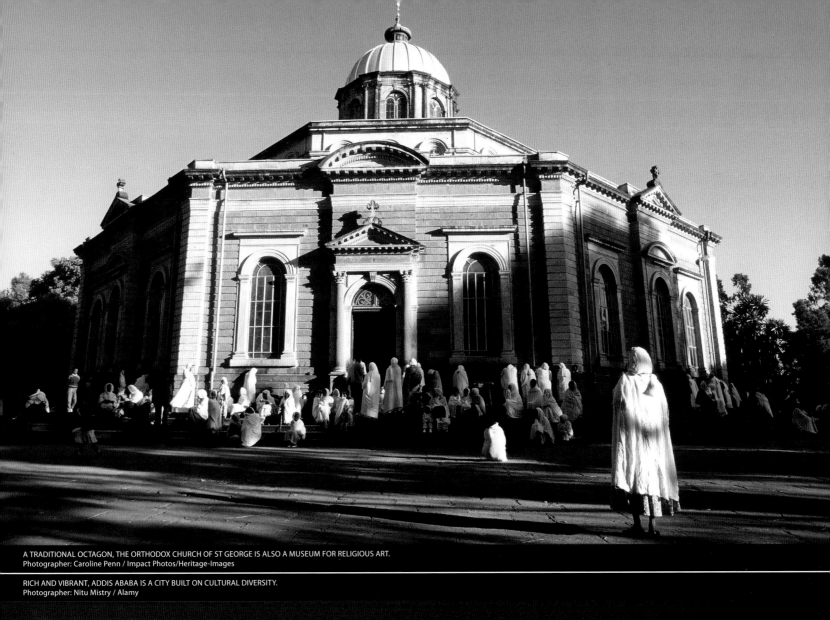

A TRADITIONAL OCTAGON, THE ORTHODOX CHURCH OF ST GEORGE IS ALSO A MUSEUM FOR RELIGIOUS ART.
Photographer: Caroline Penn / Impact Photos/Heritage-Images

RICH AND VIBRANT, ADDIS ABABA IS A CITY BUILT ON CULTURAL DIVERSITY.
Photographer: Nitu Mistry / Alamy

Agadez

VITAL STATISTICS

NAME: AGADEZ

DATE OF BIRTH: AD 1100; STEMMING FROM ITS PRIME LOCATION ON THE TRANS-SAHARAN CARAVAN ROUTES

ADDRESS: NIGER (MAP 2, C8)

HEIGHT: 529M

POPULATION: 122,000

LONELY PLANET RANKING: 152

Niger's premier ancient city, Agadez offers the romance of the Sahara and the allure of exotic mud minarets, swarming markets and nomadic culture.

ANATOMY
In Niger's central west sits Agadez. The centre of the city is taken up by the extraordinary Grande Mosquée, which affords spectacular views over the town and the surrounding desert. From here you can see the Old Town (Vieux Quartier) and to the south lies the main focus of town life – the Grand Marché (the main market). Head west for a good price on a camel or just to absorb the sights and sounds of the Tuareg Camel Market. Rising out of the Sahara to the north are the majestic Aïr Mountains, dotted with hospitable Tuareg villages, lush valleys and enough rough terrain to delight any budding mountaineer. A motley selection of minibuses, *taxis-brousses* (bush taxis) and Toyota 4WDs service the city's public-transport needs.

PEOPLE
The small but active nomadic Tuareg population has strong roots in and around Agadez, emerging from outlying areas to do business with the Hausa traders from the south at the city's Grand Marché. Pastoral populations such as the well-known Wodaabe also live in areas west of Agadez. Although French is the official language, some tribal languages are also spoken. Muslim dress is taken very seriously by Agadezers, and foreign women in particular should wear modest clothing.

TYPICAL AGADEZER
Agadezers are friendly and lively and are eager for tourism to take off in their city. They are traders, farmers and marketers – nomadic and agricultural. They are festive and as such, festivals thrive in Agadez. While they hold religion dear to their hearts and are Muslim in dress and belief, they readily indulge their liking for drinking, gambling and sport. The national obsessions of *la lutte traditionelle* (traditional wrestling) and table football are alive, well and flourishing thanks to Agadezers.

DEFINING EXPERIENCE
Wandering the labyrinth of narrow alleyways between the traditional single-storey *banco* (mud-brick) buildings of the Old Town to the small night market opposite Place de la Fraternité to eat and watch the bustle of the medicine men, food stalls and people while contemplating a game of table football or another brochette.

STRENGTHS
⊿ Camel markets
⊿ Desert trips
⊿ The nearby Aïr Mountains
⊿ Ténéré Desert
⊿ Camping
⊿ Plentiful festivals and festivities
⊿ Sealed roads going out and in
⊿ Mud-brick architecture
⊿ Grande Mosquée
⊿ The Old Town
⊿ Table football

WEAKNESSES
⊿ Agadez airport
⊿ Fierce competition (for the tourist dollar)
⊿ The distinct lack of beer
⊿ Occasional scams, thievery and armed hold-ups
⊿ Requests for a *cadeau* ('gift' or bribe)

GOLD STAR
The Grande Mosquée – standing in the centre of Agadez, this stunning mosque is for many people the single most definitive image of Niger.

STARRING ROLE IN...
⊿ *The Sheltering Sky* (1990)
⊿ *Agadez* by Jonathan Bennet
⊿ *Seven Words for Sand* by Allen Serafino

IMPORT
⊿ Camels
⊿ Tour groups
⊿ French and Middle Eastern cuisine
⊿ Beer

EXPORT
⊿ Camels
⊿ Tour guides
⊿ *Croix d'Agadez* (traditional Tuareg currency)
⊿ Local medicine and wisdom
⊿ Brochettes
⊿ 4WD expeditions

SEE the stomping bustle of the Tuareg Camel Market at sunset.

EAT home-made ice-cream surrounded by the traditional semi-open design at Restaurant Le Pilier.

DRINK nomadic Tuareg 'desert tea', strong and sugared in small glasses, in one of the scattered Tuareg villages.

DO take a camel ride through the lush valleys and rough, stony Aïr Mountains.

WATCH the artisans in action at the Centre Artisanal.

BUY *croix d'Agadez* at the Grand Marché.

AFTER DARK sit in the small night market opposite Place de la Fraternité eating brochettes and watching the world go by.

URBAN MYTH
The colourful Cure Salée event is held after the rains in August or September, when farmers take their herds to pastures rich in mineral salts. In the ceremony that's known as the Gerewol, young men of the nomadic Peul-Fulani group will adorn and beautify themselves so that only the most obstinate female can resist them. With luck, each will find a wife – a woman brave enough to move forward and demand his services, at least for a night. But furthermore, Cure Salée also involves the Soro, a virility test requiring initiates to be beaten with big sticks while maintaining an inane grin. Though it's difficult for outsiders to witness the events themselves, if you are in the region around this time you will undoubtedly run into plenty of spectacularly garbed nomads preparing for their big day.

ELEGANTLY DECKED-OUT MEMBERS OF THE WODAABE TRIBE.
Photographer: Imagestate / Austral-International

A GROCERY-LADEN CYCLIST MAKES HIS WAY HOME.
Photographer: Frans Lemmens / Getty Images

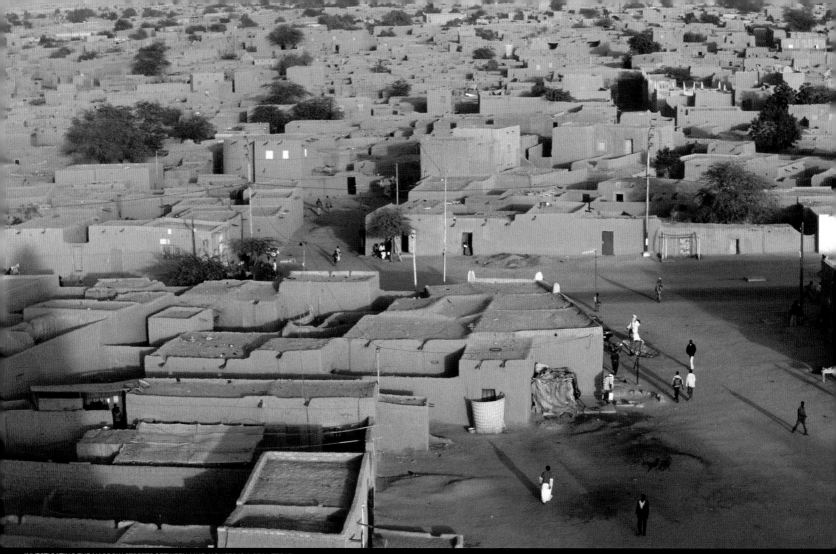

INVESTIGATING THE NARROW STREETS BETWEEN MUD HOUSES IS A REAL TREAT.
Photographer: Anthony Ham / LPI

PATIENT MOTHERS WAIT AT THE HOSPITAL.
Photographer: Alvaro Leiva / Photolibrary

Aleppo (Halab)

VITAL STATISTICS

NAME: ALEPPO (HALAB)

NICKNAME: HALAB (DERIVED FROM 'MILK' – LEGEND SAYS ABRAHAM MILKED HIS COW IN THE REGION)

DATE OF BIRTH: 1800 BC; THERE ARE RECORDS OF THE TOWN AT THIS TIME FROM THE HITTITE

ADDRESS: SYRIA (MAP 3, V16)

HEIGHT: 390M

POPULATION: 4.2 MILLION

LONELY PLANET RANKING: 114

Centre of commerce and trade since Roman times and possibly the oldest city in the world, Aleppo has a bountiful architectural heritage which has survived countless invasions and offers almost limitless opportunities for exploration.

ANATOMY

Aleppo has two distinct parts: the New City, where you stay and eat, and the Old City, where you go sightseeing. The New City is centred on sharias Al-Baron and Al-Quwatli, with the main travellers' area (containing inexpensive hotels and eating places) to the east and south. The Old City lies southeast, separated by two drab, wide avenues (sharias Al-Mutanabi and Bab Antakya). Its heart is the compress of streets making up the famed souq (market). Main thoroughfares run east–west, past the Great Mosque and terminating at the Citadel. North is the 16th- and 17th-century Christian-Armenian quarter of Al-Jdeida. Catch a microbus around town or walk.

PEOPLE

In line with the rest of the country, Aleppo's population is predominantly Arabic. There are also ethnic Syrians, who are of Semitic descent, and smaller groupings of Kurds, Armenians, Circassians and Turks. Aleppo is unique in that around a quarter of its population is Christian – one of the greatest concentrations of Christians in the Middle East.

TYPICAL ALEPPINE

Known for their hospitality, many Aleppines will welcome you into their homes for food or tea as a matter of course. Family-oriented, social life often revolves around food and bathing communally in (mostly) gender-segregated *hammams* (bathhouses). Sometimes described as serious or sober, Aleppines have a legendary mercantile bent best summed up in the proverb: 'An Aleppine can sell even a dried donkey skin.'

DEFINING EXPERIENCE

Visiting the New City's National Museum before setting off for the Old City and its souq to shop, exploring the Grand Mosque and Citadel before bathing at the Hammam Yalboughaan-Nasry, prior to dining on traditional Aleppine dishes in the Al-Jdeida quarter.

STRENGTHS

- Shopping in the souq
- Great Mosque
- Al-Jdeida quarter
- The Citadel
- Hammam Yalboughaan-Nasry
- Khan al-Jumruk and Khan an-Nahaseen
- 40 Martyrs' Armenian Cathedral
- National Museum
- Beir al-Wakil (*A Thousand and One Nights* fantasy, with added air-con and minibar)
- Qala'at Samaan
- Dead Cities – shells of ancient towns and villages
- Comparatively undeveloped city, tourism-wise

WEAKNESSES

- Political straitjacketing of cultural scene
- Litter, especially plastic bags
- Newer roads pouring traffic into neighbourhoods never designed for it
- Incongruous high-rises looming over traditional courtyard houses
- The 'Aleppo button' (ulcers from sandfly bites)

GOLD STAR

While not as extensive as Cairo's Khan al-Khalili or as grand as Instanbul's Kapali Carsi, Aleppo's souq is the most vibrant and untouristy in the entire Middle East.

STARRING ROLE IN...

- *That in Aleppo Once* by Vladimir Nabokov
- *Aleppo Tales* by Haim Sabato, Hayim Sabato and Philip Simpson

IMPORT

- Food and livestock
- Hong Kong kung-fu movies
- Trashy Indian B-movies
- Alexander the Great (took the city in 333 BC)
- Crusaders (unsuccessfully besieged Aleppo in 1118 and 1124)
- Saladin (captured the city in 1183)
- Mongols (held the city briefly under Hulagu Khan in 1260 and Timur in 1401)
- The Ottoman Empire (annexed the city in 1517)
- Agatha Christie (who wrote the first part of *Murder on the Orient Express* at the Baron Hotel)
- Machinery
- Chemicals

EXPORT

- Pistachios
- The Aleppo codex, an early manuscript of the Judaeo-Christian Bible
- Silks
- Cotton textiles
- Aleppo soap, a unique mix of olive and laurel oils
- Al-Kindo Ensemble
- Spices
- Carpets
- Muhammed Fares, Syria's first cosmonaut
- Olives
- Chess player and writer Phillip Stamma
- Poets al-Mutanabbi and Abu al-Firas
- Philosopher and scientist al-Farabi

SEE the beautifully maintained warren of Al-Jdeida's stone-flagged alleyways.

EAT cherry kebabs and mutton patties filled with fetta cheese at Beit al-Wakil.

DRINK at the Baron Hotel's bar while communing with the ghosts of guests past, including Charles Lindbergh, TE Lawrence, Theodore Roosevelt and Agatha Christie.

DO bathe at the Hammam Yalboughaan-Nasry.

WATCH whirling dervishes at the Bimaristan Arghan.

BUY gold, silver and carpets at the souq: geared to local trade, there's less pressure and better choice than in Damascus.

AFTER DARK Aleppo isn't a late-night city, but options include promenading around the Al-Azizah area or going on a bar-restaurant crawl in Al-Jdeida.

URBAN MYTH

The city is mentioned several times in Shakespeare's plays eg in *Macbeth* the witches say of a sailor's wife, 'Her husband's to Aleppo gone '.

A BEAUTIFUL DAY FOR A SONG AND A PICNIC, ST SIMEON.
Photographer: Mark Daffey / LPI

HIGH CULTURE IN THE NEW CITY: THE STATELY OPERA CINEMA.
Photographer: Wayne Walton / LPI

SUN ON THE HORIZON PAINTS THE OLD CITY A RICH SHADE OF ORANGE.
Photographer: Mark Daffey / LPI

A VETERAN TAXI TAKES A WELL-DESERVED REST OUTSIDE THE BUS STATION.
Photographer: Mark Daffey / LPI

Alexandria

VITAL STATISTICS

NAME: ALEXANDRIA

NICKNAME: THE PEARL OF THE MEDITERRANEAN

DATE OF BIRTH: 332 BC; WHEN ALEXANDER THE GREAT COMMISSIONED HIS ARCHITECT DEINOCRATES TO CONSTRUCT A NEW CAPITAL CITY ON THE COAST

ADDRESS: EGYPT (MAP 2, J2)

HEIGHT: 32M

SIZE: 300 SQ KM

POPULATION: 4.1 MILLION

LONELY PLANET RANKING: 162

A PENSIVE MOMENT ON THE TRAM.
Photographer: Bill Lyons / Getty Images

As much Mediterranean as Middle Eastern, Alexandria has stood the test of time; although its early - 20th-century European-influenced cosmopolitanism and decadence have faded, with Cleopatra's Palace and the ruins of the Pharos lighthouse emerging from the seabed and its dazzling new library, this confident Mediterranean city of cafés and promenades is making waves again.

ANATOMY

A thin, ribbonlike city, Alexandria runs along the Mediterranean coast for 20km without ever venturing more than 5km inland – a true waterfront city. The Great Corniche sweeps along the eastern harbour, with a string of city beaches. Trams travel at a snail's pace across the city, supplemented by buses and minibuses. The busy central area is small enough to walk around.

PEOPLE

Alexandria's citizens no longer include the extraordinary prerevolutionary mix of Egyptians, Greeks, English, French and Italians that gave the city its 19th- and 20th-century vitality. There were 300,000 people here in the 1940s, of whom about 40% were foreigners; today's millions are almost exclusively Egyptian.

TYPICAL ALEXANDRIAN

Alexandria is currently undergoing something of a regeneration, courtesy of an enlightened and free-spending municipality and the high-profile activities of a bunch of foreign archaeologists whose discoveries keep the city in the news. Its citizens are more laid-back than Cairenes, and have an immense pride in simply being Egyptian. Large extended families and close-knit neighbourhoods act as social support groups, strangers fall easily into conversation with each other, and whatever goes wrong, somebody always knows someone somewhere who can fix it.

DEFINING EXPERIENCE

Breakfasting at Trianon, downstairs from Cavafy's old offices, before exploring the Roman amphitheatre and Pompey's Pillar, the Catacombs of Kom ash-Shuqqafa – creepy tombs out of a horror film set – then wandering along the Corniche to the Royal Jewellery Museum for a taste of recent excess before going for a swim at Mamoura, resting in the late afternoon, and dining at the 1950s-style Elite.

STRENGTHS

- Beautiful beaches
- Antoniadis Gardens
- Old-world cafés
- Creepy catacombs
- The Biblioteca Alexandrina
- The Corniche
- The Mediterranean

WEAKNESSES

- Summer crowds
- Beautiful beaches are overcrowded
- Its rejection of cosmopolitanism

GOLD STAR

The library, with a reading room stepped over 14 terraces, re-creates the repository for literature and history founded 2500 years ago by the Macedonian conqueror of the world. It resembles a giant discus embedded in the ground at an angle, representing a second sun rising from the Mediterranean.

STARRING ROLE IN...

- *Alexandria: A History & Guide* by EM Forster
- *Death on the Nile* by Agatha Christie (film 1978)
- *Alexandria Quartet* by Lawrence Durrell
- *Lawrence of Arabia* (1962)
- *Farewell to Alexandria: Eleven Short Stories* by Harry E Tzalas

IMPORT

- Greek mathematician Euclid
- Greek poet Apollonius
- Greek scholar Aristarchus
- Greek mathematician and astronomer Eratosthenes
- Greek physician Herophilus
- Julius Caesar
- Marc Anthony
- Augustus Caesar
- Gustave Flaubert
- Hordes of Cairenes in the summer
- Millions of foreign tourists attracted to the city's jaded historical and literary mystique
- Archaeologists busy uncovering splendours on the harbour floor

EXPORT

- The great love story of Cleopatra and Marc Anthony
- Cleopatra's Needles (two red-granite obelisks), now in London and New York
- Rudolf Hess
- The exiled King Farouk
- The mass flight in the 1950s of non-Egyptians
- The poetry of Constantine Cavafy
- Omar Sharif
- Demis Roussos

SEE the ancient royal remains submerged in the surrounding sea (scuba equipment needed).

EAT the freshest seafood at Gezeirit El-Maleka and sample the whole menu – feel free to use your fingertips.

DRINK coffee at the classic and very elegant Trianon Le Salon.

DO visit the new Biblioteca Alexandrina, two millennia after the world's first library was founded here.

WATCH the Alexandrians promenading along the Corniche overlooking the sea, enjoying the cool of the evening.

BUY leather goods, including shoes, in the shopping area south and west of Mian Sa'ad Zaghool.

AFTER DARK catch the belly dancing at the Palace Suite in the Plaza Hotel.

URBAN MYTH

The theory that the original library initiated by Ptolemy I in 288 BC was destroyed by later Christian mobs – or any other group – is disputed. It is thought more likely to have gradually declined due to a lack of support.

TWILIGHT TRAFFIC FRINGES THE MEDITERRANEAN.
Photographer: Bill Lyons / Getty Images

A TRADITIONALLY DRESSED MANNEQUIN IS OUTRAGED BY HER NUDE COUNTERPART.
Photographer: Bill Lyons / Getty Images

TEA DRINKERS IN REPOSE UNDER A WATCHFULLY DECORATED RUG.
Photographer: Bill Lyons / Getty Images

TWO BUSINESSMEN PROUD OF THE WARES THEY HAWK AT THE VEGETABLE MARKET.
Photographer: Anthony Plummer / LPI

Almaty

VITAL STATISTICS

NAME: ALMATY

DATE OF BIRTH: 1854; A RUSSIAN FRONTIER FORT ON THE SITE OF THE SILK-ROAD OASIS, ALMATU

ADDRESS: KAZAKHSTAN (MAP 1, DD9)

HEIGHT: 775M

POPULATION: 1.5 MILLION

LONELY PLANET RANKING: 190

The honey pot of Kazakhstan, cosmopolitan Almaty is a city so European you would think you were in a leafy part of London, where you can sift through eclectic markets, pomp it up in fine old hotels, or make like a Soviet speed skater on the massive ice rink and best ski slopes in Central Asia.

ANATOMY

The Zailiysky Alatau Range rises like a wall along the southern fringes to form a superb backdrop to this clean, forested city. Almaty's long, straight streets are easy to navigate, running north–south and east–west, with mountains to the south and the city sloping upward from the north. There is a crowded network of *marshrutnoe* (minibus), bus and tram routes encompassing Zhibek Zholy, Almaty's pedestrianised shopping centre.

PEOPLE

Almaty's people are a typical mix of dozens of nationalities but, atypically for southern Kazakhstan, Russians and Ukrainians form the majority. To the ear, the sound of Russian, spoken even by most Kazakhs here, reveals the continuing hold of the colonising culture over the city. Several thousand Western and Asian expatriates, all after a foothold in the developing Kazakhstan economy, have also added to the mix in recent years – making Almaty Central Asia's most cosmopolitan city.

TYPICAL ALMATYAN

Almatyans are a people on the upswing. They are modern and European, having long moved away from rural Kazakhs in their dress, work habits and home life. Their former nomadic lifestyle, however, has bequeathed a certain attitude – laid-back and open – which separates them from their Russian brethren. Their middle-class incomes fuel the expansion of movie complexes, fashion shops, malls, sporting-goods stores and amusement parks. While the rich build themselves mansions up in the valleys around Almaty, some typically Kazakh traits remain and many an Almaty home will still be decorated with colourful carpets and tapestries, a tradition inherited from the brightly decorated yurts they once lived in.

DEFINING EXPERIENCE

Eating apples and *shashlyk* (kebab) in Central 'Gorky' Park before lazing on heated stone platforms at the Vostochnaya banya (Turkish baths) and then catching the infamous Otrar Sazy Kazakh Folk Orchestra and loudly discussing it afterwards.

STRENGTHS

◢ Zenkov Cathedral
◢ Altyn Adam (Golden Man)
◢ Eclectic museums
◢ Ski resorts
◢ State-of-the-art theatre scene
◢ Finest cafés and restaurants in Kazakhstan
◢ Arasan Baths
◢ Horse racing
◢ Pedestrian-friendly
◢ Cosmopolitan

WEAKNESSES

◢ Prostitution
◢ Police shakedowns
◢ Taxi scams
◢ Avalanches
◢ Waning national identity

GOLD STAR

Skiing – a hop, skip and jump from Almaty lies the powdered glory of the best skiing in Central Asia and the vertical 900m drop of Shymbulak ski resort.

STARRING ROLE IN...

◢ *Moksham* (2004)
◢ *The Place on the Grey Triangle Hat* (1993)
◢ *The Hiker's Guide to Almaty* by Arkady Pozdeyev

IMPORT

◢ The Golden Man
◢ International flights
◢ Nuclear warheads
◢ Weapons-grade uranium
◢ Ecotourism
◢ Big business
◢ Russian culture
◢ Cosmopolitan lifestyle
◢ Rich Kazakhs

EXPORT

◢ Oil
◢ Apples
◢ Vegetables
◢ Tobacco
◢ Rice
◢ Hemp
◢ Cotton

SEE the lolly-coloured, tsarist-era Zenkov Cathedral, built entirely of wood (and apparently without nails) in Panfilov Park.

EAT from the eclectic menu at PBC (RVS), the funky restaurant for the retro Soviet.

DRINK pints of beer on a crisp Sunday afternoon at the festivities in Central 'Gorky' Park.

DO catch a cable car to the viewing platform at Köktyube, the foothills of Zailiysky Alatau.

WATCH *dombra* (a two-stringed instrument) recitals at Almaty's Philharmonic Central Concert Hall.

BUY traditional Kazakh felt slippers and hats from the artisans in Sheber Aul artisans' village.

AFTER DARK line up with the young A-listers for pints of beer at the teeming Soho urban bar.

URBAN MYTH

The Golden Man is a warrior's costume. It is made of over 4000 separate gold pieces finely worked with animal motifs and a 70cm-high headdress bearing skyward-pointing arrows, a pair of snarling snow leopards and a two-headed winged mythical beast. Found in a Saka tomb near Almaty, and now Kazakhstan's greatest archaeological treasure, the Golden Man resides in the vaults of Kazakhstan's National Bank. There's some confusion about its age – the Central State Museum cites the 12th century AD but most other sources put its origins at about the 5th century BC. The real confusion however, is who, or what, this Golden Man really was. Recent studies show that Kazakhstan's adopted symbol of war and strength was mostly likely a woman.

WORSHIPPING IN THE STATELY ZENKOV CATHEDRAL, ONE OF ALMATY'S FEW REMAINING TSARIST BUILDINGS.
Photographer: Ashley Gilbertson / Aurora

FINDING THE HIDDEN RAINBOW IN THE MIDDLE OF SUMMER'S HEAT.
Photographer: Shamil Zhumatov / Reuters/Picture Media

THIS COUPLE MAKES SURE TO LOOK TIDY IN THE WINTER CHILL.
Photographer: Donata Pizzi / Getty Images

More a modern Arab city than a great ancient metropolis, Amman comes to life in its earthy and chaotic downtown district, with its markets and men smoking *nargileh* (water pipes) and playing backgammon, and in the leafy residential districts of Western Amman, with trendy cafés and bars and impressive contemporary art galleries.

ANATOMY

Amman was originally built on seven hills but has stretched out beyond these and now covers around 19. The area around the King Hussein Mosque is referred to as *il-balad* (downtown). Memorise the major landmarks or you'll find navigating the city a near impossibility, particularly in a short time. Restaurants, big hotels and shops are located around the main hill, Jebel Amman. The impressive Citadel sits atop the city's highest point, Jebel al-Qala'a. You can catch buses around town.

PEOPLE

Most of Amman's residents are Arab, including Palestinian refugees as well as Iraqi and Kuwaiti refugees who arrived after the first Gulf War of 1990–91. Amman's population is also graced by a small number of Circassians, Chechens, Armenians and Bedouins. Around 50% of Ammanians are under the age of 18.

TYPICAL AMMANIAN

Ammanians, like all Jordanians, are a welcoming bunch, and Amman, like most countries, sees a great divide between the classes. The Bedouins, who have little, will give you the hair off their camel's back in the midst of all the gentrification.

DEFINING EXPERIENCE

Wandering around the large Roman Amphitheatre, an impressive remnant of ancient Philadelphia (as the city was known under the Romans) that was cut into a hill that once served as a necropolis, and later in the day crowding round a coffee-house TV in support of Amman's football teams.

Amman

VITAL STATISTICS

NAME: AMMAN

NICKNAME: AL-HAMAMA AL-BAYDA (WHITE PIGEON)

DATE OF BIRTH: 3500 BC; THE SITE OF AMMAN HAS BEEN CONTINUOUSLY OCCUPIED SINCE THIS TIME

ADDRESS: JORDAN (MAP 2, L2)

HEIGHT: 777M

POPULATION: 2.2 MILLION

LONELY PLANET RANKING: 101

DAILY LIFE TAKES CENTRE STAGE IN JORDAN'S THRIVING FILM INDUSTRY.
Photographer: Olivier Cirendini / LPI

STRENGTHS
- Roman ruins
- Proximity to Israel
- A convenient base to travel around Jordan
- Jordanian hospitality

WEAKNESSES
- Drivers who insist that a white line down the centre of a road is just that, a white line
- Modernisation

GOLD STAR
While Amman might be a sprawling metropolis with fewer signs of the area's ancient past than its Arab neighbours, a performance in the 2000-year-old Roman Amphitheatre will have you reaching for your toga and asking for directions to the Nymphaeum.

STARRING ROLE IN...
- *Story of a City: A Childhood in Amman* by Abd Al-Rahman
- *The Desert and the Snow* by Gertrude Bell

IMPORT
- Mickey D's
- Western shopping centres
- Amman International Theatre Festival
- Fête de la Musique

EXPORT
- Coloured marble
- Amin Matalqa's short films about Jordanian life
- King Hussein
- Bedouin crafts
- Antiquities – actually it's prohibited

SEE the remains of a prehistoric Neolithic settlement near Ain Ghazal, which dates back to about 6500 BC.

EAT *mensaf* – a whole lamb, head included, on a bed of rice and pine nuts, eaten with *jameed* (sun-dried yoghurt).

DRINK coffee – Ammanians are said to have a serious caffeine addiction.

DO experience the contemporary art space, Darat al Funun.

WATCH or participate in the annual Dead Sea Ultra Marathon.

BUY hand-woven Bedouin rugs.

AFTER DARK see a free art-house film (undubbed) at Books@Cafe.

URBAN MYTH
Amman is considered the oldest capital in the world. Biblical references to the city are numerous and indicate that by 1200 BC Rabbath Ammon (as it was then known) was the capital of the powerful Ammonites. King David, after being insulted by the Ammonite king Nahash, burnt many inhabitants alive in a brick kiln. Later the city fell under the sway of Rome, and Philadelphia became the seat of Christian bishops in the early Byzantine period. But the city declined and by the time a colony of Circassians resettled here in 1878, Amman was nothing more than a sad little village amid the ruins.

CHILDREN COMING OUT TO PLAY AT THE MAGNIFICENT ROMAN THEATRE, GUARANTEED TO DRAW A CROWD.
Photographer: Anthony Ham / LPI

THE IMPRESSIVE ANCIENT CITADEL TOWERS ABOVE THE CITY FROM ATOP JEBEL AL-QALA'A.
Photographer: Clint Lucas / LPI

ALL THAT GLITTERS IS NOT GOLD, BUT LOCAL MARKETS OVERFLOW WITH INTERESTING TREASURES.
Photographer: Olivier Cirendini / LPI

Amsterdam

VITAL STATISTICS

NAME: AMSTERDAM

NICKNAME: MOKUM, VENICE OF THE NORTH

DATE OF BIRTH: 1275; WHEN THE COUNT OF HOLLAND LIFTED TOLLS FOR RESIDENTS ON THE AMSTEL DAM

ADDRESS: THE NETHERLANDS (MAP 3, H7)

HEIGHT: 1M

SIZE: 220 SQ KM

POPULATION: 755,000 (CITY); 2.2 MILLION (METRO AREA)

LONELY PLANET RANKING: 024

FRIENDS ABANDON THEIR BIKES FOR A LEISURELY JUGGLE IN VONDELPARK.
Photographer: Barry Lewis / Network

SAY CHEESE – HOLLAND'S FAMOUS YELLOW RIND VARIETY LINES THE SHELVES OF A CITY SHOP.
Photographer: Esbin Anderson / LPI

LIKE A SCENE FROM A DREAM, BUILDINGS IN KEIZERSGRACHT TILT AT BIZARRE ANGLES.
Photographer: Frans Lemmens / Getty Images

A SIGN OF THINGS TO COME AT THE ENTRANCE TO THE MODERN WING OF THE VAN GOGH MUSEUM AMSTERDAM.
Photographer: Richard Nebesky / LPI

Forget images of red lights, drug addicts and coffee shops – Amsterdam's truly liberal, laid-back atmosphere, beautiful watery setting, picturesque houses, excellent museums and infamous nightlife give it a unique appeal.

ANATOMY

The central area of Amsterdam is Centrum, home to impressive Dam Sq, great shops, and those notorious red lights. Heading east from here, you pass through the market of Waterlooplein, the museums of the Plantage, the Eastern Islands and the new residential district, IJburg. The main tourist spots are in the Southern Canal Belt, while the fashionable shops of Jordaan are west of Centrum. Not far from the Van Gogh Museum is the leafy haven of Vondelpark. Bicycles are the most popular way to get around the city.

PEOPLE

The Netherlands is one of the world's most densely populated countries. Around 47% of Amsterdam's residents come from somewhere else, mainly Suriname, Morocco and Turkey.

TYPICAL AMSTERDAMMER

About 10% of Dutch people own their own homes, but nearly all residents of Amsterdam have a bicycle (the city had 600,000 bikes at last count). The unemployment rate is under 10%. As you would expect, Amsterdammers are a pretty relaxed bunch with liberal approaches to drugs, abortion, prostitution, euthanasia and homosexuality. That said, they say what they think and can come across as rude. They like a good time and don't take themselves too seriously. Like the English, queuing is a religion – woe betide anyone who tries to jump.

DEFINING EXPERIENCE

Taking a bike ride along the canals, then visiting the Van Gogh Museum and pottering in the antiques shops of Nieuwe Spiegelstraat, before enjoying a well-earned beer on one of the many café terraces.

STRENGTHS

- 160 canals and 90 islands, all reclaimed from the sea
- 7000 registered historical buildings
- Bicycles everywhere
- Dutch-Renaissance architecture eg Bartolotti House
- Those coffee shops
- Dutch beer served frothy and cold
- Clubbing at Bloemendaal beach
- Biggest gay scene in Europe
- Golden Age painters
- Liberal attitudes (the world's first homosexual marriage and legal euthanasia)
- Van Gogh Museum
- Rijksmuseum
- Anne Frankhuis
- Blijburg Beach
- Vondelpark
- Artis Zoo
- Nederlands Scheepvaartmuseum (Maritime Museum)
- Shopping in Negen Straatjes
- Beurs van Berlage and the Amsterdam School

WEAKNESSES

- Pushy dealers
- The Heineken Experience
- Bicycle theft – 200,000 get nicked every year
- Smelly backstreets
- Turbine noise from Schiphol, Europe's fastest-growing airport
- If the dams burst, 25% of the Netherlands would flood

GOLD STAR

Liberal attitudes abound in the city.

STARRING ROLE IN...

- *Deuce Bigalow: European Gigolo* (2005)
- *Ocean's 12* (2004)
- *Traffic* (1971)
- *The Acid House* by Irvine Welsh

IMPORT

- Anne Frank
- Rembrandt
- Travel writer Lieve Joris
- Artist Marlene Dumas
- Stag nights

EXPORT

- Vincent Van Gogh
- Baruch Spinoza
- Piet Mondrian
- Jacob van Ruysdael
- Albert Cuyp
- Jan Steen
- Cornelis Troost
- Jacob de Wit
- Golden Earring
- Shocking Blue
- Jan Akkerman
- Arts and crafts
- Heineken
- Dennis Bergkamp
- Tulips
- Modern dance
- Clogs
- Cheese

SEE Dutch masterpieces by Rembrandt and others in the fantastic Rijksmuseum.

EAT spicy Indonesian cuisine to the sounds of the sax at Coffee & Jazz.

DRINK in the sun at arty Finch on one of Jordaan's most attractive squares.

DO visit Anne Frankhuis and see the attic where Anne Frank wrote her incredible diary in hiding.

WATCH the city go mad on Koninginnedag (Queen's Day), with street parties, live music and endless beer.

BUY upmarket fashion and vintage clothing along the Western Canal Belt.

AFTER DARK hit Bitterzoet to get your fix of hip-hop, roots, Latin or pulse music.

URBAN MYTH

Prostitution was legalised in the Netherlands in 1810, and brothels were made legal in 2000. Seventy-eight percent of Dutch people have no problem with prostitution. There are 380 red-light windows in the city where 1000 to 1200 prostitutes work each day. Prostitutes rent their windows for between €40 and €100 per day and pay tax on their earnings. Services rendered by prostitutes start at €30. There is a union and if a client gets violent prostitutes can press a button to alert the police. Finally, why the red light? Apparently it is so flattering it makes teeth sparkle. In the 1300s, ladies of the night carried red lanterns to welcome the sailors to shore.

TAKING THE TIME TO CATCH UP ON CURRENT EVENTS AT PEGGY'S CAFÉ.
Photographer: Brent Winebrenner / LPI

Anchorage is an outpost of wilful humanity crafting more than survival from this unforgiving yet beautiful land. In this unparalleled urban wilderness polar bears take no notice of city limits and outdoor adventure is as easy to have as theatre, great food and a rocking nightlife.

ANATOMY

Sprawling across a broad triangle of a peninsula, the city is embraced by Cook Inlet and the 1500m-plus peaks of Chugach State Park, a backyard getaway to wilderness adventure. Anchorage's excellent public-bus system shuttles you from the grid of flower-filled downtown streets where you'll find more than enough museums to keep you happy, and through the interesting Midtown neighbourhoods with their diverse eateries and lively nightlife. But get off the bus and explore the 196km of paved bicycle paths, the stunning tracts of green (or white, depending on the season) parkland and the lakes that dot the city.

PEOPLE

Fifteen years ago barely a quarter of Anchorage residents were born in Alaska but these days the city's population is a lot less transient. That said, the lure of the final frontier never diminishes, and the typical resident is young (average age is 32), mobile and often from the US West Coast. Ethnic communities are growing fast in this previously male and very Caucasian town, but Alaskan natives are the largest minority group, making up about 8% of the population.

TYPICAL ANCHORAGITE

Anchoragites have the frontier spirit of most Alaskans, but with the urban edge of big-city dwellers. They are independent, practical people who answer extreme weather with extreme living, whether it's indulging in arctic diving, bear hunting and back-country snowboarding, or just drinking until the sun goes down. Looked down upon by rural Alaskans, Anchoragites can't wait to hit the mountains on the weekend, but they always get back in time for a trip to the theatre or to catch a local band.

Anchorage

VITAL STATISTICS

NAME: ANCHORAGE

NICKNAME: LOS ANCHORAGE; THE RAGE

DATE OF BIRTH: 1914; ANCHORAGE WAS FOUNDED WHEN IT SERVED AS A HEADQUARTERS AND WORK CAMP FOR THE ALASKA RAILROAD

ADDRESS: USA (MAP 1, D6)

HEIGHT: 40M

SIZE: 4396 SQ KM

POPULATION: 280,000

LONELY PLANET RANKING: 175

TOTEMS KEEP A STERN WATCH OVER THE ENTRANCE TO THE ANCHORAGE COURTHOUSE.
Photographer: Brent Winebrenner / LPI

BRIGHT MODERN ARCHITECTURE BRINGS A RAY OF SUNSHINE TO 4TH AVE.
Photographer: Brent Winebrenner / LPI

TROPHIES THAT WOULD HORRIFY RUDOLPH AT THE GENERAL STORE.
Photographer: Brent Winebrenner / LPI

DEFINING EXPERIENCE

Wandering through the Saturday market to the Snow City Café for a breakfast of Ship Creek Benedict and a Kaladi coffee while tossing up whether to bike the Tony Knowles Coastal Trail or hike the tundra in the Chugach State Park, then heading down to the Beer Tooth Theatre Pub for an evening meal/movie/beer.

STRENGTHS

- Big, green parks
- Proximity to mountains, glaciers, lakes – this is a nature-lover's paradise!
- Alaska Zoo
- Beluga whales in Cook Inlet
- Being able to catch an 18kg salmon from under a highway bridge
- A multitude of microbreweries
- Title Wave Books
- The aurora borealis – when you can see it!
- Good music scene

WEAKNESSES

- Winter
- No major league sports teams
- 'Our Alaska' with Governor Frank Murkowski
- Ravenous summer mosquitoes
- One of the most expensive cities in the USA

GOLD STAR

You're only 20 minutes from Alaska! It's the best base location for outdoor adventures.

STARRING ROLE IN...

- *About Grace* by Anthony Doerr
- *Mystery, Alaska* (1999)
- *Sidney Laurence, Painter of the North* by Kesler E Woodward
- 'Anchorage' by Michelle Shocked

IMPORT

- Pilot bread
- 'Chicago's Best' food wagon
- Retirees from the lower 48 on cruise holidays
- Mountain men
- Nature film crews

EXPORT

- Salmon and halibut
- Oil
- Jewel
- Softball-sized radishes and giant cabbage
- Water
- Morel mushrooms
- Malamutes
- Moose 'nugget' jewellery
- Reindeer antlers

SEE the start of the Iditarod, the last great trail sled-dog race, charge up 4th Ave at the beginning of March each year.

EAT Coconut-beer–battered Spam (or not).

DRINK an ice-cold pint of Alaskan Amber on the deck of the Snow Goose and soak up the midnight sun.

DO hear ancient Alaskan songs, once thought lost forever, performed at the Alaska Native Heritage Centre.

WATCH the *Whale-Fat Follies* at Mr Whitekey's Fly by Night; a fun and raunchy musical about duct tape, spawning salmon and Alaska's official state fossil, the woolly mammoth.

BUY a Qiviut scarf or cap from the Oomingmak Musk Ox Producers' Co-operative.

AFTER DARK head to the 10 bars at Chilkoot Charlie's (Koot's) – the place for unbridled Anchorage debauchery for the last 35 years.

URBAN MYTH

US airman Ted Winnen shoots a larger than normal grizzly while out deer hunting in Prince William Sound and suddenly his escapades and photos end up in about half a million email inboxes around the world and, according to the Alaska Forest Service, the enquiries about the monster bear of impossible proportions (think 3.8m and 725kg) just keep on coming, even four years after the incident.

Antananarivo

VITAL STATISTICS

NAME: ANTANANARIVO

NICKNAME: TANA; LITERALLY 'CITY OF A THOUSAND' (WARRIORS)

DATE OF BIRTH: 1610; AFTER THE MERINA RULER, KING ANDRIANJAKA, CONQUERED SEVERAL VILLAGES IN THE AREA

ADDRESS: MADAGASCAR (MAP 2, P21)

HEIGHT: 1372M

POPULATION: 1.7 MILLION

LONELY PLANET RANKING: 193

Often eclipsed by the natural beauty of the rest of the country, Tana offers a glimpse into the edgy, urban side of Malagasy culture, plus the chance to indulge in fine French colonial cuisine.

ANATOMY

Renault 4 taxis whine up and down the cobblestone hills, belching blue exhaust fumes over the crowds of pedestrians. In spring, purple jacaranda trees blaze into life, raining nectar onto the heads of skipping children and strolling couples. Terracotta mansions are stacked on the hillsides, turning gold under the setting sun. Beyond the city sprawl, paddy fields glint in the pale sunshine.

PEOPLE

The majority group in Tana is the indigenous Merina community. They and the other indigenous groups of Tana are joined by a very few French descendants, with the languages of choice being Malagasy and French.

TYPICAL TANA CITIZEN

The typical Tana resident is rooted in traditions and community but flexible enough to make room for tourists and their beliefs. The people of Tana are proud of their illustrious history but a little reserved about sharing it. Your best understanding of the Malagasy will come from the locals you encounter in your travels – ladies selling embroidered tablecloths on the pavement, men hawking rubber stamps from improvised stalls, or taxi drivers sharing peanut cake bought from a roadside kiosk.

DEFINING EXPERIENCE

Breakfasting *à la française* with coffee and bread, spending the day shopping or selling wares at the markets, eating dinner at a *hotely* (local foodstall), sampling local rums at Restaurant Sakamanga with friends and, finally, dancing the night away to contemporary Malagasy music.

STRENGTHS

- The zoo at Tsimbazaza
- Zebu-drawn carts
- Merina history, living and dead
- Rice paddies in the middle of town
- On-foot exploration
- Antaimoro paper (tree-pulp parchment inlaid with flowers and leaves and left to dry under the moon's shade, as tradition dictates)
- The Marché Artisanal (Handicrafts Market) at La Digue
- Blended African and French heritage
- Access to the rest of Madagascar
- Views from the city down to the plains

WEAKNESSES

- Steep streets and steps
- Crowds, noise, pollution
- Only two published maps, neither of which is up to date
- Train tracks that cross the runway of the airport
- Continual advances of beggars and street vendors
- About 55% living below the poverty line

GOLD STAR

Having the most amazing names for people and places – the queen's palace at the Rova is called Manjakamiadana (A Fine Place to Rule). It was designed for Queen Ranavalona I, and is located next to a replica of the palace of King Andrianampoinimerina, founder of the Merina kingdom.

STARRING ROLE IN...

- *Madagascar* (2005)
- *Le Tricheur* (The Cheat) by Claude Simon
- *I Vola* by Andry Andraina
- *Fofombadiko* (My Fiancée) by Emilson Daniel Andriamalala

IMPORT

- Ancestor worship and rice worship from the city's Indonesian ancestors
- The African obsession with zebu
- Arabic words for books, money and music
- French pastries
- Anything that comes from European culture
- Naturalists from all over the world

EXPORT

- Tobacco
- Merina burial rituals
- A new appreciation for royalty with short names
- Textiles
- Lemurs and chameleons
- The concept of Madagascar as 'the eighth continent'

SEE the view from the Rova at sunset.

EAT at Chez Mariette – gourmet Malagasy cuisine based on the banquets served to Madagascan royalty.

DRINK tea, coffee or hot chocolate at a *salon de thé* (tearoom).

DO stroll down the steep, narrow streets to the Ave of Independence.

WATCH a traditional Malagasy performance of acrobatics, music and speeches.

BUY handicrafts from the revamped Zoma markets.

AFTER DARK dance to a mixture of American hip-hop, Malagasy chart hits, and French soft-rock anthems at Le Pandora Station.

URBAN MYTH

Everyday life in Tana is regulated by numerous *fady* (taboos), which differ from those of other regions in Madagascar. They can forbid foods (pork, lemur, turtle), wearing clothes of a particular colour, bathing in a river or a lake etc. *Fady* are attributed to ancestors, to whom the Malagasy owe a respectful worship whatever their religion. It is preferable to respect these beliefs so as not to offend.

NIGHTTIME TRAFFIC LIGHTS UP THE AVE OF INDEPENDENCE.
Photographer: David Curl / LPI

MARKET TRADERS RELAX UNDER A HOMAGE TO COFFEE.
Photographer: Jeremy Horner / Panos Pictures

PLAYTIME IN MOTION, PLAYTIME AT REST.
Photographer: Reagan Pannell / Alamy

AN AERIAL VIEW REVEALS TANA'S HAPPILY COLOURED ROOFTOPS.
Photographer: Yann Arthus-Bertrand / Corbis

Antigua

VITAL STATISTICS

NAME: ANTIGUA

DATE OF BIRTH: 1543; WHEN IT WAS FOUNDED AND SERVED AS THE COLONIAL CAPITAL FOR THE NEXT 233 YEARS

ADDRESS: GUATEMALA (MAP 4, F6)

HEIGHT: 1480M

POPULATION: 40,000

LONELY PLANET RANKING: 127

One of the oldest and most beautiful cities in the Americas, Antigua thrives as an eclectic arts hub and magnet for students of its many language schools.

ANATOMY

Nestled in the Ponchoy Valley, Antigua is dramatically set between three volcanoes: Volcán Agua to the southeast, Volcán Fuego to the southwest and Volcán Acatenango to the west. Antigua served as the capital until it was moved to Guatemala City following the 1773 earthquakes, and a few buildings remain from this era. The central point of the city is Parque Central and *calles* (streets) are labelled east and west of this point. Buses arrive at the Terminales de Buses, four blocks west of Parque Central.

PEOPLE

The majority of Antigüeños are of a mestizo (of mixed Spanish and indigenous) heritage and are practising Roman Catholics. The region's indigenous Mayan people speak Cakchiquel and continue to practise their nature-based religion along with Roman Catholicism.

TYPICAL ANTIGÜEÑO

Antigüeños typically start the day early the same way they finish it – with a meal of eggs, beans, fried plantains and plenty of tortillas. A two-hour siesta follows lunch, the main meal. They are social, polite and refined in the arts, and enjoy the marimba and mariachi music played at frequent festivals and celebrations.

DEFINING EXPERIENCE

Visiting the museums and ruins strewn about town, studying Spanish while living with a Guatemalan family, summiting Volcán Pacaya, hiking or horse-riding to the Cerro de la Cruz vista point, buying vividly coloured, traditional handmade *traje* (clothing) in the market, and watching the passing parade during elaborate religious celebrations.

STRENGTHS

- Cathedral of San Francisco
- Elaborate religious celebrations during Holy Week
- Intensive Spanish-language courses
- Climbing the stunning Volcán Agua
- Charming Spanish baroque architecture
- Parque Central
- Intricately beaded crafts
- *Huipiles* (embroided blouses)
- Unique and weathered doorknobs and knockers
- Colourful, cobblestone streets
- Shopping for Mayan crafts
- Volcanoes
- Mayan water-lily blossoms and vegetable motifs adorning the church of La Merced

WEAKNESSES

- Twisting ankles on cobblestone streets after a drink
- Leaving
- Pleading for accommodation in the busy season
- The sheer number of tourists in the busy season

GOLD STAR

Parque Central – the gathering place for locals and visitors alike. On most days the plaza is lined with villagers selling handicrafts to tourists; on Sunday it's mobbed and the streets on the east and west sides are closed to traffic. Things are cheapest late on Sunday afternoon, when the peddling is winding down. At night, mariachi or marimba bands play in the park.

STARRING ROLE IN...

- *Riotous Rhymes 'n' Remedies* by Sylvanus Barnes
- *Garden of Life* by LHC Westcott

IMPORT

- Spanish-language students
- Cafés
- Colonial architecture
- The Spanish

EXPORT

- Coffee – some of the world's best
- Ceramics
- Beaded handicrafts
- Singer Ricardo Arjona
- Handmade *traje*
- Carved ceremonial masks
- *Huipiles*

SEE Samuel Franco Arce's photographs and recordings of Mayan ceremonies and music at Casa K'Ojom.

EAT the Sunday buffet in the Café Condessa.

DRINK Zacapa Centenario (a fine Guatemalan rum).

DO enrol in an intensive Spanish-language and culture course.

WATCH the afternoon handicrafts trade around the 1738 fountain in Parque Central, to the sounds of mariachi or marimba bands.

BUY colourful beaded and embroidered handicrafts, ceramics and carved wooden masks.

AFTER DARK explore Antigua's atmospheric bars and see if you can practise some of that new-found Spanish.

URBAN MYTH

Antigua really comes alive in Semana Santa (Holy Week), when hundreds of people dress in deep-purple robes to accompany the most revered sculptural images from the city's churches in daily street processions remembering Christ's Crucifixion. Dense clouds of incense envelop the parades and the streets are covered in breathtakingly elaborate *alfombras* (carpets) of coloured sawdust and flower petals.

THE END OF A LONG DAY MAKES FOR LONG SHADOWS IN ANTIGUA.
Photographer: Paul A Souders / Corbis

FIRE AND WATER: A VIEW OF VOLCÁN AGUA OVERLOOKING THE OLD CITY.
Photographer: Alfredo Maiquez / LPI

TWO INFECTIOUSLY HAPPY DENIZENS OF THE ANTIGUA HIGHLANDS.
Photographer: Greg Johnston / LPI

SPOILT FOR CHOICE: ANTIGUA'S FRUIT AND VEGETABLE MARKET.
Photographer: Jon Arnold Images / Alamy

Apia

VITAL STATISTICS

NAME: APIA

DATE OF BIRTH: 1820S; WHEN THE RESIDENT EUROPEANS ESTABLISHED A SOCIETY IN APIA

ADDRESS: SAMOA (MAP 1, QQ18)

HEIGHT: 2M

SIZE: 1.2 SQ KM

POPULATION: 59,000

LONELY PLANET RANKING: 142

TOP BRASS – THE SAMOAN POLICE BAND BELTS OUT A MARCHING TUNE.
Photographer: Peter Hendrie / LPI

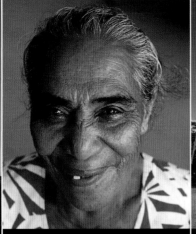

SUBMERGED SIGNPOST AT PALOLO DEEP NATIONAL MARINE RESERVE, A POPULAR SNORKELLING LOCATION.
Photographer: Mark Daffey / LPI

THE WELCOMING SMILE OF AN OLDER APIAN.
Photographer: Will Salter / LPI

THE COLONIAL GRANDEUR OF ROBERT LOUIS STEVENSON'S METICULOUSLY RESTORED FORMER RESIDENCE.
Photographer: John Borthwick / LPI

With its run-down colonial buildings, big old pulu trees and easy-going pace, Apia retains a certain shabby and romantic charm.

ANATOMY

From the centre of town, Apia's neat villages spread west along the level coastal area and climb up the gentle slopes towards the hills and into the valleys. Travelling by public bus is the most common method of getting around. Taxis are also cheap and plentiful.

PEOPLE

The indigenous people of the Samoan islands are large and robust folk of Polynesian origin. Samoans account for the majority of the population and Euronesians make up the rest. There is a substantial Chinese Samoan community centred in Apia. Most of the Europeans and Asians residing in the country are involved in UN development projects, business investment or volunteer aid organisations, such as the Peace Corps.

TYPICAL APIAN

Samoans are tradition-oriented and follow closely the social hierarchies, customs and courtesies established long before the arrival of Europeans. They are outwardly friendly and responsive people. The social system can produce as much pressure as it does wellbeing. Beneath the light-heartedness, a strict and demanding code of behaviour is upheld with expectations that can stifle individuality and creativity.

DEFINING EXPERIENCE

Spending a lazy morning exploring the Flea Market and Maketi Fou (main market) and snacking on *palusami* (coconut cream wrapped in taro leaves), visiting the churches along the city's waterfront, then snorkelling the afternoon away at Palolo Deep National Marine Reserve.

STRENGTHS

- ◢ Laid-back atmosphere
- ◢ Palolo Deep National Marine Reserve
- ◢ The Madonna-topped Catholic cathedral
- ◢ Madd Gallery
- ◢ Friendly people
- ◢ Samoan buses, with names such as 'Don't Tell Mum'
- ◢ The traditional Polynesian feast cooked in an *umu* (above-ground oven)
- ◢ Samoan *fiafia* (dance performances)
- ◢ Aggie Grey's Hotel
- ◢ Tomb of the Tu'imaleali'ifano dynasty

WEAKNESSES

- ◢ Year-round high humidity
- ◢ Cyclones
- ◢ Deforestation
- ◢ Traffic congestion due to lack of town planning
- ◢ Stray dogs

GOLD STAR

The pace of life – it's so laid-back it's only a heartbeat away from being a nice little snooze.

STARRING ROLE IN...

- ◢ *A Chief in Two Worlds* (1992)
- ◢ *Island of Lost Souls* (1993)
- ◢ *Where We Once Belonged* by Sia Figiel
- ◢ *Leaves of the Banyan Tree* by Albert Wendt

IMPORT

- ◢ Christian missionaries
- ◢ Pirates
- ◢ Robert Louis Stevenson
- ◢ Foreign aid
- ◢ Margaret Mead
- ◢ Tax breaks for foreign manufacturers
- ◢ Junk food
- ◢ The Chinese
- ◢ Rugby
- ◢ Mormons
- ◢ Peace Corps members

EXPORT

- ◢ Coconut products
- ◢ *Siapo* (bark cloth made from the inner bark of the paper mulberry tree)
- ◢ Kava
- ◢ Taro
- ◢ Writer Sia Figiel
- ◢ *Fale* (traditional thatched house)
- ◢ Va'aiga Tuigamala (the 'million dollar man') – the highest-paid rugby union player in the world in the late '90s
- ◢ Laid-back vibe

SEE Apia from the Mt Vaea Scenic Reserve, where you'll find the beautifully restored home of Robert Louis Stevenson, the botanical gardens and rainforest trails.

EAT a breakfast of Samoan pancakes (more like small doughnuts) washed down with a cup of addictive *koko Samoa* (locally grown cocoa served hot and black with lots of sugar) at the Maketi Fou or the foodstalls behind the Flea Market.

DRINK Independent Samoa's excellent locally brewed lager, Vailima, at the happening Coast Bar & Grill.

DO go snorkelling in Palolo Deep to experience the sudden drop from the shallow reef into a deep blue hole flanked by walls of coral and densely populated by colourful species of fish.

WATCH a spectacular *fiafia* at Aggie Grey's Hotel.

BUY locally made *siapo*, kava bowls and coconut jewellery at the Flea Market.

AFTER DARK see Cindy, the indomitable drag queen of Samoa, who performs at the Hotel Kitano Tusitala every Saturday.

URBAN MYTH

In December 1889 the already famous Scottish author and poet Robert Louis Balfour Stevenson and his wife, Fanny Osborne, arrived in Apia aboard the schooner *Equator*. Stevenson had left Europe in search of relief from worsening tuberculosis and the general sickliness that had plagued him all his life. He was enchanted by Samoa, and in 1890 he paid £200 for 126 hectares of land in the hills above Apia. Stevenson spent four years in Samoa before he died of a stroke. When the Samoan chief Tu'imaleali'ifano spoke of Stevenson's death, he echoed the sentiments of many Samoans: *Talofa e i lo matou Tusitala. Ua tagi le fatu ma le 'ele'ele,'* he said. ('Our beloved Tusitala. The stones and the earth weep'.)

Arequipa is a one-of-a-kind example of South American life – the lanes, museums, churches and rich culture of the town and its resilient people are resplendent after nearly 500 years of volcanic earthquakes and tumultuous politics.

ANATOMY

At over 2km above sea level, Arequipa nestles in a fertile valley under the perfect cone-shaped volcano of El Misti (5822m). The Río Chili flows around the northern boundary of the town. The city centre is easily navigable as it is based on a colonial checkerboard pattern around Plaza de Armas. Addresses, however, can be confusing, as streets change names every few blocks. Walk, cycle or catch minibuses, buses and taxis to get around the city.

PEOPLE

About half of Arequipa's population is Indian (*indígenas* is an appropriate term; *indios* is insulting). The majority of the rest of the population is mestizo, and there are also white, black and Asian minorities. As is clear from the many religious buildings and churches, Christianity is the dominant religion and a significant part of daily life. Though the Peruvian constitution allows complete religious freedom, its citizens remain almost exclusively Christian, with about 90% identifying themselves as Roman Catholic.

TYPICAL AREQUIPAN

The Arequipans are rugged and proud people, fond of intellectual debate, especially about their fervent political beliefs, which find voice through regular demonstrations in the main plaza. In fact, their stubborn intellectual independence from Lima is so strong that at one time they even designed their own passport and flag.

Arequipa

VITAL STATISTICS

NAME: AREQUIPA

NICKNAME: THE WHITE CITY

DATE OF BIRTH: 1540; REFOUNDED BY THE SPANISH AT THE SITE OF A PRE-INCAN SETTLEMENT

ADDRESS: PERU (MAP 1, M18)

HEIGHT: 2325M

POPULATION: 1 MILLION

LONELY PLANET RANKING: 140

TAXIS PATIENTLY AWAITING THEIR TURN IN THE PLAZA DE ARMAS.
Photographer: Brent Winebrenner / LPI

DEFINING EXPERIENCE

Spending the morning exploring the Museo Santuarios Andinos, the home of Juanita, 'the ice princess' and numerous other ice mummies, artefacts and curiosities, then savouring a leisurely lunch of the invigoratingly spicy *rocoto relleno* (hot peppers stuffed with meat, rice and vegetables) at one of the balcony restaurants overlooking Plaza de Armas.

STRENGTHS

- Alpaca knitwear
- *Criollo* cuisine (spicy local fare)
- Ice mummies
- Gateway to El Misti
- Dazzling *sillar* (a light-coloured volcanic rock) stonework
- The nearby Cañón del Colca and its condor residents
- River running the Ríos Chile
- Vibrant locals
- La Catedral
- Stately colonial sillar mansions

WEAKNESSES

- Petty theft
- Volcanoes
- Sparse midweek nightlife
- Animal cruelty (bullfights and cockfights)
- Illegitimate tour rip-offs

GOLD STAR

Tradition – Arequipa is a preserve of the uniquely eclectic Peruvian culture; so much more than a transit stop to the mountains, it has carved its own niche in the South American psyche.

STARRING ROLE IN...

- *Parelisa* (1999)
- *Path to Arequipa* by Mark Jacobi

IMPORT

- Spanish and African culture
- VW kombis
- Indians from Lake Titicaca and the Peruvian highlands
- Mountaineers

EXPORT

- Alpaca textiles
- Leather goods

SEE the astonishing views of Arequipa and Mt Misti flanked by its two siblings, Chachani (6075m) and Pichu Pichu (5571m) from the mirador (observation tower) in the suburb of Yanahuara.

EAT *chupede camarones* (prawn soup) or *chancho al horno* (suckling pig) at the lively Sol de Mayo.

DRINK chicha (fermented maize beer) at the tourist mecca Déjà Vu.

DO go on a guided tour of La Catedral, which dominates Plaza de Armas.

WATCH the bullfights, which are not as bloodthirsty or cruel as their Spanish counterparts (the Peruvian way is to pit two bulls against each other for the favour of a female, usually culminating in one making a sensible exit).

BUY a high-quality alpaca sweater from Patio El Ekeko.

AFTER DARK catch the very latest blockbuster movie at Cinessur el Portal.

URBAN MYTH

The Monasterio de Santa Catalina was founded in 1580 by a rich widow, María de Guzmán, who very selectively chose her nuns from the best Spanish families, who paid a hefty dowry for the privilege. Traditionally, the second daughter of upper-class families would enter a nunnery to live in chaste poverty, but in this privileged convent each nun had between one and four servants or slaves, and the nuns would invite musicians, have parties and generally live it up in the style to which they had always been accustomed. After about three centuries of these hedonistic goings-on, the pope sent Sister Josefa Cadena, a strict Dominican nun, to straighten things out. She arrived like a hurricane in 1871 and set about sending all the rich dowries back to Europe and freeing the myriad of servants and slaves, many of whom stayed on as nuns.

THE BLESSEDLY TRANQUIL EXTERIOR OF THE MONASTERIO DE SANTA CATALINA.
Photographer: Brent Winebrenner / LPI

STARING PAST STEEPLES AT THE MOUNTAINS FLANKING AREQUIPA.
Photographer: Brent Winebrenner / LPI

ALL OUT OF ICE CREAM, TWO VENDORS LUG THEIR PORTABLE MARKETS BACK TO HOME BASE.
Photographer: Brent Winebrenner / LPI

Ashgabat

VITAL STATISTICS

NAME: ASHGABAT

NICKNAME: THE CITY OF LOVE (THE MEANING OF ASHGABAT IN ARABIC)

DATE OF BIRTH: 1881; AS A RUSSIAN FORT

ADDRESS: TURKMENISTAN (MAP 1, BB10)

HEIGHT: 226M

POPULATION: 695,000

LONELY PLANET RANKING: 200

Ashgabat is a city-sized monument to Turkmenistan's former leader, the megalomaniac Saparmyrat Niyazov, self-declared 'Turkmenbashi', leader of the Turkmen. Part-Las Vegas, part-Stalingrad, this desert oasis is enjoying a new political era, but in its sprawling boulevards and wedding-cake architecture it retains no end of quirkiness

ANATOMY

The old Russian town was wiped off the face of the earth in a 1948 earthquake and the rebuilt city is entirely a product of Niyazov's dictatorship. The city's main thoroughfares are dotted with recently added white-marble residential buildings that seem permanently empty. These are broken up by fantastically elaborate palaces and monuments, including those of the stunningly weird suburb of Berzengi.

PEOPLE

The population is a mix of Russians left behind after the end of the Soviet Union and native Turkmen. Ashgabat is by far the most Russian city in Turkmenistan.

TYPICAL ASHGABAT CITIZEN

Ashgabat dwellers exhibit the spontaneous hospitality and innate generosity characteristic of Turkmen nomadic traditions. After enduring years of eccentric autocracy during the reign of Turkmenbashi, Ashgabatis are resilient and resourceful. But under the new outward-looking regime of relatively liberal Kurbanguly Berdymukhamedov they are optimistic and enjoying new opportunities – pensions and maternity benefits, the lifting of internet restrictions. Still, they are not so naive to believe that democracy is just around the corner.

DEFINING EXPERIENCE

Standing beneath the Arch of Neutrality with a golden revolving Turkmenbashi overhead and the fantastically Orwellian ensemble of marble buildings around Independence Sq.

STRENGTHS

- Irrigated greenery contrasting with the surrounding desert sparseness
- Friendly locals
- Extremely safe at all times
- The best restaurants and hotels in the country
- Almost no tourists

WEAKNESSES

- Restricted freedom of the press
- The 'companionship' of your official guide at all times
- Occasional dust storms – you're in the middle of a desert, you know
- Bugged hotel rooms

GOLD STAR

Tolkuchka Bazaar, a few kilometres outside the city in the nearby desert, is one of the most colourful and fascinating markets on earth, where you can buy anything from carpets to camels.

STARRING ROLE IN...

- There's no modern movie industry here, but Ashgabat is crying out to be used in a Bond movie of the future. Dr Evil himself appears to be on display on every street corner.

IMPORT

- Water
- Italian marble
- French architects
- BMWs
- Foreign currency (or so the new regime hopes!)

EXPORT

- Oil
- Gas (to Europe, or so EU bureaucrats hope!)
- Carpets
- Political dissidents
- *Rukhnama* (former president Niyazov's 'Book of the Soul')

SEE spectacular views of Asghabat, endless desert vistas and an 80m-high artificial waterfall from the Turkmenbashi Cableway on Kopet Dag

EAT at expat favourite the Iranian Truck Stop for a real culinary treat.

DRINK national beers Zip and Berk, both of which go down very well in the heat of the late desert afternoon.

DO some riding in the rugged countryside around the city on iconic Akhal-Teke horses.

WATCH a traditional Turkmen opera at the spanking new National Theatre.

BUY stunning Turkmen carpets at Tolkuchka Bazaar for a fraction of their price at home.

AFTER DARK your best bet is to head to the Florida nightclub (also called Kumush Ay) for Turkmenistan's one and only drum and bass night.

URBAN MYTH

Perhaps the most enduring of the many myths surrounding the former president is that of his heart bypass in 1997. Having gone in grey haired, Turkmenbashi emerged, bypass complete and his hair mysteriously jet black again. The local media, at a loss to explain such an event, immediately hailed the bypass as rejuvenating to the extent that the leader's hair had followed suit. This led to lots of local muttering about Turkmenbashi being a patient of Dr Schwarzkopf – particularly among the workers who had to spend the next few years repainting all the official portraits of Niyazov.

RELIGIOUS REFLECTIONS: THE MIRROR IMAGE OF A MOSQUE.
Photographer: Nevada Wier / Getty Images

TWO VILLAGE CHILDREN JUSTIFIABLY PROUD OF THEIR RIGHTEOUS OUTFITS, ON THE OUTSKIRTS OF ASHGABAT.
Photographer: Nevada Wier / Corbis

DAZZLING JEWELLERY ON DISPLAY AT THE SUNDAY BAZAAR.
Photographer: David Samuel Robbins / Corbis

AN ASHGABAT WOMAN DEFIES FORMER PRESIDENT NIYAZOV'S EDICT TO AVOID THE TRADITIONAL PENCHANT FOR GOLD-CAPPED TEETH – IN FULL VIEW OF HIS OWN GOLD-PLATED STATUE.
Photographer: Shamil Zhumatov / Reuters/Picture Media

Asmara

VITAL STATISTICS

NAME: ASMARA

DATE OF BIRTH: 12TH CENTURY; ENCOURAGED BY THE PLENTIFUL SUPPLIES OF WATER, SHEPHERDS FROM THE AKELE GUZAY REGION FOUNDED FOUR VILLAGES ON THE HILL THAT IS NOW THE SITE OF AN ORTHODOX CHURCH

ADDRESS: ERITREA (MAP 2, M8)

HEIGHT: 2355M

POPULATION: 500,000

LONELY PLANET RANKING: 117

EDUCATION EQUALS OPPORTUNITY FOR THESE YOUNG GIRLS.
Photographer: Patrick Ben Luke Syder / LPI

Like a film set from an early Italian movie, old espresso machines churn out macchiatos, Cinquecento taxis putt-putt about and all over town you can see outstanding examples of Art Deco architecture – Asmara is without doubt one of the safest, cleanest and most enchanting capital cities on the continent.

ANATOMY

Built according to a strict urban plan, Asmara was divided into four main areas: the administrative centre, the colonial residential quarter, the native quarter and the outbuildings. Liberation Ave, lined with majestic palms, striking architecture and busy cafés, is flanked by September 1 Sq at the eastern end and the Governor's Palace in the west. The old Italian residential quarter with its Art Deco villas is south of Liberation Ave. Central Asmara is small enough to walk everywhere, but even the locals have trouble keeping up with the changing street names.

PEOPLE

Asmarinos are a mix of nine colourful ethnic groups, each with its own language and customs. The Tigrinya make up the majority, and this is the language you'll hear widely spoken, although Arabic, English and Amharic are also prevalent. On a Sunday the clashing sound of cathedral bells and the Muslim call to prayer provide oral evidence of the communities' ability to coexist, notwithstanding all government efforts to the contrary.

TYPICAL ASMARINO

Cosmopolitan, dignified and welcoming are words often used to describe Asmarinos. Presentation is everything and it's not uncommon to see a well-groomed man walking out of his tin-roofed shack sporting a suit, leather jacket and gold galore. Locals love to dance, and the traditional style is unique, with lots of variations on shaking body parts, but if you give it a go, you'll win a lot of friends. With a small city, and such social people, Asmarinos can't walk more than a block without running into somebody they know. Cycling is popular, but bikes seem to spend more time lined up outside the cafés than on the streets.

DEFINING EXPERIENCE

Watching the world go by and enjoying a cappuccino in one of the many 1930s Italian-style cafés, then taking a *gari* (horse-drawn cart) tour of Asmara's fascinating architecture before joining in the sunset *passeggiata* (promenade; when the whole town takes a turn around the streets) to catch up with friends, hear the latest gossip, window-shop and generally take things easy.

STRENGTHS

- Sublime architecture – from Art Deco to cubist, expressionist, functionalist, futurist, rationalist and neoclassical styles
- Impressive churches
- *Mies* (local honey wine)
- Blue skies eight months of the year
- Excellent coffee and pizza
- Medeber market
- Traffic-free streets
- Incredibly clean city
- Fresh juices
- Safe to walk the streets at night
- Endless dinner/lunch invitations to strangers' homes
- Gold shops
- Lively café culture
- *Injera* (spongy bread)

WEAKNESSES

- Asmara gin
- Lack of water
- No cheap flights
- No privately owned news media
- First-day altitude sickness
- Lack of tourist infrastructure
- Not a great diversity of food once you've had your fill of pizza, spaghetti bolognese and *zigny* (a spicy meat stew)

GOLD STAR

The Cultural Assets Rehabilitation Programme (CARP) – set up in 1996 to record the city's architecture and to educate children, businesspeople and developers to look after their unparalleled urban heritage.

STARRING ROLE IN...

- *Towards Asmara* by Thomas Keneally
- *Who Said Merhawi Is Dead?* edited by Charles Cantalupo and Ghirmai Negash
- *Ciao Asmara* by Justin Hill

IMPORT

- Fiats
- Pizza
- Coffee – anyone for a macchiato or a cappuccino?
- Italian cheese and salami
- The nightly *passeggiata*
- Italian words in the vernacular
- Military materials
- Fuel

EXPORT

- Shellfish, snapper and groper
- Sesame seeds
- Salt
- Live sheep
- Gum Arabic
- Textiles
- Young football stars

SEE the entire population of Asmara strolling down the boulevards during the sunset *passeggiata*.

EAT *injera* and *tibs zil zil* (sizzling lamb) in the traditional back room of the Milano Restaurant.

DRINK an espresso from a vintage Italian coffee machine at one of the many outdoor cafés.

DO take the Eritrean State Railway steam train down the escarpment from Asmara to the Red Sea at Massawa.

WATCH a film in the 1800-seat, beautifully restored Art Deco Cinema Impero.

BUY a tailor-made leather jacket, or for something more traditional, a gorgeous basket made by ex-fighter Fattima Suleiman at Roble Gift Articles.

AFTER DARK dance up a storm with the locals at the Mocambo nightclub.

URBAN MYTH

It's hard not to stare at all the stunning women, particularly when their grins reveal tattooed gums. Fashionable teenagers prick their gums until they bleed, and then rub them with charcoal. The resulting blue colour sets off a dazzling set of teeth, and is considered a mark of great beauty.

THIS ART DECO APOTHECARY RETAINS ITS COLONIAL ITALIAN BEAUTY.
Photographer: Oliver Strewe / LPI

RELIGIOUS FESTIVITIES GIVE THIS YOUNG PRIEST SOMETHING TO THINK ABOUT.
Photographer: Frances Linzee Gordon / LPI

CHRISTIAN, MUSLIM AND ORTHODOX FAITHS LIVE SIDE BY SIDE IN ASMARA.
Photographer: Frances Linzee Gordon / LPI

Aswan

VITAL STATISTICS

NAME: ASWAN

DATE OF BIRTH: 300 BC; ELEPHANTINE ISLAND (ADJACENT TO ASWAN) WAS THE ORIGINAL SETTLEMENT AND A NATURAL FORTRESS

ADDRESS: EGYPT (MAP 2, K5)

HEIGHT: 112M

SIZE: 679 SQ KM

POPULATION: 1.2 MILLION

LONELY PLANET RANKING: 177

Once the gateway to Africa and a crossroads for the ancient caravan routes, Aswan is a mellow winter resort boasting sun-filled days, jostling markets and sweeping views of the desert on the most picturesque part of the Nile.

ANATOMY

The Nile flows down from the dams and around the giant granite boulders and palm-studded islands that protrude from the waters at the edge of Aswan. There are only three main avenues, and most of the city runs parallel to the Nile, making it easy to navigate. The train station, at the northern end of town, is only three blocks east of the river and the Corniche el-Nil, and is fronted by Aswan's market street, where the souqs (markets) overflow with colourful, tempting and aromatic wares. Running parallel to this is Sharia Abtal at-Tahrir, where you'll find the youth hostel and a few hotels. Across the river on Elephantine Island, modern Nubian culture thrives. Hire a bike or a taxi to get around.

PEOPLE

Beside the Egyptians, there are a handful of separate indigenous groups with ancient roots in Aswan. The city is finely threaded with Nubian culture. The traditional lands of Nubia, home to the tall, dark-skinned Nubian people, were drowned with the building of the High Dam in the 1970s to provide a water supply for the region. Despite this, Egyptians and Nubians live relatively harmonious, if independent, lives.

TYPICAL ASWANIAN

Aswanians distinguish themselves from the rest of Egypt by being particularly laid-back and pleasant. They love their souqs and their slice of the Nile and enjoy nothing more than watching the water move by after a long day of working numerous jobs to support their large families. Their laughter lubricates the wheels of social exchange and transactions are done with a smile. While religion cushions life's blows, in Aswan jokes and wisecracks are its parlance.

DEFINING EXPERIENCE

Spending the morning in the narrow alleyway souqs, tasting life as it has been for many centuries, before sailing gently across the Nile on a felucca to the cliffs of Elephantine Island and Nubian House for henna tattoos, Nubian music and a sunset 'tea' buffet overlooking the river and the desert beyond.

STRENGTHS

- Sunset on the desert
- The Nile
- Nubian culture
- Elephantine Island
- The tombs of the Nobles
- The Nubian Museum
- Feluccas
- Souqs
- Relaxed, friendly atmosphere
- Top-quality henna
- History-packed streets

WEAKNESSES

- Expensive tours
- Lecherous souq tattooists
- Unbearable 38ºC to 45ºC summer heat (June to August)
- Cheap camel meat
- Safflower sold as saffron

GOLD STAR

Feluccas – you haven't seen Aswan, or Egypt for that matter, until you've seen it from a felucca on the Nile.

STARRING ROLE IN...

- *Death on the Nile* by Agatha Christie
- *Elephantine: The Ancient Town* by the German Archaeological Mission

IMPORT

- Camels
- Nubians and their culture
- Western food
- Foreign guests (considered lucky) for Nubian weddings
- British design for the High Dam
- International sculptors
- Christianity
- Caravans
- Indian and African botany

EXPORT

- Camels
- Henna and henna tattoos
- Spices
- Ivory
- Granite
- Roasted peanuts
- *Karkadai* (dried hibiscus drink)
- Nubian *tahtib* (stick dancing)
- Colourful skull caps

SEE the sun set over the desert from the peaceful Ferial Gardens.

EAT *daoud basha* (meatballs in tomato sauce) as the Nile slides slowly past the Aswan Moon Restaurant.

DRINK delicious fruit cocktails and take in the views at Emy Restaurant.

DO visit the breathtaking history, art and culture of the Nubian Museum.

WATCH the *tahtib* on a winter's eve by the Aswan folkloric dance troupe.

BUY the best henna in Egypt in Aswan's colourful souqs.

AFTER DARK take a boat ride to Philae (Agilkia Island) to experience the sound and light show and wander through the temple at night.

URBAN MYTH

Mohammed Shah Aga Khan, the 48th imam of the Ismaili sect of Islam, had Aswan as his favourite wintering place. When he died in 1957, his widow, the Begum, oversaw the construction of his domed granite-and-sandstone mausoleum, opposite Elephantine Island. For over 40 years she placed a single red rose on her husband's sarcophagus each day. The Begum continued her floral tribute every day until her death in 2000. Now she lies inside, reunited with her husband for eternity.

NUBIAN DANCERS PERFORMING IN STYLE.
Photographer: Anders Blomqvist / LPI

GRAIN AND SPICE SELLERS AT THE SOUQ READY TO WRAP UP THE DAY.
Photographer: John Elk III / LPI

A CAMEL AND FRIEND TRAVERSE THE DUNES, WITH A VIEW OF THE CITY ACROSS THE NILE.
Photographer: John Elk III / LPI

DREAMS OF PAST SPLENDOUR – A SLEEPY GUIDE NODS OFF BENEATH THE SUPERB RELIEFS OF THE TEMPLE OF ISIS.
Photographer: Becca Posterino / LPI

Athens

VITAL STATISTICS

NAME: ATHENS

DATE OF BIRTH: 1400 BC; FOUNDED BY THE MYCENAEANS

ADDRESS: GREECE (MAP 3, P15)

HEIGHT: 107M

SIZE: 428 SQ KM

POPULATION: 3.7 MILLION

LONELY PLANET RANKING: 038

FATHER AND SON FROLIC ON FILOPAPPOU HILL OVERLOOKING THE ACROPOLIS.
Photographer: Scott Barbour / Getty Images

GILT-EDGED MIRRORS CATCH THE REFLECTIONS OF PASSING SHOPPERS AT THE SUNDAY PLATEIA MONASTIRAKIOU FLEA MARKET.
Photographer: Scott Barbour / Getty Images

SEEN FROM THE ACROPOLIS, THE CRADLE OF CIVILISATION NURTURES AN URBAN JUNGLE.
Photographer: Scott Barbour / Getty Images

A REMBETIKA PLAYER ENLIVENS A RESTAURANT IN PLAKA.
Photographer: Scott Barbour / Getty Images

Redolent with mythology, smeared with grime, Athens is an affable city enlivened by outdoor cafés, pedestrianised streets, parks, gardens and urban eccentrics.

ANATOMY

The city is bounded on three sides by Mt Parnitha, Mt Pendeli and Mt Hymettos. Within Athens there are eight hills, of which the Acropolis and Lykavittos are the most prominent. The city's boundary on the southern side is the Saronic Gulf. The metro system makes getting around the centre of Athens relatively painless. There's also an extensive bus and trolleybus network.

PEOPLE

A large proportion of Athens's residents today are relative newcomers to the city, who migrated here from other parts of Greece or from Greek communities around the world. Greece, which lost much of its population to mass migration, is now attracting large numbers of migrants, both legal and illegal, including many Albanians and refugees from the Balkans, the former Soviet Union, Bangladesh, Pakistan, Iran and Iraq.

TYPICAL ATHENIAN

Athenians are affable, warm and welcoming. The pace of life in Athens can be fast (the public service aside) but people still take time out for endless coffees. The younger generations of Athenians are highly literate, with a large number studying abroad. A high proportion speak English and are in tune with world trends, fashion and music. About 98% of the Greek population belong to the Greek Orthodox Church.

DEFINING EXPERIENCE

Emerging from the hectic U-Matic dance club at 5am then heading to the darkened central meat market, where the tavernas turn out huge pots and trays of tasty, traditional home-style dishes, 24 hours a day.

STRENGTHS

◢ The Acropolis standing sentinel over Athens
◢ The many city streets and squares fringed with orange trees
◢ National Archaeological Museum
◢ Refreshing your eyes and lungs in the delightfully shady National Gardens
◢ The Plateia Monastirakiou flea market
◢ Shopping for antiques in Antiqua
◢ The Bohemian Exarhia district – home to many cheap tavernas, good cafés, alternative book, music and clothing stores, *rembetika* clubs and small live-music venues
◢ *Loukoumades* (Greek-style doughnuts) served with honey and walnuts
◢ Dining on the terrace at Pil Poul, with views of the illuminated Acropolis
◢ Seeing Euripides performed in the Odeon of Herodes Atticus
◢ Lively *rembetika* clubs
◢ Benaki Museum
◢ Balconies bulging with geraniums

WEAKNESSES

◢ *Nefos* (smog)
◢ Concrete
◢ Lack of public toilets
◢ Traffic
◢ Smoking
◢ Greek bureaucracy
◢ Summer heat

GOLD STAR

The Acropolis – time, war, pilfering, earthquakes and pollution have taken their toll on the sacred hill, yet it stands defiant and dignified over Athens.

STARRING ROLE IN...

◢ *Anthismeni Amigdhalia* (Almond Trees in Bloom, 1959)
◢ *Landscape in the Mist* (1988)
◢ *The Last Temptation* by Nikos Kazantzakis

IMPORT

◻ Bad driving
◻ Mini Chinatown
◻ Haute couture
◻ Nescafé
◻ Concrete
◻ Tourists
◻ Jackie Onassis

EXPORT

◢ Souvlaki
◢ Greeks, who have migrated all over the world
◢ The Olympics
◢ Philosophy
◢ Democracy
◢ Olive oil
◢ Ouzo
◢ Shipping magnates
◢ Maria Callas

SEE dusk settle on the symbol of the glory of ancient Greece, the Parthenon (Virgin's Chamber), which stands on the highest point of the Acropolis.

EAT the best, fresh traditional-style *tiropites* (cheese pastries) in Athens (and many other tasty variations) at Ariston.

DRINK a homemade brew from one of the many on offer at Brettos, a quaint little bar with a stunning array of coloured bottles, old wine barrels and a refreshingly old-fashioned feel.

DO get lost among the little whitewashed cube houses in Anafiotika before ascending to explore the Acropolis.

WATCH a film at the outdoor cinema in the Zappeio Gardens, where you can get a wine and gourmet snack-pack to add to your viewing pleasure.

BUY a pair of traditional Jesus sandals from septuagenarian sandal-maker Stavros Melissinos' store in the market district of Monastiraki.

AFTER DARK check out Baroc'e, right next to the old Olympic Stadium, where a regular procession of well-heeled Athenians spill out onto the footpath in summer.

URBAN MYTH

Despite a popular perception, there is not much plate-smashing to be had in Greece these days. It's not the done thing in restaurants. At some bars in Athens, party animals throw stacks of paper napkins everywhere when the night heats up. But be warned – these acts of merrymaking can be rather pricey (you pay for the napkins!).

Auckland

VITAL STATISTICS

NAME: AUCKLAND

NICKNAME: CITY OF SAILS; *TAMAKI MAKAURAU* (IN MAORI)

DATE OF BIRTH: 1840; WHEN THE SETTLEMENT WAS MADE NEW ZEALAND'S CAPITAL (IT INDECISIVELY LOST THIS STATUS TO WELLINGTON IN 1865), BUT MAORI SETTLEMENT DATES BACK AT LEAST 800 YEARS

ADDRESS: NEW ZEALAND (MAP 1, OO21)

HEIGHT: 26M

SIZE: 502 SQ KM

POPULATION: 1.3 MILLION

LONELY PLANET RANKING: 068

With beaches in its backyard and an international gateway to Polynesia, Asia and, if you must, Australia – this is a truly relaxed world city.

ANATOMY

The commercial main street is Queen St stretching from QEII Sq near the waterfront to the hip wining and dining precinct around Karangahape Rd (known as K Rd to most Aucklanders). Get on the bus for posh Ponsonby Rd to the city's west, another hot spot for eating and shopping. A ferry ride across the harbour is Devonport, which is *the* Sunday afternoon spot with B&Bs, galleries and beaches. Public transport consists of buses, trains and ferries.

PEOPLE

With almost a third of the Kiwi population, Auckland has a huge cross-section of people from its traditional Maori communities to more recent Asian arrivals. Indeed, Auckland now has the world's largest concentration of Polynesians, which give the city a unique cultural make-up.

TYPICAL AUCKLANDER

Aucklanders certainly are a diverse lot, migrating from Indonesia to Invercargill. 'Jafas', as Aucklanders are called by other Kiwis, have a reputation for being smugly cosmopolitan with the migration from New Zealand's regions to the big smoke triggered by work or cultural life. The longstanding rivalry with Wellington is shrugged off by many Aucklanders who are too busy enjoying their better weather and beaches to care for the windy city to the south.

DEFINING EXPERIENCE

Brunching on K Rd before a harbour sail, catcing a ferry over to Devonport to fossick among the art galleries, cycling up to Takapuna Beach for a well-deserved laze, having a relaxed dinner in one of Ponsonby's more exclusive eateries, and gearing up for a night of clubbing along Queen St.

STRENGTHS

- Harbourside views
- Volcanic hills pocked with *pa* (fortified villages)
- K Rd dining
- Beaches
- Maori culture
- Ponsonby
- Rugby
- Multicultural population of Polynesian and Asian peoples
- Latte bowls
- Stardome Observatory
- Hauraki Gulf Islands

WEAKNESSES

- Buses suffering from privatisation
- Weather
- Rush-hour traffic
- Tough walking on hilly streets
- Howick Historical Village
- Sinking of the *Rainbow Warrior*

GOLD STAR

Yachting – they scored the America's Cup in 1995 and 2000, and the city's yachties are keen to show you why.

STARRING ROLE IN...

- *The Navigator: A Mediaeval Odyssey* (1988)
- *Whale Rider* (2002)
- *Once Were Warriors* (1994)
- *Shortland Street* (since 1992)
- *The Chronicles of Narnia: The Lion, the Witch and the Wardrobe* (2005)
- *An Angel at My Table* (1990)

IMPORT

- The America's Cup
- Over-sized latte bowls
- Polynesian people and culture
- Tim and Neil Finn
- Albert Wendt
- Bic Runga
- Scribe
- Carlos Spencer

EXPORT

- The America's Cup
- *Kina* (edible sea urchin)
- Marmite
- Mareko
- The Datsuns
- Sir Edmund Hillary
- Lucy Lawless (Xena)
- Russell Crowe
- Dave Dobbyn and DD Smash
- Deceptikonz
- Split Enz

SEE the view from Sky Tower.

EAT late-night kumara chips from the White Lady bus on Shortland St.

DRINK a glass of excellent white wine from the Marlborough region, such as Cloudy Bay.

DO the Two Volcanoes walk that takes in dormant Mt Victoria and a stunning panorama.

WATCH a cultural performance at Auckland Museum.

BUY Polynesian hip-hop bootlegs or other crafts from Otara Markets.

AFTER DARK be a doll in Papa Jack's Voodoo Lounge, a hard-rock venue complete with skulls.

URBAN MYTH

Irish rock band U2 included a song called 'One Tree Hill' on their *The Joshua Tree* album that many assume was an acknowledgement either of the 'other' One Tree Hill in the UK or the band's appreciation of the spectacular views from the obelisk on Auckland's One Tree Hill. In fact it was a tribute to Greg Carroll, a Maori roadie who worked with the band until his tragic death in 1986. Members of the band accompanied his body back to Auckland and after the funeral dedicated their new album to him. Many U2 fans believe Carroll was buried atop One Tree Hill, but that honour went to Sir John Logan Campbell, known as the father of Auckland who named the hill in 1840.

GOING ON TILT IN WAITEMATA HARBOUR.
Photographer: Fergus Blakiston / LPI

THE EXHILARATING LEAP FROM SKY TOWER.
Photographer: Peter Bennetts / LPI

CHILLING OUT AT THE MINUS 5 DEGREES BAR, PRINCES WHARF.
Photographer: Peter Bennetts / LPI

WARMING UP AT LION ROCK AND PIHA BEACH.
Photographer: Paul Kennedy / LPI

Austin

VITAL STATISTICS

NAME: AUSTIN

NICKNAME: LIVE MUSIC CAPITAL OF THE WORLD

DATE OF BIRTH: 1842; WHEN IT BEGAN LIFE AS THE VILLAGE OF WATERLOO

ADDRESS: USA (MAP 1, J11)

HEIGHT: 178M

SIZE: 651 SQ KM

POPULATION: 743,000 (CITY); 1.6 MILLION (METRO AREA)

LONELY PLANET RANKING: 169

Skip the bighorn of Houston and the Ala-ho-hum – Texas is all about its weird and wonderful capital, which hosts innovative IT, live music that's more than just alt-country, a burgeoning film industry and the best Tex-Mex you can gobble down in the state.

ANATOMY

Downtown Austin is laid out in an easily navigable grid, with Congress Ave running from the city's south, across the Colorado River and continuing to the Texas State Capitol. Parallel to Congress, Guadalupe St becomes the Drag, a student mecca for cheap eats and music stores. East 6th St – also running alongside Congress – is known as the Strip and boasts an array of clubs, bars and nightspots. The Warehouse District to the southwest of Congress is another entertainment district, catering for an older hootenanny, often with gay and lesbian nights. The city's public bus network is a solid system of inexpensive neighbourhood, express and downtown routes.

PEOPLE

Austin is relatively cosmopolitan by Texan standards with almost two-thirds of the population identifying as Caucasian. Hispanic and Latin Americans make up around 30%, with Spanish spoken amid the predominant English. African-Americans are about 10% of the population, with Asians and Native Americans also making up the diverse background of the capital.

TYPICAL AUSTINITE

After being bucked from the dot-bronco, Austinite digital cowboys have had to take a breather, but the city is still the shining star of teched-up Texas. GPS is the new cowboy hat (though the city has never been into uniforms – there's an unspoken 'no-suits' policy). Almost 50,000 residents attend UT (as University of Texas is better known), making for a massive student population to keep the music live and the art cutting edge. Yep, Austinites prize their strangeness, even going so far as to stage protests to 'Keep Austin weird', and see themselves as very different from their oil-rich, cowpoke Texan neighbours. 'I don't live in Texas', local troubadour Jerry Jeff Walker once said, 'I live in Austin'.

DEFINING EXPERIENCE

Grabbing a barbecue breakfast – a spicy start to any day – then working it off with Frisbee golf through Zilker Park, attending a seminar on film at UT, then hoeing-down at a hootenanny, sinking a few margaritas in a honky tonk on 6th St, and being spooked by the 1.5 million-strong bat colony under Congress Ave Bridge.

STRENGTHS

- South by Southwest (SXSW)
- Zilker Park and Barton Springs Pool
- McKinney Falls State Park
- UT
- Colorado River
- Bikes Not Bombs (free bikes for visitors)
- Pennybacker Bridge
- Frisbee golf courses
- Texas State Capitol
- Free Silver 'Dillo (short for armadillo) buses
- Moonlight Towers

WEAKNESSES

- Good ol' boys
- Boiling heat
- Dull chain hotels lining I-35

GOLD STAR

Live music – every other bar has tunes to get your foot tapping and your boot scooting.

STARRING ROLE IN...

- *Armadillos and Old Lace* by Kinky Friedman
- *Slacker* (1991)
- *Dazed and Confused* (1993)
- *Spy Kids* (2001)
- *Secondhand Lions* (2003)
- *Miss Congeniality* (2000)
- *Office Space* (1999)
- *Sin City* (2005)

IMPORT

- Lance Armstrong
- Michael Dell
- Sandra Bullock
- Matthew McConaughey
- Tacos, burritos and *cervezas* (beer)

EXPORT

- Hootenannies
- Richard Linklater films
- Oil
- Slacking
- Lyndon B Johnson
- Laid-back music

SEE the eerie view from the 9m-tall UT Tower.

EAT a dripping taco *al pastor* (pork and pineapple) washed down with a margarita or 12 at Guero's Taco Bar.

DRINK a few Buds at Shady Grove Café on Thursday evening with Austin's local bands rocking the stage.

DO a warm-up lap with Lance Armstrong on the Town Lake Trail, a 10-mile loop that takes in the Stevie Ray Vaughan statue.

WATCH (and maybe get dragged onto the floor yourself) for Texas dancehall at Broken Spoke.

BUY a 'Keep Austin Weird' bumper sticker from any cigar store.

AFTER DARK check out the best retro country (and the cheap brews) at Ginny's Little Longhorn, a genuine honky tonk.

URBAN MYTH

Being state capital has been a tough gig for relaxed Austin, with the title almost disappearing in 1842. Attributing the move to the danger of local Comanche attacks, President Sam Houston tried to shift the government to Houston in 1842 and later to the catchily named Washington-on-the-Brazos. The only thing sly Sam left behind were the archives of Texas, which he sneakily sent his Texas Rangers to reclaim in the dead of night. The history (a seat of government) was saved by local innkeeper Mrs Angelina Eberly, who raised the alarm by lighting a cannon with her cigar. Without the archives, the government had to return to Austin in 1845 and Sam Houston never looked at a cigar the same way again.

TIME TO SAY YOUR PRAYERS AT SIMPSON UNITED METHODIST CHURCH.
Photographer: Joe Raedle / Getty Images

PROVE YOU AIN'T NO CHICKEN BY ENTERING THE 'WHERE WILL THE POOP LAND' COMPETITION AT GINNY'S.
Photographer: Joe Raedle / Getty Images

SIX FINE LOOKIN' LEGS AT THE REGULAR JO FASHION SHOW, JO'S HOT COFFEE.
Photographer: Joe Raedle / Getty Images

TUCKING INTO SOME DAMN FINE CHICKEN, GREEN MESQUITE BBQ & MORE.
Photographer: Joe Raedle / Getty Images

GETTING SOME CHEEKY INK AT CUSTOM TATTOOS FROM THE SOUL.
Photographer: Joe Raedle / Getty Images

Baku

VITAL STATISTICS

NAME: BAKU

DATE OF BIRTH: BRONZE AGE; THERE IS EVIDENCE OF HABITATION SINCE THIS TIME, ALTHOUGH THE FIRST HISTORICAL REFERENCE TO BAKU WAS ONLY MADE IN THE 9TH CENTURY

ADDRESS: AZERBAIJAN (MAP 3, AA14)

HEIGHT: 1M

SIZE: 86,600 SQ KM

POPULATION: 2.1 MILLION

LONELY PLANET RANKING: 182

The ancient walled city at Baku's heart is a magnificently preserved collection of mosques and imposing Moorish architecture, while just outside the city fascinating relics of Zoroastrianism will astound anyone with an interest in religion.

ANATOMY

Baku curls majestically around the Bay of Baku, an inlet from the oil-rich Caspian Sea, from which the scent of black gold wafts through the city. The very heart of the town is the Içəri Şəhər, the old Muslim walled city, which contains several beautiful mosques and the famous Maiden's Tower. The modern city is congregated around the Içəri Şəhər and provides a stark contrast in its mercurial modernity. There is a range of public transport, including a metro, buses and trolleybuses.

PEOPLE

While Azerbaijan is a multicultural nation, the vast majority of Baku's population are ethnic Azeris. There are also small groups of Russians, Tatars, Lezgins, Kurds and Armenians. Azerbaijan is a Shiite Muslim nation, though Sunni Muslims and Russian Orthodox Christians comprise a significant proportion of the population. Fiercely proud of the young republic of Azerbaijan, many of the most educated people in the city nevertheless speak Russian rather than Azeri at home – a not uncommon contradiction in the post-Soviet world.

TYPICAL BAKUNIAN

Cosmopolitan and bilingual, Bakunians are well known for their sly business instincts, and the city's economic boom can be attributed as much to the character of the city's natives as it can to the oil wealth beneath the Caspian. That said, most Bakunians you meet are exceptionally laid-back, hospitable and talkative people who love nothing more than to engage in drawn-out debates and discussions. Whatever you do here, you'll come away feeling like you've got some new friends to visit on your return.

DEFINING EXPERIENCE

Leaving bustling downtown Baku with its busy oil men, glass-and-steel tower blocks and fast food, and slipping into another world entirely by wandering into the Içəri Şəhər, seeing the carpet sellers and fruit stalls, watching families going about their daily lives in the narrow backstreets and hearing the call to prayer at the grand mosques contained within the city's ancient walls.

STRENGTHS

- Cool breeze from the sea, which keeps the city pleasant even during the stifling summer months
- The friendly *çayxanə* (traditional teahouse) society will convert even ardent espresso-fans to the delights of tea
- You'll see very few tourists but plenty of Western businesspeople
- The food is delicious and markets overflow with fresh fruit and vegetables

WEAKNESSES

- The smell of oil from the Caspian
- Corrupt officials always on the lookout for some extra earnings
- The dismal political situation

GOLD STAR

The fascinating world of the Içəri Şəhər

STARRING ROLE IN...

- *The World Is Not Enough* (1999)

IMPORT

- Oil-company employees from all over the world

EXPORT

- Oil
- Rostropovich

SEE the majestic view from the top of the mysterious Maiden's Tower.

EAT fresh and delicious *lulə* (kebab) at any restaurant in town.

DRINK tea over a game of *nard* (backgammon) in a Bakunian *çayxanə*.

DO explore the fascinating Palace of the Shirvan Shahs in the Içəri Şəhər.

WATCH out when discussing politics – the war with Armenia remains a taboo subject.

BUY carpets galore at the open-air market in the Içəri Şəhər.

AFTER DARK enjoy a display of live music and belly dancing in any smart restaurant.

URBAN MYTH

The mysterious Maiden's Tower remains an object of fascination. What was it actually used for? Some claim it was a lookout tower, some a prison, and others claim the flat circular room was a place to leave the city's dead in order that vultures might clean their bones.

MODERN LIVING IS EASY IN THIS ANCIENT METROPOLIS.
Photographer: Stephane Victor / LPI

A MAZE OF NARROW ALLEYS MAKES EXPLORING THIS CITY A TREAT.
Photographer: Stephane Victor / LPI

SHOP TILL YOU DROP IN THE BEAUTIFUL DISTRICT AROUND FOUNTAIN SQ.
Photographer: Stephane Victor / LPI

FRIENDLY BREW – TRADITIONAL TEAHOUSES ARE A GREAT PLACE TO OBSERVE EVERYDAY LIFE.
Photographer: Stephane Victor / LPI

SHARING GOOD TIMES IN THE SHADE.
Photographer: Crispin Hughes / Panos Pictures

Bamako is a riot of sound and colour: women in flamboyant clothing with towers of tomatoes on their heads; men selling plastic combs, toys and bottles; table football games; the scorching sun overhead; and a rousing soundtrack of Bambara music.

ANATOMY

Sitting on the northern bank of the River Niger, Bamako city centre is a triangle formed by Ave Modibo Keita, Blvd du Peuple and the train tracks. At the heart of the city off Rue Baba Diarra is the train station. The main road out of town is Route de Ségou. You reach this by heading south from Ave Modibo Keita to Square Lumumba then taking Pont des Martyrs. Catch one of Bamako's yellow taxis or a green *dourounis* (van).

PEOPLE

The majority of Malians are Muslim, but animist beliefs are widespread. The main tribal groups in Bamako are Bambara, Malinke and Soninke.

TYPICAL BAMAKO CITIZEN

Mali is one of the world's poorest nations. Two-thirds of Mali's population struggle below the poverty line, and infant mortality is very high. The civil war in the Côte d'Ivoire, Mali's biggest trading partner, caused the country massive problems. Despite all of this, Bamako is a harmonious place. The government is stable and popular and committed to stamping out corruption, and the media is relatively free. Women are revered, although genital mutilation and polygamy are still practised. Bamako's citizens are proud of Mali's history. They are warm, friendly and as loud as their clothing. And in such a musical city it's no surprise that they like to party.

Bamako

VITAL STATISTICS

NAME: BAMAKO

DATE OF BIRTH: 1700S; WHEN THE NIARÉ CLAN ARRIVED IN THE REGION AND NAMED THE TOWN 'CROCODILE RIVER' (BAMA-KO IN BAMBARA) AFTER THE NUMEROUS CROCODILES THEY SAW IN THE NIGER

ADDRESS: MALI (MAP 1, T14)

HEIGHT: 340M

POPULATION: 1.7 MILLION

LONELY PLANET RANKING: 195

BAMAKO SITS PROUDLY ON THE NORTHERN BANK OF THE RIVER NIGER.
Photographer: John Elk III / LPI

MARKET EXTRAVAGANZAS ARE AN EXPERIENCE WORTH ENJOYING.
Photographer: Peter Ptschelinzew / LPI

THE PEOPLE OF BAMAKO REMAIN PROUD AND NOBLE DESPITE THE PRESSURES OF POVERTY.
Photographer: Finbarr O'Reilly / Reuters/Picture Media

DEFINING EXPERIENCE

Wandering through the markets, spying the dead-animal potions at the Fetish Market before buying henna decorations at the Marché de Médina and heading to Djembe for a drink and a dance to the sound of *griots* (poets, musicians and historical storytellers).

STRENGTHS

- Bambara woodcarvings, eg the *chiwara* (antelope) mask
- *Griots*
- The library and concerts at the Centre Culturel Français
- Kora (traditional 12-string instrument)
- Grand Marché
- Woodcarvings at the Maison des Artisans
- Artisans' work at the Institut National des Arts
- Fetish Market
- Bogolan (hand-painted mud cloth)
- Marché de Médina
- Musée National
- The streets at prayer time, full of genuflecting people
- Bold, colourful clothing
- The Niger
- Table football

WEAKNESS

- Muggings around the train station, riverbanks and near the Maison des Jeunes de Bamako

GOLD STAR

Live music – Bamako certainly has rhythm.

STARRING ROLE IN...

- *Bamako Sigi-Kan* (2002)
- *Je chanterai pour toi* (2002)
- *Yeleen* (1987)

IMPORT

- Damon Albarn of Blur
- Jackson Browne
- Bonnie Raitt
- Salif Keïta

EXPORT

- Film-maker Souleymane Cissé
- Musician Toumani Diabaté
- Fashion designer Xuly Bët (Kouyaté Lamine Badian)
- Photographer Seydou Keïta
- Woodcarvings

SEE the stunning views from Point de Vue Touristique above Bamako.

EAT fantastic cakes with real coffee at the Pâtisserie le Royaume des Gourmands.

DRINK at old favourite Byblos and watch male expats chatting up high-heeled hookers.

DO take drumming or dancing lessons at the Carrefour des Jeunes.

WATCH the vibrant dealings of the Grand Marché, whose stalls are crammed with dried fish, extravagant fabrics and potions.

BUY fabulous woodcarvings and jewellery from the Maison des Artisans.

AFTER DARK dance under the stars and watch Toumani Diabaté take to the stage at Le Hogon.

URBAN MYTH

Cousinage (loosely translated as 'joking cousins') is something of an institution in Mali. Certain family names or ethnic groups have other groups as counterpoints. When people are introduced they immediately know from their names whether or not they are 'joking cousins', and if they are, an exchange of mock insults ensues. But this is not just random trading of abuse; *cousinage* breaks the ice and literally ridicules the idea of animosity between different families.

Bangkok

VITAL STATISTICS

NAME: BANGKOK OR *KRUNG THEP MAHANAKHON AMON RATTANAKOSIN MAHINTHARA AYUTHAYA MAHADILOK PHOP NOPPHARAT RATCHATHANI BURIROM UDOMRATCHANIWET MAHASATHAN AMON PIMAN AWATAN SATHIT SAKKATHATTIYA WITSANUKAM PRASIT* (TRANSLATION: THE CITY OF ANGELS, THE GREAT CITY, THE ETERNAL JEWEL CITY, THE IMPREGNABLE CITY OF GOD INDRA, THE GRAND CAPITAL OF THE WORLD ENDOWED WITH NINE PRECIOUS GEMS, THE HAPPY CITY, ABOUNDING IN AN ENORMOUS ROYAL PALACE THAT RESEMBLES THE HEAVENLY ABODE WHERE REIGNS THE REINCARNATED GOD, A CITY GIVEN BY INDRA AND BUILT BY VISHNUKARN)

NICKNAME: VENICE OF THE EAST

DATE OF BIRTH: MID-16TH CENTURY; FOUNDED AS A TRADING POST

ADDRESS: THAILAND (MAP 5, K8)

HEIGHT: 2M

SIZE: 1569 SQ KM

POPULATION: 8.2 MILLION (CITY); 10.1 MILLION (METRO AREA)

LONELY PLANET RANKING: 008

It's a city of contrasts: glass and steel buildings shaped like cartoon robots standing next to glittering temple spires; wreaths of jasmine flowers dangling from the rear-view mirrors of buses and taxis; shaven-headed, orange-robed monks walking barefoot along the street beneath a bank of giant Sony screens blasting MTV Asia.

ANATOMY

Bangkok is located in the basin of the Chao Phraya River. The land is crisscrossed with canals and rivers. The sky is littered with high-rises in the form of shopping malls and major hotel chains but the side streets (sois) harbour canals and traditional Thai buildings and, perhaps, even a few teak houses. The Skyrail is an efficient and air-conditioned mode of transportation that circumnavigates the city. A túk-túk (motorised rickshaw) will take you wherever you want to go.

PEOPLE

The population is mostly Thai, although there are many Chinese immigrants and an increasing number of Indians.

TYPICAL BANGKOKIAN

About one in every 10 Thais is said to be from Bangkok. Patriotic taxi drivers will welcome you and wax lyrical about their city, with a polite smile on their face. They are down-to-earth and remarkably calm, despite the bureaucracy and traffic congestion.

DEFINING EXPERIENCE

Heralding in the day with a bit of t'ai chi in Lumphini Park and, if your muscles can manage to move after a gruelling massage at the Wat Pho school of massage, taking a spot of high tea in the Author's Lounge at the Oriental, alongside the ghosts of Joseph Conrad and Graham Greene.

STRENGTHS

- You can buy anything for a (very cheap) price, anything
- Markets around every corner
- Vegetarian cafés
- Crazy Patpong entertainment
- One-hour Thai massage for less than the price of a Happy Meal
- Five-star hotels for a song
- DVDs of films that are still making their way onto the big screen
- Open 24 hours
- Beautiful fabrics
- Gilt stupas in the centre of the madness

WEAKNESSES

- Pollution – you may as well smoke a packet a day
- *Faràng* (Caucasians) with beer guts, wearing silk shirts and with sweaty arms around young Thai boys
- Traffic congestion despite an organised Skyrail network
- Black-as-tar river (don't ask why the river taxis have covered windows)
- Count-down traffic lights

GOLD STAR

Ayuthaya Historical Park – a Unesco World Heritage site, Ayuthaya's historic temples are scattered throughout this once magnificent city and along the encircling rivers.

STARRING ROLE IN...

- *Bangkok Hilton* (1989)
- *Nang Nak* (1998)
- *The Shutter* (2004)
- *A Siamese Fairy Tale* by Somerset Maugham

IMPORT

- Japanese investment
- The flora at Rama IX Park
- Fake IDs on Khao San Rd
- Football
- Democracy
- Jim Thompson
- Virgin Radio
- Scrabble – used as a learning aid
- Zebra crossings (largely ignored by drivers)

EXPORT

- Coconut curries
- Go-go bars and ping-pong shows
- Thai massage
- Sarongs
- Exquisite silk
- Gems (read: scams)
- Red Bull (you can still get the original formula in Thailand)
- Siamese cats
- Reproduction couture

SEE the dizzying mobile-phone floor at MBK shopping centre.

EAT a bag of green mango wedges coated in sugar, lime juice and chilli – not for a weak stomach.

DRINK Singha Beer while people-watching on Khao San Rd.

DO have a heavy-duty one-hour massage on the sprawling king-sized beds at the Wat Pho school of massage.

WATCH river life and longboats cruise languidly by from a riverside café.

BUY a protective amulet from the amulet market near the Grand Palace or the funkiest clothing for your pooch at the Chatuchak weekend market.

AFTER DARK wander around Patpong and take in a show.

URBAN MYTH

According to legend, the Emerald Buddha, which was created in 43 BC in Pataliputra, India, was rediscovered when lightning struck a pagoda in a temple in Chiang Rai. It was covered in stucco but a small chip on its nose revealed a hint of green. The emerald was later revealed to be jade but the name stuck. The Emerald Buddha now resides at Wat Phra Kaew.

FROM SILVER SCREEN TO CITY SCENE, AN ARTIST APPLIES FINISHING TOUCHES TO A MOVIE POSTER.
Photographer: John Borthwick / LPI

A YOUNG MONK AT THE BUDDHA BENCHAMABOPHIT IN DUSIT.
Photographer: Richard I'Anson / LPI

ALL FIRE AND SPICE, A NIGHT MARKET HOTS UP ON THE CITY STREETS.
Photographer: Jerry Alexander / LPI

JUVENILE WATER PISTOL COMMANDOS WREAK HAVOC AT THE SONGKHRAN 'WATER-SPLASHING FESTIVAL' TO CELEBRATE NEW YEAR.
Photographer: Richard I'Anson / LPI

Barcelona

VITAL STATISTICS

NAME: BARCELONA

DATE OF BIRTH: 3RD CENTURY BC; WHEN ROMANS ESTABLISHED BARCINO

ADDRESS: SPAIN (MAP 3, G14)

HEIGHT: 93M

SIZE: 487 SQ KM

POPULATION: 1.7 MILLION

LONELY PLANET RANKING: 004

EITHER AN ALIEN SPACESHIP OR THE TORRE AGBAR FROM ACROSS THE MOTORWAY.
Photographer: Dennis Gilbert / VIEW Pictures Ltd / Alamy

The city of Gaudí and Miró captivates with its proud Catalan identity, roaring nightlife, fabulous cuisine, sunny weather, sandy beaches and sheer style – Barcelona is addictive.

ANATOMY

The wide tree-lined boulevard La Rambla is Barcelona's main thoroughfare, leading from the port up to Plaça de Catalunya where you'll find buses and taxis. East of La Rambla is the Barri Gòtic with its medieval winding streets and Catedral (cathedral). Over the road, El Raval, the more run-down part of the old quarter, is slowly being gentrified. North of here, L'Eixample is home to most of Barcelona's Modernista architecture. To the southwest stands the 173m hill of Montjuïc. Along the coast are Port Vell, the working-class district of La Barceloneta and Port Olímpic beyond.

PEOPLE

Bilingual Barcelona (Catalan and Castilian Spanish) has become a multicultural city, with around 14% of the population coming from as far afield as Ecuador, Argentina, Morocco and Pakistan. The city is not as predominantly Catalan as the rest of the region and many residents come from other parts of Spain.

TYPICAL BARCELONIN

Barcelonins who live in the city generally inhabit apartments – a lack of space means a lack of houses. All dream of an apartment with a *terrassa* (terrace). Many residents escape the city to a second property at weekends. Barcelonins are known for being serious and hard-working but party just as hard as other Spaniards. *Tapear* (tapas-bar-hopping) is popular but with rising prices, dinner parties are gaining ground. People take pride in their appearance and follow fashion. Football is almost a religion and most people support FC Barcelona. Remember that Barcelonins live in Catalonia, not Spain.

DEFINING EXPERIENCE

Breathing in the morning air on La Barceloneta beach before strolling into El Born for a coffee, then heading up to L'Eixample for Gaudí architecture at La Pedrera and a spot of shopping.

STRENGTHS

- *Bolets* (wild mushrooms)
- *Arròs negre* (rice in black cuttlefish ink)
- Late-night partying
- Festes de la Mercè, the city's main festival
- Proximity to the Pyrenees for skiing and hiking
- The Costa Brava
- Romanesque and Gothic churches
- Modernista architecture
- FC Barcelona football and basketball teams
- Reduced levels of air pollution
- Natural-gas buses
- Hosing down the street every night
- Museu Picasso
- La Sagrada Familia
- Parc Güell
- Affordable Spanish fashion
- La Pedrera
- Museu Marítim
- *Sardana* folk dance

WEAKNESSES

- Expensive real estate
- Suppression of Catalan interests within Spain
- Litter
- Dog poo
- Illegal bill posting
- Heroin abuse
- Els Boixos Nois (The Mad Boys), local football hooligans
- Noise pollution

GOLD STAR

Modernista architecture adorns the city.

STARRING ROLE IN...

- *El Gran Gato* (2003)
- *L'Auberge Espagnol* (The Spanish Apartment, 2002)
- *Todo Sobre Mi Madre* (All About My Mother, 1999)
- *Gaudí Afternoon* (2001)

IMPORT

- Purificación García
- Cruise ships
- The Olympics in 1992
- Pablo Picasso
- Jean Genet
- Stag and hen parties

EXPORT

- Antoni Gaudí
- Salvador Dalí
- Joan Miró
- Cava
- Chef Ferran Adrià
- Chupa Chups
- Joaquim Verdú
- Antonio Miró
- Custo Dalmau (aka Custo Barcelona)
- Mango clothes shop
- Seat
- Carmen Amaya

SEE Gaudí's huge architectural confection, La Sagrada Familia, unfinished and yet awe-inspiring.

EAT *melindros* (soft sugar-coated biscuits) dipped into *cacaolat* (thick hot chocolate) at Salvador Dalí's favourite dairy bar, Granja Dulcinea.

DRINK cocktails at the 1933 Art Deco Boadas whose founder served Hemingway in Havana.

DO learn about Picasso's early works at the fascinating Museu Picasso.

WATCH men offering women roses and women giving men books on Día de Sant Jordi, the feast of Catalonia's patron saint.

BUY affordable Spanish fashion at Mango or Zara in L'Eixample.

AFTER DARK bump and grind down to Port Olímpic for your pick of the clubs.

URBAN MYTH

Gaudí didn't start or finish the building for which he is probably most famous – La Sagrada Familia. Having replaced another architect in 1884, he became obsessed by the project, planning three superbly ornate façades devoted to the Nativity, Passion and Glory, each to be crowned by four towers. The design was so complicated that he only saw the creation of the Nativity. When asked why he was fussing about the top of the towers Gaudí replied, 'the angels will see them'. When funds ran out, he sold all his possessions and started sleeping on the site. In 1926 he was tragically hit by a tram and died. In 1952 work restarted and the still unfinished architectural masterpiece is visited by millions every year.

KEEPING ONE'S HEAD IS A CHALLENGE AMIDST ALL THE BEACHGOERS AT LA PLAYA.
Photographer: IML Image Group Ltd / Alamy

D IS FOR DOZING: OUTSIDE THE MUSEUM OF MODERN ART.
Photographer: Luke Peters / Alamy

THE FANTASTIC ENTRANCE TO GAUDÍ'S SURREAL PARC GÜELL.
Photographer: Martin Child / Alamy

Bath

VITAL STATISTICS

NAME: BATH

DATE OF BIRTH: 800 BC; REPUTEDLY FOUNDED BY KING BLADUD, A TROJAN REFUGEE AND FATHER OF KING LEAR

ADDRESS: ENGLAND (MAP 3, E8)

HEIGHT: 181M

SIZE: 29 SQ KM

POPULATION: 85,500

LONELY PLANET RANKING: 119

FALLING IN LOVE WITH (AND AT) THE PARADE GARDENS, BY THE RIVER AVON.
Photographer: Scott Barbour / Getty Images

BECKHAM IMPERSONATIONS ABOUND AT ROYAL VICTORIA PARK, OVERLOOKED BY THE ROYAL CRESCENT.
Photographer: Scott Barbour / Getty Images

INDIANA JONES WOULD LOVE TO EXPLORE THE GREAT BATH, CENTREPIECE OF THE ROMAN BATHS.
Photographer: Scott Barbour / Getty Images

A CONSTABLE ENSURES THAT BATH'S CREAM SUPPLY REMAINS SAFE FROM THREATS.
Photographer: Scott Barbour / Getty Images

When sunlight brightens the honey-coloured stone, and buskers and strollers fill the streets and line the river, stylish and lively Bath, England's first spa resort, reveals all its charm.

ANATOMY

Bath is nestled at the bottom of the Avon Valley in the southern Cotswolds and is famed for its seven hills, with buildings climbing the steep streets. The River Avon, tamed by a series of weirs, runs through the town centre. The town's most obvious landmark is the abbey, across from the Roman Baths and Pump Room. Walk, cycle or catch a bus to get around.

PEOPLE

The typical Bath resident is healthy, comes from a white ethnic background, has an average age of about 40, and is of the Christian faith, although around 20% of the population register no religion. The city has small populations of other ethnic groups, including Asians and blacks.

TYPICAL BATH CITIZEN

Citizens of Bath are much like their fellow countrymen – they drink tea, form orderly queues while awaiting service and enjoy a pint at the pub.

DEFINING EXPERIENCE

Strolling through the historic baths and enjoying luxurious spa treatments at Thermae Bath Spa, tasting the waters from the fountain before tea and scones in the elegant Pump Room, then visiting the Roman Baths Museum, wandering through the 500-year-old abbey, strolling through the riverside Parade Gardens and taking a boat tour at Poulteney Weir, before getting an architectural, gossip and trivia overview on a free walking tour of the city, viewing the crowning glory of Georgian Bath (Royal Crescent and The Circus), and travelling through four centuries of fashion at the Costume Museum.

STRENGTHS

- The thermal baths, which have attracted kings and queens over the centuries
- Exquisite mosaics
- Georgian splendour and original limestone buildings
- Wide parades
- The wonderful fan vaulting of Bath Abbey's nave
- The majestic sweep of Royal Crescent and the Circus
- Shopping
- Bath International Music Festival
- Abbey Ales brews
- Atmospheric restaurants and bars
- Hidden pockets of Georgiana found up steep streets
- The self-guided Jane Austen Bath Walk
- Free touch-screen information kiosks
- Carved mythical beasts in the choir stalls of the abbey
- The carnivalesque chaos of Walcot Nation Day
- Bath Fringe Festival

WEAKNESSES

- Florence-style tourist congestion
- Traffic
- Trying to read stone-carved street signs

GOLD STAR

Bath's star attraction, the Roman Baths, and their stunning mosaics.

STARRING ROLE IN...

- *Three Tenors Concert* (2003)
- *Vanity Fair* (2003)
- *Persuasion* by Jane Austen (film 1994)
- *House of Eliot* (1991–94)
- *The Music Lovers* (1969)
- *Ghost Train* (1931)
- *Northanger Abbey* by Jane Austen
- *Pickwick Papers* by Charles Dickens

IMPORT

- Richard 'Beau' Nash's 18th-century style codes
- Tourists
- Jane Austen devotees
- Organist and astronomer William Herschel

EXPORT

- Food writer and first TV celebrity chef Marguerite Patten
- Software
- New media and gaming magazines

SEE angels climbing up and down (head first!) a stone ladder on the exterior west façade of Bath Abbey.

EAT cream tea or a traditional English meal at Sally Lunn's, founded by the Huguenot refugee in 1680.

DRINK a Bellringer ale, home-brewed in Bath.

DO taste the waters in the elegant Pump Room.

WATCH the cinematic rendering of a Jane Austen classic for a view into the grand times of Georgian Bath.

BUY yourself some luxurious pampering at Thermae Bath Spa, bohemian treasures on Walcot St, or secondhand books from the covered Guildhall Market.

AFTER DARK take a 'ghost walk' of Bath, departing from the reputedly haunted Garricks Head pub.

URBAN MYTH

William Herschel arrived in Bath as an organist but was to become most noteworthy for his achievements in the field of astronomy. In 1781 he discovered the planet Uranus from the garden of his home in Bath.

Beijing

VITAL STATISTICS

NAME: BEIJING

NICKNAME: THE NORTHERN CAPITAL

DATE OF BIRTH: 500,000 YEARS AGO; WHEN THE SOUTHERN AREA OF BEIJING WAS INHABITED BY 'PEKING MAN'; THE CITY'S MODERN HISTORY DATES FROM 1045 BC

ADDRESS: CHINA (MAP 1, II10)

HEIGHT: 52M

SIZE: 750 SQ KM

POPULATION: 15.6 MILLION

LONELY PLANET RANKING: 063

The sheer size and scale of the capital of the world's most-populous nation is awe-inspiring, and if you look hard enough between the six-lane highways and skyscrapers you'll find fascinating Chinese imperial history dwarfed by everything around it.

ANATOMY

At the heart of the massive conurbation lies Tiananmen Sq and beyond it the vast imperial palace within the Forbidden City. The city's most controversial new building is the new National Theatre (dubbed 'the egg' by locals), just behind the Great Hall of the People and a stone's throw from the Forbidden City. The city is served by a small metro system (being extended for the Olympics) and an extensive bus network, but many visitors will find that the only way to truly get around is by cab.

PEOPLE

Like a magnet, Beijing attracts Chinese seeking their fortunes from all over the country, although the vast majority of the population is made up of Han Chinese speaking *beijinghua* – a dialect of the national standard dialect (Mandarin, or *putonghua*) unique to the capital. There's a big expat community centred on Sanlitun, which is a major nightlife draw and the one truly 24-hour area of town.

TYPICAL BEIJINGER

Beijingers know they live in the cultural, political and psychological centre of China. Unlike their mercurial Hong Kong and Shanghai cousins (whom they dismiss as calculating and stingy respectively), Beijingers are not showy and prefer understatement (as suggested by the city's skyline compared to those of China's two other pre-eminent economic centres). They are also extremely generous and will argue with ferocity over who gets to pay the bill in restaurants.

DEFINING EXPERIENCE

Thundering down one of the city's vast main avenues in a cab and suddenly turning into a side street where, between building sites and vast new structures, you'll be deposited at a medieval Lamasery (monastery), standing quite oblivious to the modernity around it.

STRENGTHS

- Superb food on every corner
- Pirate DVD menus available for you at restaurants while you wait for your food
- The *hutong* (side streets where traditional housing and ways of life continue as ever) give the city a human face
- Fantastic optimism and dynamism

WEAKNESSES

- Smog
- The city's sheer size and unmanageability
- Enormous building works everywhere
- The endless erosion of the *hutong* and the advance of concrete and asphalt

GOLD STAR

Coming across a genuine Beijing duck restaurant in a run-down *hutong*, and having a delicious meal without gawping tour groups present.

STARRING ROLE IN...

- *The Last Emperor* (1987)
- *Farewell My Concubine* (1993)
- *The Gate of Heavenly Peace* (1995)
- *Beijing Bicycle* (2001)

IMPORT

- Starbucks
- McDonald's
- Tour groups

EXPORT

- Pirate DVDs
- Political dissidents
- Jade

SEE the astonishing imperial apartments and temples within the Forbidden City.

EAT Beijing duck with plum sauce, knocked back by a Yanjing beer.

DRINK green tea at a traditional teahouse.

DO make the effort to get out of town to a remote stretch of the Great Wall.

WATCH Beijing Opera for an unforgettably Chinese night out.

BUY your Mao Zedong watches at the not-very-Communist gift shop outside his mausoleum.

AFTER DARK head out for a midnight boat ride on magical Houhai Lake.

URBAN MYTH

By his later years, Mao Zedong – champion of the people – had moved himself and his entourage into the Forbidden City, having turned quickly from liberator into Communist emperor. Mao's final years were spent in virtual seclusion, receiving guests in a private chamber he never left and having only one young concubine who could translate his speech into Chinese, so debilitated was he by a rare disease of the nervous system. The preserved body of this deeply contradictory man is on public display in his Tiananmen Sq mausoleum.

CHARMING SILK LANTERNS SWAY IN THE LIGHT BREEZE AT THE PANJIAYUAN MARKET.
Photographer: Andrew J Loiterton / Getty Images

HIGH TEA – A DRAMATIC DEMONSTRATION OF THE ART OF TEA POURING IN LAO SHE TEAHOUSE.
Photographer: Andrew J Loiterton / Getty Images

PENNANT-WIELDING PATRIOTS FLY THE NATIONAL FLAG IN TIANANMEN SQ.
Photographer: Andrew J Loiterton / Getty Images

RECLINING UNDER A RED CANOPY, A RICKSHAW DRIVER TAKES A WELL-DESERVED NAP IN NANYAN *HUTONG* DISTRICT.
Photographer: Andrew J Loiterton / Getty Images

The ultimate coastal chill-out zone, Beira's laid-back blend of sandy beaches, outdoor nightlife, live music and dilapidated colonial heritage bestows a subtle and authentic flavour on the city.

ANATOMY

One of Southern Africa's oldest cities, Beira is a major port and rail terminus at the mouth of the River Pungwe. The city spreads along the coast from the port to the famous lighthouse overlooking paradisal Macuti Beach. Navigation can be difficult through its unnamed maze of streets, mostly built in a Mediterranean style with colonial buildings, patios, city squares and market areas. The architecture is prettiest near the pulsating Praça (main square) where you will find the banks, shops and other handy facilities. Catch buses or *chapas* (minibuses) to get around.

PEOPLE

Ships passing through the port ensure there is always a steady flow of different nationalities in addition to Mozambique's usual array of African, Arabic, Portuguese and Chinese ethnic communities. Portuguese is the official language and Bantu and Swahili are also spoken.

TYPICAL BEIRAN

Beira emerged from nearly two decades of civil war only to be hit by catastrophic floods in 2000 and again in 2001, but remarkably the people remain sanguine and are inspiringly strong. The city is now starting to experience rapid and much-needed economic development. As a result the people are confident, positive, friendly and laid-back, even for Africa, and will often welcome the chance to practise their English and share intriguing stories over a cold beer.

Beira

VITAL STATISTICS

NAME: BEIRA

NICKNAME: THE HEART

DATE OF BIRTH: 1891; FOUNDED AS THE HEADQUARTERS OF THE PORTUGUESE COMPANHIA DE MOZAMBIQUE ON THE SITE OF AN OLD MUSLIM SETTLEMENT

ADDRESS: MOZAMBIQUE (MAP 2, L21)

HEIGHT: 10M

POPULATION: 436,000

LONELY PLANET RANKING: 198

A SHOE SELLER STARTS THE DAY OFF ON THE RIGHT FOOT.
Photographer: Ariadne Van Zandbergen / LPI

DEFINING EXPERIENCE

Losing yourself among the labyrinthine streets, stumbling unexpectedly into Largo do Municipio, playing beach volleyball under the searing sun before cooling off with a swim in the shadow of the *Macut* shipwreck on Macuti Beach, gorging on a different prawn curry every night of the week, getting blown away by the live percussion acts, and trying not to get emotional as you listen to locals telling you what life was like during the civil war.

STRENGTHS

- Awesome beaches
- Endless smiles
- Best facilities for many kilometres
- Casa Infante de Sagres
- Unofficial 'parks' everywhere
- Tropical climate
- Culturally diverse
- Gaudy 1930s-inspired Art Deco
- The shipwrecks
- Farol do Macuti, the lighthouse
- Inspiring locals

WEAKNESSES

- AIDS
- Malaria
- No street signs
- Water pollution
- Floods and cyclones
- Poverty

GOLD STAR

Beaches – dazzling hot sand, broad-leaved palm trees and spectacular shipwrecks make Beria's beaches sing like sirens.

STARRING ROLE IN...

- *Lumumba* (2000)
- *Carlos Cardosa – Telling the Truth in Mozambique* by Paul Fauvet and Marcello Mosse
- *The Veranda under the Frangipani* by Mia Couto

IMPORT

- Marxism
- Portuguese marble
- Shipwrecks
- Foreign aid

EXPORT

- Cashew nuts
- Prawns (shrimps)
- Sugar
- Lessons from tragedy

SEE the desolate shipwrecks off beautiful Macuti Beach at dusk.

EAT rice and chicken on your favourite stretch of beach.

DRINK a cup of 'real' coffee at Biques restaurant.

DO check out, but don't purchase, the contraband on sale in the market at Tchunga Moyo (literally, 'brave heart').

WATCH the masters at work in a woodcarving workshop at Makonde.

BUY a locally made drum from the market and learn to play while you're still feeling the rhythm.

AFTER DARK shake your booty to kitsch disco beats at Bar Africa.

URBAN MYTH

Rusty shipwrecks abound around Beira's port area and several more are dotted along the coast. But perhaps most surprising are the two hulking vessels washed up in the shadow of the famous red-and-white striped lighthouse on Macuti Beach. This would seem to suggest that old Farol do Macut, as they say in Portuguese, was something of a failure. However, the criticism is unfounded as the ships were intended to be breakwaters and were intentionally manoeuvred into their current beachside resting places. The 28m lighthouse is the only one in Mozambique that is close to a major town, and until recently the horizontal stripes were always painted black. It was erected in 1904 and if it hadn't been you could be pretty sure there would be more than two ships adorning Macuti Beach.

A HEADSTRONG MAN MAKES HIS WAY THROUGH THE BEACH MARKET.
Photographer: Ariadne Van Zandbergen / LPI

NO ONE EVER KICKS UP A STINK ABOUT THE DRYING FISH CARCASSES LINING THE BEACH.
Photographer: Ariadne Van Zandbergen / LPI

ART DECO HIGH-RISES PROVIDE PANORAMIC VIEWS.
Photographer: Ariadne Van Zandbergen / LPI

PUTTING ON THE FINISHING TOUCHES AT THE CRYSTAL NIGHTCLUB.
Photographer: Stephanie Sinclair / Corbis

Beirut

VITAL STATISTICS

NAME: BEIRUT

NICKNAME: THE PEARL; PARIS OF THE MIDDLE EAST

DATE OF BIRTH: STONE AGE; THE EARLIEST TRACES OF HUMANS DATE FROM THIS TIME, WHEN BEIRUT WAS TWO ISLANDS IN THE DELTA OF THE BEIRUT RIVER

ADDRESS: LEBANON (MAP 2, L1)

HEIGHT: 34M

POPULATION: 1.8 MILLION (CITY)
2.6 MILLION (METRO AREA)

LONELY PLANET RANKING: 136

Beirut is a city of contrasts: beautiful architecture exists alongside concrete eyesores, traditional houses set in jasmine-scented gardens are dwarfed by modern buildings, and swanky new cars vie for right of way with vendor carts.

ANATOMY

Bound north to south by the Mediterranean Sea, the west of Beirut is very hilly, flattening out to the east. The Hamra district in West Beirut is one of the city's hubs, where you'll find the ministry of tourism, major banks, hotels and restaurants. North of Hamra is Ras Beirut, filled with coffee bars and cheap restaurants. The Corniche is the area where Beirutis come to promenade. On the hill to the southeast is the prosperous Achrafiye; here many older buildings are still intact and it is a great place to wander. Most people use service taxis to get around, a huge number of which run like buses on set routes, carrying around five passengers.

PEOPLE

Beirut's population is around 60% Muslim and 40% Christian. Ethnic groups comprise Arabs, Palestinians, Kurds and Armenians, and Arabic, French, English and Armenian are spoken.

TYPICAL BEIRUTI

After 15 years of living in a battle zone, the typical Beiruti does their best to forget their troubled past by eating well, dancing and enjoying life, imbuing Beirut with a buzz that is absent from every other city in the region. Warm of heart, it's rare to see any interaction between people that doesn't begin with profuse greetings, inquiries into the other's health and myriad niceties. As an *ajnabi* (foreigner), if you make the effort to come up with the right expression at the appropriate moment, you'll be warmly regarded for it.

DEFINING EXPERIENCE

Exploring the shattered remains of the civil war along the city's former Green Line, experiencing 6000 years of history at the National Museum then watching dusk descend over the Mediterranean at one of the city's many seafront cafés.

STRENGTHS

- The Corniche
- The National Museum
- A city reborn at the Beirut Central District
- Ottoman houses
- American University of Beirut Museum
- Genuine hospitality
- Pigeon Rocks
- Martyrs Statue
- Souq el Barghout
- Seafront cafés
- Vibrant arts scene
- St George Cathedral
- Religious and social diversity

WEAKNESSES

- The political situation is often tumultuous and tense – stay informed
- Land mines outside of Beirut – avoid off-road and unmarked areas
- Oppressive summers
- Wild traffic
- Potholes
- Unlicensed taxis
- Lack of street numbers and conflicting street names

GOLD STAR

Optimism – a city well on the mend, visitors to Beirut can see a phoenixlike transformation in progress.

STARRING ROLE IN...

- *The Hills of Adonis* by Colin Thubron
- *A House of Many Mansions* by Kamal Salibi
- *Pity the Nation* by Robert Fisk

IMPORT

- Assorted Muslim and Christian denominations
- A glut of designer stores
- Tourists

EXPORT

- Agriculture
- Banking and finance
- Construction
- (American-Lebanese) Paul Anka and Yasmine Bleethe

SEE modern Lebanese plays in Arabic, French and occasionally English at the Al-Medina Theatre.

EAT a delicious fusion of Eastern and Western cuisines in Casablanca (Rue Ain al-Mraisse), set in one of the few intact Ottoman houses left on the Corniche.

DRINK (if you dare) three whole cups of potent Arabic coffee for the price of one at Modca.

DO peruse the traditional Palestinian embroidery at Al-Badia; the shop has garments handmade by refugee women who benefit from the proceeds.

WATCH horse racing of a Sunday at the Hippodrome, one of the only places in the Middle East where you can legally place a bet.

BUY melt-in-your-mouth baklava and other pastries from Amal al-Bohsali, Beirut's most famous pastry shop for decades.

AFTER DARK be part of Beirut's social mosaic on an evening stroll along the Corniche.

URBAN MYTH

Following the 11 September 2001 attacks, a pro-Palestine Beirut news network, Al-Manar Channel, falsely reported to Lebanon that 4000 Israelis who worked in the World Trade Center did not show up for work that day. The implication was that Israel was somehow responsible for the attack and had provided its nationals with a tip-off. The falsehood is indicative of the continuing tensions in the region.

HEAVENLY RAYS SHOW OFF THE SPLENDOUR OF THE GRAND MOSQUE.
Photographer: Bethune Carmichael / LPI

LIVING THE HIGH LIFE AT THE RIVIERA BEACH CLUB.
Photographer: Naftali Hilger / TCS / Corbis

DAY'S END AT THE CORNICHE, BEIRUT'S SEAFRONT.
Photographer: George Georgiou / Panos Pictures

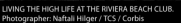

Belfast has earned its stripes; after years of violence and stagnation, there's a palpable positive energy, plus interesting industrial architecture and a slew of glorious drinking holes.

ANATOMY

Belfast's compact city centre curls around the undulating west bank of the River Lagan, with the steep slopes of Black Mountain and Cave Hill beyond. It's a child of the Industrial Revolution; imposing Victorian architecture and leafy gardens are set against the cranes of the Harland and Wolff shipyards, restored warehouses and row upon row of workers' terraced houses. Buses and trains do the job, and chartered black cabs – the people's taxis – ply the main roads of sectarian West Belfast.

PEOPLE

Historically, Belfast's only ethnic divisions were those between Catholics and Protestants. Today there is greater equality between the two groups, and sectarian tensions are often linked to issues of class. As in other large Irish cities, there are now significant migrant communities, mainly from China, the Philippines, Africa, the Middle East and Pakistan. This influx of new cultures, as well as a large student population (from the rest of Ireland and abroad), has contributed to the decreasing importance of religion. But the transition isn't an easy one, with ongoing violence towards ethnic minorities, especially those living in poorer Protestant neighbourhoods.

TYPICAL BELFASTIAN

Belfastians surprise visitors with their infectious confidence and gregariousness. Like their Dublin neighbours they take their social lives seriously but, more than anywhere in Ireland, really do dress up for a night out. They remain vitally interested in politics, but are more likely to talk about their favourite DJ or the next sun holiday to Portugal than casually discuss the peace process. They are masters at taking the piss but don't take it personally; they're also known for asking any new-found acquaintances to a party on pub closing.

Belfast

VITAL STATISTICS

NAME: BELFAST

DATE OF BIRTH: 1611; WHEN CHICHESTER'S COLONY OF ENGLISH AND SCOTTISH SETTLED HERE, THOUGH THERE WAS A NORMAN CASTLE BUILT IN 1177; CELTIC OCCUPATION DATES BACK TO THE IRON AGE

ADDRESS: NORTHERN IRELAND (MAP 3, C6)

HEIGHT: 67M

SIZE: 115 SQ KM

POPULATION: 267,000 (CITY); 645,000 (METRO AREA)

LONELY PLANET RANKING: 163

A PICTURE OF IRISHNESS: YOUNG BELFAST BOYS LOOK THE PART.
Photographer: Vehbi Koca / Alamy

DEFINING EXPERIENCE

Hitting Topshop for some gear, fixing up the fake tan then off to Spring & Airborne for that new alt-country band and wee pint before going to BT1, hanging out in the unisex toilets because it's where the action is, then heading home for a few hours' sleep and a fry-up, grabbing the steamer and heading away to the coast – the East Strand at Portrush is pumping.

STRENGTHS

- Amazing Victorian architecture: City Hall and the Grand Opera House
- Beautiful Botanical Gardens
- Views of the encircling mountains
- Queen's University
- Ulster Museum
- Compact but still resolutely urban centre
- Friendly to visitors
- Lagan Towpath
- Burgeoning restaurant scene
- City Hall
- Belfast Art College
- Resilience

WEAKNESSES

- July
- Undeserved grim reputation
- Brian Kennedy
- The marriage of old-school sectarianism and millennial xenophobia
- *Spides* (the Belfastian term for local male hoodlums)

GOLD STAR

Black, black sense of humour: Belfastians love to laugh, and the humour tends towards the surreal and sarcastic.

STARRING ROLE IN...

- *Divorcing Jack* (1998)
- *The Most Fertile Man In Ireland* (1999)
- *The Mighty Celt* (2005)
- *This Human Season* by Louise Dean

IMPORT

- Day-tripping Dubliners
- Students
- Black cabs
- Mural art
- British high-street chains
- English and Scottish footballers
- Italian craftsmen (in the 1880s)

EXPORT

- Van Morrison
- Wayward sporting stars: George Best, Alex Higgins
- Paul Hill
- Ships
- Linen
- Bushmills
- Ash
- Therapy
- Actor Stephan Rea
- James Nesbitt
- Kenneth Branagh

SEE Samson and Goliath, the giant yellow cranes of the Harland & Wolff shipyards, from a boat on the River Lagan.

EAT posh – perhaps local game cooked up by Michael Dean in his eponymous Michelin-starred restaurant.

DRINK a hot whiskey with cloves and lemon while ensconced in a snug in the high-Victorian camp of the Crown Liquor Saloon.

DO the Falls and Skankills Rds by people's taxi and take in the murals.

Watch a big-name act play the Ulster Hall or an up-and-coming one at the Limelight.

BUY an edgy new Brit label from the Clothes Agency.

AFTER DARK hear harder and heavier beats at Shine, a venerable club night at the Queen's Student Union.

URBAN MYTH

The Crown Saloon, a heavily touristed but still authentic city pub, has a sectarian love story all of its own. When the establishment was being renovated in 1885, the Catholic owner, Patrick Flanagan, argued with his Protestant wife over a new and fitting name. She eventually got her way and they opted for 'The Crown', despite the fact that it was symbolic of the British regime. Flanagan's acquiescence came with a cheeky subversion though: he ordered a crown mosaic for the doorstep so that each and every punter would trample it upon entering.

THE ORNATE MAJESTY OF BUILDINGS AT QUEEN'S UNIVERSITY.
Photographer: Richard Cummins / LPI

GLASSY WATERS REFLECT THE MODERN MASTERPIECE OF THE RIVER LAGAN WEIR.
Photographer: Richard Cummins / LPI

A REPUBLICAN MEMORIAL MURAL HONOURS THE DEAD, FALLS RD.
Photographer: Richard Cummins / LPI

THE HUSTLE AND BUSTLE OF BELGRADE'S INFAMOUS NIGHTLIFE SCENE.
Photographer: Doug McKinlay / LPI

With its underground nightlife scene and enchanting above-ground Stari Grad (Old Town), unpretentious Belgrade is like a dishevelled teenager compared with its slick European cousins, but it's fast reinventing itself.

ANATOMY

Terazije is the heart of modern Belgrade. Knez Mihailova, Belgrade's lively pedestrian boulevard, runs northwest through Stari Grad from Terazije to the Kalemegdan Citadel, which lords over the Sava and Danube Rivers estuary. Buses and a new underground metro train network will get you around town.

PEOPLE

The city is a rich tapestry of ethnicities. Over half the population is Serb, there is a significant Albanian community, plus small Montenegrin, Hungarian, Croatian, Romano and Magyar groups. The official tongue is Serbian.

TYPICAL BELGRADER

Belgraders are a proud, forthright and strong-willed bunch with a melancholic core. Tourists are only now returning to Belgrade and foreign visitors are warmly greeted. In fact, it is not uncommon for Belgraders to offer to show you round their city, and treat a newcomer to family-oriented hospitality, which revolves around eating, football and partying. Hopelessly romantic, Belgraders love to fall in love and then overdramatise it all.

DEFINING EXPERIENCE

Checking out the Kalemegdan Citadel before wandering along vibrant Knez Mihailova, a café-lined pedestrianised boulevard, and chatting with a bunch of curious university types who are likely to warmly welcome you to their student digs for a poetry reading coupled with plenty of *pivo* (beer).

Belgrade

VITAL STATISTICS

NAME: BELGRADE

NICKNAME: WHITE CITY

DATE OF BIRTH: 2300 YEARS AGO; SINCE THEN BELGRADE HAS BEEN DESTROYED AND REBUILT 40 TIMES

ADDRESS: SERBIA AND MONTENEGRO (MAP 3, O12)

HEIGHT: 132M

SIZE: 360 SQ KM

POPULATION: 1.6 MILLION

LONELY PLANET RANKING: 143

A LADY IN RED PROVIDES ANOTHER SPLASH OF COLOUR TO A GRAFFITIED STAIRWELL.
Photographer: Doug McKinlay / LPI

SLOW DESCENT AT THE KALEMEGDAN CITADEL.
Photographer: Doug McKinlay / LPI

A MOMENT OF PRAYER AT THE SVETI MARKO CATHEDRAL.
Photographer: Doug McKinlay / LPI

STRENGTHS

◢ World-class nightlife
◢ A living history
◢ Go-anywhere bus and train network
◢ Grandiose old buildings
◢ Deli central: melt-in-your-mouth *kajmak* (a salted cream turned to cheese) and delectable grilled meats (*pljeskavica* and *ražnjići*)
◢ Multilingual population
◢ Outstanding museums
◢ Polite and gregarious young people
◢ A smorgasbord of fun-filled festivals, from summer jazz to film festivals
◢ Religious celebrations held in honour of the city saint and protector, Spasovdan

WEAKNESSES

◢ A lingering postwar sadness
◢ US-wannabe gangsters
◢ Daytime traffic congestion
◢ Next to no vegetarian options (they will ask what sickness you're suffering from)

GOLD STAR

The city boasts the kind of effortlessly cool nightlife that promoters the world over can only dream of recreating. Belgraders are happy to dance all night and go straight to work the next day.

STARRING ROLE IN...

◢ *The Wounds* (1998)
◢ *Cabaret Balkan* (1998)
◢ *Loving Glances* (2003)
◢ *Underground* (1995)
◢ *Black Lamb & Grey Falcon* by Rebecca West
◢ *Balkan Blues: Writing out of Yugoslavia* edited by Joanna Labon

IMPORT

◢ All things Italian fashion: Gucci, Benneton, Sisley…
◢ All things Italian automotive: Vespa, Alfa Romeo

EXPORT

◢ Monica Seles
◢ Basketball players
◢ Serbian lovers
◢ Baby-soft leather
◢ A medley of berry fruits
◢ Top-notch cheeses
◢ Anything and everything *šlivovitz* (plum), including plum-infused *rakija* (brandy)
◢ Drop-dead gorgeous models
◢ Labour: brainy professionals to do-anything workers

SEE Belgrade's ancient Kalemegdan Citadel.

EAT the famed *burek,* a greasy pie made with *sir* (cheese), *meso* (meat), *krompiruša* (potato) or occasionally *pečurke* (mushrooms), at one of the alfresco cafés along Trg Republike.

DRINK the current apéritif of choice, bittersweet Pelinkovac, at Ben Akiba, a chic and liberal watering hole.

DO saunter along Knez Mihailova, a treasure-trove of historical buildings with great people-watching.

WATCH summer musical, theatrical and cabaret performances at Skadarska – Belgrade's answer to Paris' Montmarte.

BUY something lacy to perk up your table life; or hand-knitted woollens from the vendors in Kalemegdan Park.

AFTER DARK dance hands-in-the-air style to Belgrade's very own 'turbo folk' at one of the city's many night-owl haunts, such as Andergraund or Plastic.

URBAN MYTH

Belgrade is the meeting place of two rivers, the Danube and the Sava. Belgraders' love of all things romantic is typified in their belief that the rivers are like lovers whose passion exploded into Belgrade.

Belize City

VITAL STATISTICS

NAME: BELIZE CITY

DATE OF BIRTH: 1779; WHEN 'BELIZE TOWN' BECAME THE BRITISH HEADQUARTERS IN BELIZE

ADDRESS: BELIZE (MAP 4, G4)

HEIGHT: 5M

SIZE: 2 SQ KM

POPULATION: 70,000

LONELY PLANET RANKING: 183

ETHNIC DIVERSITY IS A PROUD HERITAGE OF BELIZE'S INTRIGUING HISTORY.
Photographer: Anthony Plummer / LPI

Belize City's ramshackle, untidy streets are alive with colourful characters representing every facet of the city's amazing ethnic variety, especially the Creoles whose culture has always been rooted here.

ANATOMY

Haulover Creek, running across the middle of the city, separates the downtown commercial area (focused on Albert St) from the slightly more genteel Fort George district to the northeast. The Swing Bridge – hub of the city – crosses Haulover Creek to link Albert St with Queen St. North up the coast from the Fort George district are the Newtown Barracks and Kings Park neighbourhoods. West of Albert St is the Southside, the poorest part of the city. There is a bus network, but walking is often your best option.

PEOPLE

Belize City enjoys a fabulous, improbable ethnic diversity. Creoles – descendants of British loggers and colonists and African slaves – now form about a quarter of the population. Racially mixed and proud of it, Creoles speak a fascinating, unique version of English, the country's official language. Over the last couple of decades, mestizos (of mixed Spanish and indigenous descent) have become Belize's largest ethnic group. The rest is a mix of the Maya, the Garifuna, 'East Indians' (people of Indian subcontinent origins), Chinese, Arabs (generally known as Lebanese), North Americans and Europeans.

TYPICAL BELIZEAN

Because of the mix of ethnicities and cultures in Belize, its people are very open, tolerant and accepting of the differences of others. Poverty is still widespread and crime is almost a way of life for some people in Belize City. You can admire lovely, large, breezy, two-storey, old-Caribbean-style wooden houses in parts of Belize City, but most Belizeans live in smaller dwellings, and new houses are often small, cinder-block boxes, while old ones may be composed of warped and rotting wood. Labour – whether washing dirty hotel sheets, cutting sugar cane or packing bananas – is poorly paid, and prices are high in comparison. It is estimated that one third of the population live below the poverty line.

DEFINING EXPERIENCE

Visiting the centre of activity in Belize City, the Swing Bridge, enjoying the traditional Belizean dish of rice and beans, then taking in the colonial architecture and cooling sea breezes of the Fort George district.

STRENGTHS

- Swing Bridge – the only remaining working bridge of its type in the world
- Multiculturalism
- Free education
- Image Factory art gallery
- Street vibe
- Crooked Tree Wildlife Sanctuary
- Lovingly cooked Creole-style fish
- Tolerance
- Calypso music
- Relaxed atmosphere
- Environmentally friendly focus

WEAKNESSES

- The 29-seat House of Representatives contained only two women at last count
- Low wages
- Poor housing
- All-too-frequent shootings and murders around the Southside district
- Heat
- Influx of cruise-ship tourists
- Divide between rich and poor

GOLD STAR

The atmosphere and street life, more than anything, are what make Belize City worth exploring.

STARRING ROLE IN...

- *The Dogs of War* (1980)
- *Mosquito Coast* (1986)
- *Heart of Darkness* (1993)

IMPORT

- Mennonites
- Football
- Cruise-ship visitors
- Bird-watching enthusiasts
- Racial diversity
- Scuba divers

EXPORT

- Punta rock
- The Garifuna
- Bananas
- Oranges
- Ecotourism
- Howler monkeys, jaguars and toucans

SEE the heart and soul of Belize City life, the Swing Bridge, which is crossed by just about everyone here just about every day.

EAT spicy jerk chicken; pork with rice, beans and vegetables; tasty shrimp Creole or a lobster-and-fish combo at Jambel's Jerk Pit.

DRINK a 'seaweed shake' sold by a street vendor – a blend of condensed milk, spices and extract of the seaweed *Eucheuma isoforme*, which grows underwater as a tangle of yellow branches.

DO encounter howler monkeys at close quarters at the Community Baboon Sanctuary.

WATCH Belize's amazing wildlife at the Belize Zoo.

BUY exquisite carvings made from the strikingly streaked wood zericote at the National Handicraft Center.

AFTER DARK catch a concert of traditional Belizean music at the 600-seat Bliss Centre for the Performing Arts.

URBAN MYTH

Some believe the name 'Belize' comes from the Mayan word *belix*, meaning 'muddy water', referring to the Belize River.

FRIDAY NIGHT LIGHTS – CLUBBING IN BELIZE IS A HIGH POINT.
Photographer: Anthony Plummer / LPI

WATCHING THE GRASS GROW – MANY OLDER BUILDINGS SUFFER FROM NEGLECT.
Photographer: Anthony Plummer / LPI

SIGHT-SEEING ON THE SWING BRIDGE IS NOT THE EXCLUSIVE DOMAIN OF TOURISTS.
Photographer: Anthony Plummer / LPI

IN A BLUR OF ACTIVITY A BARTENDER AT BERLIN'S REINGOLD BAR OFFERS BRISK SERVICE.
Photographer: Richard Nebesky / LPI

Berlin is constantly evolving, adapting, throwing up surprises and questioning its identity; while filled with history, she is determined to move ever forward.

ANATOMY

Apart from rivers and lakes, the city lacks distinctive geographical features – you're more likely to use buildings as a way of orienting yourself. Some of the city's rare hills were actually made from WWII rubble. Berlin's spread-out nature means you'll be relying on its U-bahns, S-bahns, buses and trams.

PEOPLE

Berliners enjoy a reputation for being liberal and well educated and the city itself is a patchwork of people from almost 200 countries. The most obvious immigrant group is the Turkish community. English is widely spoken, although less so among people of the former East, who will have learnt Russian as a second language.

TYPICAL BERLINER

Polite, friendly and fond of dry, sharp humour, Berliners are hard to shock. They live in high-ceilinged, airy apartments full of art and Ikea, make weekend brunches an essential experience and always seem to know where the 'scene' is and what's happening culturally.

DEFINING EXPERIENCE

Losing oneself in any of the city's blockbuster galleries and museums, keeping up with the locals by attending one of the 1500 cultural events that are crammed into Berlin's calendar, and reminding yourself that Potsdamer Platz was once 'No Man's Land'.

STRENGTHS

- History around every corner
- Willingness to make modern architectural statements
- Entrepreneurial spirit of young Berliners
- Imaginative protests
- Coffee and cake as a ritual
- Talking trash cans
- Efficient public transport
- Citywide love of new ideas
- Multiculturalism
- Vital contemporary arts scene
- Late-night kebabs
- Tiergarten (zoo)
- Schloss Charlottenburg
- Parades

Berlin

VITAL STATISTICS

NAME: BERLIN

NICKNAME: EUROPE'S BIGGEST BUILDING SITE

DATE OF BIRTH: 1307; TRADING POSTS BERLIN AND CÖLLN JOINED TO FORM A CITY

ADDRESS: GERMANY (MAP 3, L7)

HEIGHT: 55M

SIZE: 892 SQ KM

POPULATION: 3.4 MILLION (CITY); 5 MILLION (METRO AREA)

LONELY PLANET RANKING: 018

AN ABSTRACT STAR OF DAVID CRISSCROSSES THE ZINC FAÇADE OF THE JEWISH MUSEUM.
Photographer: Andrea Schulte-Peevers / LPI

URBANITES RELAX ON A SUNNY AFTERNOON IN HALENSEE PARK.
Photographer: Guy Moberly / LPI

PEACE, LOVE AND BODY PAINT – REVELLERS AT THE LOVE PARADE.
Photographer: Guy Moberly / LPI

WEAKNESSES

- ◢ 'The wall in the mind'
- ◢ Mullet hangovers
- ◢ Dog poo on the streets of Friedrichshain
- ◢ Confusing transport maps
- ◢ Needing to take public transport between attractions
- ◢ Racial tensions
- ◢ Techno doof doof when you're trying to sleep
- ◢ Weather

GOLD STAR

Nightlife – Berlin is determined to remain one of the coolest clubbing spots and her citizens throw themselves into the fray with abandon.

STARRING ROLE IN...

- ◢ *Die Fetten Jahre sind vorbei* (The Edukators, 2004)
- ◢ *Good Bye Lenin!* (2003)
- ◢ *Der Himmel über Berlin* (Wings of Desire, 1987)
- ◢ *Lola rennt* (Run Lola Run, 1997)
- ◢ *Herr Lehmann* (Berlin Blues, 2003)
- ◢ *Berlin: Sinfonie einer Großstadt* (Berlin: Symphony of a City, 1927)

IMPORT

- ◢ Ikea
- ◢ Christopher Isherwood
- ◢ David Bowie
- ◢ Lou Reed
- ◢ Iggy Pop
- ◢ Nick Cave
- ◢ U2
- ◢ Bertolt Brecht
- ◢ Stem cells for research
- ◢ Spelling changes
- ◢ Fruit and veg

EXPORT

- ◢ Marlene Dietrich
- ◢ George Grosz
- ◢ Einstürzende Neubauten
- ◢ Tangerine Dream
- ◢ Currywurst
- ◢ Nina Hagen
- ◢ Dadaism
- ◢ Leni Riefenstahl
- ◢ Techno
- ◢ Günter Grass
- ◢ Siemens
- ◢ Helmut Newton
- ◢ Squatting as a way of life

SEE what all the fuss is about at the domed Reichstag.

EAT wonderful Vietnamese food cheek by jowl with locals at Monsieur Vuong.

DRINK while checking out the other patrons at Cookies.

DO a tour of the cutting-edge galleries in the former East Berlin.

WATCH the most exciting developments in the cinematic world at the Berlin Film Festival.

BUY a GDR-era souvenir at Flohmarkt am Arkonaplatz.

AFTER DARK graffiti-bedecked Tacheles can still throw up night-time surprises for arty partiers.

URBAN MYTH

Europe's first (hand-operated) traffic light was installed in Potsdamer Platz in 1924. A replica can be found in the same spot today.

A SMART WAY TO TRAVEL – 100 YEARS AFTER E=MC² THE WILD-HAIRED PHYSICIST BEAMS FROM THE SIDE OF AN ENERGY-SAVING TRAM.
Photographer: Glenn Beanland / LPI

Bern is a charmingly quaint city despite its status as the capital of Switzerland; it boasts a medieval heart, a 15th-century town hall and a thriving alternative-arts scene.

ANATOMY

The compact town is contained within a sharp U-shaped bend, limiting some streets to pedestrian and public transport access. The main train station is at the mouth of the U and within easy reach of the main sights, and daily loan of city bikes is free.

PEOPLE

The majority of Bern's friendly residents speak Swiss German as a first language, while others speak French. Bernese German incorporates several words from *Matteänglisch*, a secret language that few people now speak, which was used in the former workers' quarter of Matte.

TYPICAL BERNESE

The typical Bern resident is modest, well-groomed, bilingual in French and German, predominantly Protestant and lives a quiet life in the pleasant Swiss capital. The Bernese enjoy the arts and regularly go to Bern's numerous cinemas to watch films in their original language.

Bern

VITAL STATISTICS

NAME: BERN

NICKNAME: BEAR (DUKE BERTHOLD V OF ZÄHRINGEN ALLEGEDLY NAMED THE CITY AFTER AN ANIMAL HE KILLED WHILE HUNTING; THE BEAR HAS BEEN BERN'S HERALDIC ANIMAL FOR SEVEN CENTURIES)

DATE OF BIRTH: 1191; WHEN IT WAS FOUNDED AS A MILITARY POST; BERN BECAME CAPITAL WHEN THE SWISS CONFEDERATION CAME TO LIFE IN 1848

ADDRESS: SWITZERLAND (MAP 3, I11)

HEIGHT: 509M

SIZE: 52 SQ KM

POPULATION: 128,000 (CITY); 660,000 (METRO AREA)

LONELY PLANET RANKING: 112

A YOUNG COUPLE SHARE A PARTING KISS ON THE BUSY BERNASTRASSE.
Photographer: Glenn Beanland / LPI

A QUICK ONE-ON-ONE WITH SOME OF THE WORLD-CLASS ARTISTS IN THE COLLECTION OF THE KUNSTMUSEUM.
Photographer: Glenn Beanland / LPI

GRAFFITI AND GIG POSTERS SIGNPOST THE WAY TO BERN'S THRIVING UNDERGROUND SCENE AT THE REITSCHULE.
Photographer: Glenn Beanland / LPI

DEFINING EXPERIENCE

Climbing the tower of Bern's Gothic Münster (cathedral) for fantastic views, joining a tour of the Bundeshäuser (Houses of Parliament), viewing the Paul Klee exhibition at the Kunstmuseum and watching the twirling figurines before the chiming of the Zeitglockenturm, an elaborate medieval clock tower with moving puppets.

STRENGTHS

- Bern's Unesco World Heritage–listed medieval city centre
- Summer rafting tours on the River Aare
- Ornate fountains every 150m or so
- Marking time at the Zeitglockenturm
- The impressively ornate Bundeshäuser
- The Bern Onion Market
- Kunstmuseum's collection, including Picasso, Hodler, Fra Angelico, Dalí and Paul Klee
- Swimming in the open-air, riverside Marzili pools
- Hotel Belle Epoque's opulent Art Deco rooms
- Reitschule's alternative scene
- Nougat-speckled Toblerone chocolate
- Covered shopping promenades

WEAKNESSES

- The thought of being eaten by the ogre in Ogre Fountain
- The Bear Pits displaying Bern's namesake (though some love it)

GOLD STAR

Stupendously vertiginous views of the medieval town, River Aare and Berner Alps from the lofty spire of Bern's Gothic 15th-century Münster.

STARRING ROLE IN...

- *An Indian Idyll* (2000)
- *On Her Majesty's Secret Service* (1969)
- Ferdinand Hodler's artwork

IMPORT

- Tourists
- Vehicles
- University students
- South American musicians
- Albanian and Kosovite refugees
- Textiles

EXPORT

- Toblerone chocolate
- Einstein's theories from the Bern patent office where he worked
- Swiss army knives
- Pockmarked Emmental cheese
- Fondue sets
- Muesli
- Painters Ferdinand Hodler and Paul Klee
- Poet Albert Bitzius
- Scientist Albrecht von Haller
- Songwriter Mani Matter
- Pharmaceuticals
- Precision instruments, including watches and clocks
- Swiss Air

SEE why the medieval town centre attained its Unesco World Heritage listing by gaining a bird's-eye view from the Münster's spire.

EAT cheese in a fondue, coupled with *rösti* (fried potatoes) and followed by smooth Swiss chocolate.

DRINK Bärner Müntschi (Bern's kiss) beer, Rivella soft drink or Apenzeller Alpenbitter (Alpine bitters), a liquor made from the essences of 67 different flowers and roots, and make sure you look into someone's eyes when you chink glasses.

DO bathe at the open-air, riverside Marzili pools.

WATCH twirling figurines celebrating the passing of time on the Zeitglockenturm.

BUY a Swiss army knife.

AFTER DARK head past graffiti-adorned buildings to the Reitschule and its vibrant alternative-arts scene.

URBAN MYTH

Though it can never be tested fully, $E=MC^2$ is no myth. Legend has it that Albert Einstein came up with his theory of relativity while gazing into space instead of tending to his tedious job at the Swiss patent office in Bern in 1907. Today this theory lives on as one of the 20th century's most important scientific pronouncements and Einstein's reputation as a ground-breaking physicist endures.

With its emerald-green lake, islet with picture-postcard church, medieval castle clinging to a rocky cliff and some of the highest peaks of the Julian Alps and the Karavanke Mountains as a backdrop, Bled is simply magical.

ANATOMY

Surrounded by mountains, Bled's focus is its idyllic 2km-long lake, its beauty enhanced by a tiny island with a red-and-white-spired belfry rising above the trees. The built-up area to the northeast is the largest of the settlements located around the lake and contains most of the hotels. Bled's main road, Ljubljanska cesta, runs eastward from here. Bled is served by a bus station and two train stations.

PEOPLE

Slovenes are polyglots, and virtually everyone in the resort town of Bled speaks some English, German and/or Italian.

TYPICAL BLED CITIZEN

For centuries Bled was a mecca for pilgrims, and since the 19th century it has attracted hordes of tourists and health devotees – you're far more likely to encounter visitors than locals. There's nothing fuddy-duddy about Bled, but given that it is a spa town renowned for its curative waters, many of its visitors are, well, older. If you're lucky enough to find a real local, chances are they'll love a good polka and regular schnapps pick-me-ups. They will also be filled with pride at the achievements of the many world-class ski champions the mountains have produced. It is obvious, from the ship-shape state of the city, that its residents are eager to preserve its history.

DEFINING EXPERIENCE

Rising early to explore the lake at its most breathtaking before embarking on a romantic gondola trip to the island to wish for what you most desire on the wishing bell, then enjoying a lunch of good home-cooked food and local wine at a countryside inn.

Bled

VITAL STATISTICS

NAME: BLED

DATE OF BIRTH: EARLY IRON AGE; BLED WAS THE SITE OF A HALLSTATT SETTLEMENT

ADDRESS: SLOVENIA (MAP 3, L11)

HEIGHT: 501M

POPULATION: 10,899

LONELY PLANET RANKING: 090

AFTER AN INVIGORATING DAY AT THE THERMAL SPA, SPIRITS ARE ENLIVENED AT THE DEVIL'S BAR.
Photographer: Richard I'Anson / LPI

STRENGTHS

- The country's best golf course, and one of Europe's most beautiful
- Bled's precipitous medieval castle
- Hikes galore
- Ice skating on the lake in winter
- Trips on the Old Timer vintage steam train
- Crystal-clear warm water
- Hot-air ballooning over the town
- The Okarina Folk Festival of folk and world music
- Summertime concerts at the castle, Festival Hall and the parish church
- Excellent bread, especially the braided loaves at Christmas
- Clean air and mountain light
- Polka dancing
- A plethora of outdoor activities
- Panoramic flights in Cessna 172s
- Charming towns such as Radovljica – an easy day trip away

WEAKNESSES

- The congestion at the top of Slovenia's highest peak, Triglav
- Droves of tourists in midsummer
- Leaving

GOLD STAR

The spectacular Vintgar Gorge, just west and slightly north of Bled, is a peaceful bit of beauty hidden by steep canyons. A wooden walkway built in 1893 hugs the rock walls of the gorge for 1600m along the Radovna River, crisscrossing the raging torrent four times over rapids, waterfalls and pools before reaching the 13m-high Šum Waterfall.

STARRING ROLE IN...

- The poetry of France Prešeren

IMPORT

- Olympic gold medal – Istok Čop and Luka Špik from the Bled Rowing Club won Slovenia's first Olympic Gold (in the double skull at the Sydney Olympic Games in 2000)
- International rowers – each year in mid-June they flock to Bled for the International Rowing Regatta
- Biathlon competitors – they arrive each winter to compete in the Biathlon World Championship of cross-country skiing and rifle shooting at the nearby Pokljuka Plateau
- Cuisine – Slovenian food is heavily influenced by Austria, Italy and Hungary

EXPORT

- Punk music in the late 1970s and early '80s
- France Prešeren, Slovenia's greatest poet, was born in Vrba, near Bled

SEE the stunning view from the summit of Velika Osojnica – over the lake, island and dramatic castle, with the peaks of the Karavanke in the background.

EAT Bled's culinary speciality, *kremna rezina* (cream cake), a layer of vanilla custard topped with whipped cream and sandwiched neatly between two layers of flaky pastry.

DRINK Zlatorog, Slovenia's best *pivo* (beer), at the friendly Pub Bled, the town's late-night venue of choice.

DO the polka – it only takes three minutes to learn.

WATCH the clouds roll by as you twirl around the lake or head to the castle in a horse-drawn carriage.

BUY a traditional beehive panel illustrated with folk motifs.

DO ring the wishing bell in the 15th-century belfry of Bled island's baroque church to ask a favour.

AFTER DARK try your luck at roulette, blackjack or baccarat at Casino Bled.

URBAN MYTH

Bled has been linked with the myths and legends of the early Slavs for centuries, particularly the ancient Slavic goddess Živa. The baroque Church of the Assumption is allegedly the site of Živa's temple, and archaeological excavations have found evidence of an ancient burial ground under the church.

A DREAMLIKE VISION AS DUSK SETTLES OVER BLED CASTLE.
Photographer: Richard I'Anson / LPI

WITH GONDOLA RIDES INCLUDED, WEDDINGS ON PICTURESQUE BLED ISLAND ARE INCREASINGLY POPULAR.
Photographer: Richard I'Anson / LPI

NESTLED IN THE PICTURESQUE MOUNTAINS IS THE CHARMING 100-YEAR-OLD TOWNSHIP.
Photographer: Richard I'Anson / LPI

THE MUSEO DEL ORO, HOME TO THE WORLD'S FINEST COLLECTION OF PRE-HISPANIC GOLD.
Photographer: Patricia Rincon Mautner / Getty Images

Bogotá

VITAL STATISTICS

NAME: BOGOTÁ

DATE OF BIRTH: PRE-COLUMBIAN; INHABITED BY ONE OF THE MOST ADVANCED PRE-COLUMBIAN INDIAN GROUPS, THE MUISCA

ADDRESS: COLOMBIA (MAP 4, L10)

HEIGHT: 2645M

SIZE: 25 SQ KM

POPULATION: 6.8 MILLION (CITY)
7.9 MILLION (METRO AREA)

LONELY PLANET RANKING: 155

Bogotá is a city of futuristic architecture, a vibrant and diverse cultural and intellectual life, splendid colonial churches and brilliant museums.

ANATOMY

Bogotá is bordered to the east by a mountain range topped by the two peaks of Monserrate and Guadalupe. Bogotá's northern sector consists mainly of upmarket residential districts, while the city's southern part is a vast spread of undistinguished lower-income suburbs, culminating in the vast shanty towns on the southernmost outskirts. The urban bus service TransMilenio is efficient and fast.

PEOPLE

About three quarters of the population is of mixed blood, composed mainly of mestizos (of mixed Spanish and indigenous heritage) and mulattos (with one black and one white parent). There are also small groups of *zambos* (of African-Indian blood) and Indians. Spanish is the official language.

TYPICAL BOGOTANO

Bogotanos are courteous, polite and hospitable. Everyday life is remarkably open and public, and much family life takes place outside the home: in front of the house, in the street, in a bar or at the market. As a result Colombians may seem indiscreet about their behaviour in public places. Someone in a bar may discuss personal problems at a volume that allows all the patrons to follow the conversation. A driver may urinate on the tyre of his bus after he has stopped for a break on the road. Couples hug and kiss passionately in parks and in the street.

DEFINING EXPERIENECE

Strolling around La Candelaria, Bogotá's charming historic quarter, and stopping off for a *santafereño* (hot chocolate served with cheese and local bread) at Pastelería Florida, then exploring the Museo del Oro (Gold Museum), before conducting a night crawl around the pubs and discos of Zona Rosa.

STRENGTHS

- Friendliness of the locals
- Museo del Oro
- Donación Botero
- Festival Iberoamericano de Teatro de Bogotá – one of the best theatre festivals in Latin America
- Colonial churches such as the Iglesia Museo de Santa Clara
- Cerro de Monserrate
- The nightlife
- Amazing variety of fruits, some of which are endemic to the country
- Futuristic architecture
- *El Señor Caído* (the Fallen Christ) statue
- Intellectual life

WEAKNESSES

- Guerrillas
- Cocaine thugs
- Vast shantytowns
- Street urchins
- Traffic
- Graffiti

GOLD STAR

The view of the city from the top of Cerro de Monserrate – on a clear day you can even spot Los Nevados, the volcanic range in the Cordillera Central, 135km away, noted for the symmetrical cone of the Nevado del Tolima.

STARRING ROLE IN...

- *The People at Universal* (1991)
- *Maria Full of Grace* (2004)
- *El Rey* (The King, 2004)
- *One Hundred Years of Solitude* by Gabriel García Márquez

IMPORT

- *Telenovelas* (soap operas)
- African rhythms of the Caribbean
- Roman Catholicism
- Columbus
- Car bombings
- Drug trafficking
- Spaniards
- Cuban salsa
- *Corrida* (bullfighting)
- Slavery

EXPORT

- Gabriel García Márquez
- Marijuana
- Shakira
- Emeralds
- Revolutionary Armed Forces of Colombia (FARC)
- Magic realism (literary genre)
- Álvaro Mutis
- Cocaine
- Illegally exported wildlife

SEE more than 34,000 gold pieces from all the major pre-Hispanic cultures in Colombia at the most important gold museum in the world, Museo del Oro.

EAT the Bogotano speciality *ajiaco* (soup made with chicken and potato) at Restaurante La Pola.

DRINK the excellent *tinto* (a small cup of black coffee) – the number one drink in Bogotá – first thing in the morning.

DO go to Galería Café Libro, a popular *salsoteca* (salsa nightclub) always packed with salsa fans.

WATCH a local theatre production at the inspiring Teatro de la Candelaria.

BUY emeralds at one of the many *joyerías* (jewellery shops) in the city centre.

AFTER DARK head to Gótica, a large nightclub offering different musical ambiences on different levels, including salsa, techno and trance.

URBAN MYTH

The Palacio de Justicia (Palace of Justice) has had a tragic history. The first court building, erected in 1921, was burnt down by a mob during El Bogotazo in 1948. A modern building was then constructed on Plaza de Bolívar, but in 1985 it was taken by M-19 guerrillas and gutted by fire in a fierce 28-hour offensive by the army in an attempt to reclaim it. The ruin stood untouched for four years until authorities decided to construct a new building.

CERRO DE MONSERRATE PROVIDES A HEAVENLY PLACE TO VIEW THE CITY.
Photographer: Patricia Rincon Mautner / Getty Images

TAKING FLIGHT IN SIMON BOLÍVAR PARK.
Photographer: Patricia Rincon Mautner / Getty Images

POMP AND CEREMONY ACCOMPANY THE CHANGING OF THE GUARD AT PLAZA DE BOLÍVAR.
Photographer: Patricia Rincon Mautner / Getty Images

Bridgetown

VITAL STATISTICS

NAME: BRIDGETOWN

NICKNAME: LITTLE ENGLAND

DATE OF BIRTH: 1628; FOUNDED BY THE BRITISH – PURPORTEDLY THE ONLY EVIDENCE OF PREVIOUS INDIGENOUS OCCUPATION WAS A SIMPLE BRIDGE (THAT PUT THE 'BRIDGE' IN BRIDGETOWN) SPANNING THE CONSTITUTION RIVER

ADDRESS: BARBADOS (MAP 4, Q6)

HEIGHT: 55M

POPULATION: 97,000

LONELY PLANET RANKING: 156

Amid the white-sand and turquoise-water tropical idyll, Barbados' only city is a modern and colonial architectural mishmash with a hubbub of side streets sprinkled with rum shops and chattel houses.

ANATOMY

Bridgetown is a busy commercial city set on Carlisle Bay, developed around an inlet known as the Careenage. True to the island's British heritage, there are obelisks, Gothic Parliament buildings, and a large Anglican cathedral. Broad and Swan Sts are thick with vendors catering to every souveniring whim. Bridgetown is easily covered on foot, while taxis can be flagged on the street.

PEOPLE

Bajan culture displays some trappings of British life, such as cricket, polo and horse racing yet, on closer examination, Barbados is deeply rooted in Afro-Caribbean tradition. The typical Bridgetown citizen's roots are African, with the rest made up of a mix of English, Scottish and East Indian cultures. Religions observed are Protestantism (around 70%), Roman Catholicism and others. Around 17% of people are atheists.

TYPICAL BRIDGETOWN CITIZEN

Like other Caribbean cultures, Bridgetown's citizens are relatively conservative and the men are macho, but the ongoing bond with London has made Barbados more socially progressive than its neighbours. Special events are carried out with a great deal of pomp and ceremony, and older ladies are fond of donning prim little hats. However, for all its surface 'Britishness', family life, art, food, music and dress have more in common with the nearby Windward Islands than with West London.

DEFINING EXPERIENCE

Snorkelling the coral-encrusted tug *Berwyn* in Carlisle Bay and lazing on Pebble Beach followed by an afternoon trip of spiritual healing, Calypso-cocktail style, at the Malibu beachfront distillery.

STRENGTHS

- Congaline Carnival (late April)
- Blissful beaches
- Rum!
- The Bridgetown Synagogue
- Payne's Bay Beach
- Barbados Museum
- Crop-Over Festival (mid-July)
- Flying-fish sandwiches
- Calypso rhythms
- Harry Bayley Observatory
- National Heroes Sq
- Workin' up (dancing)
- St Michael's Cathedral

WEAKNESSES

- Sparse accommodation
- A somewhat macho culture
- Densely populated beaches
- Berthing 'super cruise ships'
- The well-oiled pre-fab tourist machine
- Soil erosion
- Ship pollution

GOLD STAR

'British' Bridgetown is West Indian to the core – with calypso rhythms and its own quirky characteristics, it has enough local flavour to feel 'exotic' yet has enough of the familiar to feel comfortable.

STARRING ROLE IN...

- *The Castle of My Skin* by George Lamming
- *Treasures of Barbados* by Henry Fraser
- *Island in the Sun* (1957)

IMPORT

- Anglo culture
- Cricket
- Polo
- New York hip-hop fashion
- Saturday at the races
- Queen Elizabeth portraits in every scout hall and municipal building
- Around 500,000 cruise-liner passengers every year

EXPORT

- Tourism
- Sir Frank Worrell
- Sugar
- Rum
- Molasses
- Garfield Sobers
- Light manufacturing
- Calypso artist the Mighty Gabby
- Component assembly
- Agriculture
- Fishing

SEE engaging displays on all aspects of Bajan history, with exhibits on early indigenous inhabitants, slavery, emancipation, military history and plantation-house furniture at the excellent Barbados Museum.

EAT local specialities flying fish and coconut prawn (shrimp) at the Rusty Pelican – the 2nd-floor balcony affords a pleasant view over the Careenage.

DRINK with the locals at Bridgetown's many rollicking rum shops along Baxter Rd, just north of the centre.

DO tussle with the crowds on the pristine white sands of Pebble Beach on Carlisle Bay.

WATCH world-class cricket at Kensington Oval, Fontabelle, just outside Bridgetown.

BUY pottery, leather, wood and fabric handicrafts at Pelican Craft Village, between downtown and the cruise-ship terminal.

AFTER DARK view the gorgeous Caribbean night sky from the Harry Bayley Observatory, the headquarters of the Barbados Astronomical Society.

URBAN MYTH

In 1751, at age 19 – some 38 years before he would become the first US president – George Washington visited Barbados as a companion to his half-brother Lawrence, who suffered from tuberculosis. It was hoped that the tropical climate would prove therapeutic. The two rented a house in the Garrison area south of Bridgetown (where the Bush Hill House now stands) and stayed on the island for six weeks. Unfortunately, George contracted smallpox while on Barbados, which left his face permanently scarred, and Lawrence died the following year. The Barbados trip was the only overseas journey that George Washington ever made.

MAKING SHADE ON THE WAY HOME, MARHOLE RD.
Photographer: John Neubauer / LPI

INNOCENTS' PURSUITS IN POLLARD'S BAR.
Photographer: John Neubauer / LPI

A SEDATE CHATTEL HOUSE IN EVANS VILLAGE…
Photographer: John Neubauer / LPI

…AND A RIOTOUS NEIGHBOURHOOD SHOPFRONT.
Photographer: John Neubauer / LPI

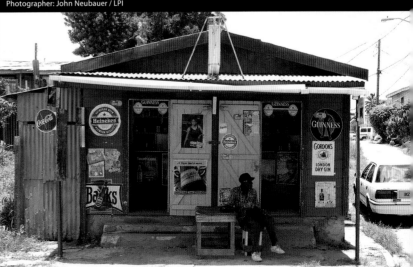

Bucharest

VITAL STATISTICS

NAME: BUCHAREST

DATE OF BIRTH: 70 BC; GETO-DACIAN TRIBES INHABITED THE REGION THAT IS NOW MODERN-DAY BUCHAREST

ADDRESS: ROMANIA (MAP 3, Q12)

HEIGHT: 92M

SIZE: 228 SQ KM

POPULATION: 2.6 MILLION

LONELY PLANET RANKING: 141

Emerging from a tumultuous and sometimes tragic past, Bucharest is blossoming into one of Eastern Europe's most cosmopolitan cities, where a flourishing music scene and lively nightlife complement the rich historical feel of the city.

ANATOMY

Despite two devastating earthquakes and allied bombings in WWII, much of Bucharest's rich and chequered history is preserved in the blend of neoclassical architecture, Romanian Orthodox churches, Parisian-style parks and the stony-faced buildings of the Communist era, including the monstrous Palace of Parliament. The main attractions cluster in the heart of the city and are easily accessible via Bucharest's transit system – one of the largest in Central and Eastern Europe – which includes buses, trolleybuses, trams and the underground urban railway, the Metro.

PEOPLE

The capital's population mirrors that of the nation and comprises some 90% Romanian citizens, while the remaining population is made up of Hungarians, Roma (formerly known as Gypsies), Germans and Ukrainians. The official language is Romanian and the vast majority of the citizens follow the Eastern (Romanian) Orthodox religion.

TYPICAL BUCHAREST CITIZEN

With a low unemployment rate most locals work and, as Bucharest is the least expensive city in Europe, the citizens of the post-Communist capital are also voracious consumers. They love to show-pony the latest-model cars in the streets of the capital, and take great pride in their personal appearance – shopping is an increasingly popular pastime. Etiquette is important, and affectionate public embraces are common. They are both a traditional and dynamic population, with a resilience and optimism born of hard-won freedom.

DEFINING EXPERIENCE

Breathing in the morning air atop the Triumphal Arch, then catching a train to the monastery by Snagov Lake to see the supposed tomb of Dracula before heading back into town to dine with expats on the terrace of the decadent Athénée Palace Hilton, and ending the evening with some sexy dance moves at Cuban club Salsa 2.

STRENGTHS

- Live music
- Ice-skating on lakes in winter
- Greenery of the urban parklands
- Mainstream and art-house cinemas
- History round every corner
- Variety of pubs, clubs and cafés
- Friendly locals
- Sailing across Herăstrău Lake in summer
- Selection of tasty, hearty local and international cuisine
- Local beer and wine
- Museum of the Romanian Peasant
- Stavropoleos Church
- Patriarchal Cathedral
- Triumphal Arch

WEAKNESSES

- Stray dogs
- Daredevil drivers and the worst potholes in Romania
- State buses for long-distance travelling
- Poorly signposted train stations
- Flirty taxi drivers (ladies: take the back seat)
- Crowded transit system during peak hour

GOLD STAR

After-dark music scene – whether it's checking out live rock, getting into the traditional sounds, dancing to your favourite '70s tunes, toe-tapping at a jazz bar or a more refined experience with the George Enescu Philharmonic Orchestra, there is something for all tastes in Bucharest. Plugging into the local scene is easy – advertisements posted around the city promote clubs and hot DJs.

STARRING ROLE IN...

- *Philanthropy* (2002)
- *The Wild Dogs* (2002)
- *Children Underground* (2000)

IMPORT

- Designer clothes
- Music from around the world
- Cars
- Oil
- Gas
- Greek olives
- American poultry and pork
- Pot plants
- McDonald's
- Tobacco
- Fruit and vegetables
- Machinery

EXPORT

- George Enescu's music
- Fashion
- Wine
- Textiles

SEE the crystal chandelier in the decadent Palace of Parliament that weighs 2.5 tonnes.

EAT exquisite French/Thai fusion at Balthazar, the best and hippest restaurant in the city.

DRINK Guinness at the Dubliner as you swap stories with other travellers.

DO head into the residential areas of Bucharest to see the old-style Bucharest housing – before the apartment blocks of Ceauşescu's era.

WATCH some fine jazz acts at the intimate Green Hours 22 Jazz Club Amzei.

BUY a bottle of the famous anti-ageing magic potion – Gerovital face cream – (allegedly used by Elizabeth Taylor and JFK) available at pharmacies.

AFTER DARK soak up the flavour of Romania's cultural scene with a ballet performance at the Opera House.

URBAN MYTH

The myth is that Michael Jackson was on the balcony of Bucharest's monumental Palace of Parliament and said 'Hello Budapest, I'm so glad to be here', though he actually made the legendary error at Bucharest's National Stadium!

ENJOY A SPOT OF SHOPPING AT THE TRADITIONAL CITY MARKETS.
Photographer: Richard I'Anson / LPI

MAGNIFICENT LAKE CISMIGIU PARK IS THE CAPITAL'S OLDEST PUBLIC GARDEN.
Photographer: Richard I'Anson / LPI

MUSIC TAKES ON A LIFE OF ITS OWN IN BUCHAREST'S LIVE MUSIC VENUES.
Photographer: Richard I'Anson / LPI

PATRIARCHAL CATHEDRAL IS THE CENTREPIECE OF THE ROMANIAN ORTHODOX FAITH.
Photographer: Richard I'Anson / LPI

One of the world's most seductive, sophisticated and cool cities, Buenos Aires is the pounding trade and cultural heart of Argentina, and is probably the only major capital you can experience *without* busting your budget.

ANATOMY

The city sits beside the Atlantic on the edge of an agriculturally rich pampas on the River Plate. It is by far Argentina's richest city and the eighth-largest in the world, with one of the highest skyscraper counts anywhere (over 1500). Buenos Aires is divided into 47 *barrios* (neighbourhoods), each with its own fascinating idiosyncrasies. Acres of parkland, wide boulevards and graceful historic architecture give the city a distinctly European edge. Buenos Aires' rail network services the suburbs surrounding the city area, while the Subte (Underground) is South America's oldest subway and still a quick, efficient and easy way to get around. Buses also ply the streets of Buenos Aires.

PEOPLE

Greater Buenos Aires holds around 40% of Argentina's population. The majority are descended from Spanish and Italian immigrants but there are also significant German, British, Jewish, central and eastern European, and Middle Eastern communities, known collectively as *turcos*. Mestizos (people of mixed Native Indian and European heritage) are a growing minority, making up over a quarter of the inner-city population. The Spanish spoken here is rhythmically closer to Italian and the locals also use colourful slang expressions known as *lunfardo*.

TYPICAL PORTEÑO

Locals refer to themselves as *porteños* (port people) and have a reputation outside Buenos Aires for being arrogant know-it-alls. They are refreshingly proud of their city and willing to sing its praises at great length. Whatever the occasion they are always meticulously turned out, earning them a further reputation as some of the sexiest people on the planet. They work hard and play harder, and exude a seductive charisma through their uniquely lyrical language.

Buenos Aires

VITAL STATISTICS

NAME: BUENOS AIRES

NICKNAME: PARIS OF THE SOUTH

DATE OF BIRTH: 1536; FOUNDED AS SANTA MARÍA DEL BUEN AIRE (ST MARY OF THE GOOD AIR) BY SPANISH SAILOR PEDRO DE MENDOZA

ADDRESS: ARGENTINA (MAP 1, N20)

HEIGHT: 27M

SIZE: 200 SQ KM

POPULATION: 3 MILLION (CITY); 13.4 MILLION (METRO AREA)

LONELY PLANET RANKING: 016

DANCERS GIVE AN IMPROMPTU PERFORMANCE ALONGSIDE BUSKERS, LA BOCA.
Photographer: Donald C & Priscilla Alexander Eastman / LPI

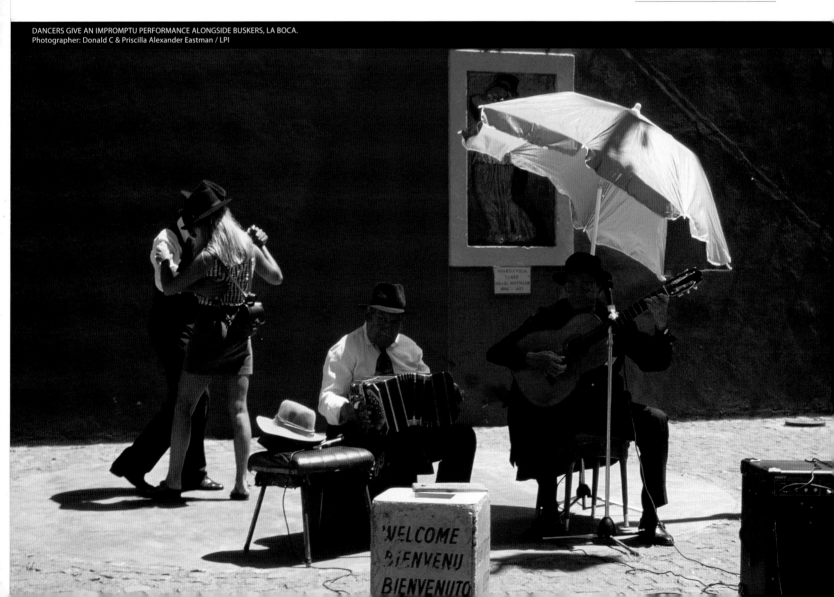

DEFINING EXPERIENCE

Feeling the world change as you go through the different neighbourhoods, rubbing shoulders with the city's elite around the Cementerio de la Recoleta, taking a cheeky siesta in one of Palermo's gorgeous parks, catching your breath on the riverside patio at club Mint, wandering 'home' via Plaza Serrano as the sun comes up, amazed at how good the *porteños* still manage to look.

STRENGTHS

- Plaza de Mayo
- Gay-friendly
- Buenos Aires International Tango Festival
- Safe neighbourhoods
- Neighbourhood diversity
- Unpredictable
- Cheap prices
- Beautiful people
- Underground jungle scene
- Hot and humid weather
- Cementerio de la Recoleta
- Succulent beef steaks
- Friendly locals
- Parks
- Botanical Gardens
- Theatre

WEAKNESSES

- Air pollution
- Crowded streets
- A few dodgy neighbourhoods
- Flooding
- Unemployment
- Can be a pedestrians' nightmare

GOLD STAR

Nightlife – the *boliches* (discos) are the throbbing heart of the city's world-famous nightlife. Dress hot, dance cool, and arrive well after 2am.

STARRING ROLE IN...

- *Evita* (1996)
- *Motorcycle Diaries* (2004)
- *A Social Genocide* (2004)
- *Pin Boy* (2004)
- *Ronda Nocturna* (2005)
- *Labyrinths; Selected Stories and other writings* by Jorge Luis Borges
- *The Flight* by Horacio Verbitsky

IMPORT

- Aristotle Onassis
- Catwalk fashion
- Latin spirit
- Drainage technology

EXPORT

- Tango
- Eva Perón
- Che Guevera
- Diego Maradona
- Latin playboy image
- Jorge Luis Borges
- Grain
- Julio Cortázar
- Biro pens – first made here in 1944
- Beef
- Champion polo players
- Shellfish

SEE Buenos Aires' hip-shakin' young things at Cocoliche, an electronic-music paradise based in a glamorous old mansion.

EAT *flan casera* (homemade flan) at Munich Recoleta, where legendary poet Jorge Luis Borges was once a regular.

DRINK maté at the trendy Nucha café.

DO hire a bicycle one weekend and check out the city's parks, including the Reserva Ecológica Costanera Sur.

WATCH majestic mayhem unfold at a Boca Juniors versus River Plate *fútbol* (football) match.

BUY outrageous sexy and crazy fashion from the weird and wonderful collection at Objeto.

AFTER DARK funk it up to some wicked hip-hop beats at Club 69.

URBAN MYTH

Nowadays the tango epitomises high-society glamour, but its origins were in the brothels of 19th-century Buenos Aires. Successive waves of immigrants, drawn to the city's 'houses of ill repute', invented the tango as a means to vent their sorrow at finding themselves 'strangers in a strange land'. The rhythm is attributed to the beats pumped out by African slaves on their drums, known as tan-go, fused with the milonga music of the pampas, and Latin sounds already familiar to the early Spanish colonists. The dance developed as an 'acting out' of the pimp-prostitute relationship, and the early tangos not only represented a kind of sexual choreography, but often a duel between men competing for the sexual favours of a woman, which resulted in the symbolic death of an opponent.

COLOURFUL AND HOT – AND THAT'S JUST OUTSIDE THE WALLS!
Photographer: Jane Sweeney / LPI

SURROUNDED BY THEIR WARES, SHOPKEEPERS AWAIT CUSTOMERS AT THE PLAZA DORREGO SUNDAY MARKET.
Photographer: Michael Coyne / LPI

ARGENTINE FLAGS FLUTTER BENEATH THE IMPASSIVE PIRAMIDE DE MAYO MONUMENT.
Photographer: Michael Coyne / LPI

Central Asia's holiest city and a place uniquely preserved from pre-Russian Turkistan, Bukhara is a sprawl of truly fascinating Islamic architecture.

ANATOMY

The *shakhristan* (old town) lies at the centre of sprawling modern Bukhara and its streets and squares probably haven't changed much in two centuries. The very centre of the city is the Lyabi-Hauz, a square with a pool in the middle of it (Lyabi-Hauz means 'around the pool' in Tajik) where people congregate for tea and conversation. Buses and taxis service the city.

PEOPLE

Bukhara is primarily Uzbek, but also has significant numbers of Tajiks and other Central Asian ethnic communities.

TYPICAL BUKHARAN

The pride the locals take in their city is hard to overstate. Its recovery in the past decade and a half of Uzbek independence has been quite amazing. Neglected by the Soviet government, for whom the city represented Islam in all its counter-revolutionary glory, the restoration programme initiated since the early 1990s has made the city a highlight of Central Asia. Bukharans are conservative but generally very hospitable and kindly people who are always happy to see visitors in their ancient city.

Bukhara

VITAL STATISTICS

NAME: BUKHARA

DATE OF BIRTH: AD 900; WHEN IT WAS THE CAPITAL OF THE SAMANID STATE AND CENTRAL ASIA'S RELIGIOUS AND CULTURAL HEART

ADDRESS: UZBEKISTAN (MAP 1, CC10)

HEIGHT: 230M

POPULATION: 300,000

LONELY PLANET RANKING: 146

SHAPING UP – UZBEKISTAN IS A COUNTRY RICH IN SPORTING ACHIEVEMENT.
Photographer: Peter Turnley / Corbis

DEFINING EXPERIENCE

Drinking tea by the Lyabi-Hauz and having a quiet chat in the shade as you watch the city bustle go on about you.

STRENGTHS

◢ Fascinating architecture
◢ The sheer scale and awe-inspiring devotion of the mosques and *medressas* (Islamic academies)
◢ Extremely open and welcoming attitude to tourists

WEAKNESSES

◢ Pushy children selling souvenirs and begging
◢ The extreme heat and dust in summer
◢ The good restaurants in the old town are block-booked by tour groups for months throughout the summer

GOLD STAR

The Char Minar, the gatehouse of a long-gone Bukhara *medressa* – this is one of the most perfect buildings anywhere in the world, surely?

STARRING ROLE IN...

◢ Bukhara has yet to grace the silver screen in any major way, although when a city is as superbly preserved as this, it really only can be a matter of time…

IMPORT

◢ Tour groups
◢ Ever-growing numbers of backpackers

EXPORT

◢ Carpets
◢ Fruit and veg

SEE the Ark, the royal town-within-a-town, for an insight into how the all-powerful emirs of Bukhara lived.

EAT delicious and cheap *laghman* (noodles) and *samsas* (samosas) at the alfresco teahouses around the old town.

DRINK tea in the blissful quiet of a summer afternoon by the Lyabi-Hauz.

DO climb the astonishing Kalon Minaret for an amazing view – Genghis Khan was so impressed that he didn't destroy it.

WATCH puppetry at the amateur theatre by the Lyabi-Hauz.

BUY jewellery, silk, carpets and trinkets from one of the fabulous bazaars.

AFTER DARK you'll be limited to a belly-dancing show or some beers in one of the few bars of the *shakhristan*.

URBAN MYTH

During the days of the 'Great Game', when the British and Russian empires ground up against each other in Central Asia, a British emissary named Charles Stoddart arrived in Bukhara to placate the emir about Britain's invasion of next-door Afghanistan. However, things didn't quite go to plan: Stoddart quickly offended the emir's vanity (he rode up to the Ark – the emir's palace – rather than dismounting, as protocol dictated) and ended up in the bug pit (the name just about says it all) for three long years. When the British finally got a second emissary to Bukhara to secure Stoddart's release, the emir (apparently offended this time at having had no reply from Queen Victoria, to whom he had written a letter earlier) executed both unfortunates in front of a huge crowd outside the Ark.

IMPRESSIVE ARCHITECTURE INSPIRES SCHOLARS AT MIR I ARAB MEDRESSA.
Photographer: Gavin Hellier / Robert Harding

EDUCATING BUKHARA'S YOUNG MINDS.
Photographer: Janet Wishnetsky / Impact Photos/Heritage-Images

THIS ROMANTIC OLD SILK ROAD CITY IS AN IMPORTANT CENTRE FOR ISLAMIC STUDIES.
Photographer: Network Photographers / Alamy

DOING THE TWIST – A WHIRLING DERVISH PERFORMS THE SACRED DANCE BEFORE AWE-STRUCK ONLOOKERS.
Photographer: Lee Foster / LPI

Cairo dominates Egypt with one of the world's highest population densities, its minarets dominate the skyline and ancient obelisks and extraordinary works of art greet you in the most unlikely places.

ANATOMY

Cairo is relatively easy to navigate. Islamic Cairo is the medieval centre of the city. Heading east, Downtown ends at Midan Ataba and the old but still kicking medieval heart of the city known as Islamic Cairo takes over. Bordering Downtown to the west is the Nile River, which is obstructed by two sizable islands. The more central of these, connected directly to Downtown by three bridges, is Gezira, home to the Cairo Tower and the Opera House complex. The west bank of the Nile is less historical and much more residential. Giza stretches some 20km west on either side of the long, straight road that ends at the foot of the pyramids. The Metro is startlingly efficient, but the masses still use minibuses.

PEOPLE

More than a quarter of Egyptians live in Cairo, Africa's largest city. The majority of its population is Egyptian, with a small number of Bedouins, Nubians from Sudan and an almost negligible number of Greeks, Armenians, Italians and French. While Muslim is the official religion, around 10% of Cairenes are Coptic Christian.

TYPICAL CAIRENE

The people of Cairo are both curious and generous. They'll gladly help you across the maddening roads with cars that never stop for anything and at the same time ask you a million questions about where you're from and even offer to show you some ancient treasures that are hidden to tourists.

DEFINING EXPERIENCE

Smoking a *sheesha* (a tobacco water pipe, often flavoured with honey or apple) surrounded by dusty gilt mirrors, tourists, travellers and locals alike at the renowned El Fishawi café in the Khan el-Khalili souq (market).

STRENGTHS

▲ Khan el-Khalili
▲ Pyramids and Sphinx at your doorstep
▲ The Egyptian Museum
▲ King Tutankhamun's relics
▲ The land of a million guides

Cairo

VITAL STATISTICS

NAME: CAIRO

NICKNAME: THE CITY OF A THOUSAND MINARETS

DATE OF BIRTH: AD 150; THE ROMAN BABYLON FORT WAS THE FIRST SETTLEMENT ON THE LOCATION OF MODERN CAIRO

ADDRESS: EGYPT (MAP 2, K3)

HEIGHT: 116M

SIZE: 214 SQ KM

POPULATION: 8 MILLION (CITY); 17.3 MILLION (METRO AREA)

LONELY PLANET RANKING: 032

SMOKE OBSCURES THE FACE OF A MAN IN THE BACKSTREETS OF CENTRAL CAIRO.
Photographer: Phil Weymouth / LPI

A LONE FIGURE POLISHES THE TILES IN THE BEAUTIFUL INTERIOR OF THE MAUSOLEUM OF BARQUQ.
Photographer: Patrick Horton / LPI

RUSH HOUR ON CAIRO'S SUBWAY: A MODERN SYSTEM SERVING AN ANCIENT CITY.
Photographer: Phil Weymouth / LPI

WEAKNESSES

◢ Guides – they'll take you anywhere, as long as you visit a papyrus 'museum', jewellery shop, camel rental etc
◢ Cars that sink into the melting bitumen
◢ The heat in June
◢ Tourist police who, for a little baksheesh, know where everything is
◢ Tourists falling out of tour buses at the Egyptian Museum wearing short shorts

GOLD STAR

The pyramids and the Sphinx – both larger and smaller than you could ever imagine, respectively.

STARRING ROLE IN...

◢ *Death on the Nile* (1978)
◢ *Gallipoli* (1981)
◢ *Malcolm X* (1992)
◢ *The Spy Who Loved Me* (1977)
◢ *The Ten Commandments* (1956)
◢ *The Purple Rose of Cairo* (1985)
◢ *The Cairo Trilogy: Palace Walk, Palace of Desire, Sugar Street* by Naguib Mahfouz
◢ *The Map of Love* by Ahdaf Soueif (1999)
◢ *Under the Same Sky – Rooftops in Cairo*, by photographer Randa Shaath (2002–2003)

IMPORT

◢ Metro German supermarket chain
◢ Pizza Hut
◢ Barbie
◢ Classical music at the Cairo Opera House
◢ Eating disorders among teenage girls

EXPORT

◢ Omar Sharif
◢ Mummies
◢ Backgammon
◢ Hand-blown glass perfume bottles
◢ Naguib Mahfouz – winner of the 1988 Nobel Prize for Literature
◢ Belly dancer Fifi Abdou
◢ The sounds of singer Om-Kalthoum
◢ Boutros Boutros-Ghali

SEE the pyramids during the heat of the day – you'll be guaranteed that there will be few tourists around and you can sit within the depths of Cheops listening only to the sound of your own beating heart.

EAT a great spread of falafel, salads, *fuul* (seasoned chickpeas), bread, tahini and omelettes at Akher Sa'a.

DRINK *karkadeh* (hibiscus tea) – found everywhere.

DO get a Coptic cross tattooed on your wrist in the Coptic Christian quarter.

WATCH feluccas sail down the Nile.

BUY pure jasmine oil in a hand-blown glass bottle from one of the many stalls in the Khan.

AFTER DARK check out the light-and-sound show at the pyramids after a spectacular sunset.

URBAN MYTH

Old Cairo is also home to the city's remaining Jewish population. The area's Ben Ezra Synagogue, Egypt's oldest, is said to be where the prophet Jeremiah gathered the Jews after they fled from Nebuchadnezzar, the destroyer of their Jerusalem temple. There is also a spring that is supposed to mark the place where the pharaoh's daughter found Moses in the reeds, and where Mary drew water to wash the baby Jesus.

Carcassonne

VITAL STATISTICS

NAME: CARCASSONNE

DATE OF BIRTH: 3500 BC; WHEN THE FIRST NEOLITHIC SETTLEMENTS APPEARED

ADDRESS: FRANCE (MAP 3, G13)

HEIGHT: 130M

POPULATION: 45,500

LONELY PLANET RANKING: 130

One of the largest and best preserved walled towns in the world, Carcassonne enfolds centuries of history within the defensive ramparts of La Cité.

ANATOMY

The River Aude separates the Ville Basse (Lower Town) from La Cité, located on a hill 500m southeast and surrounded by two concentric walls. Pedestrianised rue Georges Clemenceau leads from the train station and Canal du Midi southwards through the heart of the lower town. You can catch buses around town.

PEOPLE

The inhabitants of Carcassonne live mostly in the Ville Basse and surrounding suburbs, with only a small percentage living in La Cité itself. About 90% are Roman Catholic and some speak Catalan rather than French. In recent years the population has been greatly boosted by British migrants.

TYPICAL CARCASSONNAIS

Carcassonne's residents go about their daily lives seemingly oblivious to the hordes of tourists and the cacophony of buskers, tour guides and souvenir vendors. While celebrating their proud Cathar history at every chance, they certainly don't adopt the austere lifestyle of their predecessors, preferring to cultivate a convivial café culture and a predilection for local wine and *cassoulet* (a piping hot dish blending white beans, juicy pork cubes, sausage and – in the most popular local variant – duck).

DEFINING EXPERIENCE

Admiring the charming carousel just outside the entrance to La Cité, then literally walking around the city (along 3km of defensive ramparts), visiting Porte Narbonnaise, Basilique St-Nazaire and Château Comtal, dining on *cassoulet* at L'Écu d'Or, followed by a twilight walk outside the now-illuminated castle walls, for a different perspective.

STRENGTHS

- Your first glimpse of La Cité's witches-hat turrets as you approach
- World Heritage listing
- Basilique St-Nazaire
- 12th-century Château Comtal
- Musée Lapidaire
- Massive bastion of Porte Narbonnaise
- L'Embrasement de la Cité (Setting La Cité Ablaze) – Bastille Day celebrations
- Magnificent reconditioned 19th-century carousel
- Elaborate tombs and graves in the cemetery
- *Cassoulet*

WEAKNESSES

- Hellishly overcrowded with tourists (over two million) in high summer
- An oversupply of kitsch souvenir shops
- Cheesy/tacky private museums
- Can be expensive
- Variable quality of Château Comtal guided tour

GOLD STAR

La Cité itself, dramatically illuminated at night and enclosed within its two rampart walls punctuated by 52 towers, is simply breathtaking.

STARRING ROLE IN...

- *Robin Hood: Prince of Thieves* (1991)

IMPORT

- Tourists
- McDonald's
- Rugby

EXPORT

- Wine
- Shoes
- Rubber
- Textiles
- Tacky souvenirs

SEE graceful Gothic transept arms and superb 13th- and 14th-century windows at Basilique St-Nazaire.

EAT *cassoulet* at Au Bon Pasteur, where simple décor belies the sophistication of the cooking.

DRINK your favourite coffee from the huge selection available at La Cité des Arômes.

DO take in the view of La Cité from the Pont Neuf or Pont Vieux, straddling the River Aude.

WATCH birds of prey dive and swoop in falconry demonstrations at Les Aigles de La Cité (The Eagles of La Cité), 800m south of the city walls.

BUY kitsch souvenirs, or better yet, save your money for some of the region's wines.

AFTER DARK most tourists have left, so enjoy a quiet post-dinner stroll and experience the city anew under floodlights.

URBAN MYTH

When Carcassonne was besieged in AD 760, the inhabitants soon began to starve. But Dame Carcas, widow of one of the castle's nobles, devised a clever bluff. Feeding all their remaining grain to one pig, the fattened creature was catapulted over the walls to the army outside. When they saw that the Carcassonnais could apparently still expend large amounts of grain just to feed livestock, the besiegers became demoralised and withdrew. Bells were then rung in Dame Carcas' honour, and many historians believe this legend is the source of the city's name, 'Carcas sonne', meaning 'Carcas rings'.

THE FAIRY-TALE WALLS OF THE MEDIEVAL OLD CITY GLOW MAGICALLY AT NIGHT.
Photographer: Dallas Stribley / LPI

A HORSE MERRILY MAKES IT WAY AROUND A CAROUSEL IN THE JARDIN DU PRADO, WHILE THE TOWERS OF THE PORTE NARBONNAISE LURK OMINOUSLY OVERHEAD.
Photographer: Dallas Stribley / LPI

THE BLUE FAÇADE OF A BUILDING IN VILLE BASSE IS OFFSET BY SASSY PINK WASHING HUNG OUT TO DRY.
Photographer: Dallas Stribley / LPI

A VERY WELL CARED FOR POODLE BASKS WITH HER PERSON IN PLACE CAMOT.
Photographer: Dallas Stribley / LPI

Stunning scenery, historic, battle-scarred castles, a menu of outdoor activities, and gleaming bars and shops make the modern yet traditional capital of Wales a compelling place to visit.

ANATOMY

Central Cardiff's main landmarks are Cardiff Castle and the Millennium Stadium, by the River Taff. High St, St Mary St, Queen St, Bridge St and Charles St are a shopper's paradise, while the Civic Centre north of the castle houses government buildings. The harbour area to the south, once the world's top coal port, is now a redeveloped commercial centre called Cardiff Bay. The bus and train stations are near the stadium.

PEOPLE

Only one-fifth of Wales' population now speak Welsh and just over one-fifth of people come from England. Young people are migrating from the country to the city. Butetown is Cardiff's most multicultural area. Wales does not receive many asylum seekers.

TYPICAL CARDIFF CITIZEN

Welsh people are very proud of their national identity. They are supportive of the National Assembly, despite its limited powers, and are keen to maintain their flagging language (Welsh is taught in schools). Cardiff residents work long hours and are relatively affluent. They enjoy sport and are passionate about rugby. They are friendly and good fun, and confident and positive about Wales's future.

DEFINING EXPERIENCE

Sipping a shot of caffeine with the papers at Café Bar Europa, before wandering over to Bute Park to sunbathe near the ruins of Blackfriars Priory, then heading to Cardiff Central Market to refuel and Queen St for some retail therapy.

Cardiff

VITAL STATISTICS

NAME: CARDIFF

DATE OF BIRTH: AD 75; WHEN THE CITY BEGAN AS A ROMAN FORT – IT WAS ONLY MADE A CITY IN 1905 AND A CAPITAL IN 1955

ADDRESS: WALES (MAP 3, D8)

HEIGHT: 62M

SIZE: 120 SQ KM

POPULATION: 330,000

LONELY PLANET RANKING: 171

CHOICES, CHOICES: DIFFICULT DECISIONS AT CARDIFF MARKET'S SECONDHAND RECORD STORE.
Photographer: Neil Setchfield / LPI

STRENGTHS

- National pride
- Cardiff Festival (July/August)
- Winning the Six Nations Rugby Championship in 2005
- Millennium Stadium
- National Museum & Gallery of Wales
- Cardiff Bay
- Cardiff Castle
- Caerphilly Castle
- Castell Coch
- Roman fortress at Carleon
- Brecon Beacons National Park
- Artes Mundi Award (Arts of the World)
- Museum of Welsh Life
- National Assembly
- Rugby – Cardiff Blues and the Welsh team
- Cycling the Lôn Las Cymru trail
- St Davids Hotel & Spa
- Surfing off the Gower Peninsula
- Welsh rarebit
- Welsh cheese eg Caerphilly and Celtic Blue
- Cardiff University
- Llandaff Cathedral
- Bute Park
- Techniquest
- EU financial aid
- Lower prices than in the rest of the UK
- Royal National Eisteddfod

WEAKNESSES

- Inclement weather
- Political apathy
- Rural economic problems
- Dwindling number of Welsh speakers

GOLD STAR

Castles – Wales is famous for them and Cardiff doesn't let the side down.

STARRING ROLE IN...

- *Human Traffic* (1999)
- *Twin Town* (1997)
- *Doctor Who* (2005–)
- *Dat's Love* by Leonora Brito

IMPORT

- Sir Anthony Hopkins
- Rugby (from England originally)

EXPORT

- Dame Shirley Bassey
- Charlotte Church
- Ryan Giggs
- Ioan Gruffyd
- Griff Rhys-Jones
- Cerys Matthews
- Shakin' Stevens
- Ivor Novella
- Brains Beer
- Penderyn Single Malt Whisky
- Roald Dahl
- Coal (until World War II)
- Mail-order businesses (the first one began in Newtown)
- Kissing under the mistletoe, a druidic tradition
- S4C
- Welsh National Opera
- Captain Robert Scott (launched his expedition to the South Pole from Cardiff in 1910)

SEE Cardiff Castle complete with Great Hall and minstrel's gallery, as well as a Norman keep.

EAT innovative Welsh cuisine at the Armless Dragon Restaurant.

DRINK vodka till you drop at the Russian bar Moloko.

DO visit the National Museum & Gallery of Wales for impressionist art, volcanic eruptions and the world's largest turtle.

WATCH international football and rugby matches at the Millennium Stadium or do a tour and check out the players' tunnel.

BUY love spoons, dragons and souvenir T-shirts at Castle Welshcrafts or explore the trendy shops of High St Arcade.

AFTER DARK check out the latest local bands at Clwb Ifor Bach.

URBAN MYTH

Cardiff and Wales are awash with myths. King Arthur is said to have held his first court at Caerleon; the capstone of the Cefyn Bryn burial chamber on the Gower Peninsula is known as Arthur's stone; and legend has it that the Holy Grail hides at Llangollen's Castell Dinas Brân. Arthur's sidekick, Merlin, was apparently born in Carmarthen. In Cardiff, they say if you dance around Tinkinswood on a Sunday you will be turned to stone – and that the stones surrounding the burial chamber are, in fact, women who did just that.

WORDS AND REFLECTIONS ON THE CARDIFF BAY OPERA HOUSE.
Photographer: Neil Setchfield / LPI

STRUMMING CHORDS IN BUTE PARK – YES, THEY PROBABLY ARE SINGING TOM JONES SONGS.
Photographer: Neil Setchfield / LPI

A PEACEFUL TRIBUTE: CATHAYS PARK WAR MEMORIAL.
Photographer: Neil Setchfield / LPI

BASEBALL FANS KEEP A CLOSE EYE ON THE GAME DURING THE PLAYOFFS AT WRIGLEY FIELD.
Photographer: Ray Laskowitz / LPI

Chicago

Though it ranks third behind Los Angeles and New York size-wise, the Windy City is a vast and vibrant metropolis – a place where running shoes and a good train map are a must if you even *hope* to make a dent in the city's copious and unique attractions.

ANATOMY

The Windy City sprawls along the western side of Lake Michigan, with towering buildings constructed on swampy land forming an artificial landmark. The Loop is the city's historic heart, sitting on a small peninsula where the Chicago River meets the lake. The city and suburbs fan out across the prairie in all directions. Public transport includes trains and buses.

PEOPLE

Chicago's 'diversity index' – a percentage likelihood that two randomly chosen people in an area will be of different races – is 74%, a full 25% higher than the USA as a whole. Blacks outnumber whites in Chicago, with Latinos running a close third. Catholicism is running strong in the Windy City. Chicago has the largest Catholic archdiocese in the country, and a sizable Jewish population as well.

TYPICAL CHICAGOAN

The quintessential Midwesternness of the natives – cheerful, hard-working, and a little conservative – acts as a steadying anchor for the city's more adventurous impulses. Despite the high diversity, integrated neighbourhoods are rare in Chicago, with blacks tending to live in the city's south and west sides, Latinos showing a strong presence in Pilsen and many areas on the North Side, and Asians in Chinatown and along Argyle St in Uptown. Segregation is a fact of life in Chicago.

DEFINING EXPERIENCE

Starting a high-speed day with a laid-back breakfast at the Original Pancake House in Bellevue Plaza, followed by a quick cab ride down to the Art Institute, then to the Berghoff for lunch, followed by some top-tier window-shopping on Michigan Ave, dining on deep-dish pizza at Giordano's nearby, followed by sunset drinks way, way up on the 96th floor of the John Hancock Center's Signature Lounge.

STRENGTHS

- The lake
- Chicago Blues Festival
- Art Institute
- Navy Pier Ferris Wheel
- Chicago Mercantile Exchange
- Store-front churches
- Frank Lloyd Wright's Prairie School–style houses

WEAKNESSES

- The cold in winter
- Weather
- Rats
- Blizzards
- So much salt on the roads
- Corruption in city politics
- The cost of motel and hotel rooms
- Ice on pavements

GOLD STAR

The Art Institute of Chicago is as impressive a museum as can be found anywhere. Turn any corner and you find yet another breathtaking piece of art, from medieval armour to Mondrian abstracts. So this is where it ended up! On the shores of Lake Michigan, the institute has a wondrous collection of impressionist paintings as well as 20th-century modernist and realist works.

STARRING ROLE IN...

- *The Adventures of Augie March* by Saul Bellow
- *Nowhere Man* by Aleksandar Hemon
- *North by Northwest* (1959)
- *Blues Brothers* (1980)
- *Ferris Bueller's Day Off* (1986)
- *Chicago* (2003)

IMPORT

- Conrad Black
- Louis Armstrong
- Frank Lloyd Wright
- Al Capone
- Sara Paretsky
- Saul Bellow

EXPORT

- Oprah and *Oprah*
- John Belushi
- Hillary Rodham Clinton
- Raymond Chandler
- Sam Cooke
- Walt Disney
- Studs Terkel
- Mahalia Jackson
- Harrison Ford
- Hugh Hefner
- Herbie Hancock
- Ernest Hemingway
- *The Jerry Springer Show*

SEE Steppenwolf Theater, the legendary ensemble group that helped put Chicago theatre on the map.

EAT on Division St in Ukrainian Village, the hipster's dining paradise that includes several of the best brunch places in town – Smoke Daddy Rhythm & Bar-B-Que or Mirai.

DRINK from the hundreds of beers on offer at Quencher's.

DO check out Second City, a must-see club (John Belushi, Bill Murray, Dan Aykroyd and Elaine May got their start here) where performers give sharp and biting commentaries on life, politics and love.

WATCH the beaches in smelt season, when the tiny fish swarming into Chicago harbours to spawn are met by amateur anglers, nets and deep-fat fryers.

BUY clothes, accessories, anything on Milwaukee Ave (Wicker Park), where the funkier cousin to Damen Ave features blocks and blocks of hip stores.

AFTER DARK check out the multigenerational dance scene – Chicago was one of the hotbeds of house in the early '80s, and the audiences have aged with the music.

URBAN MYTH

It's certainly true that Chicago is windy, but meteorology is not the reason for the moniker 'Windy City'. The most popular of various legends as to the origin of the name claims it is to do with the city's politicians and journalists, who are 'full of wind'. Apparently, the name was popularised by a writer in the *New York Sun*, who claimed that despite its boasts, 'that windy city' would not beat New York in the competition to hold the World's Fair of 1893. Not only did Chicago win, but the fair was a huge success.

A SMURF'S-EYE VIEW OF THE SMURFIT-STONE TOWER ON MICHIGAN AVE.
Photographer: Richard Cummins / LPI

A COMMUTER TRAIN NEAR GRANT PARK HEADS TO THE OTHER SIDE OF THE TRACKS.
Photographer: Ray Laskowitz / LPI

HOW MUCH DO YOU LOVE CHICAGO? A BOY MAKES A SPLASH AT LAKE MICHIGAN.
Photographer: Lou Jacobs Jr / LPI

Copenhagen

VITAL STATISTICS

NAME: COPENHAGEN

NICKNAME: WONDERFUL, WONDERFUL COPENHAGEN

DATE OF BIRTH: 1167; BISHOP ABSALON CONSTRUCTED A FORTRESS ON SLOTSHOLMEN

ADDRESS: DENMARK (MAP 3, K5)

HEIGHT: 9M

SIZE: 88.3 SQ KM

POPULATION: 518,000 (CITY); 1.9 MILLION (METRO AREA)

LONELY PLANET RANKING: 120

Copenhagen is one of the few places left where the term 'fairy tale' can be used freely – from its most enduring literary legacy to its most recent royal romance. The old and the new combine to form an attractive, civilised, ergonomic and punctual confection.

ANATOMY

Copenhagen sits on the east coast of Denmark's largest island, Zealand (Sjælland). It is separated from Sweden by the Øresund and is largely low-rise, with few skyscrapers. Most of the city's obvious attractions are found near the main square of Rådhuspladsen and the islands of Slotsholmen and Christianshavn. Public transport can involve buses, boats or the shiny new metro system.

PEOPLE

The vast majority of Copenhageners seem to come from the same stock, ie the Teutonic ancestry so common to Scandinavia. However, there is also a substantial population of foreign nationals in Copenhagen, home to half of Denmark's immigrants.

TYPICAL COPENHAGENER

The clichéd local will have Jensen, Nielsen or Hansen for a surname, be tall, prepared to join a queue and fond of biting, irony-laden humour. They will have strongly held opinions on where to dine and what to dine on, and will give the impression that little else is of great importance. That and what you should sit on when you eat – beautiful chairs are a citywide obsession.

DEFINING EXPERIENCE

Thinking about your next feed, while taking advantage of even a hint of a sunny day by sitting outside at a café where the owners have thoughtfully provided blankets for their patrons, riding a bicycle across beautiful bridges such as Knippelsbro to funky Islands Brygge and taking a dip at the canal-side public baths.

STRENGTHS

- Imaginative *smørrebrod* (buttered bread) toppings at Ida Davidsen
- Timely and tidy public transport
- Christianshavn
- Royal Palaces
- Staten Museum for Kunst
- Tivoli
- Local beers
- Islands Brygge Havnebadet (harbour bathing)
- Good-looking gene pool
- Modern architecture
- An easy-going monarchy
- Bakeries

WEAKNESSES

- Licensing laws
- Taciturn locals
- Daredevil cyclists
- Stubborn refusal to do things that aren't 'the Danish style'
- Long, cold, dark winters
- Smoke-filled bars and restaurants

GOLD STAR

Design – Copenhagen is always bang on the money when it comes to marrying form with function.

STARRING ROLE IN...

- *Miss Smilla's Feeling for Snow* by Peter Høeg
- *Smilla's Sense of Snow* (1977)
- *The Idiots* (1998)
- *Open Hearts* (2003)
- *Reconstruction* (2003)

IMPORT

- Drunken Swedes
- Mary and Alexandra
- German cars
- Tropical fruit
- Solariums
- Jazz
- Chemicals
- Pizza

EXPORT

- A relaxed attitude to porn
- Pork
- Carlsberg and Tuborg
- Claus Jensen
- Dogme films
- Aqua
- Arne Jacobsen chairs
- Christiania Cycles
- Georg Jensen
- Herring
- Dairy goods

SEE the citywide panorama from atop glorious Vor Frelsers Kirke in Christianshavn.

EAT at one of the city's 10 Michelin-starred restaurants.

DRINK Carlsberg beer in Carlsberg's microbrewery.

DO a long, lazy stroll down Strøget – the world's longest pedestrian mall.

WATCH a Dogme 95 film at the Danish Filmhuset.

BUY a stunning piece of silver from the Georg Jensen flagship store.

AFTER DARK watch the fireworks display at Tivoli.

URBAN MYTH

In 1834, Hans Christian Andersen applied for work at the Royal Library in Copenhagen in order 'to be freed from the heavy burden of having to write in order to live'. Apparently the library administrators weren't too impressed with his résumé, as he was turned down. Ironically, Andersen's unsuccessful application is now preserved as part of the library's valued archives, along with many of his original manuscripts.

A BUBBLE BOY EMERGES FROM A BURROW AT THE RABBIT LABYRINTH, COPENHAGEN ZOO. Photographer: Martin Lladó / LPI

A GRID OF SHADED WINDOWS ON THE FAÇADE OF THE SALMON PINK SPIES-HOUSE. Photographer: Martin Lladó / LPI

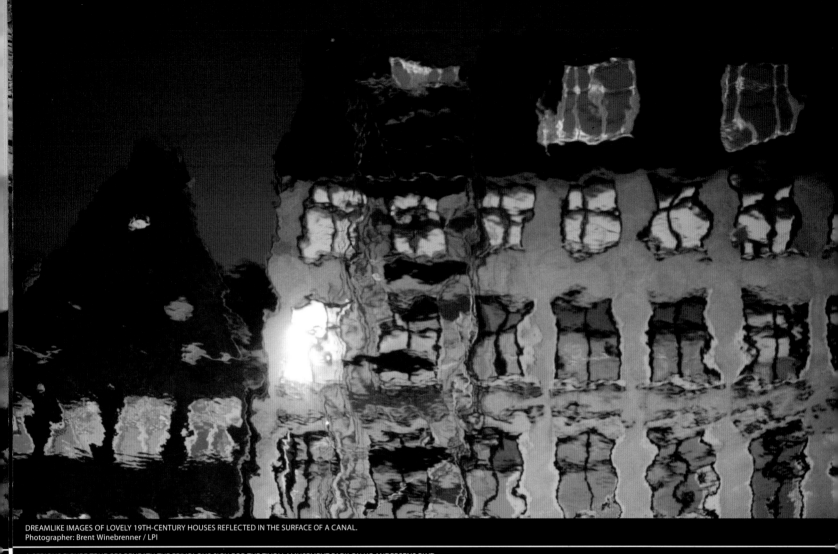

DREAMLIKE IMAGES OF LOVELY 19TH-CENTURY HOUSES REFLECTED IN THE SURFACE OF A CANAL.
Photographer: Brent Winebrenner / LPI

A SERIOUS FIGURE TRUDGES BENEATH THE FRIVOLOUS SIGN FOR THE TIVOLI AMUSEMENT PARK ON HC ANDERSENS BLVD.
Photographer: Martin Moos / LPI

By far Syria's largest metropolis, Damascus is a city of fascinating contrasts, with timeless oriental bazaars and Islamic monuments to enrapture romantics alongside the bustle of a busy capital.

ANATOMY

Damascus has two distinct parts: the Old City, tightly defined by its encircling walls, and modern Damascus, sprawled around it. The Old City is separated from the new by Sharia ath-Thawna, with the covered Souq al-Hamidiyy leading directly to the city's centrepiece, Umayyad Mosque. South of the mosque Shariah Medhat Pasha (Straight St) bisects the city on an east–west axis. Sights of interest are conveniently encapsulated within roughly 2 sq km. Handy microbuses cover set routes and the hundreds of taxis are cheap, though finding your way around this compact city on foot is simple.

PEOPLE

This ancient city has seen many previous tribes, from Mesopotamian Akkadians to the Egyptians and Hittites. Over 70% of the population are Sunni Muslim, about 16% are of Alawite, Druze and other Muslim sects, over 10% are Christian (various sects), with a tiny Jewish community remaining. Damascenes have a literacy rate of around 77%, while life expectancy is about 70 years.

TYPICAL DAMASCENE

The typical Damascene speaks Arabic, is family-oriented, enjoys socialising over a meal and bathes communally in gender-segregated *hammams* (bathhouses). While males mingle over board games and water pipes and banter at coffee houses, women generally socialise in the home. The average day of the Muslim majority is punctuated five times by calls to prayer from minarets and mosques.

Damascus

VITAL STATISTICS

NAME: DAMASCUS

DATE OF BIRTH: 3000 BC; ONE OF THE OLDEST CONTINUOUSLY INHABITED CITIES IN THE WORLD, ITS PRIME POSITION IN THE VERDANT GHOUTA OASIS AND ITS PROXIMITY TO THE SILK ROAD LED TO IT BEING COVETED BY WAVES OF CONQUERING EMPIRES

ADDRESS: SYRIA (MAP 2, L1)

HEIGHT: 720M

POPULATION: 6.5 MILLION

LONELY PLANET RANKING: 053

SHHHH! THE SOUNDLESS STEPS OF MIMES IN REHEARSAL FOR A PERFORMANCE.
Photographer: Nicolas Randall / Expuesto // Alamy

DEFINING EXPERIENCE

Getting lost in the Old City and wandering among its souqs (markets), *medressas* (Islamic academies) and khans (inns), absorbing the serenity of Umayyad Mosque, exploring the treasures of the National Museum, witnessing the fine Azem Palace, viewing Damascene houses, steaming and sweating in a *hammam*, then whiling away some time in a coffee house before heading out to dine on superb food in enchanting surrounds.

STRENGTHS

- Intricate Arabesque design
- Mysterious and exotic souqs
- Dinnertime spread of *mezze* (a selection of hot and cold starters traditionally served at the beginning of meals) among friends
- Azem Palace
- Damascene houses
- The National Museum
- Deep-rooted culture of hospitality
- *Zalabiyya* (pastries dipped in rose water)
- Being invited in to eat or drink with locals
- *Hammams*
- Umayyad Mosque
- Coffee houses

WEAKNESSES

- Attempting to find a taxi between 2pm and 4pm on working days
- Saahat ash-Shodada, an ugly chicane for speeding cars in the city's heart
- Overfuelling on Bedouin coffee
- Smoke-clogged coffee houses for the nonsmoker

GOLD STAR

Immersing yourself in the scents of spices, coffee and perfume in Damascus' souqs, which seduce the eye with colour and glitter, and assault the hearing with trader's cries and porter's warning shouts.

STARRING ROLE IN...

- *Train of Short Distances* (2003)
- *Damascus Bitter Sweet* by Ulfat Idilbi

IMPORT

- Lovingly restored '50s Buicks and Chevrolets
- Victorian adventurer Sir Richard Burton
- Indian 'B' movies
- St John the Baptist
- Egyptians
- Saul of Tarsus/St Paul the Apostle
- Hittites
- Romans
- Mongols
- Hong Kong martial-arts flicks
- Seljuk Turks
- Food and livestock
- Plastics

EXPORT

- Poet Nizar Qabbani
- Elaborate brassware
- Damascus steel (AD 900–1600)
- St John of Damascus
- Intricate, inlaid boxes
- Abbasid poet al-Mutanabi
- Singer Fairouz's first recording
- Crude oil
- Natural gas
- Damask fabric
- Figs and almonds
- The Damascus Declaration (1992)
- Damask rosewater, a prized medicine in the Arab world
- Writer/diplomat Constantine Zouraiq

SEE an *oud* (equivalent of classical guitar) craftsman at work at Sharia Bahsa in the Souq Saroujah.

EAT *tamarimoz* (pancakes with black honey and sugar, wrapped around a banana).

DRINK beer fountain-side at the Damascus Worker's Club.

DO experience the steaming and cleansing wonders of a *hammam*.

WATCH the street scene and ease into local time at Ash-Shams coffee house, formerly a *hammam*, armed with coffee and *narjileh* (water pipe).

BUY inlaid wooden boxes, Bedouin silver jewellery and elaborate copper work at the extensive Damascus Souq.

AFTER DARK team a restaurant meal with a floor show featuring whirling dervishes, musicians, singers-cum-sword fighters and human pyramid builders.

URBAN MYTH

Shariah Medhat Pasha, unique among the city's narrow winding streets, was one of the main streets of ancient Damascus and is believed to be the world's oldest known street. It's mentioned in the Bible (Acts 9:11) as a 'street called Straight', on which St Paul is supposed to have lived.

CLEANLINESS OF BODY AND PURITY OF SOUL IS THE OBJECT OF BATHING RITUALS AT THE HAMMAM EL MOKHADEM.
Photographer: Pascal Meunier / Cosmos / Aurora

SHEESHA SMOKERS BLOW THEIR TROUBLES AWAY IN A LOCAL COFFEE HOUSE.
Photographer: Nicolas Randall / Austral-International

TOOTH-ROTTING TREATS DAZZLE THE EYES AND THE TASTEBUDS AT A CITY SOUQ.
Photographer: Russell Mountford / LPI

Delhi

VITAL STATISTICS

NAME: DELHI

DATE OF BIRTH: 500 BC; HISTORICAL EVIDENCE INDICATES SETTLEMENT AT ABOUT THIS TIME; THE BRITISH MADE DELHI THE CAPITAL IN 1911

ADDRESS: INDIA (MAP 5, D2)

HEIGHT: 218M

SIZE: 1483 SQ KM

POPULATION: 12 MILLION (CITY); 17 MILLION (METRO)

LONELY PLANET RANKING: 060

Don't let your first impressions of Delhi stick like a sacred cow in a traffic jam: get behind the madcap façade and discover the inner peace of a city rich with culture, architecture and human diversity, deep with history and totally addictive to epicureans.

ANATOMY

In Old Delhi there's the main Inter State Bus Terminal (ISBT), and to the south, the New Delhi train station. Near the station is Paharganj, packed with cheap accommodation and acting as a sort of buffer zone between the old and new cities. New Delhi can be broken into the business and residential areas around Connaught P1 (the city's core) and the government areas around Rajpath to the south. Running south from Connaught P1 is Janpath, which has the tourist office, hotels and a shopping strip. Dotted around are all the big tourist sights and enough crazy local flavour to keep you occupied while you're stuck in the congestion. Take your choice of buses, auto-rickshaws, motorised rickshaws or taxis to get around.

PEOPLE

Due to Delhi's extreme cultural diversity, very few city residents can lay claim to being 'real' Delhi-wallahs. Most of the population of New Delhi comprises Hindu-Punjabi families originally from Lahore, with a constant influx of new residents. The main languages spoken in Delhi are Hindi, English and Punjabi. After the violent Partition (1947), the largely Muslim city became mostly Hindu.

TYPICAL DELHI-WALLAH

Shrewd, wily, passionate and resourceful, the typical Delhi citizen is generally tolerant of religion and the lack of personal space. They are quite entrepreneurial. Arranged marriages are still the norm, though in Delhi more residents marry for love than ever before. Delhi-wallahs share a fondness for great food, good cricket and a big shindig, with some sort of festival to be found round every corner.

DEFINING EXPERIENCE

Rambling around Old Delhi's historic Red Fort and Jama Masjid before diving into the old city's rambunctious bazaars and recuperating later on in the serene surrounds of Humayun's Tomb.

STRENGTHS

- Chandni Chowk bazaar
- The Red Fort
- Cheap, delicious cuisine
- Fatepuri Mosque
- Humayun's Tomb
- Behemoth bazaars
- Jama Masjid
- Qutb Minar
- Coronation Durbar site
- Raj Ghat
- Mysticism
- Shalimar Bagh
- Spice Market (on Khari Baoli)

WEAKNESSES

- Scams
- Touts
- Pollution
- Extreme traffic congestion
- Crooked taxi-wallahs
- Stench
- Uproar
- Fumes
- Unscrupulous travel agents
- Poverty

GOLD STAR

Delhi's beguiling charm – lose yourself while unwinding the secrets of the city's Mughal past in the labyrinthine streets of Old Delhi before emerging into the wide open spaces of imperial New Delhi with its generous leafy avenues.

STARRING ROLE IN...

- *Monsoon Wedding* (2001)
- *The Guru* (2002)
- *American Daylight* (2004)

IMPORT

- India's intelligentsia
- 'New' Delhi (courtesy of the British Raj)
- Punjabis
- Pakistanis
- KFC
- McDonald's

EXPORT

- Exquisite Bengali and Punjabi cuisines
- Mukesh Chandra Mathur
- Garments
- MF Hussain
- Textiles
- Mohammad Adil
- Crockery and silverware
- Handicrafts
- IT-enabled services (and staff)
- Spices and incense

SEE India's largest mosque, the awe-inspiring Jama Masjid, the final architectural extravagance of Shah Jahan.

EAT fat, syrupy *jalebis* (fried, sweet 'squiggles') at Jalebiwala, near the Sisganj Gurdwara.

DRINK brutally good Bloody Marys at the Imperial Hotel, as you unwind from haggling hard at the nearby Janpath Market.

DO chill out from the traffic snarls, pesky touts and other vicissitudes of life in the pleasant grounds of Humayun's Tomb, a superb example of early Mughal architecture.

WATCH Bollywood blockbusters at the Imperial Cinema.

BUY eye-popping handicrafts, *agarbathi* (incense), spices and tea from Chandni Chowk, Old Delhi's famous shopping street of bazaars.

AFTER DARK catch the Dances of India at the Parsi Anjuman Hall, a one-hour performance of regional dances that includes *bharatanatyam*, Kathakali and Manipuri.

URBAN MYTH

Popular Hindu mythology claims that Delhi was the site of the fabled city of Indraprastha, which featured in the *Mahabharata* over 3000 years ago, but historical evidence suggests that the area has been settled for around 2500 years.

PRACTITIONERS OF YOGA RELAX AND CONTORT AT A MORNING CLASS IN LODI GARDENS.
Photographer: Palani Mohan / Getty Images

HIGHWAY TO DEMOCRACY – RASHTRAPATI BHAVAN (PRESIDENT'S HOUSE) AT DUSK.
Photographer: Palani Mohan / Getty Images

AFTER A HOT DAY, TWO MEN ENJOY A SHOWER AND A JOKE NEAR INDIA GATE.
Photographer: Palani Mohan / Getty Images

A YOUNG BOY OPTS FOR A WINDOW SEAT ON A TRAIN LEAVING OLD DELHI STATION.
Photographer: Palani Mohan / Getty Images

Dhaka

VITAL STATISTICS

NAME: DHAKA

NICKNAME: CITY OF MOSQUES

DATE OF BIRTH: AD 4; AS A SMALL BUDDHIST TOWN

ADDRESS: BANGLADESH (MAP 5, H4)

HEIGHT: 8M

SIZE: 414 SQ KM

POPULATION: 12.3 MILLION

LONELY PLANET RANKING: 100

CHILDREN IMPROVISE A CRICKET PITCH IN AN ALLEYWAY OF OLD DHAKA.
Photographer: Chris Stowers / Panos Pictures

AN ELDERLY RICKSHAW WALLAH CROUCHES BY HIS VEHICLE TO WAIT FOR HIS NEXT CUSTOMER.
Photographer: Dieter Telemans / Panos Pictures

RICKSHAW GRIDLOCK ON A CITY STREET DURING A PUBLIC TRANSPORT STRIKE.
Photographer: Rafiqur Rahman / Reuters/Picture Media

MONSOON MONET – BOATMEN PICK A PATH THROUGH LUSH WATER HYACINTHS ON BURIGANGA RIVER DURING THE WET SEASON.
Photographer: Rafiqur Rahman / Reuters/Picture Media

Colourful and chaotic at a glance, Dhaka throbs with the raw (and infectious) energy of a spirited capital juggling civic deterioration, modern development and the realities of daily life as one the world's densest cities.

ANATOMY

Situated amid a maze of rivers and canals, Dhaka is both a city of relics and a melting pot of architectural styles. The frenzied – and yet curiously effective – network of bus services, trains and rickshaws will get you around town to see the main attractions. These sites are clustered in the three major sections of the city: Old Dhaka, a labyrinth of narrow streets lined with Moghul-era structures, including the premier attraction – the Lalbagh Fort on the expansive Buriganga River; Central Dhaka, which retains the whitewashed colonial buildings of its former role as the British part of the city but now forms the modern part of town and is home to the celebrated National Assembly building designed by American architect Louis Kahn; and suburban Dhaka, where the best restaurants in town are to be found.

PEOPLE

The nationality of Dhaka's citizens is almost 100% Bengali (Bengal being the regional entity that was split into West Bengal and East Pakistan at the time of Indian/Pakistani independence in 1947). The nation's official language is Bangla (also known as Bengali) and while around 16% of the population is Hindu, the vast majority is Muslim.

TYPICAL DHAKA CITIZEN

Most citizens are working-class Islamic men and women who, with indomitable patience, navigate their way through the gridlock of rickshaws to spend long hours in factories, on the river or in the fields. On the way home they may stop at one of the dilapidated floating restaurants on the river's edge for a quick bite. Despite their penchant for hard work, they are also prepared to strike, and demonstrations are common in the capital. While high unemployment is a continuing problem throughout Bangladesh, in the capital there is also a growing middle class. This stratum is made up of young, educated Bangladeshis – often found lounging in hip cafés – or families from the well-to-do inner suburbs.

DEFINING EXPERIENCE

Riding into town for a leisurely hot breakfast at the Mango Café, followed by bird-watching in the Botanical Gardens, wandering along the riverbanks to see the Lalbagh Fort and the Pink Palace, and then heading to Gulshan Ave for an indulgent meal.

STRENGTHS

- The romantic Old Dhaka region
- Bazaars
- Tea
- Rickshaw art
- Handicrafts
- Cheap public transport
- Good variety of great local, Asian and European restaurants
- Cheap clothes
- *Shankaris* (Hindu artisans)
- Diversity of Eastern and Western-influenced architecture
- Botanical Gardens
- National Museum
- 'Asian Art Biennial' – a month-long cultural event attracting top artists
- Nothing seems to stand still

WEAKNESSES

- Air pollution
- Heat and humidity during the summer months
- Poverty
- Overpopulation, leading to crowded buses and frequent traffic jams
- Locals spitting on the street
- Pickpockets
- Workers' strikes (and often violent demonstrations)
- Frequent floods
- Can be hard to get a beer (aside from expat bars, alcohol is banned in this Islamic nation)
- No bacon or pig products
- Nothing seems to stand still

GOLD STAR

Its many faces – the Eastern and Western influences of the city's past are richly woven into the challenging realities of today, giving modern-day Dhaka a uniqueness that surmounts the apparent clutter of the city.

STARRING ROLE IN...

- *The Clay Bird* (2002)
- *Tale of the Darkest Night* (2001)
- *Lajja* by Taslima Nasrin
- *The Shadow Lines* by Amitav Ghosh

IMPORT

- Coca-Cola
- Pepsi
- Fruit and vegetables
- Foreign aid
- Medical equipment
- Used cars
- International cricket

EXPORT

- Jute
- Pink pearls
- Tea
- 'Fashion for Development' fashion label
- Cheap ready-made garments
- Monica Ali (author of Man Booker prize short-listed novel *Brick Lane*)
- Fazlur Rahman Khan (structural engineer of international standing)
- Tarque Masud (film director)
- International cricketers
- Leather

SEE the vista of activity on the Buriganga River as people bathe, rest, fish and cook.

EAT Mexican at El Toro, the only Mexican restaurant in Bangladesh, and surely the best on the Indian subcontinent.

DRINK alcohol with a newly befriended expat in one of the few legal drinking establishments in Dhaka.

DO a walking tour around the historic Hindu artisan hub of Hindu St with an enthusiastic Shankari guide.

WATCH the moving gallery on Dhaka's streets as the rickshaws pass displaying the bright and varied artwork on their back panels.

BUY a personalised piece of rickshaw art from popular rickshaw artist Ahmed in Hossaini Dalan Rd.

AFTER DARK try to get into an international club.

URBAN MYTH

The famous Hindu temple Dhakeshwari, built in the 11th century, is situated at the point where Old Dhaka meets the modern Central Dhaka region. This is the oldest Hindu temple in Dhaka city and the meaning of 'Dhakeshwari' can be translated as 'Temple of the Goddess of Dhaka'. Legend has it that the city of Dhaka was named after this temple. The deity is said to have been found hidden at the site of the temple, thereby explaining the literal definition of the word 'Dhaka' which means 'concealed'.

SAVOURING THE SAND, FEMALE EMIRATI STUDENTS TAKE TIME OUT TO ENJOY THE BEACH.
Photographer: Allenby-Pratt / Panos Pictures

Dubai

VITAL STATISTICS

NAME: DUBAI

NICKNAME: DO BUY

DATE OF BIRTH: 5000 BC; WHEN TRADE IN THE AREA BEGAN

ADDRESS: UNITED ARAB EMIRATES (MAP 2, S5)

HEIGHT: 5M

SIZE: 35 SQ KM

POPULATION: 2.3 MILLION

LONELY PLANET RANKING: 115

With a slightly surreal mix of dazzling consumerism and Arabian culture with an Islamic influence, Dubai has a cosmopolitan and easy-going charm that makes it the best introduction to the Middle East.

ANATOMY

Dubai is really two towns split by the Dubai Creek (Khor Dubai), an inlet of the Gulf. North of the creek lies Deira, an older city centred on creekside Baniyas Rd, while the south has the glittering new office buildings of Bur Dubai clustered along Sheikh Zayed Rd (also known as Trade Centre Rd). There's little public transport in the city, so to negotiate Dubai you'll pay out a small fortune for taxis.

PEOPLE

More than 80% of Dubai's residents are expats (many drawn from Asia and the Philippines), who were born in other countries and have chosen to make the city their home. UAE nationals (or Emiratis) are a minority. While the official language is Arabic, you can expect to hear English, Persian, Hindi and Tagalog spoken throughout the city.

TYPICAL DUBAI CITIZEN

Emiratis like to shop and Dubai is certainly the fashionista capital, with more Porsches than you're ever likely to see in a showroom, but the city is anything but superficial. The call to prayer is probably the only thing that will get people off their mobiles, but Muslims are very devout in the city. Every neighbourhood has its own mosque and Ramadan is a month that stops DJs spinning in town. Even partying expats respect the Muslim customs and restrict their drinking to a select group of hotels.

DEFINING EXPERIENCE

Snapping up a bargain at Deira City Centre, sailing in for a closer view of Burj al Arab, sniffing the richness of Deira Spice Souq, catching a dhow to Deira, and finally relaxing with a *sheesha* (tobacco water pipe often flavoured with honey or apple) in a courtyard café.

STRENGTHS

- Burj al Arab
- Fashion
- Duty-free shopping
- Dubai Museum
- Jumeirah Mosque
- The Palm Islands
- Deira Gold Souq
- Dhows
- Deira Spice Souq
- Grand Mosque
- Endless summer sunshine
- Bootleg brands (Readbok and Adiblas, anyone?)
- Sheikh Saeed al-Maktoum House
- Emirate Tower
- Nad al-Sheba Club
- Wild Wadi Waterpark
- Jumeirah Beach Park
- Dusit Dubai
- Jumeirah Archaeological Site

WEAKNESSES

- Limited alcohol
- Hard-to-find Emirati cuisine
- Beachfront resorts
- Searing summer heat

GOLD STAR

Wacky construction projects – whether it's the world's largest indoor ski slope, biggest mall or reclaiming islands in the shape of the globe, there's always design challenges being dreamed up in Dubai.

STARRING ROLE IN...

- *Code 46* (2003)
- *Dubai Tales* by Mohammad al-Murr
- *Don't They Know It's Friday?* by Jeremy Williams
- *Father of Dubai: Shaikh Rashid bin Saeed al-Maktoum* by Graeme Wilson

IMPORT

- Tax-dodging corporations
- Accounting firms
- Tourists
- Latest fashions
- Marian Behnam
- Gold, perfume and spice
- David Beckham
- Bollywood movies

EXPORT

- Oil and gas
- Beverages, chemicals, paper, pharmaceuticals and rubber
- General Sheikh Mohammed bin Rashid Al Maktoum, the crown prince of Dubai
- Duty-free goods
- Masoud Amralla al-Ali
- Yaseer Habeeb

SEE the iconic glass sail of Burj al Arab.

EAT fish so fresh it's still flapping at the Fish Market, where you select the city's best seafood and pay by weight.

DRINK nothing but water as you sample apple or vanilla *sheesha* at Cosmo Café.

DO take a dhow cruise to see how spice, gold and perfume are still delivered to the souqs (markets).

WATCH the Bedouin dance *ayyalah* – a celebration of the tribe's courage, strength and unity – performed at the Heritage Village.

BUY spices at a souq, but only after haggling an hour to save five dirhams.

AFTER DARK hop into lush French bar Boudoir to rub shoulders with visiting supermodels.

URBAN MYTH

Even with the huge import of Ferraris and Mazeratis, dhows remain *the* vehicle of Dubai, just as they were centuries ago. The Dhow Wharfage is still piled high with assorted goods from Iran, India, Pakistan and East Africa. It's no surprise then that Dubai was once one of the most important dhow-building centres in the Gulf. The *al-galalif* (dhow builders) used basic materials and methods to construct a diverse range of vessels. The larger dhows used for long-distance journeys were called *al-boom, al-bateel* and *al-baglah,* and were up to 60m in length. Some of them have now been turned into cruise vessels and floating restaurants.

THE ART OF FALCONRY IS A PRESTIGIOUS SPORT IN THE UAE.
Photographer: Christine Osborne / LPI

STRIKINGLY BEAUTIFUL JUMEIRAH MOSQUE IS AN EXQUISITE EXAMPLE OF ARABIAN ARCHITECTURE.
Photographer: Chris Mellor / LPI

NOT YOUR AVERAGE FAMILY CAR – DUBAI'S WEALTH IS VERY VISIBLE.
Photographer: Phil Weymouth / LPI

Dublin may not be a particularly pretty city, but for poetry, pubs, sporting life and garrulous sociability, you can't do better.

ANATOMY

Dublin sprawls around Dublin Bay with the River Liffey dividing the city. North of the river, busy O'Connell St leads to Parnell Sq and, to the west, revitalised Smithfield. On the south side lie the increasingly tedious Temple Bar and the stately houses and elegant parks of Georgian Dublin. The DART train line links the seaside suburbs, and the new LUAS light-rail system connects the south to the centre.

PEOPLE

Traditionally, a Dubliner hails from between the canals, but it's now hard to put your finger on the city's physical or social boundaries. Expats returning home and migrants from the rest of Ireland are joined by significant numbers of Nigerians, Chinese, Romanians and Bosnians. A long way from the *Gaeltacht* (Irish-speaking region), Dubliners may speak a smattering of Irish, but are more famous for their own particularly colourful take on the English language.

TYPICAL DUBLINER

Dublin is one of Europe's most expensive cities, but with over half the population under 30, there's a youthful exuberance and open, optimistic spirit evident. Dubliners pride themselves on their irreverent humour, razor wit and keenness to debate. Although still overwhelmingly Roman Catholic, they tend to be relatively liberal; they're also fabulously self-deprecating and have a strong aversion to pretence of any kind. The rest of Ireland – pejoratively known as bogmen or *culchies* in the local vernacular – may not see this easy-going side, and tend to think that Dubliners are overly smug.

DEFINING EXPERIENCE

Skipping the fry-up because you can't be arsed with the weekend crowds at your local café, instead scoffing a bun and a cup of tea in Bewley's, then heading off to an international rugby test at Lansdowne Rd, seeing Ireland getting the lard beaten out of them, and then going to Ba Mizu for pints and a plate of stew, though not getting too bladdered because you've got tickets to see a gig at Whelan's.

Dublin

VITAL STATISTICS

NAME: DUBLIN

NICKNAME: DUB

DATE OF BIRTH: 6TH CENTURY; ESTABLISHED AS A MONASTIC SETTLEMENT

ADDRESS: IRELAND (MAP 3, C7)

HEIGHT: 47M

SIZE: 921 SQ KM

POPULATION: 506,000 (CITY); 1.6 MILLION (METRO AREA)

LONELY PLANET RANKING: 028

ALL HAIRSTYLES ARE WELCOME AT THE MARKET BAR.
Photographer: Jonathan Smith / LPI

STRENGTHS

- Cracking nightlife, every night of the week
- Well-preserved Georgian streetscapes
- The restaurant scene, including great Modern Irish food
- St Stephen's Green
- Proud literary heritage
- Kilmainham Gaol
- The banter
- Trinity College
- The Liffey's bridges
- Sports-obsessed culture
- Fitzwilliam Sq
- Irish Museum of Modern Art, both the collections and the site

WEAKNESSES

- City-centre traffic, especially on the quays
- Crass, soulless 'theme' bars
- Overpriced pints
- The stench of vomit in Temple Bar
- Urban planning, or lack of it
- The rain

GOLD STAR

Pub culture – despite the onslaught of gastropubs and chains, Dublin is still the best place for a pint in the world.

STARRING ROLE IN...

- *Veronica Guerin* (2003)
- *Intermission* (2003)
- *The General* (1997)
- *Circle of Friends* (1995)
- *Into the West* (1992)
- *The Commitments* (1991)
- *My Left Foot* (1989)
- *The Dead* (1988)
- *Ulysses* by James Joyce
- *Paddy Clarke Ha Ha Ha* by Roddy Doyle
- *Cowboys and Indians* by Joseph O'Connor

IMPORT

- Football
- Nurses and doctors
- Espresso
- Summer vegetables
- John Rocha
- Australian bar staff
- British stags and hens
- Damon Hill and Eddie Irvine
- Musician Phil Lynott (born in Birmingham, raised in Dublin)

EXPORT

- Guinness
- James Joyce
- U2
- Georgian door knockers
- Boyzone/Westlife/Ronan Keating
- Organic meat
- Bob Geldof
- Sinead O'Connor
- Francis Bacon
- Gabriel Byrne
- Colin Farrel
- Jameson whiskey
- Sean Scully

SEE panoramic views of the city through the bottom of a pint glass at the Gravity Bar – part of the Guinness Storehouse.

EAT a potato and mackerel terrine at Jacob's Ladder, gazing over the playing fields of Trinity.

DRINK the porter at Grogan's on South William St.

DO everything in your power to get a ticket to the All-Ireland Hurling Finals at Croke Park in September.

WATCH a play at the Abbey Theatre during the Dublin Theatre Festival.

BUY a luxe Lainey Keogh sweater from Brown Thomas on Grafton St.

AFTER DARK take advantage of the late licence and the mood lighting upstairs at Hogan's in SoDa.

URBAN MYTH

Everyone, it seems, *has* got a Bono story. Although arguably Ireland's most famous musical export, the members of U2 have continued to live in or around Dublin throughout their stellar international career. Most Dubliners will have a tale involving the seemingly ubiquitous Bono. These range from the banal to the mildly disturbing: being a waitress and serving him gravy; seeing him scribbling (a song perhaps?) on Killiney Beach; hearing him sing at the Dandelion Market in 1979; having him offer you a hand with the shopping; minding your business, sitting by the Grand Canal Docks and himself turning up in a *currach* (small boat), waving and shouting 'Thank you, Ireland!'. The phenomenon is so widespread that a novel entitled *Everyone's Got a Bono Story*, by Anne-Marie O'Connor, was based on the idea.

HURTLING THROUGH HURLING PRACTICE.
Photographer: Martin Moos / LPI

TAIL-LIGHTS BLAZE A BUSY TRAIL THROUGH DAME ST.
Photographer: Olivier Cirendini / LPI

THE HA'PENNY BRIDGE GRACEFULLY ARCHES OVER THE LIFFEY.
Photographer: Richard Cummins / LPI

Dubrovnik

VITAL STATISTICS

NAME: DUBROVNIK

NICKNAME: THE CITY; THE PEARL OF THE ADRIATIC

DATE OF BIRTH: 7TH CENTURY; WHEN THE RESIDENTS OF THE ROMAN CITY OF EPIDAURUM (SITE OF PRESENT-DAY CAVTAT) FLED TO THE ROCKY ISLET (WHICH THEY DUBBED LAUS), LOCATED AROUND THE SOUTHERN WALLS OF PRESENT-DAY DUBROVNIK

ADDRESS: CROATIA (MAP 3, N13)

HEIGHT: 49M

SIZE: 143 SQ KM

POPULATION: 45,800

LONELY PLANET RANKING: 059

The lure of the magical walled city of Dubrovnik, adorned with fine Renaissance carvings and marble-paved streets, has given a boost to the entire region, creating a 'Dubrovnik Riviera' that is welcoming to residents and visitors alike.

ANATOMY

The city extends about 6km from the mouth of the Rijeka River in the west to the Cape of Sveti Jakov in the east and includes the promontory of Lapad, a leafy residential suburb popular with tourists thanks to its rocky beaches, hostel and hotels. The old walled town lies southeast of Lapad at the foot of Srđ Hill, halfway between Gruž Harbour and the cape of Sveti Jakov. The entire old town is closed to cars and is divided nearly in half by the wide street of Placa, also referred to as Stradun. Pile Gate is the western entrance to the old town and the eastern gate is Ploče. The city boundaries also include the Elafiti Islands (Šipan, Lopud, Koločep, Olipe, Tajan and Jakljan). Walking or cycling is the best way to get around; public transport in Dubrovnik is pretty well limited to buses and taxis.

PEOPLE

Since the 1991–95 war Dubrovnik's population has been almost exclusively Croat and almost exclusively Catholic, with small minority groups of Serbs, Slovenians, Italians, Czechs and Muslims.

TYPICAL DUBROVNIK CITIZEN

Dubrovnik's residents are generally relaxed and cheerful; their Mediterranean character is evident in everything from their second language (likely to be Italian) to the casual office hours that allow people to enjoy the long hours of sunlight on a beach or in an outdoor café. They are proud of their city and its cultural heritage and generally have strong and passionate views on the 'Homeland' or 'Patriotic' war.

DEFINING EXPERIENCE

Strolling along the walls of the fortified city, taking in the patchwork of honey-coloured roofs, before making your way down the town's pedestrian promenade, Placa, where you'll be overwhelmed by the heady rush of cultural, religious and historic landmarks – not to mention some fantastic cafés.

STRENGTHS

- Dubrovnik's Summer Festival – the most prestigious in Croatia
- The visible results of a dedicated reconstruction effort since the bombs of 1991
- Fortified town walls and gleaming marble streets
- Proximity to the quiet Elafiti Islands and the beautiful beaches of Cavtat
- Vibrant street life

WEAKNESSES

- Located in a zone that is both geologically and politically seismic
- The scramble of private-accommodation owners at the bus station eager for the tourist dollar

GOLD STAR

The wide marble street, Placa, lined with businesses, cafés, churches and palaces, encourages the fusion of commerce, pleasure and faith into a vibrant community life.

STARRING ROLE IN...

- *Casanova* (2005)
- *The Ragusa Theme* by Ann Quinton
- *The Road to Dalmatia* by Christopher Dilke

IMPORT

- Cruise-ship tourists
- Investment in real estate

EXPORT

- Writer Marin Držić
- Poet Ivan Gundulić
- Scientist Ruđer Bošković
- Božidarević, Dobričević and Hamzić, Dubrovnik's finest 15th- and 16th-century artists

SEE the restored roofs of Dubrovnik from a walk around its walls.

EAT the local mussels at Kamenice, a convivial hang-out on one of Dubrovnik's more scenic squares.

DRINK a strongly brewed espresso at the inviting Café Festival, while watching the crowds ambling down Placa.

DO take the kids to the aquarium where they can 'ooh' and 'aah' at the electric rays, conger eels, scorpion fish and seahorses.

WATCH Shakespeare on the Lovrjenac fortress terrace during the Summer Festival.

BUY local products at the city's colourful market.

AFTER DARK head to the city's hippest bar, Troubadour, for Marko's jazz stylings.

URBAN MYTH

Carved in 1417, the Orlando Column in Luža Sq is a depiction of Roland, the legendary medieval knight whose fore arm was the official linear measure of the republic – the ell of Dubrovnik, which measures 51.1cm.

LOOKING OVER ROOFTOPS FROM THE CITY WALLS REVEALS AN ORANGE THEME.
Photographer: Richard I'Anson / LPI

THE CHURCH OF ST SAVIOUR'S STEEPLE TOWERS OVER THE PLAZA THAT ALSO, COINCIDENTALLY, BEARS HIS NAME.
Photographer: Richard I'Anson / LPI

A SOLITARY PRIEST WENDS HIS WAY PAST THE ARCH OF THE FRANCISCAN MONASTERY.
Photographer: Richard l'Anson / LPI

A BELLY-DANCER CREATES AN ARCH OF HER OWN AT THE TROUBADOUR CAFÉ AND BAR.
Photographer: Richard l'Anson / LPI

Since the reinstatement of the Scottish Parliament in 1999, Edinburgh has been booming with rising property prices, new building projects, and wealthy inhabitants – in financial and cultural terms.

ANATOMY

Edinburgh is very hilly and green, with Castle Rock being the most prominent inhabited hill and Hollyrood Park (home to the 251m-high Arthur's Seat) the largest green space. The only river, the water of Leith, runs along the northwestern border of New Town. New Town is characterised by regular Georgian terraces and squares. It is separated from the Old Town, which lies to the south, by the valley of Princes St Gardens. Old Town is a delightful maze of medieval alleys trickling off the Royal Mile, which climbs from the Palace of Holyroodhouse up to Edinburgh Castle. The only public transport is buses, which have the city carefully covered. Otherwise the best way to get around is on a bicycle.

PEOPLE

Edinburgh is Scotland's most cosmopolitan and middle-class city. Many Irish and English people have settled here and there are smaller ethnic communities, including Indians, Pakistanis, Bangladeshis, Italians, Poles, Chinese and Spanish. During the Edinburgh Festival the city's population swells to twice its size.

TYPICAL EDINBURGHER

Years of living almost on top of each other in densely packed tenements is often the reason given for Edinburghers' interest in each other's business. That said, people can appear shy and are unlikely to start chatting to strangers. Although Leith (Edinburgh's port) became part of the city in 1920, its inhabitants are Leithers and not Edinburghers. A typical young professional in Edinburgh probably spends his/her salary earned in financial services paying off a large mortgage on a tenement flat in the Southside. They enjoy eating out, and eschew beer and tea for wine and cappuccino. They aspire to owning property abroad and ski once a year if they can.

Edinburgh

VITAL STATISTICS

NAME: EDINBURGH

NICKNAME: ATHENS OF THE NORTH; AULD REEKIE (OLD SMOKY)

DATE OF BIRTH: 900 BC; THERE ARE SIGNS OF HUMAN HABITATION AT CASTLE ROCK AND ARTHUR'S SEAT FROM THIS TIME

ADDRESS: SCOTLAND (MAP 3, D5)

HEIGHT: 134M

SIZE: 260 SQ KM

POPULATION: 468,000

LONELY PLANET RANKING: 021

THE ROYAL MILE, AS SEEN THROUGH THE LEGS OF A DEFIANT KILT-WEARER.
Photographer: Chris Furlong / Getty Images

DEFINING EXPERIENCE

Sipping a latte in Grassmarket before wandering down the Royal Mile to Hollyrood Park and climbing up Arthur's Seat, followed by some restorative shopping in Harvey Nichols and a dish of oysters on ice at the Café Royal Oyster Bar.

STRENGTHS

⊿ Museum of Scotland
⊿ Adventure Centre
⊿ Cycling on Union Canal towpath
⊿ Elegant Georgian terraces of New Town
⊿ Arthur's Seat
⊿ Scottish Enlightenment
⊿ Scottish Parliament Building
⊿ Princes St Gardens
⊿ Victorian tenements south of the centre
⊿ More restaurants per capita than any other UK city
⊿ Modern Scottish cuisine
⊿ The cleaning of soot-blackened buildings
⊿ The Edinburgh Festival Fringe
⊿ The Military Tattoo
⊿ Hogmanay
⊿ Royal Mile
⊿ Clubbing in Cowgate

WEAKNESSES

⊿ Soaring house prices
⊿ Dearth of parking spaces
⊿ Traffic jams

GOLD STAR

The Edinburgh Festival Fringe.

STARRING ROLE IN...

⊿ *Trainspotting* (1996)
⊿ *The Prime of Miss Jean Brodie* (1969)
⊿ *Complicity* by Ian Banks
⊿ *The Falls* by Ian Rankin

IMPORT

⊿ Theatrical students for the Edinburgh fringe
⊿ MTV awards in October 2003
⊿ JK Rowling
⊿ Ian Rankin
⊿ Alexander McCall Smith
⊿ Hugh MacDiarmid

EXPORT

⊿ Sir Sean Connery
⊿ Robert Louis Stevenson
⊿ Howie Nicholsby of 21st Century Kilts
⊿ The *Encyclopaedia Britannica* and *Chambers Encyclopaedia* (first published in Edinburgh)
⊿ Sir Walter Scott
⊿ Royal Bank of Scotland and HBOS
⊿ Irvine Welsh
⊿ Sir Arthur Conan Doyle (creator of Sherlock Holmes)
⊿ Dame Muriel Spark
⊿ The Proclaimers
⊿ Finlay Quaye
⊿ The Scottish Colourists
⊿ National Gallery of Scotland
⊿ Malt whisky
⊿ Salmon
⊿ Trout
⊿ Oats

SEE Edinburgh Castle on its perfectly defensible perch, Castle Rock.

EAT chargrilled Aberdeen Angus fillet steak at the Tower, and peer over at the castle.

DRINK one or two of the 100 malts on offer at Victorian Bennet's Bar.

DO walk up Arthur's Seat for an unbeatable view of the city.

WATCH obscure plays with an audience of one at the Edinburgh Festival Fringe.

BUY exquisite, contemporary jewellery from Scottish jeweller Annie Smith.

AFTER DARK enjoy a night of theatre cabaret at the unusual Bongo Club.

URBAN MYTH

One of Edinburgh's most gruesome myths comes from the time of the plague in 1645. Legend has it that the stricken inhabitants of Mary King's Close (now the site of the City Chambers) were bricked into their houses to die and rot. Apparently when workmen eventually came to remove the bodies, rigor mortis meant limbs had to be severed in order to extricate the dead from their claustrophobic dwellings. Although this story is not true, people who lived there afterwards and who have since visited have reported sightings of grotesque ghouls and floating body parts. Spooky!

A COUPLE KISS TO A VIOLIN'S TUNE DURING FESTIVAL MONTH.
Photographer: Chris Furlong / Getty Images

A TEA HUGGER COLLECTS HER THOUGHTS AT THE FOREST CHARITY CAFÉ.
Photographer: Chris Furlong / Getty Images

THE FAMOUS CONTEMPLATION WINDOWS OF THE CONTROVERSIAL SCOTTISH PARLIAMENT BUILDING AT HOLYROOD. Photographer: Chris Furlong / Getty Images

Esfahan

VITAL STATISTICS

NAME: ESFAHAN

NICKNAME: HALF THE WORLD (FROM THE PERSIAN RHYME, 'ESFAHAN NESF-E JAHAN': LITERALLY 'ESFAHAN IS HALF THE WORLD')

DATE OF BIRTH: 1587; WHEN SHAH ABBAS I CAME TO POWER AND HE SET OUT TO MAKE ESFAHAN A GREAT CITY

ADDRESS: IRAN (MAP 2, R2)

HEIGHT: 1773M

POPULATION: 1.6 MILLION

LONELY PLANET RANKING: 082

WOMEN IN FULL CHADOR LUG SHOPPING BAGS ACROSS IMAM SQ.
Photographer: Phil Weymouth / LPI

KEEPING THE FAITH, AN ELDERLY MULLAH CLUTCHES A GOLD-EMBOSSED VOLUME OF THE HOLY KORAN.
Photographer: Clint Lucas / LPI

A MAN GAZES DOWN FROM ONE OF THE MANAR JOMBAN (SHAKING MINARETS), BUILT IN THE SAFAVIDS PERIOD.
Photographer: John Borthwick / LPI

THE BLUE-TONED MAJESTY OF IMAM SQ.
Photographer: Phil Weymouth / LPI

Iran's masterpiece, Esfahan is a stunning, colourful architectural gem, the centre of Persian arts and culture, brought to prominence by Shah Abbas the Great, set amid the desert of the central Iranian plateau.

ANATOMY

Chahar Bagh, 5km long, is the north–south artery through the centre of town. The Zayandeh River, crisscrossed by a series of historic arched bridges, runs roughly east–west. Northeast of the river are the expansive Imam Sq and the Bazar-e Bozorg (Grand Bazaar), while to the south lies the Armenian neighbourhood of Jolfa and the high-rises of the new town. Taxis and minibuses ply the main thoroughfares of the city, and if your haggling skills are good you could negotiate a private taxi.

PEOPLE

The population of Esfahan is as diverse as anywhere else in Iran. Besides Persians there are Azaris, occasionally visiting Bakhtiyari nomads, a sizable Armenian Christian community, Zoroastrians (the original monotheistic people of Persia), Afghan refugees, as well as small Jewish and Baha communities.

TYPICAL ESFAHANI

Esfahanis are fiercely proud of their home and its status as the capital of Persian arts and culture. Consequently, the typical Esfahani is likely to be articulate and urbane, educated and erudite, and as warm and welcoming as Iranians elsewhere. They will be conscious of their Muslim faith, and tend to be family oriented, living at home until – and perhaps after – they are married. An appreciation of all things artistic will be matched by a passion for football. Young people predominate in Esfahan – the majority of the Iranian population is younger than 30 years of age.

DEFINING EXPERIENCE

Wandering around the domed expanse of the Bazaar-e Bozorg, taking tea and smoking a *qalyan* (water pipe) at the outdoor tables of the Qeysarieh Tea Shop looking onto Imam Sq, poring over the exhibits at the Decorative Arts Museum of Iran, heading out to the Ateshkadeh-ye Esfahan to see the fire ceremonies of the Zoroastrians, strolling the banks of the Zayandeh River and fuelling up on tea in one of the teahouses under the bridges, musing on the elaborate frescoes of the Chehel Sotun Palace.

STRENGTHS

- ◢ The grandeur of Imam Sq
- ◢ The arts on show – calligraphy, tile making, metalwork, glassware, miniature paintings
- ◢ Carpets – where better to buy a Persian carpet?
- ◢ Haggling in the bazaar
- ◢ Teahouses and *qalyan*
- ◢ History at every turn
- ◢ Armenian cathedrals
- ◢ Architectural greatness – palaces, mosques, grand squares

WEAKNESSES

- ◢ Touts around Imam Sq
- ◢ The hard sell in the bazaar
- ◢ Scams involving impostor 'police'
- ◢ Pollution and hectic traffic
- ◢ Taxi drivers

GOLD STAR

Colour scheme – the symphony of royal blue, sunflower yellow and emerald tiles set atop the voluptuous domes and pointed arches of Imam Sq, all beneath a peerless, cloudless Persian blue sky.

STARRING ROLE IN...

- ◢ *The Road to Oxiana* by Robert Byron
- ◢ *Travels in Persia* by Sir John Chardin
- ◢ *Honeymoon in Purdah* by Alison Wearing
- ◢ *The Siege of Isfahan* by Jean-Christopher Rufin
- ◢ *Portrait Photographs from Isfahan: Faces in Transition* by Parisa Damandan

IMPORT

- ◢ Armenian artisans

EXPORT

- ◢ Carpets
- ◢ Arts and crafts

SEE the view over Imam Sq from the elevated terrace of Ali Qapu Palace.

EAT *dolme bademjan* (stuffed eggplants) with rice, or *gaz* (nougat with pistachio and other chopped nuts).

DRINK *chay* (tea) while holding a sugar lump between your teeth.

DO spend time absorbing the frescoes of Chehel Sotun Palace, including the depiction of a man kissing the foot of a half-naked maiden.

WATCH craftsmen hammering copper pots, painting miniatures or enamelling copperware in the bazaar.

BUY a carpet or any traditional craftwork in the Grand Bazaar, but come prepared to haggle.

AFTER DARK loiter over a *qalyan* in one of the teahouses.

URBAN MYTH

The great travel writer Robert Byron remarked that the ornamental lake in the centre of Imam Sq was built to prevent Bakhtiyari tribesmen from playing polo or exercising their horses there.

AFTERNOON SUN CASTS A SPELL OF LIGHT ON THE FORTIFIED WALLS OF THE ANCIENT PORT.
Photographer: Jose Manuel Navia / Network

Essaouira

VITAL STATISTICS

NAME: ESSAOUIRA

NICKNAME: WINDY CITY

DATE OF BIRTH: LATE 1500s; WHEN IT WAS FOUNDED BY THE PORTUGUESE

ADDRESS: MOROCCO (MAP 3, B18)

HEIGHT: 7M

POPULATION: 69,000

LONELY PLANET RANKING: 184

Deemed a Unesco World Heritage site, this picture-perfect town is an elegant marriage of Arabic and Mediterranean architecture. Bustling spice markets and winding whitewashed streets filled with artisan workshops combine a European sensibility with careful attention to Moroccan heritage.

ANATOMY

Essaouira has a marvellous setting between the Atlantic Ocean, a dune forest and river-mouth wetlands, and all attractions are within walking distance. The medina (old city), enclosed by walls with five main gates, is the main attraction. The walled town is pretty compact, split into the mellah (the old Jewish quarter), medina and kasbah, all laid out on a surprisingly simple grid system. The main thoroughfare, Ave de l'Istiqlal, merging into Ave Mohammed Zerktouni, runs from Bab Doukkala in the northeast to the main square, Place Moulay Hassan, in the southwest. Beyond the square is the historic port, fish market and bastion of Skala du Port, where there are panoramic views of the harbour, sweeping beaches to the east, and the offshore islands, Illes Purpuraires. The bus stations and taxis are 1km northeast of town.

PEOPLE

The official language is Arabic, but both French and Berber are spoken. As in the rest of Morocco, almost all of Essaouira's population is Muslim, with small groups of Christians and Jews.

TYPICAL ESSAOUIRA CITIZEN

The Moroccan people's love of the theatrical is most prominent in Essaouira, where you'll find a musician on every corner (some of them only just knee high…). Bodily contact plays an important role in communication: handshakes are a crucial icebreaker and affectionate public greetings are an art form. The people are also big on community. Family loyalty and responsibility extends to everyone in the neighbourhood: beggars are always offered money and a displaced woman always has a place to sleep.

DEFINING EXPERIENCE

Getting lost in the labyrinth of narrow whitewashed lanes and discovering tranquil squares, spice markets and artisans in tiny workshops, then watching the sun set behind the picturesque stone ramparts of the historic port and sating your appetite at the sizzling seafood stalls lining the harbour.

STRENGTHS

- Recently classified as a World Heritage site by Unesco
- Pedestrian-only (apart from donkeys and bicycles) medina
- Mediterranean-style architecture and atmosphere
- World-class surfing destination
- Endless sandy beaches
- All attractions are within walking distance
- Labyrinthine backstreets filled with artisan workshops and markets
- Thriving local and international music and arts scene
- Fresh seafood

WEAKNESSES

- Essaouira has become a gloriously distorted fantasy-land for countless Western baby boomers
- Hordes of day-trippers because of its proximity to Marrakech
- Relentless, strong coastal wind
- Lack of environmental awareness

GOLD STAR

Seemingly more Mykonos than Morocco, Mediterranean Essaouira has something for everyone – it is both a windsurfing mecca and a cultural hub for music and international and local art.

STARRING ROLE IN...

- *Kingdom of Heaven* (2004)
- *Alexander* (2005)

IMPORT

- Hippies in the '60s, the likes of Jimmy Hendrix and Cat Stevens
- European expats buying up picturesque medina mansions
- Internationally renowned artists
- International acts for the Gnawa Music Festival

EXPORT

- Exquisite marquetry work made from local fragrant thuja wood (now an endangered species)
- Argan-oil products
- Spices
- Raffia work made from the fibres of the doum palm
- Gnawa music (a mystical form of music that draws its roots from the Gnawas, descendants of black slaves)
- Paintings by local artists
- Skin lamps

SEE the Gnawa Music Festival, Essaouira's four-day musical extravaganza.

EAT freshly caught seafood sizzling on outdoor grills down in the port.

DRINK mint tea in Moulay Hassan Sq.

DO a camel-riding excursion through the sand dunes or break your first sweat in a classic *hammam* (bathhouse).

WATCH the sun set over the Atlantic from the historic 18th-century clifftop ramparts and turrets of Skala de la Ville.

BUY a painting by a local up-and-coming artists, or a beautifully designed raffia work.

AFTER DARK chill out at the laid-back bar on the lamp-lit roof terrace of Taros Café.

URBAN MYTH

In 1766 the Sultan Sidi Mohamed ben Abdallah commissioned a French engineer named Théodore Cornut to design a town that could compete with the rebel port of Agadir. Cornut is believed to have been a prisoner who earned his freedom through his design of the city.

MUSLIM WOMEN IN A BLUE DOORWAY – TYPICAL OF BLUE-AND-WHITE ESSAOUIRA.
Photographer: Chris Lisle / Corbis

GET SOME SPICE IN YOUR LIFE AT THE MEDINA MARKETS.
Photographer: Bruno Morandi / Photolibrary

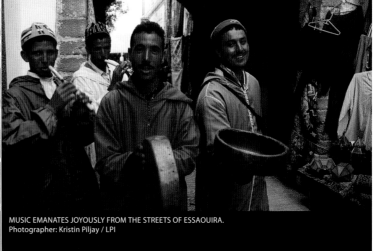

MUSIC EMANATES JOYOUSLY FROM THE STREETS OF ESSAOUIRA.
Photographer: Kristin Piljay / LPI

CONCENTRATION ON THE FACE OF A YOUNG TANNER CARRYING A CURED HIDE IN THE MEDINA.
Photographer: Jose Manuel Navia / Network

Fès

VITAL STATISTICS

NAME: FÈS

NICKNAME: ATHENS OF AFRICA

DATE OF BIRTH: AD 789; FOUNDED BY IDRIS I

ADDRESS: MOROCCO (MAP 3, D17)

HEIGHT: 378M

SIZE: 16 SQ KM

POPULATION: 1 MILLION

LONELY PLANET RANKING: 067

As the first Islamic city in Morocco, Fès is the centre of Morocco's cultural and religious life and its calls to prayer five time a day serve as a strident reminder of this fact.

ANATOMY

Fès is a hotchpotch of twisting streets that are so narrow you can barely raise a decent yawn and stretch. Even smaller alleys venture off the main paths and people brush against people, overloaded donkeys, household goods and bags of wheat at every turn. The medina of Fès el-Bali (Old Fès), which is separated from modern Fès (the Ville Nouvelle) by the ancient walls, is where the city's mosques, shops, crafts, spices, and souq (market) are located along some 9000 streets. It is closed to motorised vehicles, so strap up your donkey.

PEOPLE

The majority of Fassis are Sunni Muslims of Arab, Berber or mixed Arab-Berber lineage. The Arab culture was established when Arabs invaded Morocco in the 7th and 11th centuries. While Arabic is the official language, Berber dialects are widely spoken and French is also seen as the language of business, government and diplomacy. In (much) earlier times, Fès was the scientific and religious centre of Morocco, where Muslims and Christians from Europe came to study.

TYPICAL FASSIS

The young Fassis have cast aside the trappings of their parents' lives, adopting fashions and lifestyles more readily identified with the West. However, many remain without work, and the smart, clean Ville Nouvelle disguises the sad lot of the poorer people living on the periphery. Fès' million or so inhabitants are straining the city to the utmost, and the old city, some experts have warned, is slowly falling apart. Fès continues to act as a barometer of popular sentiment – Morocco's independence movement was born here, and when there are strikes or protests, they are always at their most vociferous in Fès.

DEFINING EXPERIENCE

Walking through one of the medina's seven ancient gateways, then exploring its labyrinthine streets and crumbling grandeur before pulling up a goat-leather stool and tucking into a traditional tagine.

STRENGTHS

- Luxurious *hammams* (bathhouses)
- *Zellij* mosaics (hand-cut tiles arranged in geometric and/or abstract patterns)
- Ancient doorways and walls
- Islamic architecture

WEAKNESSES

- The overwhelming smell from the tanneries – sniffing mint might settle the nerves
- The plundering of ancient private homes for their doors and windows for exportation

GOLD STAR

The annual World Sacred Music Festival, which celebrates music from Sufi, Andean, Sephardic, Zulu, Pakistani *ghazal* chants, Renaissance, baroque Christian, spiritual music and American gospel songs.

STARRING ROLE IN...

- *The Mummy* (1999)
- *The Amazing Race 3* (2002)
- *Aziz and Itto: A Moroccan Wedding* (1991)
- *The Jewel of the Nile* (1985)
- *Kundun* (1997)
- *The Last Temptation of Christ* (1988)
- *This Blinding Absence of Light* by Tahar Ben Jelloun
- *Living in Morocco: Design from Casablanca to Marrakesh* by Landt and Lisl Dennis

IMPORT

- French
- American soft-metal tunes
- Henri Matisse
- Tunisian stone
- Eugene Delacroix

EXPORT

- Pottery
- Cous cous
- The fez (brimless felt hat)
- Writer Tahar Ben Jelloun
- Hash
- Farsi metalwork
- Architectural antiques
- *Babouches* (pointed slippers)
- Goat leather stools
- Fiery *harissa* sauce (made from chillies and tomatoes)

SEE the Blue Gate of the Old Fès.

EAT traditional tagines, *pigeon bastila* (a large pigeon pie) and mounds of hand-blended cous cous.

DRINK bladder-bursting amounts of *atay* (mint tea).

DO take a panoramic tour of the city in a taxi.

WATCH the day unfurl from a café in Old Fès.

BUY a traditional Moroccan carpet from Hamid's Carpet Shop.

AFTER DARK be serenaded in the courtyard of La Maison Bleue before eating a sumptuous feast of local fare under superb cedar ceilings.

URBAN MYTH

The hand is seen as a means of warding off the evil eye, which is a prominent theme. The 'hand of Fatima' is seen on everything. The *al-boua* (chameleon) is also thought to have special powers. It's said that if a wife suspects infidelity, she only has to blend chameleon meat or bones in his food and he will certainly never look the other way again. Fearing misfortune of an ethereal kind, throwing the poor creature into a wood-fired oven and walking around it three times might prove useful. If the chameleon explodes, the evil is gone, if it doesn't, best find a stronger solution.

A STREET SELLER WAITS FOR CUSTOMERS UNDER ROWS OF DRYING FABRIC.
Photographer: Look GMBH / eStock Photo

FEZ-WEARING FASSIS STRAIN FOR A GLIMPSE OF THE KING ALONG A CITY STREET.
Photographer: Jack Dabaghian / Reuters/Picture Media

DYED LEATHER DRIP-DRIES UNDER THE SUPERVISION OF A PAIR OF RED LEGS.
Photographer: Jose Manuel Navia / Network

PIAZZA SANTA CROCE HOSTS THE ANNUAL FLORENTINE FOOTBALL MATCH, A TRADITIONAL 16TH-CENTURY GAME COMBINING ELEMENTS OF RUGBY, FOOTBALL AND WRESTLING.
Photographer: Tony Gentile / Reuters/Picture Media

Florence

VITAL STATISTICS

NAME: FLORENCE

DATE OF BIRTH: 30 BC; JULIUS CAESAR NAMED HIS GARRISON TOWN ON THE ARNO FLORENTIA

ADDRESS: ITALY (MAP 3, K12)

HEIGHT: 38M

SIZE: 3514 SQ KM

POPULATION: 375,000

LONELY PLANET RANKING: 027

Star of the Renaissance, Florence is an aesthetic feast of world-famous paintings and sculpture, stunning churches and palaces, and beautiful people.

ANATOMY

Florence's city centre is relatively compact. The River Arno flows through the town, with the striking dome of Florence's Duomo (cathedral) and the *centro storico* (historic centre) on the northern side. The famous Ponte Vecchio crosses the river directly south of the cathedral and not far from the main square, Piazza della Signoria, and the Uffizi. On the other side of the Arno is the Oltrarno area, which is quieter and far less touristy. Walking or catching a bus is the best way to get around.

PEOPLE

The population comprises Italians originating from Florence and other parts of Italy and migrants from Asia, Africa (Tunisia and Senegal) or the Balkans. Makeshift settlements on the edge of the city house immigrants from Albania and Kosovo. Around 85% of Florentines are Catholic, while Muslims, Protestants and Buddhists make up the rest.

TYPICAL FLORENTINE

Most Florentines are unfairly good-looking and known for taking care of their appearance. They are polite and friendly, although they can sometimes appear standoffish – with the constant invasion of tourists, this is perhaps forgivable. They tend to be conservative, and modern architectural proposals cause massive controversy. They like it if visitors attempt to speak Italian, and may even award lower prices in return. Smoking is forbidden in many bars and restaurants, but a Florentine who wants to smoke will light up anyway.

DEFINING EXPERIENCE

Craning your neck admiring the ceiling of the Duomo, before ambling through the historic centre, strolling over the Ponte Vecchio and enjoying a gelato in Piazza Pitti.

STRENGTHS

- Art everywhere you turn
- Building restoration
- Medieval historic centre
- *Bistecca alla fiorentina* (Florentine steak)
- Enviable fashion sense
- Delicious wine eg Chianti and Brunello
- Cosimo de' Medici
- Duomo
- Uffizi
- Michelangelo's *David*
- Campanile
- Ponte Vecchio
- Palazzo Vecchio
- Haggling at San Lorenzo market
- Profusion of shoes and handbags to buy
- Boboli Gardens
- Electric buses
- Fine-arts faculty at the Università degli Studi di Firenze
- Skiing the Abetone pistes north of Pistoia

WEAKNESSES

- Air pollution
- Constant restoration means things are often closed
- Crowds
- Snooty sales assistants
- Smelly streets
- Traffic
- Street prostitution
- Pigeons and rats

GOLD STAR

The Renaissance – it was born in Florence.

STARRING ROLE IN...

- *Hannibal* (2001)
- *La Vita è Bella* (Life is Beautiful, 2001)
- *Tea with Mussolini* (1999)
- *A Room with a View* (1986)

IMPORT

- Raphael
- Leonardo da Vinci
- Tourists
- Other Italians
- Michelangelo
- Galileo Galilei

EXPORT

- Leather goods
- Tuscan wines
- Pecorino cheese
- Olive oil
- Franco Zeffirelli
- Pinocchio
- Machiavelli
- Dante Alighieri
- Filippo Brunelleschi
- Gucci
- Salvatore Ferragamo
- Pucci
- Furniture
- Cheque books

SEE Botticelli's *Birth of Venus*, Leonardo da Vinci's *Annunciation* and other artistic marvels at the Uffizi (book in advance to beat the crowds).

EAT devilishly good chocolate confections on the terrace of Caffè Rivoire and savour the view of the Palazzo Vecchio.

DRINK a glass of Chianti Classico with the locals on Piazza Santo Spirito.

DO cross the Ponte Vecchio and mosey through the quieter streets of the Oltrarno.

WATCH 27-a-side football matches at the Gioco del Calcio Storico.

BUY a Pucci bikini and guarantee future beach cred.

AFTER DARK head to the outdoor dance area of Central Park and enjoy a moonlight mosh.

URBAN MYTH

Whether or not the statue of David by Michelangelo is a self-portrait, many visitors sneer at the size of his manhood. In fact, viewers are lucky to see it at all. Prudish church authorities used to insist that nudes in art had their privates hidden, either by a judiciously painted fig leaf or by removing the area altogether – Michelangelo's *Bacchus* had his bits chopped off. It's no surprise then that some artists, such as Brunelleschi with his *Crucifix*, gave up representing the naughty bits altogether.

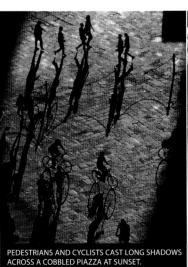

PEDESTRIANS AND CYCLISTS CAST LONG SHADOWS ACROSS A COBBLED PIAZZA AT SUNSET.
Photographer: Daryl Benson / Masterfile

MICHELANGELO'S MASTERPIECE IN MARBLE – THE EXTRAORDINARILY LIFELIKE STATUE OF DAVID IN THE GALLERIA DELL'ACCADEMIA.
Photographer: Hannah Levy / LPI

TERRACOTTA-COLOURED BUILDINGS ALONG THE ARNO BATHED IN WARM DUSK LIGHT.
Photographer: Damien Simonis / LPI

Galway

VITAL STATISTICS

NAME: GALWAY

NICKNAME: CITY OF TRIBES

DATE OF BIRTH: 1124; WHEN THE CASTLE OF BUN GAILLMHE WAS BUILT FOR THE KING OF CONNACHT

ADDRESS: IRELAND (MAP 3, B7)

HEIGHT: 21M

SIZE: 50 SQ KM

POPULATION: 73,000

LONELY PLANET RANKING: 080

Galway city is a rare confluence of elements: it's arty, romantic, youthful, eccentric and historic.

ANATOMY

Galway's tightly packed historic town centre lies on both sides of the fast-flowing River Corrib, and its curved, cobbled streets run down to the busy harbour. High St is closed to traffic most of the time, so often swarms with a festive crowd. The uninspiring Eyre Sq and the bus and train stations, as well as most of the main shopping areas, are on the river's eastern bank. To the southeast of Wolfe Tone Bridge is the historic, but now totally redeveloped, district of Claddagh; to the west is the faded beach resort of Salthill.

PEOPLE

Galway is one of Europe's most rapidly growing cities, with migrants from Eastern Europe, Asia and Sub-Saharan Africa mixing with a predominantly Irish Catholic community. Most notable, though, is the large percentage of students and a general skew towards those under 45. Although it's known as the gateway to the Gaeltacht (the Irish-speaking region), Galway has not had a solely Irish-speaking population since the 1930s.

TYPICAL GALWEGIAN

Galway has long been seen by the rest of Ireland, and beyond, as an essentially Celtic place. While Galwegians today are mostly young, and often progressive or even alternative in their outlook, it remains a city where historic cultural traditions are embraced and sustained. A local may be a musician, artist, thespian or intellectual, or combine an artistic pursuit with a boomtown professional life in IT or biotech. Galwegians have a high regard for a night out, and join the large number of students and, in the summer, tourists, in the pubs, restaurants and the streets.

DEFINING EXPERIENCE

Up early selling your hand-printed clothes at the Saturday markets, picking up some organic olives and brown bread after you've packed up your stall (it was a bit damp after all), grabbing a coffee at Bananaphoblacht, then taking your *bodhran* (traditional Celtic drum) to Taaffe's for a session and fitting in a few pints before a comedy act at the Kings Head.

STRENGTHS

- Galway Arts Festival and Galway Film Fleadh
- Lynch's Castle
- Traditional Irish music pubs
- Taibhdhearc na Gaillimhe (Irish-language theatre)
- Spanish Arch
- Salthill Golf Course
- Collegiate Church of St Nicholas of Myra
- Seafood
- The wild beauty of the surrounding landscape
- Street life in summer
- Cute painted houses

WEAKNESSES

- The rise of the super-pub
- Prodigious rainfall
- Petty crime
- Race Week crowds

GOLD STAR

Laid-back cool – Galway comfortably incorporates traditional and alternative lifestyles.

STARRING ROLE IN...

- *City of the Tribes* by Walter Macken
- *The Guards* by Ken Bruen
- *Belios* by Órfhlaith Foyle

IMPORT

- Crusties
- Spanish wine and oil in medieval times
- Folk musicians
- Students
- Jack B Yeats (poet Yeats' painter brother)

EXPORT

- Nora Barnacle
- John Lynch, signatory to the US Declaration of Independence
- Claddagh rings
- Fast-food chain Supermacs
- Connemara marble
- Aran sweaters
- Eamonn Ceannt, one of the leaders of the 1916 Easter Uprising
- Liam Mellowes
- Pottery and porcelain
- Novelist and dramatist Walter Macken
- Peter (Christopher) Yorke

SEE Galway Bay from the beach at Salthill, after eating your fill at the Oyster Festival.

EAT Cratloe Hills Gold, Irish ham and wild salmon, from Sheridans Cheesemongers.

DRINK locally made Johnny Jump-Up cider at Neáchtains.

DO a walk along the Corrib, past the Salmon Weir Bridge to the weir itself.

WATCH buskers on Shop or Quay Sts.

BUY *Anna Livia Plurabelle* by James Joyce at the Charlie Byrne Bookshop.

AFTER DARK catch a ceilidh session at Taylor's.

URBAN MYTH

A romantic icon in the hearts and songs of Irish-Americans for generations, Claddagh village was once Galway's main commercial fishing centre – up to 3000 people and 300 boats were based here. Claddagh once had its own costume and dialect, as well as its own king. Although the traditional Claddagh of thatched roofs, Irish speakers and fishing boats disappeared in the early 20th century, you will still see many people wearing Claddagh rings. The rings depict a crowned heart nestling between two outstretched hands; it signifies friendship (the hands), loyalty (the crown) and love (the heart). If the heart points towards the hand, the wearer is taken or married; towards the fingertip means that he or she is looking for a partner. It has been the wedding ring used throughout much of Connaught since the mid-18th century.

KEEPING GOOD COMPANY – LOCALS SHARE A BENCH AND A CHAT WITH ONE OF IRELAND'S MOST FAMOUS WRITERS.
Photographer: Neil Setchfield / LPI

COMPETING FOR CHANGE – ONE OF MANY TALENTED STREET MUSICIANS ENLIVEN THE CITY.
Photographer: Neil Setchfield / LPI

FLESHING OUT A THOUGHT – AN INTROSPECTIVE LOCAL DAWDLES PAST A BUTCHER'S MOSAIC.
Photographer: Neil Setchfield / LPI

LINING UP FOR WATERFRONT VIEWS – HOUSES ON THE HARBOUR AND RIVERSIDE ARE IN A HIGH DEMAND.
Photographer: Neil Setchfield / LPI

Glasgow

VITAL STATISTICS

NAME: GLASGOW

NICKNAME: GLESCA; RED CLYDESIDE

DATE OF BIRTH: 6TH CENTURY; WHEN GLASGOW GREW UP AROUND THE CATHEDRAL FOUNDED BY ST MUNGO

ADDRESS: SCOTLAND (MAP 3, D5)

HEIGHT: 8M

SIZE: 198 SQ KM

POPULATION: 580,000 (CITY); 2.3 MILLION (METRO AREA)

LONELY PLANET RANKING: 106

Scotland's largest city is the original rough diamond, with a fair share of economic pressure to create dazzling live music, a 24-carat bar scene and the hardest dialect to decipher in English.

ANATOMY

Rambling Glasgow has sights scattered throughout it, though the city centre on the north side of the Clyde River has two train stations that link even the most distant quarters of the city via the UK's second-largest metropolitan train network. The main centre is George Sq, though Sauchiehall St (running along the ridge of the northern part of the city) is a popular pedestrian mall with shops and pubs. Parallel to the river, Argyle St is another important shopping strip, along with its tributary, Buchanan St. The aptly named Merchant City is the commercial district in the city's centre, while the university is near Kelvingrove Park to the northwest, in the area deceptively known as the West End. Pollok Country Park and the Burrell Collection are in the South Side, southwest of the centre.

PEOPLE

Glasgow's population is overwhelmingly Caucasian, with a small group of Asians and Afro-Caribbeans. While English is theoretically the lingua franca, you could get confused by the slang and thick accents of Glaswegians.

TYPICAL GLASWEGIAN

Glaswegians are a tough, hard-working lot who love a pint and speak their own language, which they've cheerfully made impenetrable to visitors. There's a rough humour to it with a Glaswegian Kiss being a head butt and a lexicon that includes *wanner*, *stiffen* and *mollocate* for getting beaten up. Folk from Edinburgh refer to Glaswegians as *weegies* or *soap dodgers* – a dig at the city's working-class roots. Glaswegians are known for their fierce support of unions and the Labour Party, with huge protests against the poll tax in the 1990s, some of which ended in that other choice piece of Glaswegian patois, a *stoush*.

DEFINING EXPERIENCE

Brunching in the West End's finest cafés, strolling and spying out pirated software at the Barras, picnicking in Kelvingrove Park, sampling the best of the pubs along Sauchiehall St, and then rocking out to the next Franz Ferdinand at the Barrowlands.

STRENGTHS

- Glasgow Cathedral
- Live-music scene
- Merchant City
- Sauchiehall St
- Willow Tea Rooms
- St Mungo's Museum of Religious Life & Art
- Hunterian Art Gallery
- Burrell Collection
- Tenement House
- Mitchell Library
- Pubs and pints
- BBC Scotland studios

WEAKNESSES

- Orange marches
- Economic depression
- Unique dialect
- Neds (Non-Educated Delinquents)

GOLD STAR

Art – from Rennie Mackintosh to Franz Ferdinand there's no doubt Glasgow has made a huge impact on the arts.

STARRING ROLE IN...

- *Young Adam* (2003)
- *Wilbur Wants to Kill Himself* (2002)
- *Trainspotting* (1996)
- *My Name is Joe* (1998)
- *Shallow Grave* (1994)
- *The Borrowers* (1997)

IMPORT

- Daniel Defoe
- Ewan McGregor

EXPORT

- Franz Ferdinand
- Charles Rennie Mackintosh
- Teenage Fanclub
- Billy Connolly
- Travis, bis and Texas
- Robert Carlyle
- Irn-Bru soft drink
- Angus Young
- Robbie Coltrane
- Gregor Fisher
- Darius Danesh
- Lulu
- Sir Thomas Lipton
- Kenny Daglish
- Adam Smith

SEE the architectural canniness of Mackintosh House and get the rest of the Hunterian Art Gallery into the bargain.

EAT seasonal Scottish organic produce in a swanky Victorian-era noshery, the Buttery.

DRINK one of a hundred whiskies at Uisge Beatha (the Gaelic nickname for whisky, literally 'water of life').

DO stroll the grounds and woodland trails of Pollok Country Park and imagine you're the monarch of the glen.

WATCH Glasgow's next big things at King Tut's Wah Wah Hut, where Oasis notoriously played their debut.

BUY a designer knock-off at the Barras on Gallowgate.

AFTER DARK hang under the Arches, the city's biggest club, which attracts visiting DJs and aspiring turntablists.

URBAN MYTH

The age-old rivalry between Glasgow and Edinburgh goes way back. In the late 19th century a group of Glaswegian painters took on the domineering artistic establishment of Edinburgh. Up to this point paintings were largely historic scenes and sentimental visions of the Highlands, but the Glasgow Boys (as they became known) saw the world differently. Painters such as Sir James Guthrie, EA Hornel, George Henry and Joseph Crawhall experimented with colour and themes of rural life, shocking Edinburgh's artistic society. Like Charles Rennie Mackintosh, the Glasgow Boys achieved success in Europe, where their work met with admiration and artistic recognition, but they were largely snubbed in the UK.

LOOKING DOWN THE FOOTBRIDGE ACROSS THE CLYDE RIVER.
Photographer: Neil Setchfield / LPI

CLASSIC GLASGOW: TRADITION MEETS ATTITUDE.
Photographer: Neil Setchfield / LPI

THE SUN MAKES A RARE APPEARANCE OVER THE BUSTLE OF GORDON ST.
Photographer: Photolibrary

THE FAMOUS SCOTTISH EXHIBITION AND CONVENTION CENTRE, AFFECTIONATELY NICKNAMED 'THE ARMADILLO' FOR REASONS OBVIOUS.
Photographer: Neil Setchfield / LPI

ALMONDS AND FERRIS WHEELS – THE PERFECT COMBINATION, HAMBURGER DOM.
Photographer: Martin Lladó / LPI

Hamburg

The entertainment capital of Germany, beautiful and historic Hamburg is both economically and culturally prosperous, with strong industry, an impressive music scene and a colourful and diverse local culture.

ANATOMY

Hamburg is a large city shaped by water, with a wonderful harbour at its centre, three rivers and canals running through it, a number of lakes and around 2500 bridges. Most of the attractions cluster around the bustling urban centre, with a good number of vast green spaces to break up the intensity of the busy port city. The Alsterfleet canal splits the urban centre into the Old City, which is full of historic churches and Renaissance-style arcades, and the New City, which contains the prominent city landmark, the baroque church of Michaeliskirche. The surrounding inner suburbs house a variety of popular entertainment districts, including the notoriously seedy Reeperbahn, as well as the residential suburbs of the young and trendy and those of the wealthy. A network of ferries, trains and other public transport is available.

PEOPLE

Hamburg's citizens are mostly German, with European immigrants making up around 15% of the population. Most Hamburgers are either Lutheran or Hindu. There are small groups of Jews and Muslims, and others are unaffiliated, atheists or of other faiths. Pure German and local dialects are the main languages, though English is also widely spoken.

TYPICAL HAMBURGER

The city's population comprises more millionaires than any other German city, and the majority of Hamburgers live comfortably. They are proud of their city and relish Hamburg's green spaces. They love to shop and to eat out. Most are political with concerns ranging from social democracy to the environment, and few are shaken by the quirks of alternative subculture. While the pace in the city can be fast, they are welcoming to visitors.

DEFINING EXPERIENCE

Strolling bleary-eyed through the early-morning scene of the rowdy Fischmarkt while munching a *Bratwurst* (grilled sausage), balancing a beer and browsing for tulips and novelty T-shirts as store vendors noisily hawk their wares, then finding a bench to unload and finish breakfast while toe-tapping along to the locals joining in on the choruses of German pop tunes cranked out by bands at the market.

STRENGTHS

- Drinking holes around virtually every corner
- Excellent and free tourist maps
- Green areas of city
- Fischmarkt
- Cruises around the port
- Great music scene
- Historic buildings and churches
- Bridges
- The 'Art Mile' (string of art galleries and museums)
- Cool fashions
- Great café culture
- Flat city (good for cycling)
- German beer
- Nearby forests
- Good secondhand stores
- International cuisine
- Diverse character of the city
- Alternative scene
- Leafy streets
- Hamburger Dom festival

WEAKNESSES

- Junkies
- High cost of living
- Confusing train timetables

GOLD STAR

Entertainment central – whether you are up for clubbing, bar-hopping, a night of live music or a refined night at the theatre there are heaps of options… and it seems as though you are never more than a five-minute walk from a bar or pub in Hamburg.

STARRING ROLE IN...

- *Mirador* (1978)
- *Tomorrow Never Dies* (1997)
- *Bella Marta* (Mostly Martha, 2002)

IMPORT

- The Beatles (for a time)
- The 2006 FIFA World Cup
- Coffee
- Chain restaurants
- EU citizens
- Arab citizens
- Fuel
- Fruit and vegetables
- Building materials
- Electronics

EXPORT

- The music of Felix Mendelssohn
- The music of Johannes Brahms
- The discovery of electromagnetic waves by Heinrich Hertz
- Biotechnology
- Schwarzkopf hair products
- Shipbuilding and aircrafts
- Steinway pianos
- Philips electronics
- Siemens
- Nivea beauty products
- Montblanc fountain pen
- Car manufacturing
- Commerce
- Holsten Pilsener Beer
- Print media and publishing
- Kraftwerk

SEE the saucy exhibits at the Erotic Art Museum, which showcases a collection of erotic art from the 16th century to the modern day.

EAT gourmet French at Chez Alfred, a charming restaurant housed in an old factory where railway tracks still run through the outdoor patio.

DRINK with punks and environmentalists in the politically charged and moody Fritz Bauch.

DO check out the animated collection of bars, sex clubs, restaurants and pubs in the 'sin centre' of St Pauli.

WATCH a cutting-edge adaptation of Goethe's *Faust* at Thalia Theater.

BUY a *Bratwurst* and a beer at the boisterous Fischmarkt.

AFTER DARK pay tribute at the famous basement of the Kaiserkeller – one of the local live venues gigged by the Beatles in the '60s.

URBAN MYTH

Before they became a household name, the Beatles built their musicianship and developed their stage performances in Hamburg – where their breakthrough finally came. First playing at the Indra Club in 1960, over the next three years the Beatles put in around 800 hours of live performance at the Kaiserkeller, the Top Ten and the Star Club, and had a rollicking good time as they did it. As John Lennon famously said, 'I was born in Liverpool, but I grew up in Hamburg'.

THE HEAVILY INKED OWNER OF JUNGBLUTH PIERCING AND TATTOO SHOP POSES PROUDLY.
Photographer: Yadid Levy / Alamy

CHILE HAUS, FRITZ HOEGER'S EXPRESSIONIST TRIUMPH, MERCHANT DISTRICT.
Photographer: Andrea Schulte-Peevers / LPI

CHECKING OUT THE ACTION AT THE STRAND PAULI BEACH CLUB.
Photographer: Yadid Levy / Alamy

Hanoi

VITAL STATISTICS

NAME: HANOI

DATE OF BIRTH: 1010; WHEN IT WAS TRANSFERRED FROM THE MOUNTAINS TO ITS PRESENT LOCATION

ADDRESS: VIETNAM (MAP 5, M5)

HEIGHT: 16M

SIZE: 2146 SQ KM

POPULATION: 3.7 MILLION

LONELY PLANET RANKING: 023

Hanoi's beguiling boulevards, *belle époque* architecture and peaceful parks and pagodas are enough to recommend it, but there's also the bonus of a vibrant, optimistic population and fantastic food.

ANATOMY

Hanoi sprawls along the Red River (Song Hong), which is spanned by three bridges. The city is divided into seven central districts (*quan*), surrounded by outlying neighbourhoods called *hyyen*. Peaceful Hoan Kiem Lake lies between the imploding maze of the Old Quarter in the north, and the architecturally elegant Ba Dinh district (French Quarter) to the south. Go west for the monument-strewn former Imperial City, or north to the lovely West Lake. Here two wheels *are* better than four: motorbike, bicycle and *cyclo* (pedicab) beat the buses every time.

PEOPLE

Ethnic Vietnamese (*kihn*) dominate Hanoi, though there are a small number of ethnic minorities from around Vietnam. Second languages reflect a historical chronology: those under 30 (almost three-quarters of the population) speak English, the middle-aged may have a smattering of Russian and German and the elderly are often fluent in French.

TYPICAL HANOI CITIZEN

Hanoi residents are known for their reserve and strength of character, coupled with energy and resourcefulness. After a history of colonisation, war and Communist rule, they tend to be suspicious both of authority and of outsiders but are also hospitable and incredibly adaptive to change. Family values abound – beneath the nonchalant cool-kid-on-motorbike pop-culture persona there's usually a strong sense of Confucian responsibility and discipline. The younger generation are well educated and optimistic about the future.

DEFINING EXPERIENCE

Having your shoes shined at 5am, watching merchants setting up their stalls, then off to the flower market to buy blooms, padded bras and some plastic baskets, followed by *pho* (beef-noodle soup) for breakfast with ground pork and mushrooms at the little place next to the Binh Minh Hotel.

STRENGTHS

- Youthful energy
- Long Bien Bridge
- Temple of Literature
- Communist monuments – drab and spectacular in turn
- City lights reflecting on Hoan Kiem Lake
- Mung dumplings with sweet ginger sauce in winter
- Hotel Metropole and other French colonial architecture
- Tree-lined boulevards
- *Ga Tan* (stewed chicken with medicinal herbs, dates and grilled baguettes)
- Wacky water puppets
- One Pillar Pagoda
- Coffee – strong and sweet
- Tight-knit sense of community

WEAKNESSES

- Traffic
- Bureaucracy
- Censorship
- Over-the-top architectural styles of the newly wealthy
- Overcrowding
- Government surveillance

GOLD STAR

Bustling authentic retail landscape – the 36 streets of the Old Quarter combine hundreds of years of history with intriguing shopping and an insight into Hanoi's heart.

STARRING ROLE IN...

- *Les Filles du botaniste chinois* (2005)
- *The Quiet American* (2002)
- *Daughter from Danang* (2002)
- *Vertical Ray of the Sun* (2000)
- *Marché à Hanoi* (1903)

IMPORT

- Architecture: French and Soviet
- Canto-pop
- Buddhism
- Picasso-era modernism
- Existentialism
- Russian salads
- Catholicism
- Padma cars
- Minsk motorbikes
- Stalinist labour camps
- French food legacies: pastry, baguettes, crème caramel and yoghurt
- Confucianism
- Japanese food
- Cable TV

EXPORT

- Diaspora
- Stone carving
- Silk
- Water puppets
- *Pho*-culture

SEE the t'ai chi practice at Hoan Kiem Lake at dawn.

EAT fried squid with dill, tofu with tomatoes and grilled chicken at a *bia hoi* (beer tavern) in the old town – maybe Bia Hoi Viet on Pho Tong Dan.

DRINK *xeo* (rice wine) and hang with the Minsk motorcycle club.

DO play a game of badminton in Lenin Park.

WATCH the circus at Cong Vien Le Nin: bears, tigers, elephants and girls on roller skates.

BUY bolts of silk or order bespoke shirts along Pho Hang Gai.

AFTER DARK catch a Vietnamese pop star performing at the Hanoi Opera House then go for a motorbike ride around West Lake.

URBAN MYTH

Hoan Kiem, the name of Hanoi's enchanting lake, means 'the returned sword'. Legend has it that the 15th-century king, Le Loi, had a magical sword that proved invaluable in driving back the Chinese. One day as he was boating on the lake, a giant turtle rose from the depths and seized the sword, vowing to return it to the gods. A turtle that was found and preserved in the 1970s is thought to be more than 500 years old, making it old enough to be the turtle of the legend. There are still sightings of giant turtles in the lake, the last in 1998, and scientists believe they could be a unique species.

A SHOULDER TO LEAN ON: SCHOOLCHILDREN STICK TIGHTLY TOGETHER.
Photographer: Keren Su / Corbis

SHORT BACK AND SIDES FOR A YOUNG CUSTOMER AT A STREET SALON.
Photographer: Owen Franken / Corbis

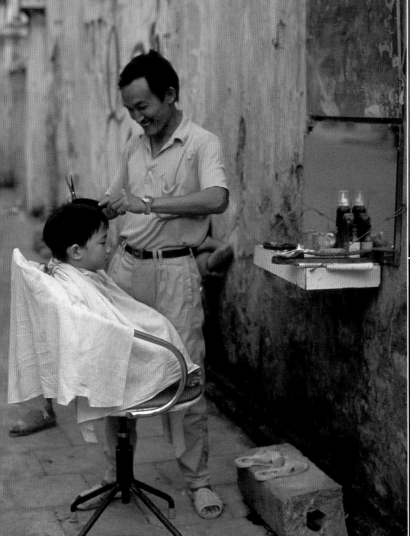

HOMEWARD BOUND, A FARMER CARRIES BASKETS OF PRODUCE THROUGH DONG ANH DISTRICT AT SUNSET.
Photographer: Kevin R Morris / Getty Images

WOMEN IN WHITE CYCLE THROUGH THE CITY STREETS AT SUNRISE.
Photographer: Jean Reay / Corbis

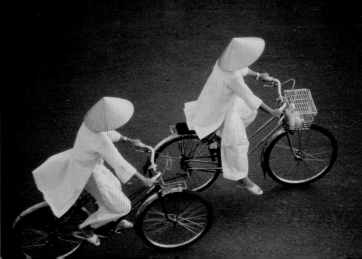

The jewel of the Caribbean, Havana's faded colonial grandeur, magnificent Malecón (waterfront promenade) and charming old town make it an instant hit with anyone lucky enough to visit.

ANATOMY

The city faces the Straits of Florida (a big temptation for many sick of Castro) with its vast seafront, the legendary Malecón, which is one of the most impressive in the world, despite the crumbling colonial buildings, peeling paint and general sense of neglect. The centre of the city is divided up into La Habana Vieja (Old Havana), a Unesco World Heritage site and the best-preserved Spanish colonial town in the Americas, and Centro Habana, the modern city and seat of most major government ministries to the west. Train is the best way to get around.

PEOPLE

Havana is almost entirely populated by Cubans, with a small business and diplomatic community. Sixty percent of citizens are of Spanish descent, 22% are of mixed race, 11% of African descent and 1% Chinese. There's almost no ethnic tension – Havana is a great example of total racial harmony. Forty-seven percent are Catholic, 4% Protestant and 2% Santería (many Catholics also practice Santería). Spanish is the official language.

TYPICAL HABANERO

Definitely a highlight of the trip, the Habaneros are great fun. Forget any preconceptions you might have of life under a totalitarian government – Habaneros carry on regardless, with an almost bloody-minded determination to be as happy and unfazed by the problems of everyday life as possible.

DEFINING EXPERIENCE

Knocking back an ice-cold *mojito* (a cocktail made of rum, lime, sugar, mint and soda water) at almost any bar in the old town, as locals stare down at you from their dilapidated balconies (a hobby among Habaneros, particularly the elderly).

Havana

VITAL STATISTICS

NAME: HAVANA

DATE OF BIRTH: 1514; WHEN THE PORT OF SAN CRISTÓBAL DE LA HAVANA WAS FOUNDED BY DIEGO VELÁZQUEZ

ADDRESS: CUBA (MAP 4, I2)

HEIGHT: 24M

SIZE: 740 SQ KM

POPULATION: 2.4 MILLION (CITY); 3.7 MILLION (METRO AREA)

LONELY PLANET RANKING: 035

RIDING IN STYLE, TWO GIRLS KEEP AN EYE ON CENTRO HABANA FROM THE WINDOWS OF THEIR CLASSIC CAR.
Photographer: Richard I'Anson / LPI

STRENGTHS

- ⊿ Extraordinarily friendly and fun-loving locals
- ⊿ Mind-blowing buildings and bright colours everywhere
- ⊿ Few better places to drink superb cocktails and listen to great live music
- ⊿ Yet to be conquered by massive American tour groups

WEAKNESSES

- ⊿ The food can be extremely unexciting after a few days
- ⊿ The appalling human-rights record
- ⊿ Beach resorts that keep Cubans apart from foreigners in a form of apartheid

GOLD STAR

La Habana Vieja – the best-preserved colonial Spanish complex in the Americas – is a joy to walk round. True, much of it has been sanitised far more than is proper, but stray into the backstreets from the revamped roads and you'll be mesmerised by the sultry Caribbean charm of Havana once more.

STARRING ROLE IN...

- ⊿ *Fresa y Chocolate* (1994)
- ⊿ *The Buena Vista Social Club* (1999)
- ⊿ *Before Night Falls* (2000)
- ⊿ *Dirty Dancing: Havana Nights* (2004)

IMPORT

- ⊿ Tour groups
- ⊿ Music lovers
- ⊿ Cigar aficionados
- ⊿ Convinced Communists
- ⊿ Fidelologists

EXPORT

- ⊿ Rum
- ⊿ Sugar
- ⊿ Political dissidents
- ⊿ Families in dinghies crossing the Straits of Florida

SEE the Capitolio Nacional, former seat of the Cuban government and one of the highlights of Havana's rich architectural heritage.

EAT ice cream at the famous Coppelia Ice Cream parlour for the true Habanero experience.

DRINK plenty of delicious *mojitos* and Cuba Libre cocktails at the fabulous neoclassical Inglaterra Hotel in Parque Central.

DO not forget that there's more to Havana than the old town – explore the further-flung parts and don't miss the Playas del Este.

WATCH the monthly display of hundreds of singers and musicians performing in Plaza de la Catedral.

BUY from an endless array of books and posters from the unofficial stands on Plaza Vieja.

AFTER DARK head to one of Cuba's famous nightspots or cabaret clubs in La Habana Vieja.

URBAN MYTH

Fidel Castro, despite having outlived entire generations of CIA staff, has remained the subject of relentlessly innovative and bizarre schemes to see him assassinated or otherwise wrested from power. Most famously there was the assassination attempt using the exploding cigar (which failed), but the CIA tried many other methods of discrediting Castro – from poisoning him so his famous beard would fall out, to impregnating a diving costume with lethal bacteria and then presenting it to Castro as a present. Amazingly, Castro has survived all these attempts on his life and has gone on to be one of the longest-serving leaders of modern times.

SHADES OF CHE – A COOL COMMIE SHOWS OFF HIS TRUE COLOURS.
Photographer: Rick Gerharter / LPI

A QUEUE FORMS BENEATH THE ARCHWAYS OF A GRACEFULLY DECAYING COLONIAL BUILDING IN THE CITY CENTRE.
Photographer: Martin Fojtek / LPI

ON THE STREETS OF THE OLD TOWN, A GLAMOROUS HABANERA PAUSES FOR A PUFF.
Photographer: Dominic Arizona Bonuccelli / LPI

Heidelberg

VITAL STATISTICS

NAME: HEIDELBERG

DATE OF BIRTH: AD 765; WHEN SETTLERS CAME TO THE AREA

ADDRESS: GERMANY (MAP 3, J9)

HEIGHT: 110M

POPULATION: 145,000

LONELY PLANET RANKING: 099

Germany's oldest university city oozes dreamy charm with pretty 18th-century buildings, an alluring semi-ruined castle and a general air of intelligentsia – Goethe was enchanted, as you will be too.

ANATOMY

The main feature of Heidelberg is the Neckar River, spanned by the Alte-Brücke at the eastern end and the Theodor-Heuss-Brücke towards the west. South of the river lies the evocative *Altstadt* (old town), whose main street, the pedestrianised Hauptstrasse, known as the Royal Mile, runs from Bismarckplatz (the old town's epicentre) through the Markt to Karlstor. Dominating the city from a hill to the southeast is the fairy-tale Schloss (castle). Public transport consists of buses and trams.

PEOPLE

Heidelberg is a student town, with one in five residents reportedly there for learning. The city receives three million visitors every year, the majority of whom come from the USA and Japan, with the UK and other European countries also contributing. There are two US military communities southwest of the *Altstadt*. Approximately 20,000 of Heidelberg's inhabitants are not German nationals.

TYPICAL HEIDELBERG CITIZEN

Heidelberg is one of Germany's great centres of intellectual study, so the fact that its inhabitants are largely well educated and cultured will hardly come as a surprise. Concerts, which are held outdoors in summer, are well attended, and foreign films are popular. Well accustomed to receiving visitors, people are very friendly and most speak some English.

DEFINING EXPERIENCE

Taking the funicular up to the Schloss and admiring the city from up high, then descending to town, hiring a bicycle and exploring the surrounding countryside before retiring to the *Altstadt* for a refreshing litre of beer and a good book.

STRENGTHS

- Neckar River
- Schloss
- Ruprecht-Karl-Universität (Heidelberg university)
- Alte-Brücke
- Heiliggeistkirche
- 19th-century romantics eg Goethe
- Architectural unity (due to a total rebuild in the 18th century after invading French troops under Louis XIV devastated the city)
- Philosophising on Philosophonweg
- Students
- Cosy pubs
- Good beer
- Friendly locals
- Heidelberger Herbst, the massive autumn festival
- Christmas market
- Fireworks festivals
- Authentic charm
- Mild winters

WEAKNESSES

- Expensive and elusive accommodation
- Dull modern part of the city to the west (well, it can't all be gorgeous)
- Dearth of cheap eating options
- Students?

GOLD STAR

Intellectual charm: Heidelberg is the thinking person's crumpet.

STARRING ROLE IN...

- *A Tramp Abroad* by Mark Twain
- *Heidelberg: Sunset* by William Turner

IMPORT

- Goethe
- Mark Twain
- William Turner
- Louis Armstrong
- Tourists
- Foreign students
- US military
- The Brothers Grimm
- Georg Wilhelm Friedrich Hegel

EXPORT

- Robert Bunsen and the Bunsen burner
- Educated people
- Printing

SEE the crumbling magic of the Schloss, one of Germany's best Gothic-Renaissance castles, and survey the town in a regal manner.

EAT 'student kisses' (chocolate-covered wafers) at Café Knösel.

DRINK dangerously addictive micro-brewed beer in the convivial bar, Vetter im Schöneck.

DO a summer German-language course at Heidelberg University and waft around the town enjoying your part in the city's academic tradition.

WATCH kaleidoscopic snap, crackle and pops at the triannual Fireworks Festivals.

BUY a ticket for a castle-spotting boat trip through the Neckar Valley.

AFTER DARK join the crooners in Germany's oldest jazz club, Cave54, where Louis Armstrong once played.

URBAN MYTH

Myths and legends are everywhere you turn in Heidelberg. The cracked iron ring by the gates of the Schloss was allegedly bitten by a witch following Ludwig V's pledge that he would give the castle to anyone who could chew through it. The footprint on the terrace apparently belongs to a knight escaping a lady's bedroom on the return of her husband, the prince. On a similar subject, the *Karl-Theodor* statue on the Alte-Brücke depicts a local legend that the prince sired 200 illegitimate offspring. If you would like the same results, touch the mice surrounding the brass monkey at the base of the bridge; touching the mirror promises wealth, and touching the fingers will ensure your return to Heidelberg.

A PARADE'S BRASH BRASS SECTION RINGS OUT AT THE MARKETPLACE BY THE TOWN HALL.
Photographer: Tina & Horst Herzig / Getty Images

WELCOMING WINDOWS THROWN OPEN TO THE NEON PROMISE OF ICE CREAM.
Photographer: Martin Lladó / LPI

A WOMAN TEARS PAST THE ALTE-BRÜCKE.
Photographer: Martin Lladó / LPI

A STYLISED GIRAFFE PEERS INQUISITIVELY AT A MODERN BUILDING BY THE HAUPTBAHNHOF.
Photographer: Martin Lladó / LPI

Ho Chi Minh City

VITAL STATISTICS

NAME: HO CHI MINH CITY

NICKNAME: HCMC; ALSO KNOWN AS SAIGON, BUT CAREFUL HOW YOU USE THIS – IT'S BEST TO STICK TO HO CHI MINH CITY WHEN DEALING WITH GOVERNMENT OFFICIALS

DATE OF BIRTH: 6TH CENTURY; WHEN THE FUNANESE CONSTRUCTED A CANAL SYSTEM THAT MOST LIKELY EXTENDED TO THE SITE OF PRESENT-DAY HO CHI MINH CITY

ADDRESS: VIETNAM (MAP 5, M9)

HEIGHT: 9M

SIZE: 2356 SQ KM

POPULATION: 6.7 MILLION

LONELY PLANET RANKING: 041

Crazy-making and seductive, HCMC (formerly known as Saigon) beats with a palpable energy, day and night.

ANATOMY

HCMC is not so much a city as a small province, with rural regions making up the majority of the land area of HCMC (but only holding a fraction of the city's population). HCMC is divided into 16 urban districts (*quan,* derived from the French *quartier)* and five rural districts (*huyen).* District 1 (once Saigon) is the downtown area and the location of most of the city's sights, while District 5 encompasses the huge Chinese neighbourhood called Cholon (Big Market). The city's neoclassical and international-style buildings and pavement kiosks selling French rolls and croissants give neighbourhoods such as District 3 an attractive, vaguely French atmosphere. Travelling the chaotic streets of HCMC is not for the faint-hearted. Metered taxis, *cyclos* (pedicabs) and motorbike 'taxis' are the most common forms of transport.

PEOPLE

HCMC has the largest ethnic Chinese community in Vietnam, mostly found in Cholon. While most fled in 1975, a small community of Indians remains; Vietnam's other minorities (Khmers, Chams and Hill Tribes) tend to live in other regions of the country.

TYPICAL HO CHI MINH CITY CITIZEN

At first sight, HCMC may seem to be populated with a million bandana-bedecked women bandits on the verge of a giant traffic accident. And, in fact, the pattern in the streets reflects a generalised, organised chaos in a city that attracts people from all over the country hoping to better their fortunes. A young office worker manoeuvres her Honda Future through rush-hour traffic, long hair flowing, high heels working the brake pedal. The sweating Chinese businessman chats on his mobile phone, cursing his necktie in the tropical heat. A desperate beggar suddenly grabs your arm – a rude reminder that this is still a developing city, despite the trimmings. It is here that the economic changes sweeping Vietnam – and their negative social implications – are most evident.

DEFINING EXPERIENCE

Strolling through the crisscross streets of historic District 1, wrangling a *cyclo* into Cholon, sniffing around local markets and browsing the sumptuous shops around Dong Khoi, before journeying further afield to the Cao Dai Temple and Cu Chi Tunnels.

STRENGTHS

- The bustling, dynamic and spirited atmosphere
- *Cyclo* drivers who give you an insight into their city
- Proximity to the Mekong Delta
- Smiling, friendly residents
- Colourful shops
- Bustling, intriguing Cholon

WEAKNESSES

- Pickpockets
- Taxi drivers who only take you to the hotels for which they receive a commission
- *Cyclo* drivers who overcharge
- Confusingly named streets
- Traffic
- Pollution

GOLD STAR

Silk boutiques – more diverse, less traditional and cheaper than those in Hanoi.

STARRING ROLE IN...

- *The Quiet American* (2002)
- *Indochine* (1992)

IMPORT

- French and Americans expats
- Rural peasants
- Pubs
- Croissants
- Joint-venture capitalists

EXPORT

- *Ao dai* (Vietnamese national dress)
- Pirated DVDs and CDs

SEE the War Remnants Museum for a graphic depiction of the impact of US military action from the point of view of 'the other side'.

EAT traditional *banh xeo* (rice-flour crepes stuffed with bean sprouts, prawns and pork), especially at the swoon-worthy restaurant Banh Xeo 46A.

DRINK cocktails while taking in the city view and cool breezes at the Rex Hotel's rooftop bar.

DO take a *cyclo* trip through the city before the municipal government phases them out.

WATCH hordes of young people checking each other out in the Dong Khoi area every weekend.

BUY a carved seal featuring your name in Vietnamese.

AFTER DARK join HCMC's fashion-conscious, alternative crowd at Q Bar near the Municipal Theatre.

URBAN MYTH

The legend goes that Quan Am Thi Kinh was a woman unjustly turned out of her home by her husband. She disguised herself as a monk and went to live in a pagoda, where a young woman accused her of fathering her child. She accepted the blame – and the responsibility that went along with it – and again found herself out on the streets, this time with her 'son'. Much later, about to die, she returned to the monastery to confess her secret. When the emperor of China heard of her story, he declared her the Guardian Spirit of Mother and Child. It is believed that she has the power to bestow male offspring on those who fervently believe in her and, as such, is extremely popular with childless couples.

HOPING FOR A LUCKY BREAK, A STREET VENDOR JOTS DOWN WEEKEND LOTTERY NUMBERS ANNOUNCED OVER THE RADIO.
Photographer: Kris LeBoutillier / Getty Images

A PASSENGER ON THE COLOSSAL FERRIS WHEEL AT DAM SEN PEERS DOWN OVER THE CITY.
Photographer: Kris LeBoutillier / Getty Images

MAN OF STEEL – STREET PERFORMERS BEND METAL AROUND A STRONGMAN'S NECK.
Photographer: Kris LeBoutillier / Getty Images

COLOURFULLY CLAD SCHOOL CHILDREN FORM A DISORDERLY LINE BEFORE CLASS.
Photographer: Kris LeBoutillier / Getty Images

Hobart

VITAL STATISTICS

NAME: HOBART

DATE OF BIRTH: 1803; WHEN EUROPEAN COLONIALISTS ARRIVED, BUT THE AREA HAD PREVIOUSLY BEEN INHABITED BY THE SEMINOMADIC ABORIGINAL MOUHENEENNER TRIBE

ADDRESS: AUSTRALIA (MAP 1, LL22)

HEIGHT: 54M

SIZE: 1360 SQ KM

POPULATION: 204,000

LONELY PLANET RANKING: 091

Small but perfectly formed Hobart pulses with the energy of a young, contemporary city proud of its well-preserved historic buildings and beautiful natural setting.

ANATOMY

Hobart has an enviable location, perched over the mouth of the Derwent River in the shadow of the imposing 1270m-high Mt Wellington. The easily-navigated city centre is arranged on a grid pattern around the Elizabeth St mall, west of which awaits retail temptation. Most of the tourist attractions are on the picturesque waterfront and Battery Point. Following the river south you meet Sandy Bay, home to the university and Wrest Point casino. Towards the north of the centre lies the Domain area, which includes the Botanical Gardens. Cars, buses, boats and bicycles nip through and around the city.

PEOPLE

The majority of Hobart's inhabitants are of European (especially British) descent. Around 2% of Hobart's population is of Aboriginal descent – a legacy of the massacres that occurred in Tasmania.

TYPICAL HOBART CITIZEN

Hobart is Australia's second-oldest city, which makes its inhabitants some of the oldest Australians in terms of generations. Their home is also the country's southernmost capital and is in one of Australia's most picturesque settings – no wonder they like where they live and are keen to conserve their environment. The setting also encourages an active life, and cycling, walking and watersports are particularly popular. They are cultured and appreciate art-house and international films as well as the Tasmanian Symphony Orchestra, whose home is in Hobart. After all that activity a glass of Tasmanian wine and some fine seafood goes down a treat.

DEFINING EXPERIENCE

Wandering through the myriad stalls of the fantastic Salamanca Market, pottering and purchasing, people-watching and enjoying the street performers, before picking up some cheap but tasty fish and chips from a barge on the dock.

STRENGTHS

- Well-preserved colonial buildings
- Natural beauty
- Compact size
- The Georgian warehouses of Salamanca Pl
- Salamanca Arts Centre
- Salamanca Market
- Mt Wellington
- Excellent seafood
- Sailing activities including the Royal Hobart Regatta
- Fish and chip barges
- Tasmanian Museum and Art Gallery
- Tasmanian Symphony Orchestra
- Battery Point
- Royal Tasmanian Botanical Gardens, housing the largest collection of mature conifers in the southern hemisphere
- Gourmet food and wine
- Organic products
- Moorilla Estate Vineyard
- Cheap car rental (lower rates than on mainland Australia)
- Tasmanian Gothic literature
- Taste of Tasmania festival
- Henry Jones Art Hotel
- Surfing at Clifton Beach

WEAKNESSES

- Relatively expensive if good accommodation
- Aesthetically challenged Federation Concert Hall
- Aboriginal massacres by the colonialists

GOLD STAR

Australian colonial architecture: there are more than 90 buildings classified by the National Trust in Hobart.

STARRING ROLE IN...

- *The English Passengers* by Matthew Kneale
- *The Tilted Cross* by Hal Porter
- *The Fatal Shore* by Robert Hughes

IMPORT

- Convicts
- Discerning tourists who bother to cross the Bass Strait
- British immigrants

EXPORT

- Errol Flynn
- Designer Patrick Hall
- Painter William Piguenit
- Pinot Noir from Stefano Lubiana Wines
- Rock lobster
- Salmon
- Abalone
- Scallops
- Wasabi
- Cascade Premium Lager and Pale Ale
- Cheddar and other Tasmanian cheeses
- Jams and sauces made from Tasmanian fruit
- Tasmanian Symphony Orchestra
- Huon pine and sassafras wood
- Lavender
- Cadbury chocolate
- Leatherwood honey

SEE the flotilla of sails at the climax of the New Year Sydney to Hobart Yacht Race.

EAT a Vietnamese salad or an all-day breakfast while watching your washing spin at the Machine Laundry Café.

DRINK a free sample or two while on a tour of Australia's oldest brewery, Cascade.

DO one of the many walks up Mt Wellington and use the spectacular view as an excuse for a rest.

WATCH the city and southwest wilderness from the cosy comfort of a seaplane.

BUY a piece of Tasmanian art or something made of Tasmanian wood.

AFTER DARK preen and pose with the in crowd at fashionable waterfront bistro-wine bar, T-42°.

URBAN MYTH

If you want a first-hand experience of Hobart's mythical underworld, take a ghost tour of the Penitentiary Chapel, offered by the National Trust. Ghost Tours of Hobart also offers nightly ghoul-spotting. With Hobart's convict history don't be surprised if you come face to face with some nasty dead characters. Good luck!

KICK UP YOUR HEELS AT THE RENOWNED SALAMANCA MARKET.
Photographer: Ian Waldie / Getty Images

THE FIRST SUNBEAMS OF THE DAY TOUCH HOUSES AT THE FOOT OF MT WELLINGTON.
Photographer: Ian Waldie / Getty Images

THE ULTRAMODERN DIGS OF THE TASMANIAN SYMPHONY ORCHESTRA.
Photographer: Ian Waldie / Getty Images

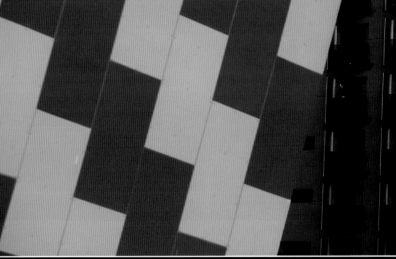

MAKING THE MOST OF HOBART'S NIGHTLIFE SCENE, SALAMANCA PL.
Photographer: Adam Pretty / Getty Images

IN THE WARM GLOW OF A GAS LAMP, TWO WOMEN PURCHASE A LATE-NIGHT CORN SNACK NEAR SULTANAHMET MOSQUE.
Photographer: Scott Barbour / Getty Images

The masterpiece of the Byzantine and Ottoman Empires in its former incarnations as Byzantium and Constantinople, and the jewel of the modern Turkish state, Istanbul is a bustling, rambunctious, energetic and bewitching city.

ANATOMY

The only city to straddle two continents, Istanbul is separated into European and Asian districts by the Bosphorus. The heart of Old Istanbul is at Sultanahmet and the nearby Bazaar district on the European side. Across the Golden Horn is the former diplomatic quarter of Beyoğlu, now a swish shopping district. Buses connect all corners of the city and yellow taxis are ubiquitous, but the best way to cross the city is on the ferries that ply the turgid waters of the Bosphorus.

PEOPLE

Istanbul is largely Turkish, but the fabric of the city and its citizens is interwoven with diverse influences. There are small Greek, Armenian and Jewish communities, as well as Russian and Georgian traders. Many Istanbul families can trace their origins to the years of the Ottoman Empire, but many villagers from Anatolia have also arrived in recent years, seeking the opportunities that the thriving metropolis provides.

TYPICAL ISTANBULLU

Istanbullus are gregarious and talkative and admirably relaxed for citizens of such an enormous city. They love a cup of çay (tea) and an opportunity to discuss the matters of the day. Istanbul residents are increasingly proud of the history and legacy of their great city. They are uniformly football mad and love green spaces in which to conduct elaborate and lengthy picnics. Family plays an integral role in everyday life, and many Istanbullus holiday in ancestral villages in Anatolia.

Istanbul

VITAL STATISTICS

NAME: ISTANBUL

NICKNAME: THE CITY OF THE WORLD'S DESIRE

DATE OF BIRTH: 657 BC; WHEN BYZAS, SON OF THE GOD POSEIDON AND A NYMPH, ESTABLISHED THE CITY

ADDRESS: TURKEY (MAP 3, R14)

HEIGHT: 114M

SIZE: 1991 SQ KM

POPULATION: 11.4 MILLION

LONELY PLANET RANKING: 010

BEER AND BANTER ARE THE ORDER OF THE DAY AT A CAFÉ IN NEVIZADE SOKAK.
Photographer: Scott Barbour / Getty Images

FLAG SELLERS WAVE THEIR WARES IN FRONT OF NEW MOSQUE, EMINÖNÜ.
Photographer: Scott Barbour / Getty Images

FOOD FOR BODY AND SOUL – A MOTHER BREAKS TO FEED HER CHILD OUTSIDE NEW MOSQUE, EMINÖNÜ.
Photographer: Scott Barbour / Getty Images

DEFINING EXPERIENCE

Contemplating the mighty soaring domes of Aya Sofya and the Blue Mosque, getting lost in the arcades of the Grand Bazaar, going underground at the Basilica Cistern beneath the heart of Sultanahmet, window-shopping on cosmopolitan İstiklal Caddesi, chilling out with a *nargileh* (water pipe), catching a ferry to Ortaköy and having a drink on the waterfront.

STRENGTHS

- Vibrant arts, music and fashion scenes
- History around every corner
- Bosphorus cruises
- Gregarious Turks
- Eating baklava and *lokum* (Turkish delight)
- Commuting on ferries
- *Meyhanes* (taverns) on Nevizade Sokak
- Topkapı Palace
- Carpets, textiles and Turkish handicrafts
- Architecture – from Byzantine to ultramodern
- Old books and maps at Sahaflar Çarşısı
- The Fish Market at Beyoğlu
- Wrought-iron balconies and cobbled streets
- Sea views

WEAKNESSES

- Carpet-shop touts
- Traffic
- Smokers everywhere
- Old neighbourhoods being swallowed up
- Wooden houses, dripping with character, falling into disrepair

GOLD STAR

The interaction of air, water, land and architecture – to truly appreciate this, climb the Galata Tower at twilight to watch the sun retreat across two continents and silhouette the voluptuous skyline of Old Istanbul.

STARRING ROLE IN...

- *From Russia with Love* (1974)
- *Topkapi* (1964)
- *Hamam* (1996)
- *Distant* (2003)
- *The Black Book* and *Istanbul: A Memoir* by Orhan Pamuk
- *The Birds Are Also Gone* by Yashar Kemal
- *Portrait of a Turkish Family* by Irfan Orga
- *The Turkish Embassy Letters* by Lady Mary Wortley Montagu
- *Istanbul the Imperial City* by John Freely
- The Inspector Ikmen crime novels of Barbara Nadel

IMPORT

- Anatolian workers and their families

EXPORT

- Guest workers to Germany
- Rifat Özbek
- Hussein Chalayan
- Cars, appliances, consumer goods
- Carpets, leather, ceramics

SEE the treasures of the Ottoman sultans at the Topkapı Palace.

EAT a fish sandwich from the vendors on the boats at Eminönü.

DRINK *rakı* (aniseed spirit) accompanied by savoury *meze* (selection of hot and cold starters traditionally served at the beginning of Middle Eastern meals).

DO a Bosphorus cruise, bumping between rickety piers on the European and Asian shores.

WATCH commuters at Eminönü in the late afternoon – the whole world is on the move.

BUY carpets or traditional craftwork in the Grand Bazaar – come prepared to haggle.

AFTER DARK head across to Beyoğlu to the bars and clubs around İstiklal Caddesi.

URBAN MYTH

English prime minister Benjamin Disraeli spent time in Istanbul in 1830, claiming 'the life of this people greatly accords with my taste, being somewhat indolent and melancholy... To repose on voluptuous ottomans, to smoke superb pipes, daily to indulge in the luxuries of the bath...is I think a far more sensible life...'

Jaipur

VITAL STATISTICS

NAME: JAIPUR

NICKNAME: THE PINK CITY

DATE OF BIRTH: 1727; WHEN JAI SINGH DECIDED TO MOVE HIS CAPITAL FROM AMBER

ADDRESS: INDIA (MAP 5, C3)

HEIGHT: 390M

POPULATION: 3.3 MILLION

LONELY PLANET RANKING: 092

Acid-bright colours punctuate the streets: crouched porters group by the station in red shirts and turbans, billowing saris catch the eye like butterflies and shopfronts glitter with fierce fabrics.

ANATOMY

The walled Old City is in the northeast of Jaipur, while the new parts spread to the south and west. The main tourist attractions are in the bazaar-lined old city and taxis and auto-rickshaws are the best way to get around.

PEOPLE

Jaipur's population is predominantly Hindu, with a sizable Muslim minority. There are small communities of Jains, Sikhs and Christians. Tribal (Adivasi) groups were the first inhabitants of this region, and today they form about 12% of the population – the national average is around 8%. The main languages are Hindi and Rajasthani.

TYPICAL JAIPURIAN

Heirs to a rich intellectual heritage, Jaipurians, Hindu and Muslim men alike have bright Rajput turbans and swashbuckling moustaches while the women wear colourful saris. Jaipurians go about their business among streets jam-packed with cars, cows, rickshaws, snuffling pigs, motorcycles and death-defying pedestrians. Street children beg outside huge jewellery shops and palatial hotels.

DEFINING EXPERIENCE

Taking a trip out to Amber Palace to see the elephants and architecture, lunching at Copper Chimney in the middle of the day and exploring the City Palace, then wandering through town to look at the Havelis, taking in a little shopping – textiles, carpets, handicrafts or jewellery – before eating on MI Rd and catching a Hindi film at Raj Mandir Cinema, with its shell-pink interior.

STRENGTHS

◢ Elephant Festival
◢ Gangaur (Harvest) Festival
◢ Teej festival
◢ Jantar Mantar, Jaipur's remarkable observatory
◢ Hawa Mahal (Palace of the Winds)
◢ Old City
◢ Maharaja Sawni Mansingh II Museum
◢ Central Museum
◢ Rajasthan Astrological Council & Research Institute
◢ Modern Art Gallery
◢ Nahargar (Tiger Fort)
◢ Amber Fort and Palace
◢ *Havelis* (traditional ornate residences)

WEAKNESSES

◢ The hassle
◢ The pressure to buy
◢ Gem scams
◢ Traffic jams
◢ Overzealous rickshaw wallahs
◢ Persistent hotel touts

GOLD STAR

The old city, which is partially encircled by a crenellated wall, is notable for its town planning: avenues divide the Pink City into neat rectangles, each of which specialises in certain crafts. At dusk the sunset-shaded buildings have a magical glow.

STARRING ROLE IN...

◢ *A Princess Remembers* by Gaytari Devi and Santha Rama Rau
◢ *Jaipur: The Last Destination* by Aman and Samar Singh Jodha

IMPORT

◢ The Raj
◢ Tourists
◢ Irrigation scientists

EXPORT

◢ Ex-royals
◢ Textiles
◢ Handicrafts

SEE a film at Raj Mandir Cinema, the world's only meringue-shaped film house.

EAT *lal maas* (mutton in a thick spicy gravy) at Copper Chimney, a classy place with the requisite waiter army and a big rollicking horse mural.

DRINK at the Polo Bar in the Rambagh Palace Hotel with its arched, scalloped windows overlooking perfect lawns.

DO make the trip out to the magnificent delicate-pink, fort-palace of Amber, a beautiful, ethereal example of Rajput architecture.

WATCH a polo match at the enormous polo ground next to the Rambagh Palace.

BUY precious and semiprecious stones – gold, silver and fine, highly glazed enamel work known as *meenakari*, a Jaipur speciality.

AFTER DARK head for the DJ bar Hightz in Mansingh Hotel; however you might find a Hammond organ as entertainment rather than the promised DJ.

URBAN MYTH

Jaipur's legendary pink colour was first instituted in 1876 when Maharaja Ram Singh had the entire old city painted pink – a colour associated with hospitality – to welcome the Prince of Wales (later King Edward VII).

CHARMED I'M SURE – A SNAKE CHARMER HYPNOTISES A COBRA AT THE GATES OF THE CITY PALACE.
Photographer: Paul Beinssen / LPI

PREENING PALACE GUARDS FLAUNT COLOURFUL UNIFORMS IN FRONT OF THE LEGENDARY PEACOCK DOOR OF THE CITY PALACE.
Photographer: Liz Thompson / LPI

THE STATELY WIND PALACE LOOKS DOWN OVER A BUSTLE OF ACTIVITY IN BADI CHAUPLE SQ.
Photographer: Noboru Komine / LPI

A MOTHER ADDS FINISHING TOUCHES TO HER DAUGHTER'S FACE PAINT AHEAD OF THE GANGAUR FESTIVAL.
Photographer: Paul Harris / Getty Images

Kabul

VITAL STATISTICS

NAME: KABUL

DATE OF BIRTH: 1772; WHEN IT WAS MADE THE CAPITAL OF AFGHANISTAN, THOUGH THERE HAS BEEN HUMAN HABITATION SINCE PREHISTORIC TIMES

ADDRESS: AFGHANISTAN (MAP 1, CC10)

HEIGHT: 1827M

SIZE: 250 SQ KM

POPULATION: 2.9 MILLION

LONELY PLANET RANKING: 118

A precious preserve of thriving Afghan culture, Kabul is one of the world's most ancient cities and continues to sparkle through tumultuous change.

ANATOMY

Kabul sits on a plain ringed by the mountains of the Hindu Kush. Little remains of the old city. The Koh-e Sher Darwaza mountains run south, topped by the old city walls, and then lead eastwards to the royal citadel of Bala Hissar. The Kabul River divides the capital. To the north is the prosperous Shahr-e Naw area, centred on its eponymous park and Pashtunistan Sq.

PEOPLE

Afghanistan's location at the crossroads of Asia has produced a jigsaw of nationalities. The largest ethnic groups are the Pashtun, Tajik and Hazara, but over a dozen smaller nationalities also live within Afghanistan's borders, from the Uzbek Baluchi and the blue-eyed Nuristanis, to the nomadic Kuchi and Kyrgyz. The majority of the population is Sunni Muslim, another 15% (mainly the Hazaras) follow Shiite Islam. Sufism has always been an important strand in traditional Afghan Islam.

TYPICAL KABULI

Through the many manmade disasters, tragedies and rebuilding, the people of Kabul have maintained a reputation of generosity and hospitality. However, travellers that have returned since in recent years have noted that these experiences have somewhat hardened the local people. Though encouraged by modern changes, many Kabulis remain fearful.

DEFINING EXPERIENCE

Brunching on a tasty chicken kebab from one of the many vendors on Cinema Zainab Rd while strolling through the park on your way to the Afghan Handicrafts Centre to peruse the local wares.

STRENGTHS

- Chicken St Markets
- Darulaman Palace
- Mausoleum of Abdur Rahman Khan
- Kabul Zoo
- Pul-e Khishti Mosque
- OMAR Land Mine Museum
- Ariana Graveyard
- The fortress of Bala Hissar
- The bird market
- Musical instrument makers

WEAKNESSES

- Sparse nightlife
- Few streetlights
- Strong presence of foreign armies
- Land mines
- Restricted drinking
- Fuzzy directions

GOLD STAR

Preservation of Afghan culture – Kabul has retained an ancient culture through a myriad of oppressions, rising above the terrible reputation given to the Afghani people by the Taliban and other extremist groups.

STARRING ROLE IN...

- *Kandahar* (2001)
- *Osama* (2003)
- *Little Game* by Timor Shah

IMPORT

- Extremist rule
- Refugees from the provinces
- Land mines
- Foreign aid

EXPORT

- Heroin
- Musical instruments
- Refugees
- Terrorists
- Afghan carpets and rugs

SEE the bird markets and musical instrument makers in the old city for a taste of traditional Afghan life.

EAT *Qabli pulao* (pilaf of rice and fried vegetables topped with almonds, raisins and grated carrot) from any street vendor.

DRINK a discreet beer on the terrace bar of the Deutscher hof.

DO suck black tea through a sugar cube as you overlook the city from the beautifully restored terraces of Babur's Gardens, created in the 16th century as the last resting place of the first Mughal ruler.

WATCH the concerts of Afghan music and poetry recitals on Saturdays at the FCCS (Foundation for Culture & Civil Society).

BUY a genuine Afghan rug from the Carpet Bazaar.

AFTER DARK on Thursday is kebab night at the Mustafa Hotel, which includes a rooftop barbecue.

URBAN MYTH

Various regimes, most famously the Taliban, each took their turn to erode the rights of women. However, this hasn't always been the case; pictures from the 1920s show Queen Soraya unveiled and wearing a sleeveless dress. In the early 1970s, Afghan womens' rights were included in the national constitution. At the time, women were seen on the streets of Kabul in skirts, they attended university and studied to be doctors, while holding over 40% of government jobs. Afghanistan's former king Zahir Shah has said, 'Any country that covers the eyes of its women makes itself blind'. Then, in September 1996, the Taliban took Kabul. The numerous edicts they imposed were medieval and the punishments for breaking these were brutal. The burka was made mandatory from head to toe, a mere flash of ankle could result in a fatal beating. Womens' voices (even laughter) and footsteps were not to be heard by strangers. They could not buy from a male shopkeeper and were forbidden to leave their homes unless accompanied by a *mahram* (male relative).

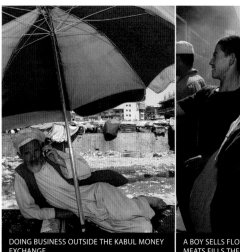

DOING BUSINESS OUTSIDE THE KABUL MONEY EXCHANGE.
Photographer: Paula Bronstein / Getty Images

A BOY SELLS FLOWERS AS SMOKE FROM GRILLED MEATS FILLS THE AIR.
Photographer: Paula Bronstein / Getty Images

A 12-YEAR-OLD GIRL CARES FOR HER TWO-YEAR-OLD COUSIN IN AN ABANDONED, WAR-RAVAGED BUILDING.
Photographer: Paula Bronstein / Getty Images

A TOILET-PAPER VENDOR DODGES SHOPPERS AS SHADOWS LENGTHEN AT THE MARKET.
Photographer: Paula Bronstein / Getty Images

Khartoum

VITAL STATISTICS

NAME: KHARTOUM

DATE OF BIRTH: 1821; ESTABLISHED AS AN
EGYPTIAN ARMY CAMP

ADDRESS: SUDAN (MAP 2, K8)

HEIGHT: 390M

POPULATION: 4.3 MILLION

LONELY PLANET RANKING: 174

LOCAL BOYS SPOT THE CAMERA WHILE FILLING UP THEIR WATER TANKS.
Photographer: Eric L Wheater / LPI

A BUSINESSMAN STRIKES A JAUNTY POSE OUTSIDE HIS JEWELLERY SHOP.
Photographer: Eric L Wheater / LPI

THE EVERYDAY BUSTLE OUTSIDE AL-KABIR MOSQUE, SHARIA AL-JAMI.
Photographer: Anthony Ham / LPI

A REFUGEE FROM DARFUR WITH SOMETHING TO SMILE ABOUT.
Photographer: Finbarr O'Reilly / Reuters/Picture Media

Where the azure and pale waters of the Blue and White Niles meet lies Sudan's modern capital – Khartoum is a haven of hospitable people, tree-lined boulevards and bustling souqs (markets) lining the banks of the legendary river.

ANATOMY

The two Niles converge in the centre of Khartoum, splitting the capital into three main wedges: Khartoum, Bahri (Khartoum North) and Omdurman. Omdurman is Khartoum's most traditional suburb and home to the largest souq in the country. Buses, minibuses and shared taxis cover most points in the city and it is a short ride from the airport to central Khartoum and UN Sq, south of which are countless informal joints serving up Sudanese classics.

PEOPLE

As much of Sudan's population, including around two million nomads, live in rural areas, the residents of Khartoum form an urban minority. More than 100 languages are spoken around the country, but Arabic is the official language and the mother tongue of Khartoum, and Islam is the predominant religion, in keeping with much of northern Sudan. English, widely used here, is by no means universal.

TYPICAL KHARTOUMAN

For Khartouman read hospitality. Khartoumans will pay for everything, share their meals and even invite you to stay in their homes. They are among the friendliest people in Africa, with a natural generosity that entirely belies their poverty. They are strictly Islamic nondrinkers but will discreetly enjoy a chicha (a water pipe infused with apple or tobacco) after a meal. Frequent street clashes and revolts reflect a city whose people, justifiably or not, remain passionate about past and present conflicts and continue to fight for their beliefs.

DEFINING EXPERIENCE

Eating ta'amiya (falafel) while picking through the wares at the souq in Omdurman, watching the colours of the Blue and White Niles swirl into one from the White Nile Bridge, and then going to Hamed el-Nil Mosque to see the traditional Nubian wrestlers going through their paces for the last two hours before sunset.

STRENGTHS

⊿ Convergence of the Niles
⊿ Nubian history
⊿ The National Museum
⊿ Omdurman
⊿ The souq
⊿ The camel market
⊿ Mahdi's Tomb
⊿ The Ethnographical Museum
⊿ Cheap (if basic) hotels
⊿ Fast, low-priced internet
⊿ Pyramids

WEAKNESSES

⊿ War zone
⊿ Death penalty (maximum) for homosexuality
⊿ Extreme poverty
⊿ Nonexistent nightlife
⊿ 40°C summer heat

GOLD STAR

The souq – this market is a dusty, vibrant relic of Sudanese life. At home in Khartoum's traditional suburb of Omdurman, it is the largest souq in the country.

STARRING ROLE IN...

⊿ Khartoum (1966)
⊿ Triumph of the Sun by Wilbur Smith
⊿ The Translator by Leila Aboulela

IMPORT

⊿ Camels
⊿ Internet
⊿ Islam
⊿ Christianity
⊿ English texts
⊿ US missiles (unwanted)
⊿ Colonialism
⊿ The water of the Blue and White Niles

EXPORT

⊿ Camels
⊿ Chicha
⊿ Nubian wrestlers

SEE the sun setting on the narrow pyramids that fill the ancient royal cemetery of Meroe.

EAT fuul (beans) and ta'amiya on the riverside at El-Shallal.

DRINK the famously fresh fruit juices at Lem Prost restaurant.

DO ride the fast-moving Ferris wheel in the Al-Mogran Family Park for an original perspective of the converging Niles.

WATCH the Halgt Zikr stir up the dust in celebration of Allah at the Hamed el-Nil Mosque every Friday afternoon.

BUY almost anything from the amazing variety of wares at the Khartoum souq.

AFTER DARK enjoy a postdinner smoke at the tiny chicha terrace on Sharia as-Sayed Abdul Rahman.

URBAN MYTH

Mahdi's Tomb, housed in a striking postwar onion-domed building, is not the original. According to Muslim prophesy, the Mahdi would rid the world of evil and when, in 1881, Mohammed Ahmed proclaimed himself to be the Mahdi he carried out the legacy by ridding Khartoum of General Gordon, the British-appointed governor. The Mahdists then ruled Sudan until 1898. They were defeated by Lord Kitchener and his Anglo-Egyptian army who ordered Mahdi's tomb to be destroyed. General Gordon's nephew 'Monkey' then carried out the deed by, somewhat unsportingly, throwing the Mahdi's ashes into the Nile!

Kolkata

A CONTEMPLATIVE RICKSHAW WALLAH WAITS FOR A FARE OUTSIDE VICTORIA MARKET.
Photographer: Tony Wheeler / LPI

VITAL STATISTICS

NAME: KOLKATA

NICKNAME: CITY OF JOY

DATE OF BIRTH: 1690; WHEN IT WAS FOUNDED AS A TRADING POST FOR THE BRITISH EAST INDIA COMPANY; IT LATER SERVED AS THE CAPITAL OF BRITISH INDIA UNTIL 1912

ADDRESS: INDIA (MAP 5, G5)

HEIGHT: 6M

SIZE: 1036 SQ KM

POPULATION: 7.7 MILLION (CITY);16.7 MILLION (METRO AREA)

LONELY PLANET RANKING: 065

Kolkata is the centre of Bengali intellectual life and the cultural capital of India – the country's five Nobel Prize winners all come from Kolkata.

ANATOMY

Kolkata sprawls north–south along the eastern bank of the Hooghly River. South of the Howrah Bridge are BBD Bagh (the hub of the CBD, the central business district) and Chowringhee Sts. A new one-way system with streets flowing in different directions depending on the time of day, mean taxis, crowded trolleybuses or the subway (the oldest in Asia) are the way to get around.

PEOPLE

More than 80% of the population is Hindu. Muslims and Christians constitute the largest minorities, but there are also Sikhs, Jains, and Buddhists, and small Jewish and Christian communities.

TYPICAL KOLKATAN

Kolkatans are the poets and artists of India, with a penchant for art and culture and a level of intellectual vitality and political awareness unsurpassed in the rest of the country. No other Indian city can draw the kinds of thronging crowds to book fairs, art exhibitions and concerts. There is a lively trading of polemics on walls, which has led to Kolkata being dubbed the 'city of posters'. Elsewhere in India, the many millions of poor are largely shut out of this cultural life.

DEFINING EXPERIENCE

Soaking up an education at the Indian Museum and popping down to Park St (Mother Teresa Sarani) for a refreshing cappuccino or hot *kati* roll (marinated fillings in bread) and browsing in the Oxford Book Shop, then strolling along the east bank of the Hooghly River, passing several Hooghly Ghats, and finally, heading to the river for a ferry trip across the Hooghly for views of the Hooghly Bridge before dining at Peter Cat, a Kolkata institution.

STRENGTHS

- St Paul's Cathedral
- India Museum
- MP Birla Planetarium
- Asiatic Society
- Academy of Fine Arts
- Graveyard at St John's Church
- Eden Gardens
- Howrah Bridge
- Botanical Gardens

WEAKNESSES

- Traffic jams
- *Bandhs* (strikes), which happen with monotonous regularity
- Flooding

GOLD STAR

The Indian Museum covers an impressive range of subjects, from natural history to modern art. Highlights include a world-class gallery of religious sculptures and a life-sized reproduction of the Barhut Gateway, built by Bihari Buddhists in the 2nd century BC. Also interesting – and possibly unique – is the gallery on plants and horticulture. The displays describe the varied uses of all the plants and crops grown in India.

STARRING ROLE IN...

- *The Missionary Position: Mother Teresa in Theory and Practice* by Christopher Hitchens
- *Calcutta Chromosome* by Amitav Ghosh
- *City of Joy* by Dominique Lapierre
- *A Suitable Boy* by Vikram Seth

IMPORT

- Hindus from East Bengal at Partition
- Muslims from East Pakistan in the war of 1971
- Marxism
- Chronic labour unrest
- Mother Teresa and the Missionaries of Charity

EXPORT

- Nobel prize–winning author Rabindranath Tagore
- Satyajit Ray
- William Makepeace Thackeray
- Vikram Seth
- Author Amitav Ghosh
- Sri Aurobindo
- Photographer Julia Margaret Cameron
- Nobel prize–winning economist Amartya Sen

SEE a Bengali or foreign art-house film at the Nandan Cinema.

EAT sweets, Kolkata's culinary contribution to India, at a *mishtir dokan* (sweets shop).

DRINK at Cud Corner, where they whip up some of the best curd and lassis in town.

DO catch Kolkata's beautiful young things in their finest at Tantra or Shisha where you can dance and puff on a hookah.

WATCH the crowds stream over the Howrah Bridge and the flower sellers below.

BUY beautifully embroidered clothes and fabrics at the Women's Friendly Society.

AFTER DARK take in a dance-drama performance or Bengali poetry reading at Rabnidra Sadan.

URBAN MYTH

The Black Hole of Calcutta isn't a description of current living conditions. Having established a new trading post in Calcutta (now Kolkata) in 1690, the British expanded their trading activities rapidly, under the apprehensive gaze of the nawab (local ruler). Eventually, the nawab decided that British power had grown far enough. In June 1756 he attacked Calcutta and, having taken the city, locked some 70 British prisoners in a tiny cell. The space was so cramped and airless that by the time the prisoners were released the next morning, 43 had perished, and the cell became infamously known as the 'Black Hole of Calcutta'.

FAMILIES GATHER TO CELEBRATE THE NEW YEAR TOGETHER AT KALIGHAT TEMPLE.
Photographer: Richard I'Anson / LPI

CURRY AND CONVERSATION AT THE BUSTLING FOOD MARKET IN FRONT OF THE TIPPU SULTAN MOSQUE.
Photographer: Richard I'Anson / LPI

SEEN FROM ABOVE, THE FLOWER MARKET BENEATH HOWRAH BRIDGE BLAZES WITH COLOUR.
Photographer: Richard I'Anson / LPI

Kraków

VITAL STATISTICS

NAME: KRAKÓW

NICKNAME: POLAND'S ROYAL CITY

DATE OF BIRTH: 7TH CENTURY; WHEN SETTLEMENT WAS FIRST RECORDED HERE

ADDRESS: POLAND (MAP 3, N9)

HEIGHT: 209M

SIZE: 327 SQ KM

POPULATION: 756,000 (CITY); 1.2 MILLION (METRO AREA)

LONELY PLANET RANKING: 030

Kraków is a whimsical, beautiful city: tatters of the iron curtain can still be found in the city's grey, identikit suburbs, but these only throw into relief the pale, lazy loops of the Vistula River curling around the old town, or the flower stalls, which make the centre of the old town and its marketplace so vivid.

ANATOMY

Relatively flat, save for some scattered rocky formations, Kraków is bisected by the Vistula River, Poland's longest river (wending its way 1047km to the Baltic). Most districts, including the historic quarter, are on the northern, left bank and very walkable. The Old Town is only 800m wide and 1200m long, with the Main Market Sq in the middle. Both buses and trams are used to travel further out.

PEOPLE

Ethnically homogeneous, Poles make up 98% of Kraków's population. The current Jewish population is relatively small, compared with 70,000 in the late 1930s. About 95% of the population is Roman Catholic.

TYPICAL KRAKÓW CITIZEN

Residents of Kraków are more conservative than their fellow countrymen in Warsaw. They are friendly and hospitable but polite and formal – they are passionate hand-shakers. They are firmly religious.

DEFINING EXPERIENCE

Reflecting on Poland's long Catholic tradition at St Mary's Church in Rynek Glowny, then leisurely strolling around the Main Market Sq, passing through the Cloth Hall, finding an appetising lunch on ul Grodzka, then heading to the Czartoryski Museum before ambling to Wawel Royal Castle and watching the stunning views over the Vistula River.

STRENGTHS

- Wawel Palace
- Wawel Cathedral
- Czartoryski Museum
- Rynek Glowny
- Cloth Hall
- The jazz scene
- Wieliczka salt mine
- A vast collection of artworks
- Wierzynek, Poland's oldest restaurant, dating from 1364

WEAKNESSES

- Weather
- Nowa Huta
- Sauerkraut with everything

GOLD STAR

Main Market Sq – the largest medieval town square in Poland (and reputedly in all of Europe) – and the Cloth Hall. The 1257 layout has been retained to this day – the façades might look neoclassical, but most of the buildings are much older.

STARRING ROLE IN...

- *La Double vie de Véronique* (The Double Life of Véronique, 1991)
- *Schindler's List* (1993)

IMPORT

- Capitalism
- Nigel Kennedy
- Karol Wojtyla (Pope John Paul II)
- Nowa Huta
- *Lady with the Ermine* by Leonardo da Vinci
- Lenin

EXPORT

- Pope John Paul II
- Copernicus
- Film-maker Roman Polanski
- Musician Zbigniew Preisner

SEE the Chapel of the Blessed Kinga, a church deep in the salt mine at Wieliczka.

EAT excellent Polish fare at Restuaracja pod Aniolami in vaulted cellars, beautifully decorated with traditional household implements and old crafts.

DRINK beer (Zywiec, Okocim or EB) or vodka (clear, or flavoured with juniper berries, cherries or rowan berries).

DO make the trip out to Auschwitz, possibly the most moving experience in the whole of Poland.

WATCH experimental theatre (knowledge of the language is not necessary).

BUY amber in striking colours – from ivory and pale yellow to reddish and brownish hints.

AFTER DARK vaulted cellar pubs and bars are the place to head for; there are 100 pubs and/or bars in the Old Town alone.

URBAN MYTH

According to legend, once upon a time there lived a powerful prince, Krak or Krakus, who built a castle on a hill named Wawel on the banks of the Vistula and founded a town named after himself. It would have been paradise if not for a dragon living in a cave underneath the castle. This fearsome and ever-hungry huge lizard decimated cattle and sheep, and was not averse to human beings, especially pretty maidens. The wise prince ordered a sheep's hide to be filled with sulphur, which was set alight, and the whole thing was hurled into the cave. The voracious beast devoured the bait in one gulp, only then feeling the sulphur burning in its stomach. The dragon rushed to the river, and drank and drank and finally exploded, giving the citizens a spectacular fireworks display. The town was saved. The dragon has become the symbol of the city, immortalised in countless images, and the dragon's monument has been placed where the beast once lived.

A LOCAL WOMAN AND A HOTEL ADVERTISEMENT COME FACE TO FACE ON A STREET CORNER.
Photographer: Bruce Yuanyue Bi / LPI

LOVERS LOUNGE BENEATH THE OPULENT FRIEZES OF ST MARY'S CHURCH.
Photographer: Bruce Yuanyue Bi / LPI

PIGEONS AND FAMILIES ALIKE FLOCK TO MAIN MARKET SQ, THE HEART AND SOUL OF THE CITY.
Photographer: Bruce Yuanyue Bi / LPI

COLD BEER AND WARM ATMOSPHERE DEFINES KRAKÓW'S PERSONABLE PUB SCENE.
Photographer: Bruce Yuanyue Bi / LPI

Kuala Lumpur

VITAL STATISTICS

NAME: KUALA LUMPUR

NICKNAME: KL

DATE OF BIRTH: 1857; WHEN A TROUPE OF TIN PROSPECTORS LANDED AT THE JUNCTION OF THE KLANG AND GOMBAK RIVERS AND DUBBED IT KUALA LUMPUR (MUDDY CONFLUENCE)

ADDRESS: MALAYSIA (MAP 5, L12)

HEIGHT: 39M

SIZE: 243 SQ KM

POPULATION: 1.9 MILLION (CITY);7.2 MILLION (METRO AREA)

LONELY PLANET RANKING: 052

A SALESWOMAN MELTS INTO A BACKGROUND OF EMBROIDERED SCARVES IN A FABRICS ARCADE IN LITTLE INDIA.
Photographer: Greg Elms / LPI

A BOY COPS AN OUTDOOR SHOWER AT SWIMMING POOLS BENEATH THE SOARING PETRONAS TOWERS.
Photographer: Greg Elms / LPI

THE QUIRKY COLONIAL ARCHITECTURE OF THE KUALA LUMPUR TRAIN STATION BUILT IN 1911.
Photographer: Greg Elms / LPI

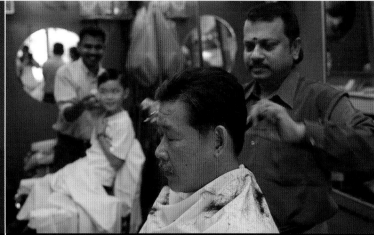
AN IMPROMPTU BARBERSHOP QUARTET AT A HAIRDRESSING SALON IN LITTLE INDIA.
Photographer: Greg Elms / LPI

A triumphant and forward-looking city, KL vibrantly accommodates its traditional Malay, Chinese and Indian cultures with the buzz of thriving industry.

ANATOMY

KL's traditional heart beats at Merdeka Sq, marked by the world's tallest flagpole (100m), while the Golden Triangle represents modern KL; the Petronas Towers (now the world's *second* tallest, topped by Taipei 101) are dazzling beacons of industry. Southeast of Merdeka lies bustling Chinatown and southward is Masjid Negara (National Mosque) and the historic KL Train Station. Stretching west is KL's 'green belt', with the Lake Garden and Malaysian Parliament House. Beyond its mall culture, KL's maze of motorways can frustrate pedestrians – it's often easier to nab a cab or ride the slick LRT (Light Rail Transit) system.

PEOPLE

Kuala Lumpur truly is 'Little Asia', with 65% Malays, 20% Chinese, 10% Indians and 5% of other mostly Asian cultural groups. The official national language is Malay (Bahasa Melayu), and other languages spoken are Hokkien/Fukien, Cantonese, Hakka, Teochew, Tamil, Telugu, Malayalam, Hindi and English. Predominantly Muslim, Buddhists, Hindus, Sikhs and Christians all form part of KL's rich tapestry.

TYPICAL KUALA LUMPUR CITIZEN

Kuala Lumpur's citizens are proud, respectful and tolerant of different beliefs and cultural practices. They have triumphed at building a metropolis that retains local traditions and colour. Oppressed by dripping humidity, the citizens know how to relax, be it enjoying great food or bargain-hunting for fashion and electronic gadgets in KL's many air-conditioned malls.

DEFINING EXPERIENCE

Picnicking at the Lake Gardens among butterflies, birds and orchids, serenading your true love on a Tasik Perdana (Premier Lake) rowing boat, topped off by a balmy banquet and good-natured haggling at Chinatown's night market.

STRENGTHS

- Multiculturalism and diversity
- Tolerance
- Dazzling Petronas Towers
- Local colour and vibrancy
- Hawker markets and foodstalls
- Halal fast food
- Chinatown
- Little India
- Luscious gardens
- Bargain-hunting
- Exquisite pewter
- Nearby Batu Caves
- 'World's tallest' (flagpole *and* – almost – building)

WEAKNESSES

- Dripping humidity (though great for orchids)
- Traffic congestion and narrow streets
- Lack of sidewalks
- Unreliable bus service
- Smog
- Poor water quality
- The invasion of 'mall culture'
- (Some) less-than-honest cab drivers, preferring to go 'off meter'

GOLD STAR

Cheap, delicious and culturally diverse food – a hearty meal can be found in any one of KL's nooks, crannies and basements.

STARRING ROLE IN...

- *Entrapment* (1999)
- *Connecting Faith* (2004)
- *The Big Durian* (2004)

IMPORT

- Chinese people
- Indian people
- British manicured gardens
- Moorish, Islamic and Buddhist architecture
- Japanese pop culture
- Rampant consumer culture
- LV and Gucci bags (the real deal)
- Shark fins (in brine and dried)

EXPORT

- Rubber
- Palm oil
- Tin/pewter
- Orchids
- PGA golfer Danny Chia
- Hollywood action star Michelle Yeoh
- LV and Gucci knock-offs
- Textiles
- Cheap (read 'pirated') DVDs

SEE the city lights from the Petronas Towers before getting a ride an hour northwest of KL to see the natural light show of *kelip-kelip* (fireflies) in the mangroves, best viewed on a river tour from Kuala Selangor.

EAT *bak kut teh* (a broth containing pork ribs and spices) from Jalan Petalin.

DRINK with friendly locals at *mamak* stalls (hang-out spots) dotting the city; run by Muslim Indians they are a great place for night owls to hang out late.

DO brave the indoor rollercoaster at Berjaya Times Sq if the heat gets too much.

WATCH Malay dance, Indian classical dance, Chinese dance and t'ai chi performances every weekend at the open-air Central Market.

BUY electronic gadgets, especially games, cheap DVDs, and mobile phones at Low Yat Plaza.

AFTER DARK doof-doof into the wee hours at Bangsar, KL's hub for clubs.

URBAN MYTH

It is rumoured that people have suffered strokes, aneurisms and heart attacks from mixing durian fruit (a popular if *very* malodorous treat) with alcohol. Purportedly, a deadly yeast can result when the two are added together. This is all unproven, and to the unseasoned but daring traveller, the best precaution taken before quaffing a durian-infused cocktail would be a peg on the nose.

A TOUCH OF MADNESS HELPS THESE WINTER BATHERS BRAVE THE COLD.
Photographer: Stringer / Reuters/Picture Media

Kyiv

VITAL STATISTICS

NAME: KYIV

NICKNAME: NORTHERN ROME

DATE OF BIRTH: AD 5–6; THE STORY ABOUT THE ORIGINS OF THE CITY ARE DISPUTED, BUT ACCORDING TO OFFICIAL SOVIET HISTORY THE CITY WAS FOUNDED AT THIS TIME

ADDRESS: UKRAINE (MAP 3, S8)

HEIGHT: 179M

SIZE: 780 SQ KM

POPULATION: 2.8 MILLION

LONELY PLANET RANKING: 145

This ancient city has undergone a face-lift in the wake of the nation's independence around 20 years ago, and modern Kyiv is a fast-paced capital – glamorous, consumerist, cosmopolitan and rich in the treasures of history and culture.

ANATOMY

Situated on the Dnipro River, Kyiv's city centre and old city are on the western bank, while grey residential blocks sit on the eastern bank. The old town lies along the high bank, with the main commercial centre of town sitting behind it. The city's wide boulevards are lined with a curious mix of architecture that reflects the rich historical influences in the capital: plain Stalinist buildings and stunning medieval, baroque, Gothic, Russian and Byzantine monuments and churches. As the main attractions are mostly found beyond the centre of town, the Kyiv Metro is a good way to get around, with river cruises, buses and car hire also available.

PEOPLE

The capital's population is composed of a Ukrainian majority, as well as Russians and a small percentage of Eastern European immigrants. The majority of the population belongs to one of several national Orthodox churches or to the Russian Orthodox Church, with minority faiths including Roman Catholicism, Judaism and Islam. Ukrainian is the official language, but English is also quite widely spoken in Kyiv.

TYPICAL KYIVAN

The city attracts more than its fair share of wealthy and talented Ukrainians as well as the political elite and stunning fashionistas. These moneyed groups are flashy. They are pushy and don't like to queue. They are fast and frantic and voracious consumers. They love to be seen at the hot clubs, bars and restaurants of Kyiv. They do, however, like the more 'ordinary' people of the city, have strong social connections and are proud of their culture and city.

DEFINING EXPERIENCE

Indulging with a lavish breakfast and jaw-dropping views of Kyiv's golden church domes on the 18th floor of the Premier Palace Hotel, then meeting friends at Independence Sq for some quick shopping before going to see a high-stakes match featuring the resident football team, Dynamo Kyiv.

STRENGTHS

- Culinary capital of Ukraine
- Very cheap food
- Beer considered a soft drink and can be drunk on the streets
- St Andrew's Church
- Caves Monastery
- Street performers during Kyiv Days celebrations
- Mosaics and frescoes at the 11th-century St Sophia Cathedral
- Museum of the Great Patriotic War
- Mariyinsky Palace
- Independence Sq
- Pyrohovo Museum of Folk Architecture
- Street-food kiosks
- River cruises
- Kitsch-themed restaurants
- Wild nightlife
- Shevchenko Opera & Ballet Theatre
- Clean Metro

WEAKNESSES

- Wild traffic
- Swinging glass doors on the metro
- Pushy locals in queues
- Confusing street numbers
- High cost of living
- Covert sex industry

GOLD STAR

Caves Monastery – to Orthodox pilgrims this site is holy land, the holiest in the country, and to all other visitors this place is at the very least something truly spectacular. With the earliest buildings dating from as far back as AD 1051, the monumental monastery is set on grassy hills above the river and clustered with gold-domed churches, fascinating museums and monks' quarters. Underground is an intriguing labyrinth of caves lined with the naturally preserved bodies of monks.

STARRING ROLE IN...

- *Mamai* (2003)
- *A Prayer for Hetman Mazepa* (2002)
- *Est-ouest* (East-West, 2000)
- *Defending the Honour of Kyiv* by Andy Dougan
- *The White Guard* by Mikhail Bulgakov

IMPORT

- SUVs and luxury cars
- Catwalk fashion
- Eurovision Song Contest
- Fast-food chains

EXPORT

- Chemicals
- Fur products
- Vodka
- Fashion models
- Machinery and transport equipment
- Vehicle manufacture
- Fuel
- Mail-order brides
- Football stars
- Chicken Kiev (Kyiv)

SEE the mummified monks by candlelight in the underground passages of the Caves Monastery.

EAT traditional Ukrainian food served up in Cossack-themed Kozak Mamay, one of Kyiv's best restaurants.

DRINK 'real coffee' at Kaffa, one of the few cafés that don't just serve instant coffee.

DO meet at the ever-lively and noisy, fountain-filled Independence Sq, the meeting place it seems for every citizen in Kyiv, day or night.

WATCH the 'walruses' (swimmers) wake up to themselves with a winter swim in the freezing Dnipro River.

BUY tasty *Kievsky Tort* (a nutty, layered sponge) at the train-station stalls.

AFTER DARK get into the latest hip-hop and R&B at the glam Tchaikovsky club.

URBAN MYTH

In summer the beaches on the mid-river islands of the Dnipro are packed with thousands of locals and tourists. The river is contaminated to some unknown extent with radioactive silt from Chornobyl, and an enduring urban myth is that the waters are inhabited by a family of huge, mutated crocodiles. While this story is unlikely, it is probably better just to sunbathe than to swim.

STATELY ST MICHAEL'S MONASTERY IS SURE TO LEAVE A LASTING IMPRESSION.
Photographer: Peter William Thornton / LPI

MAKING A SPLASH IN THE PARKS OF CENTRAL KYIV.
Photographer: Gleb Garanich / Reuters/Picture Media

EXTINCT IS FOREVER – SIGNS OF REMEMBRANCE FOR THE MANY TOWNS LOST TO CHORNOBYL.
Photographer: Carol Ann Wiley / LPI

Kyoto

VITAL STATISTICS

NAME: KYOTO

DATE OF BIRTH: 7TH CENTURY; LITTLE MORE THAN A VAST, FERTILE PLAIN, KYOTO – THEN KNOWN AS YAMASHIRO-NO-KUNI – BECAME HOME TO THE HATA CLAN FROM KOREA

ADDRESS: JAPAN (MAP 1, KK10)

HEIGHT: 41M

SIZE: 610 SQ KM

POPULATION: 1.5 MILLION

LONELY PLANET RANKING: 045

Cultural heart of Japan, Kyoto's raked pebble gardens, sensuously contoured temple roofs and latter-day geishas fulfil the Japanese fantasy of every Western cliché hunter.

ANATOMY

The city is divided into five sections designating the central (raku-chu), eastern (raku-to), northern (raku-hoku), western (raku-sai) and southern (raku-nan) areas, plus raku-gai, the city's outskirts. With a rectangular grid system, it's easy to navigate. The main business district is in the south and centre; the less populated northern parts have a greener feel, with rice fields sandwiched between apartment buildings. Although many major sights are in the centre, the best sightseeing is on the fringes in the north, east and west. It's easy to get around by walking, cycling, taking the bus or subway.

PEOPLE

Kyoto is home to one of the largest concentrations of colleges and universities in Japan, however, the majority of students leave after graduation for the bigger economic centres of Tokyo and Osaka. There are also an estimated 33,000 Japanese-Koreans living here, particularly in the neighbourhood south of Kyoto station.

TYPICAL KYOTOITE

Kyotoites are sometimes described as cold, unnecessarily formal and snobbish towards outsiders, though short-term tourists are made to feel welcome. The Kyoto dialect can be extremely vague, masking true feelings behind veiled smiles and nebulous wording. Known for their sense of style, Kyotoites prefer small and refined over large and flashy.

DEFINING EXPERIENCE

Visiting Nanzen-ji temple and its expansive grounds, including the classic Zen garden, then viewing the cherry blossoms in bloom (April only) in Kyoto Imperial Palace Park, before relaxing in a sentō (public bath) as a prelude to an evening stroll around Ponto-chō's restaurants, bars and teahouses.

STRENGTHS

◢ Japan's cultural treasure-house – 17 ancient structures and gardens are World Heritage sites
◢ 1600 Buddhist temples
◢ 400 Shintō shrines
◢ Three palaces
◢ Dozens of gardens and museums
◢ Cherry-blossom festival (April)
◢ Nightlife in Ponto-chō and Gion's 'floating world'
◢ 500 matsuri (festivals) every year
◢ Growing environmental awareness among young Kyotoites
◢ Kyoto station

WEAKNESSES

◢ Ugly urban development
◢ Widespread environmental apathy
◢ Kyoto Tower – great views, not so great to look at

GOLD STAR

Nanzen-ji Temple, for the combination of temple, grounds, Zen garden and hidden shrine in a forest hollow behind the main precinct

STARRING ROLE IN...

◢ Katakuri-ke no kôfuku (The Happiness of the Katakuris, 2001)
◢ The Pillow Book (1996)
◢ Ai no corrida (In the Realm of the Senses, 1976)
◢ Rashômon (1950)

IMPORT

◢ Beer
◢ Western junk food
◢ Soccer
◢ Baseball
◢ Doughnuts
◢ Foreign artists, musicians, teachers, scholars, writers and people 'just passing through'
◢ Whisky
◢ Coffee

EXPORT

◢ The sensu (folding fan)
◢ Kiyomizu-yaki pottery and ceramics
◢ Nintendo
◢ Film director Jūzō Itami
◢ Kyocera cameras
◢ Kyō-ryōri (cuisine emphasising subtlety, utilising fresh seasonal vegetables)
◢ Shōjin-ryōri (vegetarian cuisine with origins in Buddhist asceticism)
◢ Film director Oshima Nagisa
◢ Kyō-yūzen (silk-dyeing method)
◢ Kyō-komon (stencil dyeing)
◢ Tie-dyeing (kyō-kanoko shibori), in the 6th century
◢ Kyō-ningyo (handcrafted dolls)

SEE a panoramic 360-degree view of the city from Kyoto Tower.

EAT sukiyaki in a traditional tatami room at Morita-ya.

DRINK sake at Ing, a favourite spot for a drink in Kyoto.

DO belt out a number or three at Jumbo Karaoke Hiroba.

WATCH a traditional kabuki performance at Minami-za, the oldest kabuki theatre in Japan.

BUY distinctive ceramics at To-ji market, held on the 21st of every month.

AFTER DARK wander the 'floating world' of traditional entertainment areas Gion and Ponto-chō.

URBAN MYTH

Kyoto's fortune in escaping US bombing during WWII is commonly believed to be due to American scholar Langdon Warner, said to have urged US military authorities to spare the city, thereby preserving its artistic and historical treasures. Despite this popular account, other theories have surfaced, along with documentation pointing to an elaborate conspiracy to quell anti-American sentiment. Some historians now suggest that, in fact, Kyoto was on a list of 180 cities earmarked for air raids, and was also a prime target for atomic annihilation.

'AND DON'T FORGET TO PUBLISH YOUR MEMOIRS' – AN APPRENTICE GEISHA RECEIVES ADVICE FROM AN OLDER WOMAN.
Photographer: Oliver Strewe / LPI

THE EXTRATERRESTRIAL KYOTO TOWER LOOMS OVER THE CITY AT NIGHT.
Photographer: Martin Moos / LPI

LIKE A BRUSH PAINTING COME TO LIFE, THE BLOSSOMING BANKS OF THE KAMO GAWA RIVER PRESENT AN IDYLLIC SCENE.
Photographer: Frank Carter / LPI

HELLO KITTY – PUNK PUPPIES IN GANG COLOURS.
Photographer: Frank Carter / LPI

Las Vegas

VITAL STATISTICS

NAME: LAS VEGAS

NICKNAME: SIN CITY

DATE OF BIRTH: 1821; WHEN ANTONIO ARMIJO TOOK A DETOUR EN ROUTE TO LOS ANGELES, BUT NATIVE AMERICAN SETTLEMENTS HAVE BEEN HERE SINCE ANCIENT TIMES

ADDRESS: USA (MAP 1, H10)

HEIGHT: 612M

SIZE: 293 SQ KM

POPULATION: 599,000 (CITY); 2 MILLION (METRO AREA)

LONELY PLANET RANKING: 046

A PINK LIMOUSINE PROWLS FOR A PARK UNDER A GAUDY CANOPY OF CASINO LIGHTS.
Photographer: Chris Cheadle / Getty Images

THE BRIGHT LIGHTS OF FREMONT ST LURE FORTUNE-SEEKERS LIKE MOTHS TO THE FLAME.
Photographer: Curtis Martin / LPI

PAST ITS PRIME, A GIGANTIC W RESTS IN PEACE IN THE NEVADA DESERT.
Photographer: Neil Emmerson / Getty Images

SEQUIN-POPPING SHOWGIRLS GLAM IT UP AT THE CIRCUS HOTEL AND CASINO.
Photographer: Ray Laskowitz / LPI

There's nowhere like Vegas, baby – come here to marry a stranger you met on the plane, gamble your life savings away or just lap up the glorious oddness and kitsch of the whole place.

ANATOMY

Centred on the world-famous strip (or Las Vegas Blvd to purists), the city can seem to be little else for those just in town for a few days. Las Vegas proper is centred on Fremont St and the downtown area to the north of the big hotel-casino complexes of the strip.

PEOPLE

The vast majority of Las Vegans were born outside Nevada. It's impossible to define this mixed bunch. There's a Bible-toting Elvis bumming smokes from the guy hawking his first hip-hop album in what appears to be Tuscany. At the strip joint off the strip the drunken guy on his last fling is throwing dollars at the perky-breasted gal dancing on the pole. She's telling him the money's so good she commutes from the West Coast.

TYPICAL LAS VEGAN

Your typical Las Vegan loves this city, as they've chosen to live here, coming from other towns in the US and beyond. The population loves its sport (particularly golf and tennis) and is oblivious to the tourist crowds on the strip, avoiding them by living and hanging out downtown, and so experiencing a very different lifestyle (despite many working in the casinos and hotels of the strip) from that enjoyed by most visitors to the city.

DEFINING EXPERIENCE

Strolling down the strip through the animated crowds in the summer evening heat, wandering from Venice (the Venetian Hotel) to Polynesia (the Mirage Hotel, complete with on-site erupting volcano) to Paris (the Paris-Las Vegas Hotel) to New York (New York-New York) to Egypt (the Luxor Hotel) in the space of half an hour, constantly being amazed at what an insane place Las Vegas is.

STRENGTHS

- 24-hour gambling and drinking
- Huge choice of hotels, all with their own ridiculous theme
- Delicious food and extraordinarily attentive service
- No need to worry about being rained out

WEAKNESSES

- Sometimes you just want some normality and a little less neon
- The need to take a taxi almost everywhere
- The heat makes staying in an air-conditioned casino such an attractive idea
- There's nothing to make you feel you should be having anything but fun…

GOLD STAR

There's only one reason for Vegas being here – it's the undisputed gambling capital of the world, with more choice and more casinos than anywhere else on earth.

STARRING ROLE IN...

- *Viva Las Vegas* (1964)
- *Rain Man* (1988)
- *Leaving Las Vegas* (1995)
- *Casino* (1995)
- *Oceans Eleven* (1960 and 2001)

IMPORT

- Gamblers from all over the world
- Nicolas Cage (he's made more films here than anywhere else)
- Water
- Divas on their last legs (Liza, Céline, Elton)

EXPORT

- Andre Agassi
- Broke gamblers
- The Killers
- Newlyweds

SEE the incredible dancing fountains outside the Bellagio Hotel.

EAT in vast hotel buffets – the only way Vegas can realistically feed its teeming thousands of hungry gamblers.

DRINK for free as you play – just grab a cocktail waitress and don't forget to tip.

DO get married to someone you barely know at short notice in one of the hilarious chapels on the strip.

WATCH the neon-clad city from the sky by ascending the Stratosphere at night.

BUY more chips, regularly…and remember, the house always wins.

AFTER DARK bring your sunglasses out with you to deal with all the fabulous neon.

URBAN MYTH

It's actually a myth that you can pitch up at any chapel in Las Vegas and get married there and then. You need to go first to the Clark County Court House and obtain a marriage licence. The courthouse is open daily, but only until midnight, so it's not always plain sailing and you can't just drunkenly arrive at the chapel and demand an instant union.

A WOMAN SQUINTS AT A CELEBRATION OF LOSAR, THE TIBETAN NEW YEAR.
Photographer: Maria Stenzel / Getty Images

Lhasa

NAME: LHASA

NICKNAME: HOLY CITY; SUNLIGHT CITY

DATE OF BIRTH: 7TH CENTURY; WHEN LOCAL RULER SONGSTEN GAMPO MADE LHASA HIS CAPITAL

ADDRESS: TIBET (MAP 5, H2)

HEIGHT: 3595M

SIZE: 30,000 SQ KM

POPULATION: 257,000

LONELY PLANET RANKING: 089

The resilient heart of a nation and a city of unique heritage, Lhasa sits literally on the top of the world, seen by many as the homeland and jewel in the crown of Buddhism.

ANATOMY

The city divides clearly into a western (Chinese) section and an eastern (Tibetan) section. The Chinese side holds most of Lhasa's upmarket accommodation options, along with Chinese restaurants, bars and the Nepali consulate. The Tibetan eastern end of town is more colourful and has all the budget and midrange accommodation popular with independent travellers. The main drag is the east to west–running Dekyi Nub Lam, which then becomes Dekyi Shar Lam in the east of town (in Tibetan, *nub* means west and *shar* means east). Jokhang Temple and Barkhor Sq are in between Dekyi Shar Lam and Chingdröl Shar Lam (Jiangsu Lu) and are connected to these two main roads by the Tibetan quarter – a web of winding alleyways lined with the whitewashed façades of traditional Tibetan homes. Bicycle is without a doubt the best way to get around (once you have acclimatised to the altitude). Otherwise, you'll find privately run minibuses are frequent on Dekyi Shar Lam and taxis are plentiful.

PEOPLE

The official figures for Lhasa's population are 87% Tibetan and just under 12% Han Chinese, though these are generally discounted by all except the Chinese government, which released them. More realistic estimates put the percentage closer to 50/50. The population of the city before the Chinese takeover was less than 30,000 and the recent influx of Han Chinese has been nicknamed 'China's second invasion'. There is also a 2000-strong Islamic community, based mostly in the Muslim Quarter.

TYPICAL LHASAN

Understanding the basics of Buddhism is essential in understanding any Tibetan and the citizens of Lhasa even more so. They are gentle in spirit, deeply religious and quietly unshakable in their resolve. Though they have lost so much to outside influence, they remain remarkably open and generous.

DEFINING EXPERIENCE

Following the flow of pilgrims around the Barkhor circuit with sustenance stops at nearby restaurants for *momos* (Tibetan dumplings) washed down with steaming yak-butter tea.

STRENGTHS

- ◢ Potala, the deserted citadel of the Dalai Lama
- ◢ Jokhang and its shrines
- ◢ Walking tours
- ◢ The nearby Drepung Monastery
- ◢ Nam-tso Restaurant
- ◢ Buddhist history
- ◢ Tibet Museum
- ◢ Barkhor Sq
- ◢ A plethora of chapels
- ◢ The Norbulingka

WEAKNESSES

- ◢ Chinese cultural dominance
- ◢ Altitude sickness
- ◢ Modernisation
- ◢ Chinese propaganda
- ◢ Limited cuisine

GOLD STAR

To the Tibetans – for holding tight to what's left of Tibetan cultural and religious heritage after half a century of brutal and restrictive Chinese rule.

STARRING ROLE IN...

- ◢ *Windhorse* (1998)

IMPORT

- ◢ Buddhism
- ◢ Chinese culture
- ◢ Pilgrims

EXPORT

- ◢ Lamas in exile
- ◢ Buddhist teachers and teachings
- ◢ Traditional handicrafts
- ◢ Yak hair and leather

SEE the Potala, the deserted citadel of the Dalai Lamas.

EAT the local fare such as *momos*, *thugpa* (soup) and *shemdre* (potatoes and yak meat) at the Pentoc Tibetan Restaurant.

DRINK *bö cha* (Tibetan yak-butter tea).

DO cycle to the Drepung Monastery for an afternoon of exploring what remains of its 6th-century history.

WATCH traditional performances at the Tibetan Dance & Drama Theatre.

BUY a prayer wheel from one of the many stalls lining the Barkhor circuit.

AFTER DARK try the Music Kitchen or any of the other bars near the Lhasa Hotel for a good night out.

URBAN MYTH

It was Princess Wencheng, the Chinese wife of King Songtsen Gampo, who divined the presence of a vast, supine demoness whose body straddled all the high plateau. Through Chinese geomantic calculations she established that the heart of the demoness lay beneath a lake in the centre of Lhasa, while her torso and limbs lay far away in the outer dominions of the high plateau. It was decided that the demoness would have to be pinned down. The first task was to drain the lake in Lhasa of its water (read lifeblood of the demoness) and build a central temple that would replace her heart with a Buddhist heart. The temple built there was the Jokhang. A stake through the heart was not enough to put a demoness of this size out of action, however, and a series of lesser temples, in three concentric rings, were conceived to pin the extremities of the demoness forever.

PILGRIMS COMPLETE THEIR RITUAL CIRCUMAMBULATION OF JOKHANG MONASTERY.
Photographer: Angelo Cavalli / Getty Images

NOVICE MONKS AT DREPUNG MONASTERY CROWD IN FOR A GROUP SHOT.
Photographer: Dennis Cox / Alamy

SUNBEAMS FILTER INTO THE RUSTIC SLEEPING QUARTERS OF A MONASTERY NEAR THE CITY.
Photographer: Hannah Levy / LPI

Lisbon is as romantic as Paris, as fun as Madrid, as laid-back as Rome, but small enough to fit into their handbags.

ANATOMY

Lisbon sits atop seven hills on the northern side of Portugal's finest natural harbour, the wide mouth of the Rio Tejo (Tagus River). On each hill is a castle, church or stunning *miradouro* (viewpoint). Many of the medieval buildings were destroyed in a huge earthquake in 1755 and the city was rebuilt in a baroque style along a formal grid. The ancient mazelike Alfama district, relatively unscathed, still exists near the narrow streets of the Bairro Alto's *fin-de-siècle* decadence with snaking cobbled streets. Trams, both very old and very new, and funiculars exist alongside an extensive metro system.

PEOPLE

Portugal's population breakdown has seen dramatic changes in the last few decades. The country's emigration rate has long been among Europe's highest, but its immigration rate shot up during the mid-1970s when around one million African *retornados* (refugees) immigrated from former Portuguese colonies. They have especially big communities in Lisbon. Another influx resulting from Portugal's empire building is of Brazilians. There's a small resident Roma (formerly known as Gypsies) population and there are also increasing numbers of immigrant workers from central and Eastern Europe.

TYPICAL LISBONITE

Lisbonites, like most Portuguese, return to home villages in August, drawn by family ties and a longing for home. They are known to suffer bouts of *saudade*, a particularly Portuguese melancholia, or longing, for something past. The city and its inhabitants have benefited greatly from EU membership, with floods of foreign investment and an overhaul of the city centre. Despite this, recent studies have declared the Portuguese the laziest people and heaviest drinkers in Europe. Lisbonites will have none of it.

Lisbon

VITAL STATISTICS

NAME: LISBON

DATE OF BIRTH: 1000 BC; WHEN THE PHOENICIANS FIRST SETTLED HERE

ADDRESS: PORTUGAL (MAP 3, B15)

HEIGHT: 77M

SIZE: 87 SQ KM

POPULATION: 565,000 (CITY); 2.6 MILLION (METRO AREA)

LONELY PLANET RANKING: 050

ONE OF LISBON'S TRADEMARK TRAMS PREPARES TO POUNCE FROM A NARROW STREET CORNER.
Photographer: Bruno Morandi / Photolibrary

DEFINING EXPERIENCE

Wandering Baixa (Lower Town), Lisbon's heartbeat, taking a tram to Belém for a custard tart, then spending the afternoon with art and antiquities at the Museu Calouste Gulbenkian before choosing from an eclectic range of restaurants in Bairro Alto (some as big as a dining room).

STRENGTHS

- ◢ The Lisbon metro – an art gallery in itself
- ◢ *Azulejos* – the decorative glazed tiles found everywhere
- ◢ Mosteiro dos Jerónimos
- ◢ Torre de Belém
- ◢ Royal Palaces
- ◢ Mammoth baroque Palacio Nacional de Mafra
- ◢ Gare do Oriente
- ◢ 17km-long Ponte de Vasco da Gama
- ◢ African jazz scene
- ◢ Laid-back clubs
- ◢ Dining late
- ◢ Custard tarts
- ◢ Rickety trams
- ◢ Cobblestone streets

WEAKNESSES

- ◢ The rivalry between Cape Verdean and Angolan gangs
- ◢ *Bacalhau* (salt cod) – there is such a thing as too much
- ◢ Mateus Rosé

GOLD STAR

A city in thrall to its past, Lisbon has baroque cafés, 1960s diners, velvet-lined bars and Art Deco bakeries. This city has not been renovated into oblivion.

STARRING ROLE IN...

- ◢ *The Lisbon Story* (1994)
- ◢ *The Book of Disquiet* by Fernando Pessoa
- ◢ *The Last Kabbalist of Lisbon* (2000)
- ◢ *A Small Death in Lisbon* by Robert Wilson
- ◢ *Caitaes de Abril* (April Captains, 2000)
- ◢ *Requiem* by Antonio Tabucchi

IMPORT

- ◢ EU funds
- ◢ Citizens of its former colonies
- ◢ Investment money from John Malkovich
- ◢ Chillies
- ◢ Gold from South America

EXPORT

- ◢ Prince Henry the Navigator
- ◢ Vasco da Gama
- ◢ Catherine of Bragança
- ◢ Tea to the rest of Europe
- ◢ Five million people to Brazil from 1884 to 1963
- ◢ Painter Paula Rego
- ◢ Billions of natural cork bottle-stoppers each year
- ◢ Nobel prize–winning Author José Saramago
- ◢ The films of Manoel de Oliveira

SEE the central city from the low vantage point of 45m – the frilly, wrought-iron 19th-century oddity, the Elevador de Santa Justa.

EAT custard tarts from a secret recipe – they taste as though made by angels – at Pasteis de Belém.

DRINK *vinho verde* (green wine) – light, crisp dry wine (Portugal's signature wine).

DO take a stroll through Alfama, starting on tram No 28 to Miradoura da Senhora do Monte to avoid the uphill slog.

WATCH free Sunday-morning music and dance performances at Centro Cultural de Belém.

BUY *azulejos* and ceramics, sold all over, but check out styles first at the Museu Nacional do Azulejo.

AFTER DARK seek out the *fado* (Portuguese blues) experience in Bairro Alto or Alfama.

URBAN MYTH

The Portuguese don't actually drink much port – it's more of an English drop. The foreigners from the north were instrumental in the development of this wine, which is still commonly trod by human foot, and they've always been its chief market.

SIMPLE ELEGANCE CHARACTERISES BAYSIDE BUILDINGS IN A CITY OF AMAZING ARCHITECTURAL DIVERSITY.
Photographer: Ludovic Maisant / Corbis

TOWEL SPACE IS AT A PREMIUM ON PRAIA DA CONCEIÇÃO, A POPULAR CITY BEACH.
Photographer: Julia Wilkinson / LPI

AN ELDERLY LISBONITE RESTS AT THE WINDOW OF HER HOUSE IN BAIRRO ALTO.
Photographer: Doug Scott / Photolibrary

CORREIO

UNIFORMED STUDENTS STRIKE A POSE OUTSIDE THE TOWN'S EPONYMOUS SCHOOL.
Photographer: Dave Bartruff / Corbis

Africa's adventure capital, the humble, dusty city of Livingstone is only a stone's throw from the magnificent Victoria Falls, where bungee-jumping, white-water rafting and abseiling end in sunset booze cruises on the mighty Zambezi.

ANATOMY

Livingstone lies only 11km north of one of the world's greatest natural wonders: the Victoria Falls. Mosi-oa-Tunya Rd is the city's tourist mecca, with shops, banks, *bureaux de change*, a post office, the Zamtel public-phone office and, most importantly, travel and tour agents. South of the town centre is Livingstone's main produce market (Maramba Township). Past the train station the town fizzles out but the trail of minibuses and taxis heading south lead to the Zambezi River, Victoria Falls and the Zambia–Zimbabwe border.

PEOPLE

More than half of Zambia's population lives in urban areas such as Livingstone, which lies on the border of the traditional territories of the Lozi, Tonga and Leya peoples. Although the main language group and people are Lozi, English is the official language and widely spoken due to Livingstone having become a major hub for travellers in southern Africa. The dominant religion is Christianity, though the majority also adhere to the traditional Zambian beliefs.

TYPICAL LIVINGSTONIAN

If Zambians have a reputation for being laid-back, Livingstonians are decidedly tranquil. They are notoriously friendly and easy-going and live happily in the present. They are blasé and indifferent to the buzz and hype of the falls and more interested in what tourism has done for Livingstone than what Livingstone has done for the tourist. They party hard and won't begrudge you a space on the dance floor. They are both colonial and very African.

Livingstone

VITAL STATISTICS

NAME: LIVINGSTONE

NICKNAME: MARAMBA

DATE OF BIRTH: 1905; FOLLOWING THE COMPLETION OF THE RAILWAY BRIDGE ACROSS THE ZAMBEZI RIVER

ADDRESS: ZAMBIA (MAP 2, I21)

HEIGHT: 985M

POPULATION: 97,000

LONELY PLANET RANKING: 161

A STATUE OF DR LIVINGSTONE (WE PRESUME), KEEPING WATCH OVER VICTORIA FALLS.
Photographer: Adrian Arbib / Network Photographers // Alamy

THE VICTORIA FALLS BRIDGE'S BUNGY-JUMP STATION COMMANDS A SPECTACULAR VIEW OF THE WATERFALL.
Photographer: Andrew Woodley / Network Photographers / Alamy

GRUBBY HANDS GET CLEANED UP BEFORE MEAL TIME.
Photographer: Jenny Matthews / Network Photographers / Alamy

DEFINING EXPERIENCE

Waking up in a lush oasis, having a light breakfast with strangers discussing spine-tingling adventures, then sharing a minibus to the adrenaline junkie's paradise, bungee-jumping into the Batoka George, and white-water rafting through the seething turmoil that is the Zambezi.

STRENGTHS

- Victoria Falls
- Gateway to Zambia's wildlife parks
- Vast array of activities
- Laid-back atmosphere
- Tourist-friendly layout
- A raw-edged Africa
- Stone's throw from Zimbabwe
- Livingstone Museum
- Mukuni Village
- Wooden sculpture
- Great backpacker accommodation

WEAKNESSES

- Regular muggings between Livingstone and Victoria Falls
- Touts
- Rougher-than-usual wilderness
- It-can-wait attitude
- Losing capital-city status (to Lusaka)

GOLD STAR

Victoria Falls on the Zambezi River – the mesmerising waterfall spans nearly 2km, drops a dramatic 100m over a cliff and accommodates an amazing range of activities, from the tranquil to the terrifying.

STARRING ROLE IN...

- *Stanley and Livingstone* (1939)

IMPORT

- Adventure seekers
- David Livingstone
- Christianity
- Tourism
- English
- US dollar
- Victorian-era names
- Pizza

EXPORT

- Safaris
- Tours
- Batik fabrics
- Wooden sculptures
- Locally made furniture
- Falls activity T-shirts
- Visas

SEE the natural wonders of the Victoria Falls section of Mosi-oa-Tunya National Park.

EAT the Friday barbecue at Hippo's open-air restaurant.

DRINK as much as you can handle on a sunset booze cruise on the Zambezi.

DO a heart-stopping gorge swing over Batoka Gorge.

WATCH traditional dance performances from Zambia and neighbouring countries at Falls Craft Village.

BUY carved-wood pieces by the Leya people at Mukuni Village craft market.

AFTER DARK rock to the roof with Western hits and Congo rumba at the loud and gregarious Ravestone.

URBAN MYTH

Before being asked that famous question ('Dr Livingstone, I presume?'), British explorer David Livingstone travelled up the Zambezi River. It was the 1850s and Livingstone hoped to introduce Christianity and commerce to combat the horrors of the slave trade. In 1855 local people showed him a magnificent waterfall of torrents of water thundering into the Zambezi, which Livingstone later described as 'the ceaseless roar of the cataract, with the perpetual flow, as if pouring forth from the hand of the Almighty'. This natural wonder was called 'Mosi-oa-Tunya' (smoke that thunders). To Dr Livingstone, however, Victoria Falls seemed a more appropriate name, and Victoria Falls it remains.

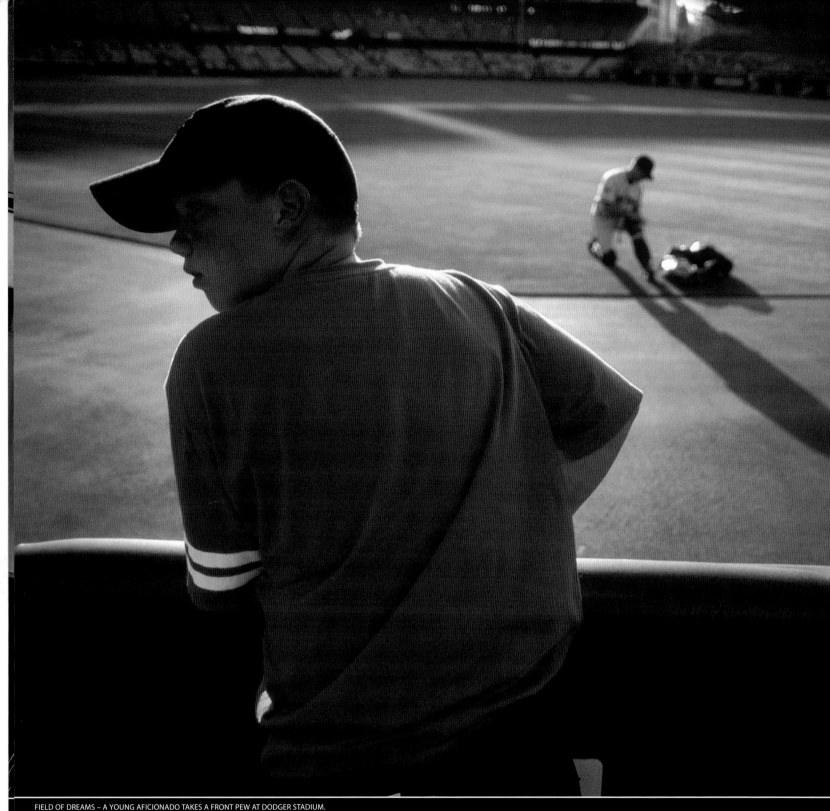

FIELD OF DREAMS – A YOUNG AFICIONADO TAKES A FRONT PEW AT DODGER STADIUM.
Photographer: Ray Laskowitz / LPI

Los Angeles

Los Angeles may be the world capital of myth-making but it thrives beyond its own highly constructed clichés with a mosaic of cultures and a beautiful setting between desert and sea.

ANATOMY

Los Angeles, in fact an enormous concatenation of independent cities, stretches down the Pacific coast, and is sandwiched inland by the Santa Monica and San Gabriel Mountains. Inland, the skyscrapers of Downtown are the only recognisable centre. East LA, a Latino-dominated area, edges against Downtown, as do the historically African-American neighbourhoods of South Central and Compton. Westward are iconic Hollywood, West Hollywood, Bel Air and Beverly Hills. The car is king, but there is a large bus and limited light-rail network.

PEOPLE

Angelinos are a diverse lot. Almost half the population are Hispanic by birth or heritage, and Spanish is spoken almost as widely as English. There is a fast-growing Asian and Pacific Islander population, who join significant African-American and Native American communities.

TYPICAL ANGELINO

Angelinos don't care what the world thinks of them (narcissistic, vapid, flaky and superficial), or their city (dystopian, ugly, soulless) because they are too busy keeping fit, self-actualising, working the room, or just out there enjoying the place. They will admit to their notoriety for aggression behind the wheel, and are all too aware of the appalling economic disparities on display (and the simmering tensions it can generate), but that's because they are generally a tolerant, open-minded and cosmopolitan lot.

DEFINING EXPERIENCE

Running along the beach, then off to morning service at a happening little nondenominational (spirituality is on the list of things to improve this year), grabbing some cheddar enchiladas at the Venice Cantina before going to a Lucha Libre match (those wrestler's masks are *so* hot…), stopping by Wordtheatre's reading to check out your actor friend doing Raymond Carver, and then heading home to blog all the latest gossip.

STRENGTHS

- 300-plus days of sunshine per year
- Excellent contemporary-art museums and galleries
- Nuevo-Latino cuisine
- Downtown renewal
- Walt Disney Concert Hall
- LA Metro
- Getting into trouble at the Marmont
- Hollywood Forever Cemetery
- Griffith Park
- David Lynch's online weather report
- Farmers Market
- Midcentury modern furniture on tap
- Las Posadas and other Mexican festivals
- Thriving alternative art scene
- Jacarandas in bloom
- Kilometres of beaches
- Kelly Wearstler's OTT interiors
- Vibrant Latino culture

WEAKNESSES

- June gloom
- Sprawl
- Cooler-than-thou bouncers and shop assistants
- Stop-and-go freeways
- Persisting racial inequality
- Bad pizza
- Aggressive surfers
- Gang violence
- New York 'transplants' who do nothing but criticise
- San Andreas fault line

GOLD STAR

Built environment – for fans of modernist architecture, LA is the most innovative and diverse city in the USA.

STARRING ROLE IN...

- *Double Indemnity* (1944)
- *The Big Sleep* (1946)
- *Sunset Boulevard* (1950)
- *Rebel without a Cause* (1955)
- *Touch of Evil* (1958)
- *Point Blank* (1967)
- *Chinatown* (1974)
- *Barfly* (1987)
- *La Bamba* (1987)
- *Boyz n the Hood* (1991)
- *The Player* (1992)
- *Short Cuts* (1993)
- *LA Story* (1991)
- *Pulp Fiction* (1994)
- *LA Confidential* (1997)
- *Mulholland Drive* (2001)
- *Crash* (2004)

IMPORT

- Eucalypts
- Actors
- Film and TV industry workers
- Charles and Ray Eames
- Igor Stravinsky
- Water
- Mexican domestic labourers
- William Faulkner
- F Scott Fitzgerald
- Bertolt Brecht
- Richard Neutra
- Chet Baker
- Mike Davis

EXPORT

- Film
- TV
- Porn
- Surf and skate culture
- McDonald's
- The word 'smog'
- Charles Bukowski
- San Pedro punk (Minutemen et al)
- Bikram yoga teachers
- Art Pepper
- Cobb salad
- NWA
- California rolls *(kashu-maki)*
- MFK Fisher
- Beach Boys

SEE nature *and* culture: the mountain and sea views plus David Hockney's Californian scenes at Richard Meier's glorious Getty Center.

EAT meat and drink vodka, Atkins-style, in the rococo-camp surrounds of the Lincoln Steakhouse Americana, Santa Monica.

DRINK an apple martini holed up in a poolside pleasure pod on the rooftop at the Standard Downtown.

DO a Friday-night yoga session with live DJs at Bala Yoga on La Brea, the ultimate in LA chill.

WATCH a Hollywood blockbuster in Hollywood, at the hipster-favoured ArcLight on Sunset Boulevard.

BUY preloved rock-and-roll lifestyle clothing – perhaps an ultra-rare Ziggy Stardust T-shirt – from Lo-Fi in West Hollywood.

AFTER DARK entertain or be entertained by Marty and Elayne at the Dresden Room in Los Feliz.

URBAN MYTH

Kenneth Anger's 'delicious box of poisoned bonbons', *Hollywood Babylon* dishes the dirt on the world's most self-mythologising city, purporting to uncover the seedier side of LA's entertainment industry. From the Fatty Arbuckle rape trial in the '20s and Errol Flynn's predilection for underage girls to Marilyn Monroe's death and the Manson murders, the book is full of half-truths, unsubstantiated rumour and outright fiction, but has gone on to inspire a whole genre of ironically tabloid-style 'LA uncovered' books.

THE SURF-INSPIRED ARCHITECTURE OF THE GETTY CENTER.
Photographer: Richard Cummins / LPI

SURFER DUDES CARVE UP THE WEEKEND WAVES WITH PANACHE.
Photographer: David Peevers / LPI

A CHEVY SHAKES ITS BOOTY AT A CAR DANCE-OFF WHERE VEHICLES WITH HYDRAULIC AXLES SHIMMY FOR SHOW.
Photographer: Robert Yager / Getty Images

Luang Prabang

VITAL STATISTICS

NAME: LUANG PRABANG

DATE OF BIRTH: 1512; WHEN THE CITY-STATE OF MUANG XIENG THONG (CITY OF GOLD) BECAME KNOWN AS LUANG (GREAT OR ROYAL) PHABANG (PRABANG)

ADDRESS: LAOS (MAP 5, L6)

HEIGHT: 287M

POPULATION: 103,000

LONELY PLANET RANKING: 054

Encircled by mountains and situated at the confluence of the Khan and Mekong Rivers, the city's stunning mix of gleaming temple roofs, crumbling French provincial architecture and multiethnic inhabitants is enthralling.

ANATOMY

Luang Prabang is dominated by Phu Si, a large hill near the middle of the peninsula formed by the confluence of the two rivers. Most of the longer roadways through Luang Prabang parallel the river. Shorter roads – once mere footpaths – bisect the larger roads and lead to the riverbanks, serving as dividing lines between different villages. Most of the historic temples are located between Phu Si and the Mekong, while the trading district lies to the south of the hill. The airport, speedboat landing and northern bus terminal are all northeast of the city, while the southern bus terminal and Sainyabuli terminal are to the southwest. Most of the town is accessible on foot and you can catch *jumbos* (motorised three-wheeled taxis).

PEOPLE

Lao is the official language, but Lao dialects (closely related to Thai) are also spoken, as are French and English. Sixty percent of the population is Buddhist, with 40% made up of animist and spirit cults.

TYPICAL LUANG PRABANG CITIZEN

Laid-back, relaxed, cruisey, slow paced, serene, unfussed and easy-going, the locals commonly express the notion that 'too much work is bad for your brain' and often say they feel sorry for people who 'think too much'. They avoid any undue psychological stress, choosing not to participate in any activity, whether work or play, unless it contains an element of *múan* (fun).

DEFINING EXPERIENCE

A morning spent playing *kátâw* (a game with a cane ball) with the locals, cruising through scenic villages on a motorcycle to the stunning Tat Kuang Si waterfalls and indulging in a soothing massage at the Lao Red Cross, before enjoying the tasteful chinoiserie décor and a sumptuous dinner of Lao, Thai and Pacific Rim cuisine at one of Luang Prabang's best restaurants, the Apsara.

STRENGTHS

- Gilded temple roofs
- Multiethnic marketplaces
- The ubiquitous Beer Lao
- Charming French colonial architecture
- The famous Pak Ou caves, crammed with images of the Buddha in all styles and sizes
- The wide, many-tiered waterfall of Tat Kuang Si, tumbling over limestone formations into a series of cool, turquoise pools
- Peaceful Buddhist traditions
- Lao women's more-or-less equal status in the workforce, inheritance, land ownership and so on
- Low cost of living/lazing
- Picturesque riverside setting
- The quaint Royal Palace Museum
- Trekking, rafting and cycling

WEAKNESSES

- Smoke from slash-and-burn agriculture in the surrounding mountains, causing red, watery eyes and breathing difficulties
- Crack-of-dawn roosters
- The high number of serious speedboat accidents, including fatalities, on the rivers

GOLD STAR

The traditional herbal sauna and/or hour-long Swedish-Lao massage at the Lao Red Cross.

STARRING ROLE IN...

- Short story 'The Boatman's Gift' by Pamela Michael
- *Het Bun Dai Bun: Laos Sacred Rituals of Luang Prabang* by Hans Georg Berger

IMPORT

- Theravada Buddhism
- French bread and pastries
- UXO (unexploded ordnance), which litters northeastern Laos and kills around 130 people each year
- *Nâm pạa* (a thin sauce of fermented anchovies from Thailand)
- Chinese and Vietnamese food

EXPORT

- Poached animals
- Teak and other hardwoods
- Garments
- Wood products
- Coffee
- Electricity
- Tin

SEE Wat Xieng Thong, Luang Prabang's most magnificent temple.

EAT *phák nâm* (a delicious watercress that's unique to Luang Prabang) and *khào nîaw* (the ubiquitous sticky rice).

DRINK *khào kam* – a local red, sweet, slightly fizzy wine made from sticky rice.

DO a walking tour around Luang Prabang's northeastern quarter to take in most of the historic attractions and sightseeing spots.

WATCH the boat races during Bun Awk Phansa (the End of the Rains Retreat) in October.

WATCH local performers put on a show that includes a *bqasĭi* (spirit-blessing) ceremony, traditional dance and folk music at the Royal Theatre.

BUY beautiful handmade *săa* (mulberry bark) paper, naturally dyed house-woven Lao silk and cotton, handcrafted silverware, silk-lined cushions and embroidered rice mats.

AFTER DARK join a young Lao crowd dancing to bands playing Lao and Thai pop or DJs spinning rap and hip-hop in the cavernous club of Dao Fah.

URBAN MYTH

Inside the Royal Palace Museum (Ho Kham), a Buddha statue cast of a gold, silver and bronze alloy stands 83cm tall and is said to weigh 53.4kg. According to legend, the image was cast around the 1st century AD in Sri Lanka and later presented to Khmer King Phaya Sirichantha, who in turn gave it to King Fa Ngum in 1359 as a Buddhist legitimiser of Lao sovereignty. The Siamese twice carried off the image to Thailand (in 1779 and 1827) but it was finally restored to Lao hands by King Mongkut (Rama IV) in 1867. Persistent rumours claim that the image on display is a copy and that the original is stored in a vault either in Vientiane or Moscow. The 'real' one supposedly features a bit of gold leaf over the eyes and a hole drilled through one ankle.

GOTCHA! A CHEEKY CHILD PICKS A WATER FIGHT DURING CELEBRATIONS FOR THE LAO NEW YEAR.
Photographer: Chris Sattlberger / Panos Pictures

A NOVICE MONK WITH A BIG GRIN TELLS YOU WHAT THE WORD IS.
Photographer: Jamie Marshall / Tribaleye Images / Alamy

ANOTHER HEAVENLY DAY AT WAT XIENG THONG, LUANG PRABANG'S MOST FAMOUS TEMPLE.
Photographer: Bill Wassman / LPI

ENTHUSIASTS WATCH A NIGHT MATCH OF PALENQUE, A POPULAR BOWLING GAME SIMILAR TO BOULES.
Photographer: Peter William Thornton / LPI

Lübeck

VITAL STATISTICS

NAME: LÜBECK

DATE OF BIRTH: AD 1000; WHEN THE WENDS ESTABLISHED A ROYAL SEAT CALLED LIUBICE

ADDRESS: GERMANY (MAP 3, J6)

HEIGHT: 17M

POPULATION: 214,000

LONELY PLANET RANKING: 131

Lübeck's medieval architecture is as mouth-watering as its marzipan, and for a relatively small city it packs a powerful punch – it's a Unesco World Heritage site and in days gone by its famous Holstentor (gate) used to grace the DM50 note.

ANATOMY

The twin, pointy-roofed circular towers of the Holstentor form the main entry to Lübeck's *Altstadt* (old town) on the western side. The northern and eastern parts of the *Altstadt* belonged to craftspeople in the Middle Ages. Now this area is characterised by small low-rise homes in *Höfe* (courtyards) that are accessed by little *Gänge* (walkways) from the street. Not far from the Holstentor is the *Markt* (marketplace), where you'll find the *Rathaus* (town hall) and the Marienkirche, Germany's third-largest church. The pedestrian-ised shopping area leads off from here. The whole of the *Altstadt* is surrounded by the Trave River and its canals. Travemunde ferry port is 16km from the *Altstadt*. Buses and trains service the city.

PEOPLE

Lübeck still calls itself a Hanseatic city, referring to the commanding medieval Hanseatic League that united more than 150 merchant cities in an 'association'. It may now be a provincial city, but the people of Lübeck have powerful roots.

TYPICAL LÜBECK CITIZEN

Lübeck is the main attraction for visitors to Schleswig-Holstein, Germany's answer to the Côte d'Azur (weather aside), and inhabitants of Lübeck escape the crowds by sailing to islands offshore and relaxing on the attractive beaches along the coast. The city may be old and picturesque, but it also hums with life, particularly in the warm and inviting bars that are popular with the locals. The people also enjoy culture and the city has con-nections to two Nobel prize-winning authors – Thomas Mann, who was born in Lübeck in 1875, and Günter Grass, who is a current resident.

DEFINING EXPERIENCE

Musing on creative genius in the Günter Grass-Haus, then seeking inspiration for your novel among the fairy-tale architecture of the *Altstadt*, before taking the kids to the *Marionettentheater* (puppet theatre).

STRENGTHS

- Marzipan
- Holstentor
- Medieval merchant's homes
- 1000 historical buildings
- Hanseatic League
- Marienkirche and its shattered church bells, now a peace memorial
- *Rathaus*
- Museum für Puppentheater
- Literary tradition
- Café Niederegger
- Füchtingshof and Glandorps Gang
- Nearby beaches
- Boat trips through the canals
- Gothmund, a charming fishers' village

WEAKNESSES

- Lots of temptation for those on a diet
- Cold winds and dark clouds (even in summer)

GOLD STAR

Marzipan – don't you just love those chocolate-covered marzipan delights…

STARRING ROLE IN...

- *The Buddenbrooks* by Thomas Mann
- *Holstentor* by Andy Warhol

IMPORT

- Günter Grass
- Discerning tourists

EXPORT

- Willy Brandt
- Thomas Mann
- Horst Frank
- Marzipan

SEE the magical city gate, Holstentor, and imagine letting down your Rapunzel hair from the circular towers.

EAT modern German cuisine in Markgraf, a perfectly elegant historic restaurant.

DRINK home-brewed beer in Brauberger, which has made and served its own since 1225.

DO a boat tour of the canals that surround the *Altstadt* – well, with all that water you have to really, don't you?

WATCH a spellbinding organ concert in the Marienkirche, home to the world's largest mechanical organ.

BUY some of that lovely sweet stuff at Café Niederegger – and, yes, we're talking about marzipan.

AFTER DARK watch a play in the Art Nouveau Theater Lübeck.

URBAN MYTH

The Hanseatic League is a legendary part of Lübeck's history. Its initial aim was to protect shipping and trade in the North Sea and Baltic regions, but as more and more members signed up its sheer size made it a powerful political force in Europe. During meetings in Lübeck, the league effec-tively dictated policy by fixing prices of commodities such as grain, fur and ore or threatening to withhold trad-ing privileges. It was known to bribe foreign officials and in 1368 it even went to war with Denmark after being challenged by Danish King Vlademar IV for control of the south-western Baltic. In general it was a positive force, though, and provided stability and prosperity to members. In the 16th century the league started to erode and the 17th-century Thirty Years' War was the final nail in the cof-fin. Bremen, Hamburg and Lübeck still call themselves Hanseatic cities despite no meeting of the league taking place since 1669.

THE VIEW FROM ABOVE REVEALS HOW LÜBECK'S CATHEDRAL ANCHORS THE OLD TOWN.
Photographer: Manfred Gottschalk / LPI

A DARK FIGURE CONTEMPLATES THE LIGHT SIDE AS SUN SETS ON HEILIGEN-GEIST-HOSPITAL.
Photographer: Martin Lladó / LPI

A MANNEQUIN COOLLY AWAITS FINAL SALE.
Photographer: Martin Lladó / LPI

Luxembourg City

VITAL STATISTICS

NAME: LUXEMBOURG CITY

DATE OF BIRTH: AD 963; WHEN COUNT SIGEFROID OF ARDENNES ERECTED A CASTLE HERE

ADDRESS: LUXEMBOURG (MAP 3, H9)

HEIGHT: 330M

POPULATION: 90,000

LONELY PLANET RANKING: 179

The entire ancient core of this 1000-year-old city has been preserved and provides spectacular vistas over lush parklands and atmospheric old quarters, spanned by a series of imposing bridges.

ANATOMY

The Alzette River passes through Luxembourg City and gives the capital its geographic charm. A medieval street plan mixes with 18th- and 19th-century buildings in the Old Town. The city's central area is divided by gorges; the lower town is at the base of the Old Town's Bock fortifications. Walking is the best way to get around.

PEOPLE

Lëtzebuergesch, closely related to German, was proclaimed the national language in 1984. French and German are also official languages. A whopping 97% of the population is Roman Catholic. The population is about 30% foreigners, predominantly Italian and Portuguese, the highest ratio of any EU country.

TYPICAL LUXEMBOURGER

Luxembourgers are wealthy; the country's per-capita GDP is one of the word's highest and the standard of living consistently rates among the best. Luxembourgers are likely to work in the new service-based economy, as the country has morphed from an industrial producer by wooing big spenders from abroad with favourable banking and taxation laws. Luxembourgers are a confident lot. Their motto? *'Mir wëlle bleiwe wat mir sin'* (We want to remain what we are.)

DEFINING EXPERIENCE

Wandering the pedestrianised heart of the Old Town, investigating history and art in the new Musée National d'Histoire et d'Art, delving into the dark Bock Casemates and taking the lift (elevator) carved into the rock at Plateau du St Esprit to Grund for an apéritif before returning to the Chemin de la Corniche and dining outside for a fabulous view.

STRENGTHS

- Place d'Armes
- Musée National d'Histoire et d'Art
- Chemin de la Corniche
- Breedewee
- The equality of three official languages: French, German and Lëtzebuergesch

WEAKNESSES

- Conservative attitudes
- Very Eurocentric
- Eurocratic

GOLD STAR

With its impressive state-of-the-art museums, its Moorish Palais Grand-Ducal, its cathedral and free lift dug into the rock, the pedestrianised centre is a pleasant way to while away the time. Unesco obviously thought so when it added the fortifications and older quarters of the city to its list of World Heritage sites.

STARRING ROLE IN...

- *The Moon of the Big Winds* by Claudine Muno
- *Aleng* by Cathy Clement

IMPORT

- Employees from neighbouring countries
- The Commission of the European Community
- The Court of Justice of the European Communities
- The General Secretariat of the European Parliament
- The European Investment Bank
- The Nuclear Safety Administration

EXPORT

- Edward Steichen
- Richard Schuman
- Happy personal investors
- Busy Eurocrats

SEE the startling white building of the Musée d'Histoire et d'Art, with collections of prehistoric relics and contemporary local and international artists.

EAT the national dish, *judd mat gaardebounen* (slabs of smoked pork served in a thick, cream-based sauce with broad beans and huge chunks of potato).

DRINK local specialist brews, Gamorinus, a blond beer and Diekirche's Grand Cru.

DO promenade on the Chemin de la Corniche and the pedestrianised heart of the Old Town.

WATCH the city from the terrace of Breedewee, perched high on the Corniche, the French-cuisine restaurant with an unbeatable view.

BUY porcelain from the House of Villeroy & Boch, the world-famous manufacturer of china and crystal.

AFTER DARK try out the techno and house at funky nightclub Didjeridoo in Hollerich.

URBAN MYTH

When the founder of Luxembourg City, Count Sigefroid, married the beautiful Melusina, he was so smitten with his new bride that he agreed to her request to spend one day and one night alone every month. As the years went on, though, the Count's curiosity grew and grew. One day the Count could take it no more – he peeked into Melusina's room. What the Count saw was his wife lying in the bath with a mermaid's tail draped over the edge. Melusina repaid the intrusion by leaping out of the window into the Alzette River. Occasional sightings of mysterious beautiful women with fish tails in the Alzette persist.

A NEON SIGN ON CASINO LUXEMBOURG REMINDS US THAT EVERYTHING WAS NEW ONCE.
Photographer: Martin Lladó / LPI

SUNRISE REFLECTS OFF THE SPIRE OF NEUMÜNSTER ABBEY.
Photographer: Martin Lladó / LPI

CAFÉ-GOERS THRONG PLACE D'ARMES.
Photographer: Richard Elliott / Getty Images

MODERN GLASS ARCHITECTURE BEDECKS PLACE GUILLAUME II.
Photographer: Richard Klune / Corbis

Madrid

VITAL STATISTICS

NAME: MADRID

DATE OF BIRTH: AD 854; WHEN MOHAMMED I, EMIR OF CÓRDOBA, ESTABLISHED A FORTRESS HERE

ADDRESS: SPAIN (MAP 3, D14)

HEIGHT: 660M

SIZE: 607 SQ KM

POPULATION: 3.2 MILLION (CITY); 7 MILLION (METRO AREA)

LONELY PLANET RANKING: 036

Madrid's city centre is the most vibrant, versatile and exciting in Europe – La Movida may technically be over, but you'll be hard-pressed to believe it on a weekend night at 4am.

ANATOMY

Madrid is Europe's highest capital. Most major sights are within walking distance of a very short metro ride. The historic centre features a mix of old and new low-rise buildings and hundreds of plazas, with skyscrapers predominantly in the northern part of the city. Madrid's metro is the quickest and easiest way to get around the city, with *cercanías* (regional trains) and buses close runners-up.

PEOPLE

Many locals aren't from Madrid proper, and often come from all over Spain. Some 600,000 foreign migrants live in the Comunidad de Madrid (the region around Madrid) – more than two-thirds of them in the city. The biggest groups include Ecuadorians, Colombians and Moroccans. In the working-class neighbourhoods of Lavapiés and around, you will encounter North Africans rubbing shoulders with Pakistanis, black Africans and Latin Americans.

TYPICAL MADRILEÑO

Doesn't seem to need any sleep! They might be *gatos* (born-and-bred locals, from the Spanish word for 'cat') or they might be from somewhere else in Spain or North Africa, but they'll work long hours, spend a fortune on keeping a roof over their heads and appreciate that none of it's worth it without regular tapas-fuelled catch-ups with friends and family.

DEFINING EXPERIENCE

Waking up late, having coffee and *churros* (doughnuts), then browsing for trash (maybe treasure) at El Rastro flea market before enjoying a long Sunday lunch in a nearby restaurant, having a rest in El Retiro afterwards, and then waiting to hear if your plans for the evening come to fruition.

STRENGTHS

- Tolerance
- Chatty locals
- Efficient public transport
- Cheap taxis
- Thousands of tapas bars
- Regional Spanish and ethnic cuisine
- Siesta
- Nightlife
- Major art museums
- Los Austrias, La Latina and Lavapiés *barrios* (neighbourhoods)
- Plazas brimming with friends and neighbours catching up
- Green parks in the early morning
- Real Madrid
- Acoustics at Teatro Real

WEAKNESSES

- Endless roadworks
- Noise pollution
- Dog poo on the streets
- Traffic jams at 4am
- Late-night/early-morning rubbish collection
- Packed peak-hour metro trains in summer
- Freezing winters and hellish summers
- Drunken teens on the streets at weekends
- The exodus to Valencia on Friday
- Trying to score Real Madrid tickets

GOLD STAR

Art – Madrid has three blockbuster museums in the Museo del Prado, the Museo Thyssen Bornemisza and the Centro d'Arte Reina Sofía.

STARRING ROLE IN...

- *Abre los Ojos* (Open Your Eyes, 1997)
- *Amantes* (The Lovers, 1991)
- *Live Flesh* (1997)
- *Bad Education* (2003)

IMPORT

- Expensive footballers
- Flamenco
- Asian cuisine
- Picasso's *Guernica*
- Queen Sofía
- Asturian cider
- Galician octopus
- Basque *pintxos* (tapas)
- Navarran wine
- Air-conditioning units

EXPORT

- Gal lip balm
- Colourful fans
- Real Madrid strips
- Lladró porcelain
- Pedro Almodóvar
- Capes
- Tapas
- Bullfighting posters
- Sexy actresses

SEE Picasso's *Guernica* and weep.

EAT tapas every chance you get.

DRINK eye-crossingly potent cocktails in any of the party *barrios*.

DO as the locals do and take it easy for the siesta with a long lunch.

WATCH a soul-stirring flamenco performance at a backstreet *tablao* (flamenco bar).

BUY a beautiful embroidered and fringed silk *mantón* (shawl) from El Corte Ingles.

AFTER DARK try staying awake for as long as the Madrileños – say 6am on weekends.

TRADITIONAL CÓRDOBAN HATS COME IN MANY COLOURS AT A CARNIVAL COSTUMERY NEAR PUERTA DEL SOL.
Photographer: Christopher Wood / LPI

THE STUNNING SYMMETRIES OF THE PATIO DE LOS EVANGELISTAS IN THE PALACE OF SAN LORENZO EL ESCORIAL.
Photographer: Michael George / Impact Photos

URBAN MYTH

Full-blooded Madrileños are often known as *gatos* (cats); a nice image to reflect their city savvy. The term quite appeals to the locals, as it has come to reflect their tendency to crawl around the city like cats until all hours. They say the term was coined as one of Alfonso VI's soldiers artfully scaled the formidable walls of Muslim Magerit (now Madrid) in 1085. 'Look', cried his comrades, 'he moves like a cat!'

NEWSPAPER IN HAND, A LOCAL MAN STROLLS PAST THE ELABORATE TILE WORK ON THE FAÇADE OF A CITY SHOP.
Photographer: Patrick Ward / Corbis

GIGGLING FOR FORGIVENESS – CHEEKY WOMEN PENITENTS AT THE EASTER HOLY WEEK PROCESSIONS.
Photographer: Juan Carlos Rojas / Corbis

Male'

VITAL STATISTICS

NAME: MALE'

DATE OF BIRTH: 2000 BC; EVIDENCE OF THE EARLIEST SETTLEMENT ON MALE'

ADDRESS: THE MALDIVES (MAP 5, C12)

HEIGHT: 2.1M

SIZE: 2KM

POPULATION: 104,000

LONELY PLANET RANKING: 147

ISLAM IS THE DOMINANT RELIGION OF MALE'.
Photographer: Hilarie Kavanagh / Getty Images

The only city in this Indian Ocean archipelago nation, Male' is the transit point for divers and honeymooners: a laid-back stop atop a coral reef.

ANATOMY

Two kilometres long and only one wide, the island is flat but half of it has been reclaimed in the last century as the reef has been filled in with dredged coral to create more land. The atoll is now all filled in, packed to the edges with buildings, roads and a few well-used open spaces, and there's nowhere to go but up – high-rises are growing. Taxis are the way to get around, if not on foot. The increasing number of cars is causing the not unexpected but wholly unwelcome inconvenience of traffic jams. Male' experienced only minor flooding from the tsunami in the Indian Ocean in December 2004. International and domestic flights and boat services around the islands resumed almost immediately after the disaster.

PEOPLE

Male''s citizens are liberal Muslims. They start their families at a young age and population growth is quite high, compounded by urbanisation and by Maldivians flocking to the capital for education and work opportunities. A century ago only 5000 people lived on the much smaller land area of Male'.

TYPICAL MALE' CITIZEN

Maldivians make up at least 75% of the city's population. They are laid-back, friendly, sober and accustomed to living in fairly cramped quarters. Other ethnic groups include South Indians, Sinhalese and Arabs.

DEFINING EXPERIENCE

Strolling around the island on Boduthakurufanu Magu, one of the loveliest street names, late in the afternoon, watching a game of football, basketball or maybe cricket, on the manmade sports grounds at the eastern end, then stopping for refreshments at a teahouse.

STRENGTHS

- The *dhoni* (a traditional all-purpose vessel now usually powered by a diesel engine) ride from the Male' airport island, Hulhule
- The gold-domed Grand Friday Miskiiy (mosque)
- The coral-stone–walled Hukuru Miskiiy, which dates from 1656
- Curious street names rather than numbers – watch for Crabtree, Sweet Rose, Sun Dance, the grand River Nile, the strange Ozone or even Aston Villa
- The Artificial Beach built on reclaimed land at the eastern end of the island

WEAKNESSES

- Traffic
- No alcohol

GOLD STAR

The Hukuru Miskiiy (Old Friday Mosque), which dates from 1656. Its walls, built with coral stones, are intricately carved with Arabic writings, ornamental patterns and expert lacquer works, especially in the domes.

STARRING ROLE IN...

- *The Strode Venturer* by Hammond Innes

IMPORT

- Land reclamation
- Tourists
- Motor vehicles
- Almost all food other than fish
- Aid workers

EXPORT

- Happy honeymooners
- Bronzed holidaymakers

SEE the rounded corners of walls and buildings so vehicles can negotiate tight corners more easily.

EAT *hedhikaa* (short eats) – a selection of sweet and savoury counter items including rice pudding, tiny bananas, curried fish cakes and frittered dough balls, which are usually fishy and mostly spicy.

DRINK *raa*, the local brew, a sweet and delicious toddy tapped from the crown of the palm-tree trunk.

DO dive to the wreck of the *Maldive Victory*, with its wheelhouse underwater at around 15m and propeller at 35m.

WATCH football or cricket at the National Stadium.

BUY fine-woven *kunaa* (mats) with elegant, abstract geometric patterns and subdued natural colouring.

AFTER DARK catch a movie or hang out in a teashop.

URBAN MYTH

The accent in the city's name isn't an 'e' acute, although pronunciation would suggest it. Pronounced *Mah*-leh, the most common local spelling has an apostrophe following the 'e' – a contraction of the name of an early dynasty, Malei. It is often assumed the apostrophe was used because there was no acute accent on the old English typewriter; however, even with modern software, local publishers still prefer the apostrophe ending.

LOCALS WATCH THE SUN BID A FLASHY FAREWELL TO THE DAY.
Photographer: Anuruddha Lokuhapuarachchi / Reuters/Picture Media

THE STRIKING GOLD DOME OF THE GRAND FRIDAY MISKIIY RISES ABOVE THE BUILDINGS OF A MALE' STREET.
Photographer: Luca Romano / Impact Photos/Heritage-Images

OVERCROWDED CITY LIVING CAN'T DAMPEN THE GENEROUS MALDIVIAN SPIRIT.
Photographer: Dominic Sansoni / Impact Photos/Heritage-Images

Manchester

VITAL STATISTICS

NAME: MANCHESTER

DATE OF BIRTH: AD 70; WHEN THE ROMANS ESTABLISHED A FORT CALLED MAMUCIAM

ADDRESS: ENGLAND (MAP 3, E6)

HEIGHT: 73M

SIZE: 1286 SQ KM

POPULATION: 458,000 (CITY); 2.5 MILLION (METRO AREA)

LONELY PLANET RANKING: 126

THE CASTLEFIELD CANAL BOAT WAITS TO TAKE IT TO THE NEXT LEVEL.
Photographer: Neil Setchfield / LPI

Manchester's pioneering spirit started the Industrial Revolution, a musical revolution and the *Guardian* newspaper, and its resilience shook off an IRA bomb to rise triumphant, with excellent museums, fine dining and top shopping.

ANATOMY

The city centre is easily navigable on foot or using the efficient Metrolink. The latter's hub is in Piccadilly Gardens, east of the cathedral. North of here is the hip Northern Quarter. To the southeast you'll find Canal St and the Gay Village, with Chinatown next door. Nineteenth-century canalside industrial buildings have been trendily developed at Castlefield and Deansgate Locks southwest of the centre. Further south are the Salford quays embellished by the fabulous Imperial War Museum North and the Lowry Centre. Old Trafford (the 'Theatre of Dreams') is nearby. Compact Manchester is fairly foot-friendly, but if you're not pounding the pavements you can either catch one of the many buses or trams that weave across the city or one of the trains that skirt the inner city area.

PEOPLE

Manchester's population is predominantly of British heritage, although the number of Pakistani and Bangladeshi inhabitants is increasing.

TYPICAL MANCUNIAN

Mancunians are justifiably proud of their city, from its industrial history as 'Cottonopolis' through to the musical mayhem of 'Madchester'. They believe Manchester is the best city in England, and are friendly and welcoming to visitors. The city of Hacienda fame knows how to party, and people are fun-loving and stylish. Despite housing Manchester United, the hugely successful football club and global brand, most people support Manchester City, its far less successful neighbour. In addition to a general rivalry with London, Manchester and Leeds sit on opposite sides of the historic Lancashire-versus-Yorkshire clash, which is reinterpreted every year with the Roses cricket match. The city bounced back after the 1996 IRA bomb and many now say the city looks much better for it.

DEFINING EXPERIENCE

Breathing in the view of the city from little-visited Godlee Observatory before heading down for some shopping heaven in the Northern Quarter, followed by a reviving beer in Bar Centro and a spot of live music at the Manchester Roadhouse.

STRENGTHS

◢ Civic pride
◢ Harvey Nichols
◢ Successful urban regeneration
◢ Canals
◢ Manchester Pride
◢ Football
◢ Imperial War Museum North
◢ Lowry Centre
◢ Manchester Art Gallery
◢ Manchester Smithsonian
◢ University of Manchester
◢ Old Trafford
◢ Canal St after dark
◢ Lancashire County Cricket Club
◢ Large choice of restaurants
◢ Manchester airport
◢ Granada TV studios

WEAKNESSES

◢ Working conditions in the 19th century
◢ Weather
◢ Lack of low-cost airlines
◢ Manchester City Football Club

GOLD STAR

Pioneering and resilient spirit.

STARRING ROLE IN...

◢ *24-Hour Party People* (2002)
◢ *Cold Feet* (1998–2003)
◢ *Coronation Street* (1960–)
◢ *The Queen is Dead* by the Smiths

IMPORT

◢ Footballers' wives
◢ Students
◢ Friedrich Engels (to work in a family cotton factory)
◢ Scientist Ernest Rutherford

EXPORT

◢ Manchester United
◢ Oasis
◢ The Stone Roses
◢ Happy Mondays
◢ The Smiths
◢ Artist LS Lowry
◢ Cotton (but not since World War II)
◢ *Guardian* newspaper
◢ Caroline Aherne
◢ Steve Coogan
◢ Mick Hucknall
◢ Anna Friel
◢ Joanne Whalley-Kilmer

SEE the Daniel Libeskind–designed Imperial War Museum North and the audiovisual displays inside.

EAT at the best Indian restaurant on Curry Mile, Shere Khan.

DRINK a whisky in Temple of Convenience, a converted public toilet.

DO a tour of Old Trafford and imagine wearing one of those red shirts.

WATCH the heavens above and the city below from the Godlee Observatory.

BUY stylish clothes and must-have accessories in Millennium Quarter.

AFTER DARK don your dancing shoes for a club night at Music Box.

URBAN MYTH

The origins of 'Madchester' can be traced to Tony Wilson, founder of factory records – the label that in 1983 released New Order's *Blue Monday*, Britain's bestselling 12-inch single. With his pockets getting fatter, he opened the Hacienda nightclub but it was slow to take off. The turning point came with house music from Chicago and Detroit, DJs Mike Pickering, Graeme Park and Jon da Silva, and ecstasy – everyone in town became 'mad for it'. Local bands the Stone Roses, Happy Mondays and the Charlatans joined in. But the party couldn't last forever. In 1992 the Hacienda closed and the bands went quiet, making room for Manchester's most successful band, Oasis. Today new groups expound their individuality, reluctant to belong to a particular movement. Madchester is no more, but it has gone down in legend as a wild time.

PLENTY OF SPACE TO CONTEMPLATE: THE JANE BROWN EXHIBITION AT SALFORD QUAY'S LOWRY CENTRE.
Photographer: Neil Setchfield / LPI

THE JAUNTY PEAK OF THE URBIS, MANCHESTER'S URBAN MUSEUM.
Photographer: Neil Setchfield / LPI

MURAL DEPICTING VARIOUS FAMOUS MANCUNIANS.
Photographer: Neil Setchfield / LPI

The urban hub of the Philippines' 7000 islands, Manila is a megacity of skyscrapers, shantytowns and shopping malls with the ghosts of a Spanish colonial past lurking in the alleyways.

ANATOMY

Manila is huge. The so-called Metro Manila area is a vast district comprising 17 sprawling municipalities. At the centre of it all is the City of Manila, which gazes westward over the ocean. Intramuros is the oldest district in the city, perched on a thin peninsula that juts out into Manila Bay. This was the site of the original Muslim settlement, on top of which the Spanish built their walled fortress. From here you can venture east into the rest of the metropolis on foot or by *Jeepney* (local bus).

PEOPLE

Most Manilans are Catholic, and although the majority belong to the Tagalog ethnic group, Manila has become something of a microcosm of the Philippines ever since internal immigrants from all quarters of the archipelago settled in the city.

TYPICAL MANILAN

Manilans have a reputation for being warm and relaxed but they're never afraid to express their feelings or opinions. And it's hardly surprising. The city has been occupied successively by the Spanish, Americans and Japanese, and residents are well accustomed to struggling for their sense of self and political freedoms. The influence of the West remains strong, yet Manilans have adapted rather than surrendered to the outside world. Some locals speak 'Taglish', a dialect of Tagalog that subsumes elements of English vocabulary. The distinctly Filipino Jollibee restaurants are many times more popular than the imported fast-food chains they originally emulated.

Manila

VITAL STATISTICS

NAME: MANILA

NICKNAME: PEARL OF THE ORIENT

DATE OF BIRTH: 1571; WHEN IT WAS FOUNDED BY SPANIARD MIGUEL LOPEZ DE LEGAZPI, ALTHOUGH A MUSLIM SETTLEMENT HAD ALREADY EXISTED ON THE SITE FOR CENTURIES

ADDRESS: PHILIPPINES (MAP 5, R8)

HEIGHT: 14M

SIZE: 38.55 SQ KM

POPULATION: 11.6 MILLION

LONELY PLANET RANKING: 069

A COLOURFUL *JEEPNEY* GRIDLOCK ALONG THE MAIN ROAD AT DIVISORIA MARKET.
Photographer: Greg Elms / LPI

DEFINING EXPERIENCE

Paying your respects at the bizarre Chinese Cemetery with its air-conditioned houses for the dead, strolling through the weird and wonderful markets and side streets of Quiapo, Santa Cruz and Binondo, then wandering along the walls of Intramuros in the evening and appreciating the legendary sunset over Manila Bay.

STRENGTHS

◢ *Jeepneys* – multicoloured local buses reconstructed from ex-US army jeeps
◢ Chinese Cemetery
◢ Dr José Rizal – national hero of the Philippines
◢ Intramuros – the walled Spanish city
◢ Fast-changing nightlife of the Malate and Ermita areas
◢ Fantastic clothing off the rack
◢ Extraordinary markets
◢ Trendy eateries
◢ Karaoke

WEAKNESSES

◢ Shantytowns
◢ Poverty
◢ Prostitution
◢ Traffic
◢ Stifling heat
◢ Pollution
◢ Overpopulation
◢ Ferdinand Marcos

GOLD STAR

Sunset – geographically Manila is perfectly poised to witness the brilliant sunsets over the bay, and the pollution in the air only enhances the light show!

STARRING ROLE IN...

◢ *Seed of Contention* (2006)
◢ *Homecoming* (2003)
◢ *Too Hot to Handle* (1977)

IMPORT

◢ Mobile phones – Manilans love them
◢ Machinery
◢ Fuel
◢ Legal systems – from Spain and the US
◢ Hopeful workers from other parts of the Philippines

EXPORT

◢ San Miguel beer
◢ Kitsch religious souvenirs
◢ Herbal medicines
◢ *Parols* (traditional lanterns)
◢ *Barongs* (embroidered men's shirts)
◢ Electronic goods

SEE Intramuros, the old walled city that guarded Spain's Asian empire.

EAT typical dishes from all over the Philippines at a cheap and cheerful *turo turo* (a fast-food restaurant where patrons point to what they want to order).

DRINK San Miguel beer, the finest in Asia.

DO a tour of the Chinese Cemetery where mausoleums have running water and flush toilets for the deceased.

WATCH the sun set over Manila Bay.

BUY just about anything you can imagine – and much that you'd rather not – at a city market.

AFTER DARK hit the karaoke bars with the rest of Manila.

AS DUSK FALLS OVER MANILA BAY A TEENAGE GIRL SHOOTS OFF A QUICK TEXT MESSAGE.
Photographer: Greg Elms / LPI

WINDOWS IN THE CRUMBLING WALLS OF THE SPANISH-BUILT FORT OF INTRAMUROS PROVIDE A PERFECT TRYST FOR LOVERS. Photographer: Greg Elms / LPI

TWO SOON-TO-BE-COMPETING ROOSTERS AT LA LOMA COCKFIGHTING ARENA.
Photographer: Greg Elms / LPI

One of Africa's most alluring cities for rest and relaxation, Maputo has a distinctly Mediterranean atmosphere, white sandy beaches and friendly locals that give the busy capital a resort feel.

ANATOMY

Set on a small cliff overlooking the large harbour in Maputo Bay, the city is circled by stunning beaches, the scenic Inhaca and Portuguese Islands, the 'reed cities' – the overpopulated slums – various sized farm plots as well as species-rich coastal wetlands. The city's ample avenues, lined with red acacia and lilac jacaranda trees, are populated by worse-for-wear colonial buildings – the result of almost two decades of civil war – many modern constructions and a flourishing café culture. The best way to see Maputo is by foot, but minibus tours and car hire are options. It's only been a couple of years since traffic lights arrived in Maputo and many drivers have a relaxed observance of road laws, so take care.

PEOPLE

Indigenous tribal groups comprise almost the entire population, with Europeans and Indians making up the rest. Around 50% of the population adheres to indigenous beliefs, about 30% is Christian and 20% Muslim. Although Portuguese is the official language, there are many local dialects spoken, and English is quite common in the city.

TYPICAL MAPUTO CITIZEN

Unlike their rural counterparts, these urban Mozambicans have disposable income, which they like to spend. Going out for coffee is a popular pastime, as is hanging out at the beach. They have strong religious beliefs, are resilient and optimistic, enthusiastic about music and love to dance and play sport. They are always smiling and friendly towards visitors.

Maputo

VITAL STATISTICS

NAME: MAPUTO

DATE OF BIRTH: 1787; THE TOWN DEVELOPED AROUND A PORTUGUESE FORTRESS, WHICH WAS COMPLETED AT THIS TIME

ADDRESS: MOZAMBIQUE (MAP 2, K24)

HEIGHT: 59M

POPULATION: 1.2 MILLION

LONELY PLANET RANKING: 181

BREAKIN' IT DOWN AT XIPAMANINE MARKET.
Photographer: Ariadne Van Zandbergen / LPI

DEFINING EXPERIENCE

Sunbathing with a book on the white sands of Praia de Maceneta beach, then taking in the bustling street life over a protracted beer and spicy tiger-prawn feast, picking up the Latino rhythm with some hot moves at the Mini-Golfe disco and cutting it up almost till dawn…before hot-footing it to the bay to take in a glorious sunrise.

STRENGTHS

- Locals
- Relaxed atmosphere
- Beach weather year-round
- Cheap-as-chips seafood
- Huge, colourful street murals
- Excellent water sports
- Palm tree–lined beaches
- Lively nightlife
- The Portuguese fort Nossa Senhora da Conceiao (Our Lady of Conception)
- Maputo Bay sunrises
- Café culture
- Maputo Elephant Reserve
- Colourful markets
- National Art Museum
- Local football matches
- Species-rich wetlands close by
- National Company of Song & Dance

WEAKNESSES

- Street crime
- Dodgy police officers
- Lawless drivers
- Poverty
- Central Railway Station
- Expensive supermarkets
- Poor-quality souvenir items

GOLD STAR

Pristine beaches – they're full of marine life and coral reefs, are within close reach of the city centre and have heaps of water sports available, including snorkelling, surfing, diving, fishing and windsurfing.

STARRING ROLE IN...

- *Ali* (2000)
- *The Gaze of the Stars* (1997)
- *Under the Frangipani* by Mia Couto
- *Half a Life* by VS Naipaul

IMPORT

- Lots of South African tourists
- Fast-food chains
- Food
- Foreign aid
- Western-style billboards
- Clothing
- Mobile phones
- Farm equipment
- Petrol
- Air-conditioning

EXPORT

- Aluminium
- Cashews
- Prawns (shrimp)
- Cashews
- Cotton
- Sugar
- Citrus fruits
- Timber
- Electricity

SEE the impressive 95m-long mural opposite the Praça dos Heróis Moçambicanos, commemorating the Revolution.

EAT spicy *piri-piri* (a sauce made from a particular type of chilli) chicken at the famous 1960s-feel Restaurante Piri-Piri.

DRINK the local beers – Laurentina, Manica and 2M – street-side, under the shade of an acacia tree.

DO a camping trip to Inhaca Island and explore its offshore coral reefs.

WATCH an energetic performance of the first-rate National Company of Song & Dance.

BUY up-to-the-minute import items delivered straight from the docks of Maputo Bay to the city's air-conditioned shopping centres.

AFTER DARK check out the local jazz scene at Cinema Gil Vicente.

URBAN MYTH

The imposing Central Railway Station is an enormous palacelike structure. The story goes that the building was designed by Alexandre Gustav Eiffel (of Eiffel Tower fame), but as Eiffel himself never stepped foot in the city, some suggest it was in fact designed by one of his associates.

A POOL SHARK CONSIDERS HIS NEXT MOVE.
Photographer: Ariadne Van Zandbergen / LPI

BROWSING THROUGH AN ASSORTMENT OF TRADITIONAL MEDICINES AT THE MARKET.
Photographer: Ariadne Van Zandbergen / LPI

STREET MURAL DEPICTING THE CHAOS OF THE CIVIL WAR.
Photographer: Ariadne Van Zandbergen / LPI

Marseille is not pretty or quaint like some of its Provencal neighbours – it's a real, vibrant, cosmopolitan city with an endearing old port, great seafood and a ticking nightlife.

ANATOMY

Marseille's main artery is the wide boulevard of La Canebière, which carves through the city east from the Old Port. Bohemian cours Julien buzzes with trendy cafés, restaurants and theatres south of the boulevard. Further south stands the Basilique Notre Dame de la Garde, which proudly surveys the city from its spot on a hill. West from the Old Port and out to sea, boats sail to Corsica, Sardinia, Tunisia, Spain and Algeria. Also out to sea but closer to home stands Château d'If, the 16th-century fortress-turned-jail immortalised in Alexandre Dumas' *Le Comte de Monte Cristo*. Rumbling beneath the city are two metro lines, while buses cruise around above the surface. The overland train station is north of La Canebière.

PEOPLE

Due to its proximity to Tunisia and Algeria, Marseille is France's most North African city, with many immigrants from these countries. Immigrants also come from the Mediterranean basin and Indochina.

TYPICAL MARSEILLAIS

As citizens of France's second city and the capital of Provence, the Marseillais are predictably and justifiably proud. The city used to have a reputation for violence and racial tensions, but development projects and the TGV link to Paris are leaving this image behind. Smart Parisians are snapping up weekend homes and plugging into the cultural scene. In general, people are welcoming of visitors, but they do have a defensive streak, which can allow them to close ranks if they choose to. The people of Marseille were enthusiastic supporters of the revolution, and France's national anthem, 'La Marseillaise', was named after local revolutionaries who sang it on their march to Paris. Finally, the Marseillais are big fans of football and hip-hop.

Marseille

VITAL STATISTICS

NAME: MARSEILLE

DATE OF BIRTH: 600 BC; WHEN GREEK MARINERS FOUNDED A TRADING POST CALLED MASSILIA

ADDRESS: FRANCE (MAP 3, H13)

HEIGHT: 4M

POPULATION: 839, 000 (CITY); 1.6 MILLION (METRO AREA)

LONELY PLANET RANKING: 124

THE TINY FISHING PORT OF VALLON DES AUFFES HAS A BIG REPUTATION FOR CHARMING SEASIDE RESTAURANTS.
Photographer: Eric Bouvet / Getty Images

DEFINING EXPERIENCE

Delving into the city's Greek and Roman past at the Musée d'Histoire de Marseille, before tasting some *pastis* (a 90-proof, anise-flavoured cousin of absinthe) at La Maison de Pastis, grabbing some bouillabaisse down at the port and then making for place Jean Jaurès to pick up some vintage clothing.

STRENGTHS

- France's most important seaport
- Shopping heaven on rue Paradis
- Musée d'Histoire de Marseille
- Basilique Notre Dame de la Garde
- Château d'If
- Sunbathing at Calanques
- Îles du Frioul
- Musée des Beaux-Arts
- Musée de la Mode
- Centre de la Vieille Charité
- Harbourside restaurants
- Cosmopolitan vibe
- Old Port
- Bustling markets eg the fish market
- Tasty seafood
- TGV link to Paris
- Marseille Euroméditerrannée
- Hôtel le Corbusier
- Fiesta des Suds

WEAKNESSES

- Expensive car parks
- Some street crime
- Smelly backstreets

GOLD STAR

Bouillabaisse.

STARRING ROLE IN...

- *La Vie est Tranquille* (2002)
- *Baise-Moi* (2000)
- *Taxi* (1998)
- *The French Connection* (1971)
- *Le Comte de Monte Cristo* by Alexandre Dumas

IMPORT

- Parisian weekenders
- Thriller writer Lee Child
- Marcel Pagnol

EXPORT

- Zinédine Zidane
- Eric Cantona
- Sébastien Grosjean
- Bouillabaisse
- Fish and seafood
- Olive-oil soaps
- IAM
- Hip-hop
- Tarot cards
- 'La Marseillaise'

SEE the absorbing view of Marseille from the highest point in the city, the Romano-Byzantine Notre Dame de la Garde.

EAT inventive cuisine at Une Table au Sud, and take a break from bouillabaisse.

DRINK homemade *pastis* or, if you're feeling brave, absinthe at L'Heure Verte.

DO stroll around the Old Port and spy the fishing craft, pleasure yachts and ferries.

WATCH or join in a game of *pétanque* (aka boules – similar to lawn bowls but played with heavy metal balls on a sandy pitch) in the late afternoon.

BUY African woodcarved animals at Marseille's best market, Marché aux Puces (flea market).

AFTER DARK salsa, samba and prop up the bar at steamy Le Cubaila Café.

URBAN MYTH

Heated discussions over the best way to prepare Marseille's speciality, bouillabaisse, are legendary in the city. Standard ingredients are fish, onions, white wine, tomatoes, fennel, saffron and croutons, and brief, vigorous boiling of the soup followed by simmering over a low heat are universally accepted practices. Most people agree that five or six types of Mediterranean fish plus crab or prawn (shrimp) should be included. However, to some people's horror, there are those who add mussels, lobster or langoustines to the mixture. Others dare to pop potatoes in. And the serving of the stew divides everyone – should the broth and the stew be served separately, or together?

WITH FIST-PUMPING ENTHUSIASM MARSEILLE SOCCER CLUB SUPPORTERS REACH FEVER PITCH IN THE STANDS.
Photographer: Eric Bouvet / Getty Images

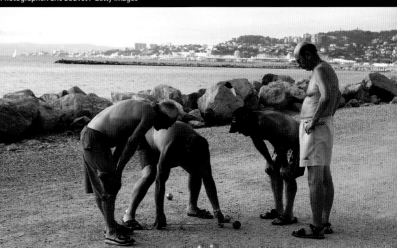

EVEN FROM THE HARBOUR THE GILDED 'GOOD MOTHER' OF NOTRE DAME DE LA GARDE CAN BEEN SEEN WATCHING OVER THE CITY. Photographer: Eric Bouvet / Getty Images

ARGUING THE TOSS – A SUMMER AFTERNOON'S GAME OF *PÉTANQUE* HEATS UP WHEN THE TAPE MEASURE APPEARS.
Photographer: Eric Bouvet / Getty Images

Melbourne

VITAL STATISTICS

NAME: MELBOURNE

NICKNAME: PARIS OF THE SOUTHERN HEMISPHERE

DATE OF BIRTH: 1835; BY TASMANIAN ENTREPRENEURS KEEN ON A MAINLAND BASE

ADDRESS: AUSTRALIA (MAP 1, LL21)

HEIGHT: 35M

SIZE: 2025 SQ KM

POPULATION: 3.8 MILLION

LONELY PLANET RANKING: 011

LOOKING INTO DECEPTIVELY PLAIN-JANE PELLIGRINI'S, ONE OF MELBOURNE'S HIGH TEMPLES TO CAFFEINE.
Photographer: Nic Lehman

Suave, sophisticated, and stark-raving sports mad, Melbourne is an arty powerhouse with an eye on the Melbourne Cup and a mouthful of world-class cuisine.

ANATOMY

Melbourne lines Port Phillip Bay and stretches into the plains to the west and east and out to the foothills of the Dandenong Ranges. The city is divided by the muddy Yarra River, with the CBD on the north bank, set in a neat grid that suits its kitschy tram transport perfectly. To the CBD's north is the dining precinct of Carlton and grungy Fitzroy, which vies for coolest-suburb honours with St Kilda to the south of the Yarra with its ace of beaches and backpackers. Trams and trains are the best way to get around the city.

PEOPLE

Melbourne's population is drawn from around the world, with postwar migrations of Italian, Greek and Jewish people giving it a unique cultural make-up. Melbourne, famously, has the highest population of Greeks of any city outside of Greece itself. More recently Vietnamese, Indonesian and Malaysian people have arrived, with Melbourne having a particularly high population of international students (the fourth-largest in the world). Melbourne's original people, the Wurundjeri, have survived all of these waves of immigration.

TYPICAL MELBURNIAN

Dressed in black and swilling a coffee, Melburnians have been known to argue about their city's best restaurant for hours and spend most of Monday talking about how their footy team went. You could say lifestyle is more important than career, but Melburnians are passionate about their politics, with the city holding the largest protests against federal government change to industrial relations reforms. While many talk about the 'great divide' between the north and south side of the Yarra, many more live in suburbs far from the river.

DEFINING EXPERIENCE

Running a lap of the Botanic Gardens, then catching a tram to the Melbourne Cricket Ground (MCG) for Saturday's big (Australian Football League) AFL game, hunkering down in a Fitzroy pub to watch local band the Lucksmiths, then spotting possums in Carlton Gardens on the way home.

STRENGTHS

- Flinders St Station
- Trams
- Secret city laneways and back alleys
- St Kilda beaches
- Live music
- Federation Sq
- Melbourne Zoo
- Sports-obsessed culture
- National Gallery of Victoria
- MCG, or more simply, the G
- Esplanade Hotel (The Espy)
- Royal Exhibition Buildings and Carlton Gardens
- Snazzy new Docklands
- 'Paris end' of Collins St
- St Kilda bars and restaurants
- Melbourne Museum
- Diverse cuisine
- Funky Fitzroy
- Lygon St cafés
- Artsy Southgate

WEAKNESSES

- Tricky traffic hook turns
- St Kilda beaches
- Tea-coloured Yarra River
- Controversial Crown Casino

GOLD STAR

Multiculturalism – from postwar Italian and Greek immigrants to more recent Vietnamese and Eritrean families, Melbourne has a diverse ethnicity.

STARRING ROLE IN...

- *Ghost Rider* (2006)
- *Three Dollars* (2005)
- *The Wog Boy* (2000)
- *The Bank* (2001)
- *Malcolm* (1986)
- *Proof* (1991)
- *Crackerjack* (2002)
- *Mallboy* (2001)
- *The Castle* (1997)
- *Love and Other Catastrophes* (1996)
- *Death in Brunswick* (1991)
- *Dogs in Space* (1987)
- *Harvie Krumpet* (2003)
- *Street Hero* (1984)

IMPORT

- Paul Kelly
- Great coffee
- Cathy Freeman
- Formula One Grand Prix

EXPORT

- AFL
- *Neighbours*
- Kylie Minogue
- Peter Carey
- AC/DC
- Nick Cave
- Melbourne Cup
- The Australian Ballet
- Jet
- Heidelberg School
- Dame Edna Everage and her alter-ego, Barry Humphries
- Adam Elliot
- Lonely Planet

SEE the patchwork design of Federation Sq.

EAT the sumptuous Peking duck at the Flower Drum, Melbourne's foodie apogee.

DRINK an espresso (anything else isn't *autentico*) at Pellegrini's, Mario's or a fabulous new place that absolutely no-one has ever heard of.

DO the adrenaline rush of kite-surfing at St Kilda Beach.

WATCH local band Architecture in Helsinki at the iconic live-music venue, the Corner Hotel.

BUY an edgy outfit on Chapel St, only to spot a bargain knock-off on Bridge Rd.

AFTER DARK check out the back alleys that hide bars like the Croft Institute and Double Happiness.

URBAN MYTH

On 17 December 1967, Australia's prime minister Harold Holt popped out for a swim on Cheviot Beach not far from Melbourne and disappeared without a trace. Speculation was rife about what happened to the head of state, with theories ranging from suicide to defection to China. The latter conspiracy theory speculated that Holt had arranged to be picked up by a Chinese submarine as a pay-off for creating closer trade relationships with Asia. When told of this idea, his wife, Zara, reputedly scoffed that Holt 'didn't even like Chinese food'. Regardless of his diet, Holt's disappearance remains a part of Melbourne culture through the rhyming-slang expression 'to do a Harold Holt' (or bolt) and Glen Iris' ironic Harold Holt Swimming Centre.

WORSHIPPERS CONGREGATE AT THE MCG, THE GREAT CATHEDRAL OF AUSTRALIAN RULES FOOTBALL, MELBOURNE'S ORTHODOX RELIGION.
Photographer: Dallas Stribley / LPI

A MAN JOGS ALONG SOUTH MELBOURNE BEACH BENEATH BROODING STORM CLOUDS.
Photographer: Regis Martin / LPI

NOT JUST FOR SQUARES – AWESTRUCK DEVOTEES OF MELBOURNE'S OTHER RELIGION AT THE AUSTRALIAN CENTRE FOR CONTEMPORARY ART. Photographer: Phil Weymouth / LPI

Mexico City

VITAL STATISTICS

NAME: MEXICO CITY

NICKNAME: EL DF; CHILANGOTLÁN; CHILANGOLANDIA; LA CIUDAD DE LOS PALACIOS (CITY OF PALACES); LA CIUDAD DE LA ESPERANZA (CITY OF HOPE)

DATE OF BIRTH: 1325; WHEN THE AZTECS RULED IT AS TENOCHTITLÁN, BUT IT WAS REBUILT AS NUEVA ESPAÑA BY THE CONQUISTADORS AROUND 1550

ADDRESS: MEXICO (MAP 4, C4)

HEIGHT: 2309M

SIZE: 5000 SQ KM

POPULATION: 19.8 MILLION

LONELY PLANET RANKING: 029

For sheer scale, Mexico City impresses; it's also North America's oldest metropolis, and its layering of European nostalgia, rich indigenous culture and modern urban energy are as exhilarating as its size.

ANATOMY

Set in a high, flat valley, Mexico City's 350 crowded *colonias* (neighbourhoods) sprawl. The heart of the city, El Zócalo, and its surrounding museum-packed neighbourhoods and green expanses of the Alameda, form the Centro Histórico. Architectural styles range across the spectrum, from the baroque to early-20th-century delights, from millennial-gated communities to the outer rings of slum dwellings. There is horrendous traffic congestion, despite a metro, a large network of buses and trolley cars, and countless (and infamous) taxis.

PEOPLE

The majority of *capitalinos* or *chilangos,* as residents are known, are Spanish-speaking mestizos, a typically Mexican melange of Spanish and indigenous ancestry, often with some European or African-slave heritage in the mix as well. The city's enormous population continues to be swelled by immigrants from other parts of the country, usually from the rural south.

TYPICAL CAPITALINO

Young *capitalinos* from the fashionable inner neighbourhoods tend to be politically engaged (though cynical), culturally switched on, and a little hedonistic. Although deep-held values – family, machismo, Catholicism – still endure, for the middle class at least, there are profound shifts in social attitudes, particularly around gender equality. *Capitalinos* may know they are living in a city that is safer than ever, increasingly stylish and certainly cosmopolitan, but not all of them get to share in the glamour; over 20% of citizens live in poverty, mainly in the dire outer sprawl.

DEFINING EXPERIENCE

Brunching late at El Pendulo, listening to the guitarist and discussing the presidential election, taking a stroll around the Mercado de la Merced with your *abuela* (grandmother), then having a prickly-pear ice cream at Neveria Roxy, stopping by Chic By Accident and bargaining for that antique mirror you've been coveting for the conversion in El Centro, followed by drinks on the rooftop at Condesa DF.

STRENGTHS

- Improving air quality
- Museo Nacional de Antropología
- The new 'Mexican chic' epitomised by Hotel Habita and Condesa DF
- Palacio de las Bellas Artes
- Self-deprecation
- Thousands of taco stands
- Photography collection at Galería Casa Lamm
- Camino Real's Mex-modernist décor
- Colour
- Art Deco in Condesa
- Art Nouveau in Colonia Roma
- Casa Azul and Museo Casa Estudio Diego Rivera y Frida Kahlo (key cult-of-Kahlo sites)
- Church of Santa Veracruz and the baroque Church of San Juan de Dios
- Castillo de Chapultepec
- The pyramids at Teotihuacán Tenochtitlán
- Never-say-die nightlife

WEAKNESSES

- Sprawl
- Pollution
- Decrepit infrastructure
- Extreme social inequalities
- It's sinking
- Happy-handed rush hour commuters on the metro
- The 5am trumpet wake-up call in the Zócalo
- Altitude

GOLD STAR

Murals: Mexico City's spirited, incendiary murals, especially those by Rivera, Siqueiros and Orozco, which capture the history and psyche of the city and the nation.

STARRING ROLE IN...

- *Los Olvidados* (1950)
- *The Falcon and the Snowman* (1985)
- *Love in the Time of Hysteria* (1991)
- *The Beginning and the End* (1993)
- *Amores Perros* (2000)
- *Y Tu Mama Tambien* (2001)
- *Frida* (2002)
- *The Death of Artemio Cruz* by Carlos Fuentes

IMPORT

- Leon Trotsky
- André Breton
- Baseball
- Luis Buñuel
- Bullfighting
- Tina Modotti
- US fast-food chains
- Gabriel García Márquez
- Sushi
- Football

EXPORT

- Mural art
- Octavio Paz
- Cement
- Textiles
- Silver
- *Antojitos* (small tortillas with various fillings)
- Musicians Rodrigo y Gabriela
- Plastics
- Hammocks
- Hugo Sánchez

SEE the Gothic, baroque *and* neoclassical Catedral Metropolitana and the Aztec Templo Mayor from the balcony bar of the Holiday Inn.

EAT Patricia Quintana's *nueva cocina mexicana* (new Mexican cuisine) at Izote: Mexican standards and indigenous ingredients (think yucca flower) get a considered reworking.

DRINK *pulque* (maguey liquor) at Las Duelistas, a traditional working-class *cantina* (bar).

DO escape to the shaded waterways of pre-Hispanic Xochimilco and take in the music from aboard a *trajinera* (a gondolalike vessel).

WATCH Astrid Hadad skewer the powerful in her bawdy take-no-prisoners cabaret, upstairs at Condesa's La Bodega.

BUY vintage embroidered dresses and antique silver at the Bazar Sábado in San Angel.

AFTER DARK grab a *pinindia* (cocktail that includes tequila and pineapple juice) at Prima, then get to the Dos Naciones for contemporary sounds and *cantina* atmosphere, finishing up at a 24-hour café on 5 de Mayo.

URBAN MYTH

Frida Kahlo is one of Mexico's most well-known artists. Kahlo's exquisitely sensuous work uses the pain and heartbreak of her life as a central motif. Her physical pain was all too real, the result of appalling injuries sustained in a bus accident. The teenage Kahlo's leg and spine were shattered and she was impaled by a handrail's steel shaft ('I lost my virginity', she wryly observed). Kahlo lay naked, the force of the crash having torn off her clothes, bleeding profusely and covered in the gold powder paint that a fellow passenger had been carrying. Surreally, she came to resemble a figure from a gruesome *santa sangre* (a form of Mexican folk painting), an image that would later haunt her work.

A COOL CUSTOMER CUTS A GLAMOROUS FIGURE IN A CONDESA DISTRICT SHOP.
Photographer: Lynsey Addario / Corbis

COLUMNS OF PINK AND FLUFFY CANDY FLOSS FOR SALE ON A STREET CORNER IN COLONIAL COYOACAN.
Photographer: Mireille Vautier / Alamy

¡QUÉ PADRE! DANCERS OF THE BALLET FOLCLÓRICO KEEP TO A TRADITIONAL TEMPO.
Photographer: David Ryan / LPI

A YELLOW VOLKSWAGEN BEETLE TAXI PROCLAIMS ITS INDIVIDUALITY AMONG THE MASSES.
Photographer: Chris Cheadle / Getty Images

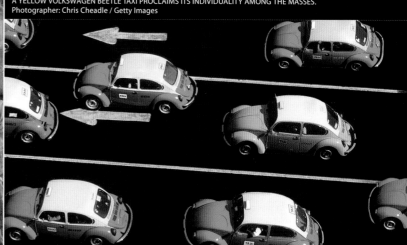

A thriving port city, Mombasa is a steamy, tropical entrepôt where life unfurls languidly.

ANATOMY

Mombasa is an island, connected to the mainland by causeways to the north and west and a ferry to the south. Digo Rd, and its southern extension, Nyerere Ave, is the main north–south thoroughfare. East of Digo Rd is the main market, which then leads on to the warren of narrow streets of the Old Town. On the fringe of the Old Town, overlooking the old harbour, are the fish markets and the almighty bulk of Fort Jesus. *Matatus* (minibuses, always jam packed) buzz around town, and connect Mombasa to the beach resorts to the north and south.

PEOPLE

As befits a port city, Mombasa has seen peoples – Persian, Omani and Portuguese, all of whom mixed with local African populations – come and go for millennia. The city is now one of the biggest Swahili cities, with a distinctive coastal culture that is a melange of African, Asian and Arabic influences. Along with the mosques of the Swahili populace there are Hindu and Sikh temples. There is a sizable English community as well as refugee communities from the Horn of Africa – Somalis, Eritreans and Ethiopians.

TYPICAL MOMBASAN

A tropical, coastal people, the Mombasans approach life at a languid pace. The humidity and a laid-back mind-set mean that there is no need to rush. That said, Mombasa is the biggest port in East Africa and it bustles (albeit at its own pace). Locals are convivial and gregarious – life occurs on the street, particularly in the evening as the cool descends. Etiquette is paramount, and greetings are long and elaborate. Mombasa is one of the oldest settlements in Kenya, so locals have a strong sense of identity.

Mombasa

VITAL STATISTICS

NAME: MOMBASA

DATE OF BIRTH: AD 150; WHEN PTOLEMY PLACED THE CITY ON HIS MAP OF THE KNOWN WORLD

ADDRESS: KENYA (MAP 2, N15)

HEIGHT: 16M

SIZE: 30 SQ KM

POPULATION: 660,000

LONELY PLANET RANKING: 191

GOING FOR A STROLL UNDER DRYING RAIMENTS.
Photographer: Carl & Ann Purcell / Corbis

DEFINING EXPERIENCE

Strolling the streets of the Old Town, admiring the ornately carved doorways, window frames and fretwork balconies of the coastal colonial houses, stopping for chai, then exploring the battlements of Fort Jesus, including Omani House, which dates back to the late 18th century, heading north to watch the comings and goings at the dhow harbour, or turning south on Mama Ngina Dr, passing the mighty baobab trees and gazing out across the Indian Ocean.

STRENGTHS

- Chai flavoured with cardamom
- Lazily spinning fans as you sleep under a mosquito net
- The scent of frangipani flowers in tropical rain
- The elaborate (slightly fading) glory of Swahili architecture
- Starched tablecloths on the Mombasa–Nairobi train
- Football on the gravel beneath Fort Jesus
- Lateen sails of dhows putting out to sea
- Tropical fruits – mangoes, pawpaws, pineapples

WEAKNESSES

- Street hassle from touts
- Mosquitoes when you're trying to sleep
- Humidity during the monsoon
- Disappearance of dhows from the dhow harbour
- Security after dark – some areas are best avoided
- Sex tourism

GOLD STAR

Coastal indolence – Mombasa is the place to take life languidly and watch the world pass by.

STARRING ROLE IN...

- *The Portuguese Period in East Africa* by Justus Strands
- *A Tourist in Africa* by Evelyn Waugh
- *Lunatic Express* by Charles Miller
- *The Weather in Africa* by Martha Gellhorn

IMPORT

- Arabic and Persian architectural styles
- Indian know-how and industriousness
- Expats looking for a coastal idyllic life

EXPORT

- Any and all produce from East Africa
- Oil
- Coffee
- Tea

SEE the sun rise over the Indian Ocean.

EAT traditional Swahili fare: grilled fish, beans in coconut milk, spiced pilau.

DRINK delicious lime soda in Fort Jesus.

DO a luxury dhow cruise around the harbour.

WATCH the colourful floats and parades at the annual carnival.

BUY a *kanga* or a *kikoi* (colourful traditional woven cloths).

AFTER DARK check out the bars on Moi Ave or Mama Ngina Dr.

URBAN MYTH

An Arab visitor in 1400 noted that Mombasa was being held to ransom by gangs of roaming monkeys. It was alleged the apes 'attack men in their own homes' and 'when they enter a house and find a woman they hold congress with her'.

SQUEEZING INTO THE SHOT DURING A BREAK FROM SCHOOL.
Photographer: Eric L Wheater / LPI

A GAME OF FOOTBALL AT SUNSET AT FORT JESUS.
Photographer: Robert Caputo / Getty Images

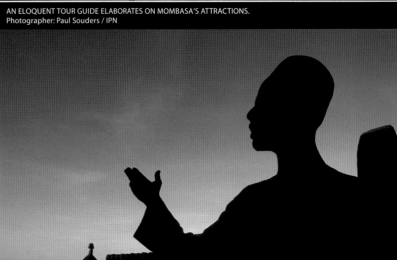

AN ELOQUENT TOUR GUIDE ELABORATES ON MOMBASA'S ATTRACTIONS.
Photographer: Paul Souders / IPN

Montevideo

VITAL STATISTICS

NAME: MONTEVIDEO

DATE OF BIRTH: 1726; WHEN THE SPANISH FLEET ESTABLISHED A CITADEL IN THE SHELTERED PORT OF MONTEVIDEO REACTING TO THE BURGEONING PORTUGUESE IN THE RIO DE LA PLATA AREA

ADDRESS: URUGUAY (MAP 1, O21)

HEIGHT: 22M

POPULATION: 1.3 MILLION

LONELY PLANET RANKING: 138

A picturesque blend of colonial Spanish, Italian and Art Deco styles paired with superb sandy beaches on the city's outskirts, Montevideo is South America's well-kept secret.

ANATOMY

Lying almost directly east of Buenos Aires on the west bank of the Río de la Plata (River Plate), Montevideo's Ciudad Vieja (Old Town) attracts most visitor attention. The Rambla (riverfront road) rambles eastward past numerous public parks (including Parque Rodó) at the southern end of bulevar Artigas. Well within the city limits are the sandy beaches, a little further east. Montevideo's bus fleet is reliable, but most stop running by 11pm. If you're out late, taxis are safe and on the meter but a little pricey.

PEOPLE

Predominantly white with around 8% mestizo (with mixed Spanish and indigenous blood) and 4% black, Montevideo's population includes many European immigrants, mostly from Spain and Italy. Economic stagnation and political decline in the mid-20th century also saw many rural folk flood into Montevideo's city slums.

TYPICAL MONTEVIDEANOS

A city of lovers (of the arts and big drinking) not fighters (bar-room brawls are rare), Montevideanos pride themselves on being the opposite of the hot-headed Latin-American stereotype. Sunday is family day, a time to throw half a cow on the *asado* (spit roast), sip some maté and stroll along the river.

DEFINING EXPERIENCE

Perusing the opulent furnishings of Montevideo's 19th-century elite at the Museo Romántico, riding the No 64 bus along the riverfront Rambla, then tucking into a seriously sumptuous steak in the Mercado del Puerto.

STRENGTHS

- Historical Ciudad Vieja
- Laid-back atmosphere
- Museo Histórico Nacional
- White sandy beaches
- Mercado del Puerto
- Rich artistic and cultural heritage
- Teatro Solís (superb acoustics and a quality roster of local and international performers)
- Spanish, Art Deco and Italian styles
- The neoclassical Palacio Legislativo (Parliament)

WEAKNESSES

- A throbbing decades-old hangover from economic stagnation
- Dependency on Argentine tourism
- Increasing social divide
- Shabby (not chic) city appearance
- Rising street crime

GOLD STAR

Montevideo's port market, Mercado del Puerto – it was the continent's finest when it opened back in 1868. The impressive wrought-iron superstructure bustles with craftspeople, street musicians, outstanding seafood restaurants and traditional *parrillas* (steakhouses).

STARRING ROLE IN...

- *State of Siege* (1973)
- *Burnt Money* (2000)
- *Between the Moon and Montevideo* (2001)

IMPORT

- The Spanish
- The Italians
- *Candombe* (an African-derived rhythm brought to Uruguay by slaves)
- Argentine holidaymakers

EXPORT

- The football World Cup in 1930 (well, Uruguay were the first-ever hosts and winners)
- Beef
- Writer Juan Carlos Onetti
- Painter Juan Manuel Blanes
- Playwright Mauricio Rosencof
- Tango legend Carlos Gardel
- Software and IT services

SEE the crumbling vestiges of grand 19th-century neoclassical buildings, legacies of the beef boom, in Ciudad Vieja.

EAT obscenely big steaks at *parrillas* inside the Mercado del Puerto.

DRINK *medio y medio* (a knockout blend of local sparkling and white wines) in Bartholomew Mitre, Montevideo's most happening bar precinct.

DO ride bus No 64 along the riverfront Rambla – Montevideo's beaches get better the further you go.

WATCH local football rivals Nacional and Peñarol at Montevideo's Estadio Centenario stadium.

BUY everything from antique knick-knacks to fried fish at Montevideo's sprawling outdoor market, the Feria de Tristán Narvaja.

AFTER DARK whip that rose between your chompers and take on the tango at Fun Fun in the Mercado Central.

URBAN MYTH

Montevideo's full name is San Felipe y Santiago de Montevideo. According to one definition, it's derived from the Portuguese *'Monte vide eu'* (I see a mountain). Another definition is that Spanish cartographers noted the location as *'Monte VI de Este a Oeste'* (The sixth mountain from east to west). Regardless, Montevideo's moniker has something to do with mountains and absolutely nothing to do with that thing that killed the radio star.

MEN CLUSTER ROUND TO FIND OUT WHAT'S NEWS IN THE CIUDAD VIEJA.
Photographer: Michael Coyne / LPI

IT TAKES TWO TO ATTEND CLASSES AT THE JOVEN TANGO (YOUNG TANGO) DANCE SCHOOL.
Photographer: Michael Coyne / LPI

A SOLITARY PALM LENDS SOME SHADE TO THOSE WORKING WITHIN THE INDEPENDENCE BUILDING AT PLAZA INDEPENDENCIA.
Photographer: Michael Coyne / LPI

THE ART OF MARRIAGE – A BRIDE CELEBRATES *LAYYAT AL-HENNA* ON THE EVE OF HER WEDDING.
Photographer: James L Stanfield / National Geographic Image Collection

Muscat

VITAL STATISTICS

NAME: MUSCAT

NICKNAME: THE THREE CITIES

DATE OF BIRTH: 1741; IMAM AHMED BIN SAID, HAVING EXPELLED IRANIAN RULE, MADE MUSCAT THE CAPITAL OF THE NEWLY INDEPENDENT OMAN

ADDRESS: OMAN (MAP 2, T5)

HEIGHT: 5M

POPULATION: 1 MILLION

LONELY PLANET RANKING: 107

Elegance in a concealed harbour – Muscat is a dichotomy of tradition and progression, where camels cruise through the city on the back of Toyota pick-ups and the domed buildings of the walled city are inhabited by modern Omanians with mobile phones.

ANATOMY

Wedged between the sea and a jagged spine of mountains, Muscat comprises a string of suburbs, each with its own attractions. The gated city of Muscat sits on a natural harbour and is flanked on the coast by Mutrah, which stretches along an attractive corniche of latticed buildings and mosques. Inland lies Ruwi, Oman's 'little India', the commercial and transport hub of the capital. Plentiful public transport (buses) runs through the three cities. The giant sculptures on the roundabouts provide much-needed navigational aids for the city's unnamed streets, while the well-marked highway parallels the coast and passes through its main attractions.

PEOPLE

Although the city's population is predominantly Arab and Arabic speaking, an Indian merchant community has existed in Muscat for at least 200 years, and English is also enthusiastically spoken. Muscatians follow the Ibadi sect of Islam and are tolerant of other religious groups. Under the auspices of a progressive leader, Sultan Qaboos, the city has reawakened into a modern culture.

TYPICAL MUSCATIAN

Muscatians are as paradoxical as their beloved three cities. They will fashionably wear a headscarf and silk *abeyya* (black outer robe) over Western clothing; receive text messages on eating well while becoming increasingly obese on fast food; and contemplate genetically modified crop rotations, while looking at the cloudless sky and realising that they haven't been praying loud enough. They are hard-working and modern, the women motivated and politically active. They embrace rapid change with a healthy scepticism.

DEFINING EXPERIENCE

Visiting the Marina at dawn to inspect the daily catch, enjoying fresh juice and *shwarma* (meat stuffed in a pocket of pita-type bread with chopped tomatoes and garnish) at the souq (market), then stocking up on savoury pastries, *halwa* (halva) and dates to picnic like royalty by the water (or that old Muscatian favourite: the sewage farm) discussing the afternoon's wet-pitch football game.

STRENGTHS

- ◢ Sultan Qaboos
- ◢ Fishing-village feel
- ◢ (Almost) endless stretches of beach
- ◢ Domed buildings
- ◢ Mutrah's souq
- ◢ International-standard health care
- ◢ Walled city of Muscat
- ◢ Mountain walks
- ◢ Water sports
- ◢ The Muscat festival (mid-Janurary to mid-February)
- ◢ Excellent bird-watching
- ◢ Spotlessly clean streets
- ◢ Progressive attitudes

WEAKNESSES

- ◢ High cost of living
- ◢ Public beaches (which may make women feel uncomfortable)
- ◢ Long distances
- ◢ Limited shopping and entertainment
- ◢ Lack of Arabic coffee

GOLD STAR

Mutrah's souq – an outdoor warren of isle-like alleyways selling everything from frankincense to fruit juice, the souq is the essence of Muscat.

STARRING ROLE IN...

- ◢ *The Icarus Agenda* by Robert Lidlum

IMPORT

- ◢ Islam
- ◢ Western medicine
- ◢ Portuguese rule
- ◢ Internet cafés
- ◢ Ships
- ◢ Camels
- ◢ Fast food
- ◢ Football
- ◢ Street names (in progress)

EXPORT

- ◢ Frankincense
- ◢ Slaves
- ◢ The arms trade
- ◢ Oman Today
- ◢ The Oman Bird List
- ◢ Fine-bone china
- ◢ Tableware
- ◢ Pottery skills
- ◢ Textiles
- ◢ Gold
- ◢ Kitsch knick-knacks
- ◢ Moving-forward attitude

SEE 125 years of graffitied records left by visiting sailors on the harbour walls.

EAT sizzling kebabs at the Khargeen Café.

DRINK snake coffee, which the head waiter performs by setting fire to an orange peel, at Mumtaz Mahal.

DO visit the perfect bathing spot at picturesque Jissah Beach.

WATCH the fireworks and dance displays at the fabulous Muscat Festival.

BUY and bargain for frankincense in Muscat's Mutrah souq.

AFTER DARK pop down to Al-Ghazal for some pub-grub, a quiz night and other expat festivities.

URBAN MYTH

The walled city of Muscat's gates remained resolutely locked and bolted against the inevitable encroachments of the outside world until 1970, when Sultan Qaboos opened the city again. To facilitate the growing number of cars needing access to the city, a hole was driven through the city walls. Goods and services flooded in and Muscat flooded out to occupy the surrounding coastline. Touchingly, the city gates continued to be locked at a specific time every evening, despite the adjacent hole in the wall, until the gates were replaced with an archway – a fitting metaphor for a city that has given access to modern conveniences while it holds on to the integrity of its character.

FISH FOR SALE AT ONE OF MUSCAT'S MANY MARKETS.
Photographer: Peter Jordan / Network

THE STRIKING WATCHTOWER MONUMENT ONCE FORMED PART OF THE CITY'S ANCIENT FORTIFICATION.
Photographer: Thierry Bouzac / Impact Photos

CUBS AND SCOUTS FIND COMMON GROUND THE WORLD OVER.
Photographer: Piers Benatar / Panos Pictures

Nairobi

VITAL STATISTICS

NAME: NAIROBI

NICKNAME: SAFARI CAPITAL OF THE WORLD

DATE OF BIRTH: 1901; AFTER EMERGING AS THE ADMINISTRATIVE CENTRE FOR THE UGANDA RAILWAY, NAIROBI BECAME THE CAPITAL OF THE BRITISH PROTECTORATE

ADDRESS: KENYA (MAP 2, M15)

HEIGHT: 1820M

SIZE: 680 SQ KM

POPULATION: 2.9 MILLION (CITY); 4 MILLION (METRO AREA)

LONELY PLANET RANKING: 135

From a rugged iron-roofed frontier town with rhinos and lions roaming in the streets, Nairobi has, in the last 100 years, emerged as a bustling cosmopolitan city set among the vast wilderness of Africa.

ANATOMY

As the gateway to East Africa, the busy Kenyan capital is surrounded by the breathtaking snowcapped Mt Kenya and the open plains of the Masai Mara National Reserve. This young city, with its ultra-modern skyline and few remaining colonial-era buildings, spreads out from the city centre – where the main touristy sights are located – into the energetic working-class suburbs, the wealthy garden suburbs of expats and the notorious sprawl of shantytowns. Getting around Nairobi is easy, but sometimes treacherous: there are crowded but cheap and plentiful speed-demon *matatus* (shared minibus taxis), trains and frequent buses.

PEOPLE

The population comprises many indigenous tribes, a significant number of expats and an increasing number of refugees from surrounding nations. Besides English (the official language) and the widely spoken Swahili, there are also many ethnic languages. Most of the population is either Protestant, Roman Catholic or Muslim, and a small percentage are animist.

TYPICAL NAIROBIAN

Narobians are largely working-class, even though there are extremely rich and poor elements of the population. They like going out for a drink after work and socialising in cafés, restaurants and clubs. Sport is very popular – especially athletics, golf, rugby and cricket – as are Indian and mainstream movies, and shopping in the malls and markets.

DEFINING EXPERIENCE

Sharing a table with locals while enjoying coffee, cake and a newspaper at the overpopulated Nairobi Java House, then heading *Out of Africa* to wander around the colonial house and gardens of the Karen Blixen Museum before heading down the road to the fashionable pub and stylish restaurant in the Karen Blixen Coffee Garden.

STRENGTHS

- Excellent nightspots and good music scene
- Hot, but not extreme, temperatures (due to the high altitude)
- Air-conditioning
- Westlands Triangle Curios Market
- White-water rafting on the Tana River
- Western luxuries in malls
- Many craft emporiums
- Good selection of restaurants and bars
- Text Book Centre (one of the best bookshops in East Africa)
- Excellent outdoor activities

WEAKNESSES

- Poverty
- Rampant crime (the city is often referred to as Nairobbery by the locals)
- Few laundrettes
- Political instability (and attendant violent demonstrations)
- Ever-present prostitutes
- AIDS epidemic

GOLD STAR

Proximity to Africa's natural wonders – just a few kilometres from the air-conditioned luxury of the city is the species-rich Nairobi National Park, full of famous African beasts, hundreds of species of birds and exotic plant life, while only an hour out of town the thrills and spills of white-water rafting await the adventurous. Trekking and mountain-climbing fun on Mt Kenya (5199m) is also close by – only a couple of hours out of town.

STARRING ROLE IN...

- *Nowhere in Africa* (2003)
- *Nairobi Affair* (1988)
- *Out of Africa* (1985)
- *Present Moment* by Marjorie Oludhe Magoye

IMPORT

- Indian and Western blockbusters
- Fast-food chains
- International cuisine
- Air-conditioning
- Heaps of expats

EXPORT

- World-champion athletes
- Coffee
- Exotic flora and fauna
- Batteries
- Textiles
- Flour
- Chemicals
- Beer
- Tea

SEE Western blockbusters cheaply in open-air Africa at the Belle-Vue drive-in.

EAT excellent Swahili stews and curries at the Smart Place.

DRINK an ice-cold Tusker on the rooftop of the Wheels Restaurant & Bar.

DO some lion- and rhino-spotting at Nairobi National Park.

WATCH a range of lively African bands at popular bar-restaurant Simmers.

BUY wonderful – albeit pricey – African souvenirs at Kumbu Kumbu.

AFTER DARK join the steamy drinkin' and dancin' mayhem at the bizarre spacecraftlike New Florida, locally known as the 'Mad House'.

URBAN MYTH

While robbing from churches is unfortunately not an uncommon event in Nairobi, one singular tale goes that a middle-aged man received divine retribution when he was killed after accidentally running in front of a bus. At the time he was escaping from the Nairobi All Saints Cathedral after stealing the contents of collection plates.

SHARE A DRINK AT THE LORD DELAMER BAR IN THE NORFOLK HOTEL.
Photographer: Mark Daffey / LPI

NAIROBIAN CHILDREN CLAP TO THEIR OWN TUNE.
Photographer: Eric L Wheater / LPI

THE CURIOSITY OF YOUTH SPARKS AN UNUSUAL FRIENDSHIP IN THE NAIROBI NATIONAL PARK.
Photographer: David Wall / LPI

MAASAI FOR THE MASSES – THIS COLOURFUL JEWELLERY IS POPULAR WITH TOURISTS.
Photographer: Tom Cockrem / LPI

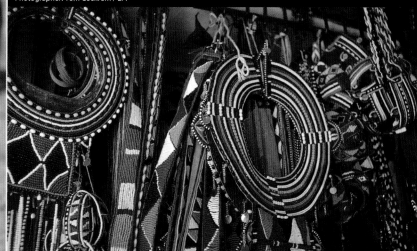

Naples

VITAL STATISTICS

NAME: NAPLES

DATE OF BIRTH: 474 BC; WHEN GREEKS FROM NEARBY CUMAE FOUNDED NEOPOLIS

ADDRESS: ITALY (MAP 3, L14)

HEIGHT: 110M

SIZE: 117 SQ KM

POPULATION: 1 MILLION (CITY); 3 MILLION (METRO AREA)

LONELY PLANET RANKING: 097

Naples is a city for those who relish the intense urban experience: raucous, polluted, crowded and chaotic, but never dull.

ANATOMY

Naples has a heart-wrenchingly beautiful, if precarious, setting. Facing a crescent-shaped bay, Italy's largest port is watched over by a still-active volcano, Mt Vesuvius. The chaotic *centro storico* (inner city) follows the grid of its ancient counterpart that lies below: Via Toledo, Naples' main street, leads north from Piazza Trieste e Trento, next to the waterfront's central landmark, Castel Nuovo. Funiculars and the metro service residential neighbourhoods; in the rest of the city foot and scooter are more efficient than bus or, heaven forbid, cars.

PEOPLE

Naples' history is one of both occupation (as the local dialect flush with Arabic, Spanish, French and English words attests) and emigration (as the Neapolitan diaspora demonstrates). Neapolitans now stay, and although they imagine themselves as a homogeneous Italian-born group, they are increasingly joined by immigrants from Asia, North Africa and Eastern Europe.

TYPICAL NEAPOLITAN

Neapolitans embrace the Italian stereotype – noisy, theatrical, food-obsessed and passionate. They don't earn as much as most other Italians, but that doesn't stop them enjoying eating out and staying up late. They also manage to go to the theatre, rack up astronomical mobile-phone bills and drive like maniacs. The notion of family is still strong, and once young Neapolitans marry and move out of home, they will have more children than anywhere else in Italy.

DEFINING EXPERIENCE

Waking up after a siesta to a short, sweet, strong espresso, a chat with the local barista, hopping on your Piaggio and heading down to Mergellina for the evening *passeggiata* (promenade), grabbing a pizza and folding it in quarters, eating it as you stroll along staring out to Capri, then trying a new flavour of gelati.

STRENGTHS

- *Sfogliatella* – the staple *dolce* (sweet) of Naples, flaky and ricotta-filled
- The late-night *passeggiata*
- A Unesco-listed *centro storico* that's certainly historical, but also vividly alive
- Ferries to Capri, Genoa, Palermo or Tunisia
- *Mozzarella di bufala* (buffalo-milk mozzarella)
- Feeling like you have the Museo Archeologico Nazionale to yourself
- Leg- and lung-saving funiculars
- Ospedale delle Bambole – the delightfully kooky doll's hospital

WEAKNESSES

- The Camorra (Naples' home-grown Mafia)
- Cavalier attitude to the preservation and display of priceless artefacts
- Filthy and crumbling historic treasures
- Chaotic traffic
- Street hustlers and petty criminals
- Air pollution
- Soulless international hotels

GOLD STAR

Street life – Neapolitans take to the piazze and the *vicoli* (backstreets) for breakfast, lunch and dinner, and for a lot of the time in between.

STARRING ROLE IN...

- *Paisà* (Paisan, 1946)
- *L'Oro di Napoli* (The Gold of Naples, 1954)
- *Vito e gli altri* (Vito and the Others, 1991)
- *Il Postino* (The Postman, 1994)
- *The Talented Mr Ripley* (1999)
- *The Volcano Lover* by Susan Sontag
- *Midnight in Sicily* by Peter Robb

IMPORT

- In chronological order: Greeks, Romans, Normans, Saracens, Angevins, Napoleonic French and Bourbon Spanish
- Virgil
- Caravaggio
- South American soaps
- Bottled water
- Milanese and Roman media
- Poet Giacomo Leopardi
- Military bases: US Navy's 6th Fleet Naval Support Activity and the NATO Joint Force Command South
- Diego Armando Maradona

EXPORT

- Sophia Loren
- Domenico Scarlatti
- Totò
- Pizza
- Enrico Caruso
- Coral jewellery
- Bud Spencer
- The literary fairy tale – Giambattista Basile's *Lo cunto de li cunti*, published in Neapolitan dialect in 1634, was the first integral collection of fairy tales to appear in Western Europe
- Actor and director Massimo Troisi
- Shoes and leather goods
- Casertana, Salernitana and Pontina cheese, to Roman restaurants every morning

SEE the chaos below, and Vesuvius beyond, from the peaceful piazze of the Vomero.

EAT a *margherita* pizza at Da Michele, and wonder why it can't always be this good.

DRINK a locally made *limoncello* (lemon-based liqueur) on ice at Bar Lazzarella.

DO a run around Parco di Capodimonte.

WATCH the dancing to electro-pop on the beach at Arenile di Bagnoli on a hot July night.

BUY *presepi* (nativity scene) figures in Via San Gregorio Armeno – will you go trad with shepherds and sheep or cheeky with Berlusconi?

AFTER DARK stumble across the Argentinian tango dancers in the Galleria Umberto, and join them if your tango is up to it.

URBAN MYTH

Every year thousands of Neapolitans cram into the Duomo to witness the blood of their patron saint San Gennaro miraculously liquefy. Of course, few believe that it's a real miracle, and science has a ready explanation. To verify the theory of thixotropy, though, scientists would have to analyse the blood, something the church has effectively blocked by refusing permission to open the phial. Still, the fact remains that when the blood liquefies the city breathes a sigh of relief – another year safe from disaster. A coincidence maybe, but when the miracle failed in 1944, Vesuvius erupted and when it happened (or didn't happen) again in 1980 an earthquake struck.

NOT THE BEST PLACE TO GET A HANDLE ON THE BASICS – PIAZZA PLEBISCITO'S OBSTACLES INCLUDE PERFORMERS AND LARGE HERDS OF NERVOUS TOURISTS.
Photographer: Paolo Sacchi / Getty Images

THE PRESTIGIOUS 16TH-CENTURY PROMENADE OF SANTA LUCIA NOW PLAYS HOST TO THE MOST EXCLUSIVE HOTELS IN THE CITY. Photographer: Paolo Sacchi / Getty Images

A NEAPOLITAN SHOPKEEPER PROUDLY INFLATES ONE OF ITALY'S MOST FAMOUS FACES.
Photographer: Paolo Sacchi / Getty Images

A GREENGROCER AMONG HIS PRODUCE IN THE ANCIENT ROMAN MARKETPLACE OF VIA TRIBUNALI.
Photographer: Paolo Sacchi / Getty Images

IN THE CITY'S FRENCH QUARTER, A LOCAL PO BOYS SHOP SETS A NEON SCENE.
Photographer: Jerry Alexander / LPI

New Orleans will always seduce with soulful jazz wafting out of saloon doors, people leaning over wrought-iron balconies on sultry summer nights and masked party-goers turning up the heat at Carnival.

ANATOMY

New Orleans lies in reclaimed swampland sandwiched between the Mississippi to the south and Lake Pontchartrain to the north. The heart of the original city is the historic French Quarter (the Vieux Carré). Southwest of here is the Central Business District (CBD). The arty Warehouse District and bohemian Lower Garden District are upriver (paradoxically this is south) of the French Quarter. Adjacent to the Lower Garden District are the historic homes of the Garden District. Faubourg Marigny to the east attracts a mostly gay crowd, while the mainly black neighbourhood of Faubourg Tremé to the north is known for its music. Catch a local bus or streetcar to get around town.

PEOPLE

Well over half of New Orleans' population is black. Whites make up 35% while Hispanics number around 3%. A group of Asian immigrants lives mainly in the Versailles area and on the West Bank. Thanks to its French and Spanish heritage, the population is predominantly Roman Catholic.

TYPICAL NEW ORLEANIAN

New Orleans is a fairly poor city with a small tax base to support its social services and education. Wages in Louisiana, as measured in income per capita, are the lowest in the USA after Mississippi and Arkansas, and one in four people live on or near the poverty line (most of the poor people are black). New Orleanians are a friendly bunch and welcoming towards visitors (although you're not really part of the club unless you have generations of New Orleans blood coursing through your veins). Life in the Big Easy is for enjoying and service can occasionally be slow. But New Orleanians don't worry about that – they know that having a good time is more important than having a quick time!

New Orleans

VITAL STATISTICS

NAME: NEW ORLEANS

NICKNAME: THE BIG EASY; CRESCENT CITY

DATE OF BIRTH: 1718; WHEN SIEUR DE BIENVILLE FOUNDED NOUVELLE ORLÉANS

ADDRESS: USA (MAP 1, K11)

HEIGHT: 2M

SIZE: 468 SQ KM

POPULATION: 1 MILLION

LONELY PLANET RANKING: 039

CARNIVAL BEADS AND JAZZY TRINKETS OVERLAY AN EMBLEMATIC IMAGE OF MARDI GRAS.
Photographer: Richard Cummins / LPI

CAJUN COOKING IN THE BUSY KITCHENS OF NOLA'S RESTAURANT IN THE FRENCH QUARTER.
Photographer: Jerry Alexander / LPI

THE FURIOUS SOUNDS OF NEW ORLEANS JAZZ RAISING THE ROOF AT PRESERVATION HALL.
Photographer: John Elk III / LPI

DEFINING EXPERIENCE

Starting the day with a coffee at Café du Monde before wandering around the French Quarter, relaxing in Jackson Sq and gearing up for an evening of live music at Funky Butt on Congo Sq.

STRENGTHS

- New Orleans Jazz & Heritage Festival
- Mardi Gras
- Gay and lesbian scene
- The beautiful Garden District
- Audubon Zoo
- Riverboat calliope music
- Buskers in Jackson Sq
- St Charles Ave streetcar
- The balconies and courtyards of Royal St
- St Louis Cemetery No 1
- Creole restaurants of Royal St and Bourbon St
- The French Market
- The French Quarter
- Ursuline Convent
- Aquarium of the Americas
- Tranquil Bayou St John
- New Orleans Museum of Art

WEAKNESSES

- Racial inequality during the Civil War and Reconstruction
- Risks of flooding and sudden storms – Hurricane Katrina devastated the city in 2005
- Faint petroleum smell in parts of the city

GOLD STAR

Jazz.

STARRING ROLE IN...

- *JFK* (2001)
- *Dead Man Walking* (1996)
- *Easy Rider* (1969)
- *A Streetcar Named Desire* (1951)
- *The Big Easy* (1987)

IMPORT

- Professor Longhair
- Trent Reznor
- Benjamin Henry Latrobe
- Tennessee Williams
- William Faulkner
- King Oliver

EXPORT

- Louis Armstrong
- Buddy Bolden
- Truman Capote
- Harry Connick Jr
- Fats Domino
- Randy Newman
- Lee Harvey Oswald
- Aaron Neville
- Jelly Roll Morton
- Anne Rice
- Grain
- Steel
- The cocktail (allegedly invented in New Orleans)

SEE the city from aboard a riverboat.

EAT gumbo at local favourite K-Paul's Louisiana Kitchen.

DRINK in the candlelit Lafitte's Blacksmith Shop, apparently an old pirate haunt.

DO wander through the French Quarter, discovering New Orleans' history at the Louisiana State Museum and soaking up the atmosphere.

WATCH the parades, floats, seminaked revellers and dazzling debauchery of Mardi Gras.

BUY local tunes from the Louisiana Music Factory, which also has live music on Saturday.

AFTER DARK Donna's Bar & Grill is hopping with the best local jazz musicians – if they're not on the bill they'll pop in to jam.

URBAN MYTH

Shotgun houses can be found all over the city and are popular for their high ceilings and Victorian styling. They are called 'shotgun' not because of the speed of their construction as you might think but because of their shape. With each room back to back and the whole house one room wide, they were specifically designed in the 19th century so as to allow a bullet to pass through the house without stopping. There are also double-shotguns (duplexes with a separately owned mirror-image) and even camel-back shotguns, with a 2nd floor above the back of the house.

Nuuk

VITAL STATISTICS

NAME: NUUK

NICKNAME: GODTHÅB (LITERALLY 'GOOD HOPE' IN DANISH)

DATE OF BIRTH: 1728; THE TOWN WAS FOUNDED BY THE NORWEGIAN MISSIONARY HANS EGEDE AS THE FIRST ALL-YEAR EUROPEAN COLONY AND TRADING POST IN GREENLAND

ADDRESS: GREENLAND (MAP 1, O5)

HEIGHT: 20M

SIZE: 87,000 SQ KM

POPULATION: 16,000

LONELY PLANET RANKING: 165

Nuuk is the perfect base for discovering Greenland and its culture – explore the Inuit culture and people, then head off into the mountains or onto the fjords for spectacular adventure tourism.

ANATOMY

Situated on the mouth of the Godthåbsfiord, Nuuk commands an impressive if spread-out fjord system and is backed by a splendid panorama of mountains, particularly Mt Sermitsiaq. The architecture is a mix of older homes of real Greenlandic charm and rows of spirit-crushing housing. Explore the world's northernmost capital city by boat and snowmobile.

PEOPLE

This city's population is bicultural, with Greenlanders (Inuit) forming the majority and Danes the minority. The two thought systems are often almost diametrically opposed, but Greenlanders of Danish, Inuit and mixed origin share a bond of objective, philosophical realism, and they mock incoming Danes and foreigners alike for their unrealistic belief in clocks, appointments and deadlines. Danish is the official language.

TYPICAL NUUK CITIZEN

Nuuk's inhabitants have adapted to the development from a traditional Greenlandic society to a modern industrial town in a unique way. The economy functions for and because of administrators, but tools lie where they're dropped once the cash arrives on payday. Time will be spent with friends, but in comfortable silence – the key is in the body language. Smiles are common, but don't always mean pleasure. Adults in villages will ignore you, but children won't stop examining you. Your race and origins will be observed, but you'll be judged on your actions. Nuuk is the only place to be for family, friends and the hunt.

DEFINING EXPERIENCE

Morning fishing on the fjords, then *kaffemik* (coffee and, usually, seven types of cakes or biscuits) with the entire community, sitting in blissful silence with friends and leaving when you've had you're second cup of coffee, eating your day's catch, then heading out for a night of live music and dancing at the pub.

STRENGTHS

- Vibrant Inuit culture
- Aurora borealis
- Braedet Market (fresh fish and game sold on open-air tables)
- World's hardest golf course
- Photogenic Qornup Suvdula fjord
- Traditional costumes worn on the first day of school
- Snow, ice and water sports galore
- Oldest rocks (3.8 billion years old) ever discovered on earth
- Ghosts of Herrnhut missionaries in the University of Greenland
- Humpback whales in the harbour
- Greenlandic modern art

WEAKNESSES

- Long-slab apartment blocks, such as Block P
- Pervasive sense of economic apartheid
- Children on the streets all night from parental neglect
- Alcoholism
- *Perlerorneq* ('the burden' in Greenlandic) – depression during the long, dark winters

GOLD STAR

The Arctic Marathon – Nuuk hosts the world's most challenging snow-bound marathon for locals and internationals.

STARRING ROLE IN...

- *Nuuk* (2004)
- *Miss Smilla's Feeling For Snow* by Peter Høeg
- *Smilla's Sense of Snow* (1977)
- *Last Places* by Lawrence Millman
- *Tales and Traditions of the Eskimo* by Henry Rink
- *Eskimo Folk-tales* collected by Knud Rasmussen
- *An African in Greenland* by Tété-Michel Kpomassie

IMPORT

- Anything (product or food) that can't be made from Arctic critters or territory
- Beer
- Ridiculously expensive hashish
- Vikings
- Missionaries
- Danish welfare payments
- Evangelical Lutheran beliefs and hymns
- Music styles

EXPORT

- Fish, prawns and other fish products
- Inuit culture
- Fur craft and clothing
- Mummified six-year-old girls on the cover of *National Geographic*
- The Nuuk Declaration on Arctic nations and its role in protecting the Arctic environment
- Nuuk Posse, Greenland's most popular hip-hop band
- Big-budget Arctic tourism
- Santa Claus
- Packaged whale steaks

SEE Kolonihavn – an 18th-century fishing village in the heart of Nuuk.

EAT gourmet Arctic gastronomy (like musk steak) at Restaurant Nipisa.

DRINK genuine Greenlandic coffee at Café Tuap.

DO explore ancient and modern Inuit art at the Katuaq Cultural Centre.

WATCH snow sculptors at work at the annual Nuuk International Snow Festival.

BUY a piece of black *Nuummiit*, the 'Greenland opal', found only in the Nuuk region.

AFTER DARK drink up in Kristinemut, Greenland's first pub, then party on in the electro-throbbing rock bar Afterdark.

URBAN MYTH

An indefinable distance from Nuuk is Kongsgaarden, a world-famous workshop full of consumer goods that are given away on a seasonal basis, especially in late December. This behaviour brings unprecedented popularity to the manager, a certain Mr S Claus, who receives more mail than anyone else in the whole of Greenland. Alas, reindeer-sleigh services are notoriously unreliable, so Santa Claus can only be accessed via the web (www .santa.gl) or through mail posted in the world's biggest postbox, located outside the post office in Nuuk.

BASKING IN THE AFTERNOON SUN – UNIFORM APARTMENT BLOCKS ARE A COMMON SIGHT IN NUUK.
Photographer: Anders Blomqvist / LPI

SEAL MEAT IS A STAPLE OF THE LOCAL DIET, ON SALE HERE IN THE BRAEDET MARKET.
Photographer: Anders Blomqvist / LPI

THE INUIT PEOPLE TRY TO PRESERVE THEIR CULTURE DESPITE THE CRUSH OF MODERNISATION.
Photographer: Anders Blomqvist / LPI

GOLFERS DO IT TOUGH AGAINST THE BACKDROP OF SERMITSIAQ PEAK.
Photographer: Anders Blomqvist / LPI

At once relaxed and energetic, remote and cosmopolitan Oaxaca City is one of Mexico's most vibrant cultural capitals where ancient indigenous culture and modern artistic innovation intermingle in a charming colonial setting.

ANATOMY

Situated at a comfortable altitude at the juncture of three valleys, the city enjoys a sunny and stable climate, which suits its cheerfully laid-back vibe. Oaxaca City's Spanish colonial heritage is visible as much in the stunning stone buildings as in the town's gridlike planning. Streets open out into public gardens and airy plazas then disappear again into narrow cobbled lanes and winding back alleys. Oaxaca City's heart and soul is the broad *zócalo* (town square), a meeting place for its citizens and venue for its many cultural events. Most points of interest in the city are within walking distance of each other, but you can use city buses if your feet get tired.

PEOPLE

Almost all of Oaxaca City's citizens are descended from the indigenous Zapotec and Mixtec peoples who remain fiercely proud of their heritage; many continue to observe pre-Hispanic traditions, from cooking and music to healing practices.

TYPICAL OAXACAN

Oaxacans have the best of everything. They are well educated (thanks in part to the town's historic hero, Benito Juárez), artistically appreciative, discerning in matters culinary and lacking in the macho boisterousness that tends to confront visitors in other parts of Mexico. Locals are self-confident and friendly. They are as comfortable yelling at a football match as they are chatting at a café or wandering quietly through an art gallery. Nobody is in much of a hurry in Oaxaca. With thousands of years of colourful history behind it, what's the rush?

Oaxaca City

VITAL STATISTICS

NAME: OAXACA CITY

NICKNAME: IN THE NOSE OF THE SQUASH; THE LITERAL MEANING OF 'HUAXYÁCAC', OAXACA'S EARLIER AZTEC NAME

DATE OF BIRTH: 1529; WHEN THE SPANISH OFFICIALLY FOUNDED THE CITY, ALTHOUGH AN INDIGENOUS SETTLEMENT HAD ALREADY EXISTED AT THE SITE OF PRESENT-DAY OAXACA CITY FOR SEVERAL MILLENNIA

ADDRESS: MEXICO (MAP 4, D5)

HEIGHT: 1550M

POPULATION: 260,000

LONELY PLANET RANKING: 079

COWBOY-HATTED LOCALS FRAMED AGAINST THE CHARACTERISTIC PASTEL COLOURS OF A CITY DWELLING.
Photographer: Jeffrey Becom / LPI

DEFINING EXPERIENCE

Getting up early and heading straight for the rowdy market to enjoy an invigorating bowl of hot *cacao* (chocolate) and sweet bread, stepping out again into the clear light that has inspired some of Mexico's most respected contemporary artists, crawling the galleries and the cafés for the rest of the day before losing yourself in the joyful mania of a festival.

STRENGTHS

- Chocolate
- Extraordinary arts and crafts
- Stunning galleries
- Indigenous culture
- Explosive festivals
- Unbeatable local cuisine
- Modern art
- Día de los Muertos (Day of the Dead) celebrations
- Colonial architecture
- Benito Juárez
- Handicrafts
- VW beetle taxis

WEAKNESSES

- Heavy-handed police
- Political unrest
- Former dictator Porfirio Díaz
- Traffic

GOLD STAR

Nowhere is the Mexican festival Día de Muertos taken more seriously than in Oaxaca City and the surrounding villages. In this Zapotec celebration, which has fused with Catholic traditions, Oaxacans honour their dead by setting off fireworks in the cemeteries, eating sugared skulls and dressing up in outrageous costumes.

STARRING ROLE IN...

- Día de Muertos iconography

IMPORT

- Camera-happy tourists
- International fine-arts students
- Handicraft collectors
- American products
- Rural workers looking for a big-city break

EXPORT

- *Calaveras* (whimsical sculptures or images on a skeleton motif, abundant at markets prior to Día de Muertos)
- *Mole* (a sauce made with unsweetened cocoa and chilli)
- Benito Juárez' philosophy
- Pirated CDs
- Contemporary art
- Chocolate

SEE the Iglesia de Santo Domingo, the most splendid of Oaxaca's many churches.

EAT spiced grasshoppers from a street stall.

DRINK sickly sweet hot chocolate with cinnamon and crushed almonds.

DO a round of the contemporary art museums and wind up in an atmospheric café.

WATCH frenetic dancing at the Guelaguetza festival.

BUY Mexico's best folk art.

AFTER DARK hit Candela to catch some of the best live salsa you'll ever experience.

URBAN MYTH

Benito Juárez (1806–72) is literally synonymous with the city itself, as Oaxaca City was once named Oaxaca de Juárez in his honour. A Zapotec orphan, he began his impoverished childhood as a bookbinder and later rose to become justice minister. His liberal reforms, which reduced the power of the church and the military, provoked the War of Reform and briefly forced him into exile. One of Juárez' main political achievements was to make primary education free and compulsory. Today countless statues, streets, schools and plazas preserve his name and memory, and his sage maxim 'Respect for the rights of others is peace' is widely quoted.

IN A BLUR OF MOVEMENT A GRINNING DANCER STEPS TO A TRADITIONAL BEAT.
Photographer: Greg Elms / LPI

SANTO DOMINGO CATHEDRAL RISES MAJESTICALLY ABOVE THE PALM LINED *ZÓCALO* IN THE TOWN CENTRE.
Photographer: Richard I'Anson / LPI

PLASTIC BASKETS IN TRADITIONAL INDIGENOUS DESIGNS LINE THE COBBLESTONES OUTSIDE OAXACA MARKET.
Photographer: Greg Elms / LPI

Panama City

VITAL STATISTICS

NAME: PANAMA CITY

NICKNAME: PANAMÁ, THE NAME OF THE FORMER CITY, RAZED TO THE GROUND BY THE PIRATE HENRY MORGAN IN 1671

DATE OF BIRTH: 1519; WHEN IT WAS FOUNDED ON THE SITE OF AN INDIAN FISHING VILLAGE BY THE SPANISH GOVERNOR PEDRO ARIAS DE ÁVILA

ADDRESS: PANAMA (MAP 4, J8)

HEIGHT: 13M

SIZE: 2561 SQ KM

POPULATION: 470,000

LONELY PLANET RANKING: 108

The bottleneck of the world's shipping routes, Panama City is a teeming capital in the heart of Latin America, touched by transient influences from all over the globe – sooner or later, everything comes to town.

ANATOMY

Panama City stretches about 20km along the Pacific coast, with the Bahía de Panamá to the south, the Panama Canal to the west, protected forest to the north and the stone ruins of Panamá Viejo (Old Panama, the city's original site) to the east. You can trace the history and personality of the city by walking from the crumbling old town neighbourhood of Casco Viejo through the hotel district of La Exposición to arrive eventually at the vertiginous skyscrapers of El Cangrejo, the thriving banking district. Panama City has a good network of local buses (nicknamed *diablos rojos* – or red devils). Taxis are also plentiful.

PEOPLE

Most of Panama City's population is mestizo (of mixed Spanish and indigenous ancestry). There is also a sizable Chinese community, and a considerable proportion of the population is descended from English-speaking West Indians.

TYPICAL PANAMANIAN

Just as the colonial decay of old-town Casco Viejo is thrown into sharp relief by the modern excess of new-town El Cangrejo, your typical citizen of Panama City is equally contradictory. The exceptionally tolerant Panamanian character weathers many disjunctions – the old and the new, the grave disparity between rich and poor, and the gorgeous natural environment and its rapid destruction. Much of this tolerance begins in the family, which is the cornerstone of Panamanian society and plays a role in nearly every aspect of a person's life.

DEFINING EXPERIENCE

Wandering aimlessly through the heavily atmospheric old-town district of Casco Viejo, peering in the doorways of old churches to admire the altar displays and escape the midday sun, rambling on towards the bustling market and finishing up with a sangria or coffee at an outdoor café.

STRENGTHS

◢ Bicycle-riding police
◢ Fabulously decorated public buses
◢ Mireya Moscoso, the country's first female president
◢ Artistic postage stamps
◢ Scrumptious international food
◢ The Panama Canal
◢ Diverse museums

WEAKNESSES

◢ High crime
◢ Psychotic drivers
◢ General Manuel Noriega
◢ Unemployment
◢ Government corruption

GOLD STAR

The Panama Canal, one of the seven wonders of the industrial world, is just a short distance from the city. Its construction was considered as early as 1524 and its early-20th-century system of giant lock gates remains a marvel of engineering.

STARRING ROLE IN...

◢ *The Tailor of Panama* (2001)

IMPORT

◢ Shopping malls
◢ American fashions
◢ High-rolling entrepreneurs
◢ Manufactured goods
◢ Panama hats – actually made in Ecuador
◢ Illegal drugs
◢ Sailors
◢ Container ships laden with everything from the four corners of the Earth

EXPORT

◢ Bananas
◢ Fish
◢ Sugar
◢ Coffee
◢ Reggae – the earliest recordings were made by Jamaican labourers in Panama City
◢ Reggaeton – the hard-core new upstart in the Latin music scene, pioneered in Panama City
◢ Illegal drugs
◢ Sailors
◢ Container ships laden with everything from the four corners of the earth

SEE a ship passing through the giant locks of the Panama Canal.

EAT cuisine from all over the world.

DRINK sangría in Casco Viejo.

DO a dance course at the Latin Dance Company; this skill will get you places.

WATCH the thunderous, booty-shaking *carnaval* parade.

BUY bargain jewellery.

AFTER DARK hit one of Panama City's pumping clubs and be prepared to dance till you drop.

URBAN MYTH

It is said that when the Welsh pirate Henry Morgan sacked Panamá in 1671, the only object of value that was salvaged was the Altar de Oro (Golden Altar) in the Iglesia de San José. According to local tales, when word came of the pirate's impending attack, a priest painted the altar black to disguise it. The priest told Morgan that the famous altar had been stolen by another pirate and even convinced Morgan to donate handsomely for its replacement. Morgan is said to have told the priest, 'I don't know why, but I think you are more of a pirate than I am'.

STRIKING A POSE, PANAMA-STYLE.
Photographer: Richard Quataert / Photolibrary

THE SPARKLING VIEW DOWN BALBOA AVE AT NIGHTTIME.
Photographer: José Fuste Raga / Photolibrary

LOCALS RELAX IN THE CRUMBLING BEAUTY OF CASCO VIEJO.
Photographer: Alfredo Maiquez / Photolibrary

FISHING BOATS GET A REST AFTER DELIVERING THE DAY'S CATCH.
Photographer: Danny Lehman / Corbis

Paris

VITAL STATISTICS

NAME: PARIS

NICKNAME: CITY OF LIGHT

DATE OF BIRTH: 52 BC; WHEN JULIUS CAESAR ESTABLISHED LUTETIA ON THE BANKS OF THE SEINE

ADDRESS: FRANCE (MAP 3, G9)

HEIGHT: 75M

SIZE: 105 SQ KM

POPULATION: 2.2 MILLION

LONELY PLANET RANKING: 001

Paris has it all: celebrity monuments, manicured parks, taste-bud–tingling cuisine, endless museums, frenetic flea markets and *haute couture* – and like its well-groomed citizens, it always looks good, with no hair out of place.

ANATOMY

Ringed by the terrifying blvd Périphérique, France's capital city is made up of 20 *arrondissements* (districts). The Seine River flows through the city and around two islands, Île de la Cité (site of Notre Dame) and Île St-Louis. The arty, intellectual Left Bank (south of the Seine) houses the Sorbonne University, the vibrant, touristy Latin Quarter and upmarket St-Germain. The Right Bank is home to the Champs-Élysées and the Louvre, as well as trendy shopping in the Marais, nightlife in the Bastille district and Paris's two opera houses. Overlooking the city to the north is the 126m-high Butte de Montmartre (Montmartre hill), the Moulin Rouge and Pigalle (the red-light district). The Eiffel Tower is directly south of the Arc de Triomphe on the southern side of the Seine. Walk or take the wonderfully efficient Métro.

PEOPLE

Officially, 17% of Paris' population are immigrants, with the largest numbers arriving from Algeria, Portugal, Morocco, Tunisia, China and Mali (in descending numerical order). The rest are French.

TYPICAL PARISIAN

Parisians are typically crazy drivers and park with their handbrakes off to allow their neighbouring parker the inevitable bumping. They are stylish, chic and will wear lipstick for putting the rubbish out. They can come across as snooty and see the rest of France as rather provincial. Etiquette is very important and one false move will meet a barely detectable raising of the eyebrows and semiaudible sigh. They are well educated and ambitious, but never brash. They are also expert conversationalists and very respectful and proud of French cuisine and culture. Finally, despite burgeoning nonsmoking laws, Parisians still smoke – a lot.

DEFINING EXPERIENCE

Coffee and croissants on Place de la Contrescarpe, then strolling through the Latin Quarter and over the river to the quietly charming Île St-Louis, on to the Marais for some retail indulgence then lunch and a *vin rouge* (red wine) on Place des Vosges.

STRENGTHS

- Successful modern masterpieces eg the Eiffel Tower, the Louvre Pyramid and the Centre Pompidou
- Musée du Louvre
- Musée d'Orsay
- Sacré Cœur
- Dazzling department stores – La Samaritaine, Galeries Lafayette
- Shakespeare & Co bookshop
- *Haute couture*
- Cathédrale de Notre Dame de Paris
- Cimetière du Père Lachaise
- Château de Versailles
- *Café terrasses* (café terraces)
- Quirky museums eg the Musée des Égouts de Paris (sewers) and Catacombes de Paris (catacombs)
- Philosophers and intellectuals
- Paris Plage
- French Open
- Compulsory cleaning of building façades every 10 years
- Art in the Métro
- Heavenly food and wine

WEAKNESSES

- Mad drivers
- Underwhelming Eurostar terminal
- Tiny, expensive hotel rooms
- Rude waiters
- Dog poo
- Strikes
- August – much of Paris closes as Parisians flee the city

GOLD STAR

Landmarks – so much of Paris is iconic.

STARRING ROLE IN...

- *Before Sunset* (2004)
- *Le Fabuleux Destin d'Amélie Poulin* (Amélie, 2001)
- *Subway* (1985)
- *Last Tango in Paris* (1972)
- *À Bout de Souffle* (1959)
- *Les Misérables* by Victor Hugo

IMPORT

- Valentine's Day visitors
- James Joyce
- Samuel Beckett
- Henry Miller
- Ernest Hemingway
- Pablo Picasso
- Man Ray
- Salvador Dalí
- Jim Morrison

EXPORT

- Existentialism
- Jean-Paul Sartre
- Marcel Proust
- Brigitte Bardot
- Serge Gainsbourg
- Simone de Beauvoir
- Johnny Halliday
- Charles Baudelaire
- François Voltaire
- Molière
- Édith Piaf
- Jacques Chirac
- Claude Monet
- The French Revolution
- Auguste Rodin
- The Statue of Liberty

SEE Leonardo da Vinci's *Mona Lisa* at possibly the world's best art gallery, the Louvre.

EAT delectable patisseries and creamy confections at historic Ladurée on rue Royale, founded in 1862.

DRINK martinis or mojitos (a cocktail made of rum, lime, sugar, mint and soda water) at the classy China Club and imagine you're in a gentleman's club.

DO sunbathe by the Seine at Paris Plage (imported sand and pebble beaches complete with plastic palm trees).

WATCH the Eiffel Tower light up from the balcony of Georges restaurant in the Centre Pompidou.

BUY Hermès and Yves Saint Laurent on rue du Faubourg St-Honoré.

AFTER DARK take to the water with a techno night at Le Batofar, a tugboat-turned-club on the Seine.

URBAN MYTH

Who actually uttered the infamous phrase 'let them eat cake' is a source of much debate. It is usually attributed to Marie Antoinette, who apparently suggested cake as a response to riots about bread shortages in 1789. The mob, seething with hunger and rage, stormed the Château de Versailles, forcing Marie Antoinette to flee down a secret passage. The story, as we know, ends badly for the lady. Whether or not she said 'let them eat cake', she and her husband Louis XVI had become sufficiently unpopular as to lose their role as monarchs and were summarily guillotined a few years later.

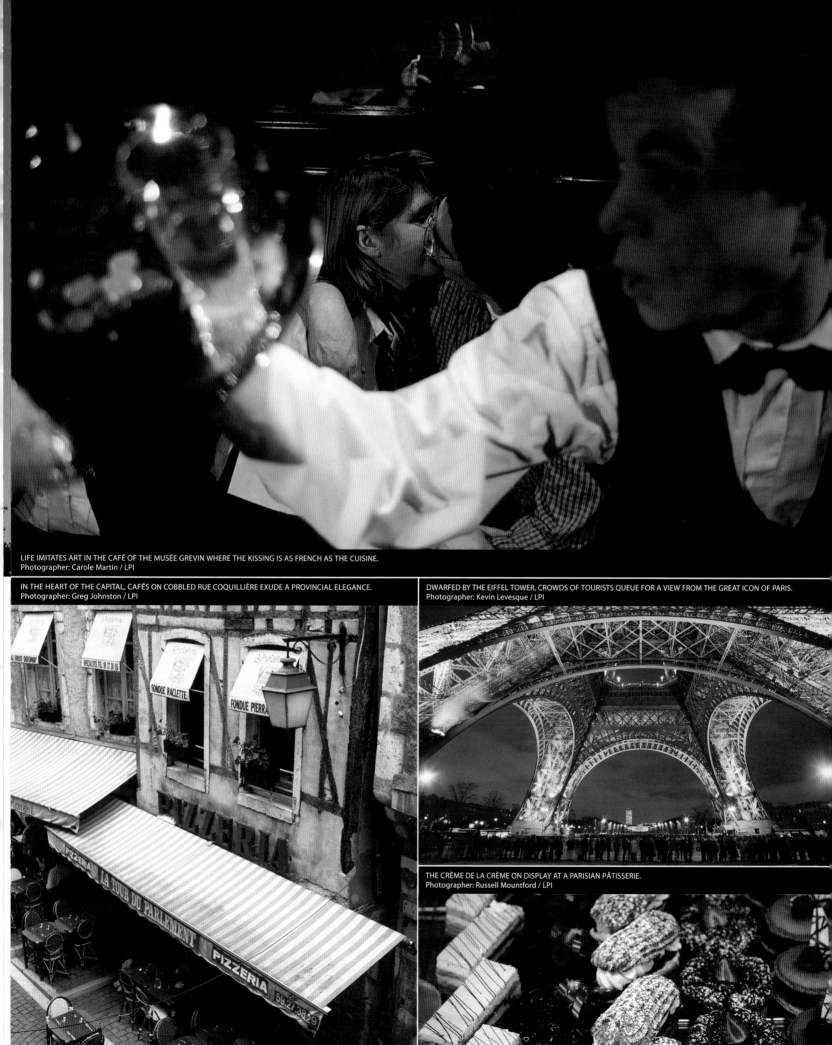

LIFE IMITATES ART IN THE CAFÉ OF THE MUSÉE GREVIN WHERE THE KISSING IS AS FRENCH AS THE CUISINE.
Photographer: Carole Martin / LPI

IN THE HEART OF THE CAPITAL, CAFÉS ON COBBLED RUE COQUILLIÈRE EXUDE A PROVINCIAL ELEGANCE.
Photographer: Greg Johnston / LPI

DWARFED BY THE EIFFEL TOWER, CROWDS OF TOURISTS QUEUE FOR A VIEW FROM THE GREAT ICON OF PARIS.
Photographer: Kevin Levesque / LPI

THE CRÈME DE LA CRÈME ON DISPLAY AT A PARISIAN PÂTISSERIE.
Photographer: Russell Mountford / LPI

Prague

VITAL STATISTICS

NAME: PRAGUE

NICKNAME: MATIČKA PRAHA (LITTLE MOTHER PRAGUE)

DATE OF BIRTH: 4000 BC; WHEN FARMING COMMUNITIES WERE ESTABLISHED BY GERMANIC AND CELTIC TRIBES; THE SLAVS ARRIVED AROUND AD 600

ADDRESS: CZECH REPUBLIC (MAP 3, L9)

HEIGHT: 262M

SIZE: 496 SQ KM

POPULATION: 1.2 MILLION (CITY); 1.9 MILLION (METRO AREA)

LONELY PLANET RANKING: 014

With its fairy-tale cityscape, solid cultural heritage and perfect pilsner, Prague continues to captivate.

ANATOMY

Prague straddles the Vltava River, its two halves joined by the Charles Bridge, one of the world's loveliest. The centre consists of five historical towns: Hradčany, the castle district, on a hill above the west bank; Malá Strana (Little Quarter), between the river and castle; Staré Město, the Gothic 'Old Town' on the east bank; adjacent Josefov, the former Jewish ghetto; and Nové Město (New Town – new in the 14th century, that is), to the south and east. This compact maze is best appreciated on foot, aided by Prague's fine Soviet-era metro, tram and bus system.

PEOPLE

Prague has a significant Czech population, as well as Slovak and Roma groups – the latter, formerly known as Gypsies, are often the target of vicious racism. Significant numbers of German and American expatriates also call Prague home.

TYPICAL PRAGUER

Praguers pay dearly for the privilege of living in one of Europe's best-preserved and most-visited cities – at least half their wages can go on rent, and many restaurants, bars and consumer goods are out of their reach. They still manage to drink enormous amounts of beer, and indulge decidedly highbrow cultural tastes (and dress up for the symphony). First impressions may suggest mild manners and old-fashioned values, but Praguers often harbour a surreal sense of humour, and a steely sense of their rights and their place in history.

DEFINING EXPERIENCE

Taking the dog for a run through Vrtbovska Gardens and up Petřín Hill, refuelling on strudel and browsing for antique books in Staré Město, then drinking beer and scoffing sausage at riverside Letenske sady, laughing about David Černý's latest stunt and deciding whether it's to be an all-nighter at Akropolis or a jazz jam at Little Glen's.

STRENGTHS

- A thousand years of well-preserved European architecture
- Pilsner, pilsner and more pilsner
- Poignant, picturesque Josefov
- Old Town Sq, despite the tack
- Fab futurist Metro stations
- The Velvet Revolution
- The Havel/Pistek-designed uniforms of the castle guards
- Jan Švankmajer
- The morally instructive Astronomical Clock

WEAKNESSES

- Shuffling crowds of camcorder-wielding tourists
- Jazz-fusion fanatics
- Grumpy service
- Pickpockets
- Tacky souvenir shops
- Meter-meddling taxi drivers

GOLD STAR

Romance – despite the tourists, Prague's riverside setting and architectural heritage cannot fail to pull the heart strings.

STARRING ROLE IN...

- *Comfortably Numb* (2005)
- *Van Helsing* (2004)
- *A Knight's Tale* (2001)
- *Mission: Impossible* (1996)
- *The Unbearable Lightness of Being* (1988)
- *Metamorphoses* by Franz Kafka

IMPORT

- Coca-Cola
- American trustafarians (a marijuana-smoking, rich, white university student)
- Soviet-era watches and fur hats
- Mexican restaurants
- British and Irish stag parties

EXPORT

- Animation
- Pilsner
- Franz Kafka
- Antonin Dvořák
- Absinthe
- Textiles
- Milan Kundera
- Ivan Klima

SEE the splendid gilt-set slabs of semiprecious stones in the Chapel of St Wenceslas in St Vitus Cathedral, then take in the splendid view from the ramparts outside.

EAT posh pork and dumplings at the Kolkovna in Staré Město, a modern take on the trad beer hall.

DRINK light, dark or waywardly flavoured Czech lager, made on the premises at Nové Město's Pivovarský Dům.

DO a Sunday afternoon football match at AC Sparta Praha's stadium.

WATCH Smetana performed at the glorious, golden-roofed Národní Divadlo, a living monument to the Czech National Revival.

BUY a 16th-century aquatint of an angel at Antikvariát U Karlova Mostu, right near the Charles Bridge.

AFTER DARK dance with the Bohemians, or discover the lethal combination of *pivo* (beer) and poetry, at the venerable Radost FX, near Wenceslas Sq.

URBAN MYTH

Those who were involved in the Velvet Revolution – '89ers – often tell a story about 'the Japanese guy'. Student activists where having a hard time keeping under the police radars and were using ancient 300-baud modems to communicate via Fidonet, an early internet bulletin-board system, but it wasn't an easy task. Out of the blue, a quiet Japanese man turned up at the university and presented the students with a suitcase full of brand-new 2400-baud Taiwanese modems. No-one got his name or saw him again, although everyone agrees he existed. The modems were vital to the cause and were used to coordinate demonstrations, circulate manifestos and keep one step ahead of the secret police. Soon the older-generation dissident intelligentsia joined in and the rest, as they say, is history.

LOVERS SHARE AN INTIMATE EMBRACE ON THE CITY'S NUMBER ONE MUST-SEE MONUMENT, THE STONE GOTHIC CHARLES BRIDGE .
Photographer: Sean Gallup / Getty Images

A MAN WAITS FOR
Photographer: Ant

THE MYSTERIOUS S
AT SUNRISE. Phot

THE PLAYFUL ARCHITECTURE OF THE DANCING HOUSE.
Photographer: Sean Gallup / Getty Images

A DAILY STREAM OF PRAGUERS CROSS CHARLES BRIDGE INTO PICTURESQUE MALÁ STRANA AT THE FOOT OF
PRAGUE CASTLE. Photographer: Sean Gallup / Getty Images

REVAMPED SOVIET-ERA METRO STATIONS GIVE THE CITY'S TRANSPORT SYSTEM A LIFT.
Photographer: Sean Gallup / Getty Images

Pyongyang

P

VITAL STATISTICS

NAME: PYONGYANG

DATE OF BIRTH: AD 427; WHEN THE GOGURYEO DYNASTY BUILT ITS CAPITAL HERE

ADDRESS: NORTH KOREA (MAP 1, JJ10)

HEIGHT: 27M

SIZE: 200 SQ KM

POPULATION: 3.2 MILLION

LONELY PLANET RANKING: 187

ON GUARD IN THE DEMILITARISED ZONE – NORTH KOREAN SOLDIERS ON PATROL AT TRUCE VILLAGE.
Photographer: Lee Jae-Won / Reuters/Picture Media

KIM JONG IL IS A CULT FIGURE IN HIS COUNTRY.
Photographer: Lee Jae-Won / Reuters/Picture Media

A LONE WORKER WALKS BY JUCHE TOWER, THE DEFINING SYMBOL OF NORTH KOREAN COMMUNISM.
Photographer: Anthony Pletts / Alamy

THE STRANGE BALLET OF THE MASS GAMES IS A WELL CHOREOGRAPHED SPECTACLE.
Photographer: Tony Wheeler / LPI

Monumental and monolithic, the North Korean capital is one of the most impressive and unique cities on earth.

ANATOMY

Clustered around the massive Taedong River, Pyongyang's streets are eerily empty of traffic – most people walk or take buses, but only the privileged few have access to private motor cars. The centrepiece is Kim Il Sung Sq, the vast public space where military parades of fanatic precision take place under the shaded gaze of Communist emperor Kim Jong Il.

PEOPLE

Pyongyang must be one of the most homogeneous cities on earth. Its scant foreign population is billeted in the restricted diplomatic quarter, while the Chinese workers who run some of the city's hotels are unable to leave the establishments they work as it is feared they may adversely influence the locals. Pyongyang inhabitants are therefore fascinated by any foreigner, and will wave and smile, but rarely dare speak to you. Only those of an ideologically pure background are given permits to live in the capital, so the people you see here are among the most privileged in the country.

TYPICAL PYONGYANGER

Despite their relatively high status in North Korean society, the vast majority of Pyongyang's inhabitants live austere lives. Every household will have a portrait of Kim Il Sung and his son Kim Jong Il. While food is no longer scarce, most people will live on a frugal diet of rice and noodles. Electricity is in short supply and the capital is often pitch black at night. Whenever the lights go off, locals shout 'blame America!' in response.

DEFINING EXPERIENCE

Finding Pyongyang's heart and soul is challenge indeed. So much of what you see is façade designed to interpret the government's vision of the country, but often bearing nothing in common with reality. In itself this is the defining experience of the city – trying to see through the cracks and chinks in the city's ideological armour.

STRENGTHS

◢ The North Koreans, when you are lucky enough to spend time with them, are delightful
◢ Lack of traffic pollution
◢ No crime problems

WEAKNESSES

◢ Appalling human-rights record
◢ No contact with locals (you'll mainly speak to your North Korean guides)
◢ You can't leave the hotel without your guide
◢ Little nightlife beyond pool and karaoke in your hotel
◢ Bugged hotel rooms

GOLD STAR

Monumental buildings: few cities can compete with Pyongyang's exceptional ability to produce vast socialist-realist-meets-Asia architecture.

STARRING ROLE IN...

◢ *The Game of Their Lives* (2002)
◢ *State of Mind* (2004)

IMPORT

◢ Aid workers
◢ Chinese weekenders looking to relive the Cultural Revolution in all its glory
◢ UN food relief

EXPORT

◢ Plutonium
◢ Refugees escaping over the border to China
◢ Diplomatic endgame

SEE the view of this incredible city from the top of the Tower of the Juche Idea.

EAT at the Pyongyang Boat Restaurant, which cruises the Taedong River while you eat.

DRINK Taedong beer, and reflect that it was made in a factory bought and shipped wholesale from Trowbridge, England.

DO make an effort to learn the Korean for 'hello' and 'thank you', as it will mean the world to any North Korean with whom you do have fleeting contact.

WATCH the annual 'Mass Games' – a weird North Korean team sport in which thousands of participants perform ideological worship as ballet.

BUY plenty of propaganda, including exquisite hand-painted agitprop posters.

AFTER DARK enjoy the facilities in your hotel, as you're unlikely to be going anywhere else.

URBAN MYTH

Most visitors are taken to see the Pyongyang metro as part of their city tour. However, the fact that groups are only ever taken to two stations and ride between them has fuelled rumours that the entire system normally lies dormant due to electricity shortages, only rumbling into life (complete with conscripted passengers hurrying about purposefully) when tour groups pay the system a visit.

Québec City

VITAL STATISTICS

NAME: QUÉBEC CITY

DATE OF BIRTH: 1608; FOUNDED BY SAMUEL DE CHAMPLAIN ON THE SITE OF STADACONA, A FIRST NATIONS SETTLEMENT

ADDRESS: CANADA (MAP 1, M8)

HEIGHT: 90M

SIZE: 93 SQ KM

POPULATION: 491,000 (CITY); 716,000 (METRO AREA)

LONELY PLANET RANKING: 095

IT'S ALL ABOUT OLD-FASHIONED SERVICE AT NORTH AMERICA'S OLDEST GROCERY STORE, JA MOISAN, FOUNDED IN 1871.
Photographer: Mario Tama / Getty Images

Cradle and protector of French culture in North America and the heart that first beat the province's blood, captivating, historic Québec City is Canada's most European-flavoured destination.

ANATOMY

The city itself is surprisingly small, with nearly everything of interest packed into one compact, walkable district. Part of the city sits atop the cliffs of Cap Diamant (Cape Diamond), and part lies below. Québec City is thus divided into Haute Ville (Upper Town) and Basse Ville (Lower Town), each with old and new sections. The Citadelle, a fort and landmark, stands on the highest point of Cap Diamant. Together, the 10 sq km of these historic upper and lower areas, within the stone walls, form the appealing Vieux Québec (Old Town). Québec City is covered by a reasonably priced and efficient bus system.

PEOPLE

Québec City has a predominantly European population of French, British, Italian and Irish origin. The vast majority of people are white, with a small percentage of Arab, Hispanic and Asian inhabitants. Many residents are bilingual, though most speak French and about 94% claim French ancestry.

TYPICAL QUÉBÉCOIS

In general French Québécois tend to be down-to-earth and not big on ceremony or pretence. There is a sense of not wanting to seem better than others, and many project an earthy quality of straightforwardness often missing in their Anglophone counterparts. Francophones also have a reputation for being more fun-loving and raucous at get-togethers.

DEFINING EXPERIENCE

Breakfasting at Casse Crêpe Breton; exploring the old Haute Ville, including the fortifications, Parc de Champs de Bataille (Battlefields Park) and the Citadelle; then spending the afternoon wandering the old Basse Ville, before drinking beer at L'Oncle Antoine and later dining at a Basse Ville patio.

STRENGTHS

- Winter Carnival
- La Citadelle
- Parc de Champs de Bataille
- Musée du Québec
- Fortifications of Québec National Historic
- Parc d'Artillerie
- Festival de la Neige
- Musée d'Art Inuit
- Cathedrale de la Sainte Trinité (Cathedral of the Holy Trinity)
- Latin Quarter
- Basilica Notre Dame de Québec
- Musée de l'Amérique Française
- Le Château Frontenac
- Terrasse Dufferin
- Place Royale
- Musée de la Civilisation
- Antique shop district

WEAKNESSES

- Exploitation of fauna reserves by the forest industry
- World's second-largest exporter of asbestos
- Xenophobic government hiring policies

GOLD STAR

With its striking architecture and well-organised permanent and temporary exhibits that cover both historical and contemporary concerns, the Musée de la Civilisation is not to be missed.

STARRING ROLE IN...

- *Le Confessional* (1995)
- *Black Robe* (Robe Noire, 1991)

IMPORT

- Tourists
- French culture
- 'New-economy' high-tech enterprises in photonics, geomatics, biotechnology and nutraceuticals
- Demonstrators against globalisation

EXPORT

- Maple syrup
- Celtic-tinged Québécois folk music
- Asbestos
- Dairy products
- Fruit
- Vegetables
- Cheeses, especially Oka and cheddar
- Paper
- Hydroelectricity

SEE newcomers or the occasional big name at Chez son Père, one of the best *boîtes à chanson* (informal singer-songwriter clubs).

EAT provincial fare including pea soup, duck or trout followed by maple-syrup pie at Aux Anciens Canadiens.

DRINK a selection of beers at L'Inox in the Old Port area, the city's only brewpub.

DO tweak snowman/mascot Bonhomme's nose at the Winter Carnival (January).

WATCH a classical concert at the Grand Théâtre de Québec.

BUY Inuit art from Galerie Brousseau et Brousseau.

AFTER DARK chill out (literally) at North America's first Ice Hotel, half an hour from central Québec City.

URBAN MYTH

When explorer Jacques Cartier left Stadacona (a village predating Québec City on the same site) he took with him basketfuls of iron pyrite (fool's gold) and quartz crystals, thinking they might be valuable. From this came the expression *'voilà un diamant de Canada'* (there's a diamond from Canada), meaning 'something's fake'.

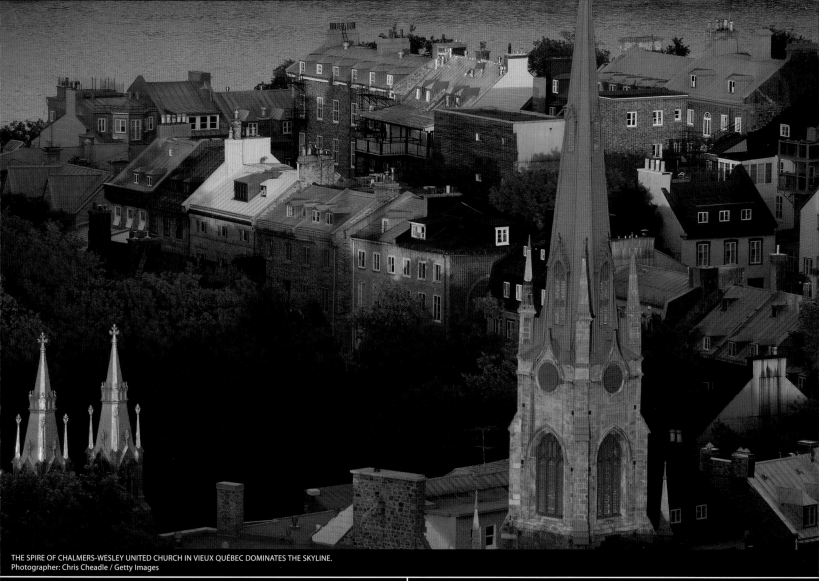

THE SPIRE OF CHALMERS-WESLEY UNITED CHURCH IN VIEUX QUÉBEC DOMINATES THE SKYLINE.
Photographer: Chris Cheadle / Getty Images

DUSK SETTLES ON VIEUX QUÉBEC.
Photographer: Chris Cheadle / Getty Images

A WOMAN STROLLS IN FRONT OF A PAINTED MURAL IN THE LOWER TOWN SECTION OF VIEUX, QUEBEC.
Photographer: Mario Tama / Getty Images

Quito

VITAL STATISTICS

NAME: QUITO

DATE OF BIRTH: PRE-COLUMBIAN; EARLY INHABITANTS OF THE AREA WERE THE PEACEFUL QUITU PEOPLE, WHO GAVE THEIR NAME TO THE CITY

ADDRESS: ECUADOR (MAP 1, L16)

HEIGHT: 2879M

SIZE: 17KM LONG AND 4KM WIDE

POPULATION: 1.4 MILLION

LONELY PLANET RANKING: 104

A HILLSIDE DESCENT REVEALS SPOTLIT QUARTERS OF THE OLD CITY.
Photographer: Pablo Corral / Corbis

A SWEET TOUCH – CANDIED APPLES RIPE FOR THE PICKING.
Photographer: Alison Wright / Corbis

THE CHRISTIAN IDEALS OF THE CONQUISTADORS ARE EMBEDDED IN LOCAL FAITH.
Photographer: Owen Franken / Corbis

THREE QUITEÑO TEENS GET ALL DOLLED UP FOR THE ARTS FESTIVAL, PLAZA DE SANTO DOMINGO.
Photographer: Pablo Corral Vega / Corbis

Tucked amid a high Andean valley and flanked by majestic mountains – when it comes to setting, Quito has it made.

ANATOMY

Quito lies along the central valley in a roughly north–south direction. It can be divided into three segments: the centre (El Centro) is the site of the old town, with its whitewashed, red-tiled houses and colonial churches; north is modern Quito, the new town, with its major businesses, airline offices, embassies, shopping centres and banks; and south of Quito consists mainly of working-class residential areas. The local bus network runs north–south. The speedy and efficient *El Trole* (the trolleybus) is Quito's most comfortable and useful transportation system. Trolleys run along Av 10 de Agosto, through the old town to the northern end of the southern suburbs.

PEOPLE

About 25% of the population is Indian, and another 65% is mestizo (of mixed Spanish and indigenous ancestry). Most of the rest of the population is either white or black, with a small number of people of Asian descent. Quechua and Spanish are spoken.

TYPICAL QUITEÑO

Quiteños are warm, welcoming and polite. Class division is an issue and blacks and indigenous people are sometimes discriminated against and treated as second-class citizens. While most of the population is Catholic, the Indians tend to blend Catholicism with their traditional beliefs.

DEFINING EXPERIENCE

Strolling along the old-town streets, where you'll pass an interesting sight on almost every block, then stopping at the hole-in-the-wall Heladería San Agustín, a 140-year-old ice-cream parlour, for a couple of scoops of nourishment before walking from the narrow colonial streets of the old town into the openness of Plaza San Francisco, revealing one of the finest sites in Ecuador – a sweeping cobblestone plaza backed by the long whitewashed walls and twin bell towers of Ecuador's oldest church, the Monasterio de San Francisco.

STRENGTHS

- ◢ Plaza San Francisco
- ◢ Vibrant indigenous cultures
- ◢ Spectacular setting
- ◢ World Cultural Heritage site status
- ◢ Virgin of Quito on El Panecillo
- ◢ Avenue of Volcanoes
- ◢ *Salsotecas* (salsa nightclubs)
- ◢ Monasterio de San Francisco
- ◢ Museo del Banco Central
- ◢ La Mitad del Mundo (The Middle of the World) monument
- ◢ Well-preserved colonial architecture

WEAKNESSES

- ◢ Altitude sickness
- ◢ Political unrest
- ◢ Class division
- ◢ Pickpockets, especially in the Ipiales market area
- ◢ Economic instability
- ◢ Deforestation

GOLD STAR

El Panecillo ('The Little Bread Loaf') – from the summit of this much-loved hill there are marvellous views of the whole city stretching out below, as well as views of the surrounding volcanoes.

STARRING ROLE IN...

- ◢ *Between Marx and a Naked Woman* (1996)
- ◢ *Proof of Life* (2000)
- ◢ *The Villagers* by Jorge Icaza

IMPORT

- ◢ *Fútbol* (football)
- ◢ Armed rent-a-cops
- ◢ Colonial architecture
- ◢ Roman Catholicism
- ◢ Spaniards
- ◢ Colonial religious art
- ◢ Foreign debt
- ◢ Corrida (bullfighting)
- ◢ Volunteer organisations

EXPORT

- ◢ Oil
- ◢ Bananas
- ◢ Panama hats
- ◢ Coffee

SEE marvellous views of Quito by climbing the tower of La Basílica high on a hill in the northeastern part of the old town.

EAT *yaguarlocro* (potato and blood-sausage soup) for lunch at Tianguez, under the Monasterio de San Francisco.

DRINK the local firewater, *aguardiente* (sugar-cane alcohol), at the cozy *peña* La Taberna del Duende while listening to traditional *música folklórica* (folk music).

DO take a few salsa dance lessons at Ritmo Tropical before hitting the dance floor of one of Quito's *salsotecas*.

WATCH the spectacular Ballet Folklórico Nacional Jacchigua at Teatro Aeropuerto.

BUY superb Andean textiles on the weekend at Quito's biggest crafts market and sidewalk art show at the northern end of Parque El Ejido.

AFTER DARK head to Reina Victoria, around Santa María and Pinta, where there are several wildly popular bars with packed dance floors on weekends.

URBAN MYTH

New Year's Eve in Quito is celebrated by burning elaborate, life-sized puppets (often representing politicians) in the streets at midnight.

Rīga

VITAL STATISTICS

NAME: RĪGA

NICKNAME: THE PARIS OF THE BALTICS; PARIS OF THE EAST

DATE OF BIRTH: 1201; WHEN BISHOP ALBERT OF LIVONIA FOUNDED THE LIVONIAN KNIGHTS

ADDRESS: LATVIA (MAP 3, P4)

HEIGHT: 3M

SIZE: 307 SQ KM

POPULATION: 790,000

LONELY PLANET RANKING: 116

The Baltic States' biggest and most cosmopolitan city, Rīga exudes both medieval charm and contemporary cool, combining these qualities seamlessly in a welcoming environment that has not gone unnoticed by European tourists, who already flock here for weekend breaks.

ANATOMY

Rīga lies slightly inland from the massive Bay of Rīga, on the massive Daugava River. On the eastern bank is Vecrīga (Old Rīga), the city's historical heart, with a skyline dominated by three steeples: St Peter's, Dome Cathedral and St Jacob's. The river is crossed by three huge bridges, and joins Vecrīga to the city's more modern left bank and to the nearby seaside resort of Jūrmala. You can get around by bus, minibus, tram or trolleybus.

PEOPLE

Just as Latvia is the most Russian of the Baltic States, Rīga is the most Russian of the Baltic capitals, with close to half of the city's residents being ethnic Russians. Many of the Latvians resident in the city also speak fluent Russian, too, so unlike Tallinn or Vilnius the city has an extremely Russian feel. Most Latvians are Lutheran, while the Russian population is generally Russian Orthodox Christian.

TYPICAL RĪGAN

Despite a very real Latvian feeling of colonisation and resentment towards Russians in general, anti-Russian feeling is hardly ever expressed by Rīgans – a rare case of two very different peoples sharing a city in almost total harmony. While Latvians have a very Scandinavian approach to life – and this is evident in the incredible pace of change over the past two decades – the Eastern-looking Russian Rīgans have also been caught up in the developmental frenzy and profited from it equally. Your typical Rīgan will have both Russian and Latvian friends, be confident in both languages and be extremely proud of Rīga's pre-eminent position among the Baltic capitals.

DEFINING EXPERIENCE

Wandering the charming streets of Vecrīga, stumbling across ancient churches and colourful houses, always being surprised by something.

STRENGTHS

- Extremely clean streets
- Friendly people
- Easy to negotiate
- Superb Art Nouveau architecture

WEAKNESSES

- Some would say that Rīga has been cleaned up and restored into sterility
- Those freezing winters limit most visitors to just a few sunny months during the summer
- The stodgy and greasy national cuisine of Latvia leaves many people cold

GOLD STAR

The cleanliness of the city, its charming inhabitants and their extraordinarily good manners – this is a city where people clean up after themselves, always open doors for you and drivers bend over backwards to give way to each other at junctions. If nothing else, this will convince you just how Scandinavian Rīga is.

STARRING ROLE IN...

- *The Dogs of Riga* by Henning Mankell
- *The Merry Baker of Riga* by Boris Zemtzov

IMPORT

- Oil
- Natural Gas
- Machinery

EXPORT

- Timber
- Paper
- Agricultural products

SEE the stunning Art Nouveau architectural creations that line the streets of Vecrīga.

EAT everything infused with garlic (including dessert) at Kiploka Krogs.

DRINK the local lethal tipple, Rīga Black Balsam, only if you dare…

DO visit the Dome Cathedral, the largest in the Baltics.

WATCH a production at the stunning National Opera House.

BUY exquisite amber jewellery from the Rīga Central Market.

AFTER DARK enjoy the sleek restaurants and cool bars of Vecrīga.

URBAN MYTH

It has often been claimed that Rīga is the home of the original Christmas tree, created by Martin Luther while he took a winter walk in the woods near the city. The truth is slightly different – the story has, in fact, two parts. The Latvians at the time were pagan and one of their rituals was worshipping the winter solstice (known as Yule), when they burned a log in honour of the sun. This later developed into a ceremony in which an evergreen tree was placed outside the town hall, decorated by men in black hats and later burned. Martin Luther, generally considered to have been the man who introduced the tradition to Europe, probably came across this annual ritual during the Christmas period while on his travels to Rīga in the early 16th century. To this day there's a magnificent Christmas tree in Vecrīga Sq every year.

TWO GUARDS TAKE THEIR JOBS AT THE FREEDOM MONUMENT VERY SERIOUSLY.
Photographer: Bruce Yuan-Yue Bi / LPI

AN EQUALLY STERN ART NOUVEAU FAÇADE HANGS OVER AN OLD TOWN DOORWAY.
Photographer: Bruce Yuan-Yue Bi / LPI

'LOOK, MA: I CAN FLY!' – A PERFORMANCE AT THE WATER PEACH INTERNATIONAL VIDEO FESTIVAL.
Photographer: Bruce Yuan-Yue Bi / LPI

SOAKING UP THE NIGHTLIFE OUTSIDE THE RĀTSLAUKUMS (TOWN SQUARE), WITH THE HOUSE OF BLACKHEADS LIT UP IN THE BACKGROUND.
Photographer: Bruce Yuan-Yue Bi / LPI

THE TIMELESS FACE OF THE DIOSCURI STATUE LOOKS TO ROME'S GLORIOUS PAST.
Photographer: Martin Moos / LPI

Whether they're romantics, art-lovers, gourmands or historians, when you tell people you're going to Rome, they'll sigh – even if they haven't been there.

ANATOMY

Rome's best-known geographical features are its seven hills: the Palatine, Capitoline, Aventine, Caelian, Esquiline, Viminal and Quirinal. Two other hills, the Gianicolo, which rises above Trastevere, and the Pincio, above Piazza del Popolo, were never part of the ancient city. From the Gianicolo you can see how the River Tiber winds through town. Rome has myriad bus routes that cover the city and a semi-useless two-line metro system (Linea A and Linea B) which traverses the city in an X-shape.

PEOPLE

The majority of Romans (over 80%) still consider themselves Catholic, although church attendance isn't what it used to be. Of the non-Catholics in the city, it's the Muslims who are making the furthest inroads – 36.5% of immigrants to Italy are Muslim. The Muslim community in Rome is based around the city mosque, inaugurated in 1995.

TYPICAL ROMAN

The typical Roman works for the government, drives rather than catches public transport, lives at home with the family despite being over 30 years old and is fairly conformist when it comes to matters of style, preferring to look like most other Romans – stylish, groomed and labelled. They share their city with millions of tourists and 150,000 stray cats.

DEFINING EXPERIENCE

Taking your morning espresso at Caffè Sant'Eustachio, walking the streets and getting lost only to stumble upon the perfect trattoria and losing all sense of time over *saltimbocca alla romana* (jump-in-the-mouth veal) and a good wine, crossing Piazza del Popolo and having your breath taken away by Caravaggio's the *Calling of St Matthew*.

STRENGTHS

◢ History everywhere you look
◢ Stylish dressing as a widespread art form
◢ Gelato
◢ Passeggiata di Gianicolo walk for beautiful views of the city
◢ AS Roma
◢ The Pantheon
◢ The Forum
◢ Domus Aurea
◢ Via del Governo Vecchio
◢ Villa Borghese
◢ Baroque architecture
◢ Morning coffee on a piazza
◢ Crossing the Tiber on foot
◢ Al dente pasta
◢ Trastevere

Rome

VITAL STATISTICS

NAME: ROME

NICKNAME: THE ETERNAL CITY

DATE OF BIRTH: 21 APRIL 753 BC; ANCIENT ROMANS DATED THE CITY FOUNDATION FROM THIS DATE

ADDRESS: ITALY (MAP 3, K13)

HEIGHT: 17M

SIZE: 150 SQ KM

POPULATION: 2.7 MILLION

LONELY PLANET RANKING: 006

THE COBBLED DISTRICT OF TRASTEVERE IS ALWAYS A BLUR OF ACTION.
Photographer: Glenn Beanland / LPI

BERNINI'S COLONNADE, THE GRAND GATEWAY TO THE VATICAN, PIAZZA DI SAN PIETRO.
Photographer: Martin Moos / LPI

TWO OLD FRIENDS BASK IN THE SUNSET GLOW OF PIAZZA GARIBALDI, WITH CENTRAL ROME IN THE BACKGROUND.
Photographer: Martin Moos / LPI

WEAKNESSES

- Overcrowded buses and an all but useless metro
- Too many menus in English/French/German
- Bureaucracy
- Tame nightlife
- Trying to walk in stylish shoes on cobblestones (unless you're a local)
- Tripe
- Dreary modern high-rise buildings in the outer suburbs
- Lack of public toilets

GOLD STAR

History – Rome knows that no-one's coming here for the modern architecture, and so a lot of money gets spent on keeping the past alive for tourists.

STARRING ROLE IN...

- *Roma, città aperta* (Rome, Open City, 1945)
- *Ladri di biciclette* (The Bicycle Thief, 1948)
- *Roman Holiday* (1953)
- *La Dolce Vita* (1961)

IMPORT

- Other countries' citizens
- Irish theme pubs
- Caravaggio
- Helmet laws for Vespa and motorcycle riders
- Smart cars
- Knock-off handbags
- John Keats
- The current Pope
- Drugs
- Telecommunications technology

EXPORT

- Rules and regulations
- Pasta
- Roads
- Bread-and-circuses politics
- Conservation techniques
- Roman numerals
- Toga parties

SEE the Vatican.

EAT Rome's favourite pizza at Da Baffetto.

DRINK a glass of Torre Ercolana, an opulent local red from Anagni, in a little *enoteca* (wine bar).

DO as the Romans do.

WATCH some of the tightest reverse parking you'll ever see.

BUY something beautiful from a household name on Via dei Condotti.

AFTER DARK go sightseeing when everyone's in bed and the traffic's negligible – you won't get inside the big sights, but you will get to see the outside with no hassles.

URBAN MYTH

According to the legend of Romulus and Remus, the twin sons of Rhea Silvia (a Latin princess) and the war god Mars were raised by a she-wolf after being abandoned on the banks of the River Tiber. The myth says Romulus killed his brother during a battle over who should govern, and then established the city of Rome on the Palatine, making himself the first king. Later he disappeared, poetically taken up by the gods or, more prosaically, secretly murdered by senators.

Salvador da Bahia

VITAL STATISTICS

NAME: SALVADOR DA BAHIA

NICKNAME: BAHIA; SALVADOR; BLACK ROME

DATE OF BIRTH: 1549; WHEN TOMÉ DE SOUZA LANDED ON PRAIA PORTO DA BARRA UNDER PORTUGUESE ROYAL ORDERS TO FOUND BRAZIL'S FIRST CAPITAL

ADDRESS: BRAZIL (MAP 1, Q17)

HEIGHT: 19M

SIZE: 324 SQ KM

POPULATION: 2.9 MILLION

LONELY PLANET RANKING: 062

CAUGHT MOMENTARILY AGAINST THE SETTING SUN, A BOY LEAPS INTO THE BAY WHILE HIS FRIENDS QUEUE FOR THEIR TURN.
Photographer: David W Hamilton / Getty Images

A MILITARY POLICEMAN MAKES A CALL FROM A PUBLIC PHONE SHAPED LIKE A *BERIMBAU*, A TRADITIONAL CAPOEIRA INSTRUMENT.
Photographer: Gianni Muratore / Alamy

TWO CHICKENS RE-ENACT A TIMELESS CLICHÉ IN THE HISTORIC QUARTER OF PELOURINHO.
Photographer: Sylvain Grandadam / Robert Harding

SPONTANEOUS DRUMMING AND DANCING EXPLODES IN THE FORMER SLAVE DISTRICT AS A PRELUDE TO *CARNAVAL*.
Photographer: Peter Turnley / Corbis

Salvador da Bahia is known as the African soul of Brazil: here, the descendants of African slaves have preserved their cultural roots more than anywhere else in the New World. This beautiful city thrives with culinary, religious, musical, dance and martial-art traditions.

ANATOMY

Salvador can be difficult to navigate as there are many one-way, no left-turn streets that wend their way through the hills and valleys. The centre is on the bay side of the peninsula and is divided by a steep bluff in two parts: Cidade Alta (Upper City) and Cidade Baixa (Lower City). The heart of historic Cidade Alta is the Pelourinho (or Pelô), which is also the heart of Salvador's tourism and nightlife. Cidade Baixa contains the Comércio (the city's commercial and financial centre), the ferry terminals and port. Linking Cidade Alta and Cidade Baixa are the historic Elevador Lacerda (four lifts that travel a set of 72m vertical cement shafts in about 20 seconds, shuttling 50,000 passengers daily) and the Plano Inclinado Gonçalves (funicular railway). You can catch buses around town.

PEOPLE

Bahia is Brazil's most Africanised state, and many inhabitants were forcibly brought here as part of the slave trade, while other ethnic groups were lured by the Portuguese to mine for gold. About 70% of the population is Roman Catholic, with a significant proportion either belonging to various cults or practising Indian animism. Portuguese is the official language.

TYPICAL SALVADORENOS

Fun-loving, joyous, sensual and mystical all describe typical Salvadorenos, as does paradoxical. They are spiritual people who devoutly dedicate time to the activities of their church or *terreiro* (place of worship). On Sunday everyone dons something skimpy and heads outdoors to ogle the local eye-candy and, in turn, be ogled.

DEFINING EXPERIENCE

Drinking in a panoramic bay view from the Praça Municipal, then marvelling at the off-kilter icons in the baroque Igreja e Convento São Francisco before attending a Candomblé (an African-American religion, chiefly practised in Brazil) service at a *terreiro* in Casa Branca.

STRENGTHS

- Exciting, exhilarating *carnaval*
- Forbidden dances
- Capoeira
- Churches, churches, churches
- Idyllic white-sand beaches
- Colourful colonial façades
- Warm waters
- Enthusiastic, energetic locals
- Charming cobblestone streets

WEAKNESSES

- Sleazy, dangerous, volatile *carnaval*
- Rampant poverty
- Scams
- Muggings
- Pickpocketing
- Sexual harassment
- Begging
- Dengue fever

GOLD STAR

Mojo – Salvador da Bahia has a culture rich in hypnotic drum beats, fragrant spices, inherent sensuality and *axé* (divine energy that brings good luck).

STARRING ROLE IN...

- *That's My Face* (2002)
- *Dona Flor e Seus Dois Maridos* (Dona Flor and Her Two Husbands by Jorge Amado; film 1976)
- *Tenda dos Milagres* (1977)
- *Robinson Crusoe* by Daniel Defoe

IMPORT

- The Portuguese
- A rich African culture
- Tourism
- Party-goers
- Catholicism
- European luxury goods

EXPORT

- Petroleum
- Capoeira
- Chemicals
- Sugar
- Author Jorge Amado
- *Carnaval*
- Transport
- Tobacco
- Gold
- Diamonds
- Silver jewellery
- Leather goods
- Handicrafts

SEE city streets from the windows behind the lift (elevator) entrances at the beautifully restored Art Deco Elevador Lacerda.

EAT steaming plates of *bobó de camarão* (shrimp cooked in yucca cream) lowered down to you on a tray from the kitchen above in tiny Dona Chika-ka.

DRINK exquisite cocktails on the open-air patio at popular Cantina da Lua.

DO attend Salvador's raucous *carnaval*, the second largest in Brazil.

WATCH Bahia's beautiful people, skimpy togs and all, on beachside Praia Porto da Barra, bustling with vendors selling everything imaginable along the clear, calm waters.

BUY local handicrafts ranging from embroidery to musical instruments at Mercado Modelo on Praça Cayru.

AFTER DARK a long evening of Candomblé in Casa Branca, Salvador's oldest *terreiro*, is quite an experience.

URBAN MYTH

Forced to build their masters' church, the baroque Igreja e Convento São Francisco, and yet prohibited from practising their own religion, African slave artisans responded through their work: cherubs' faces are distorted, some angels are endowed with huge sex organs, while others appear pregnant.

San Cristóbal de las Casas

VITAL STATISTICS

NAME: SAN CRISTÓBAL DE LAS CASAS

NICKNAME: SAN CRISTÓBAL

DATE OF BIRTH: 1528; WHEN DIEGO DE MAZARIEGOS FOUNDED THE CITY AS A SPANISH REGIONAL BASE

ADDRESS: MEXICO (MAP 4, E5)

HEIGHT: 2163M

POPULATION: 142,000

LONELY PLANET RANKING: 086

In the heart of Mexico's southernmost state, San Cristóbal de las Casas is a light and airy city; diverse indigenous communities flock here to trade goods and ideas among crumbling colonial churches and pastel-coloured houses.

ANATOMY

Although San Cristóbal de las Casas is elevated several thousand metres above sea level, it still manages to rest in a broad, fertile valley. The town grid is framed on all sides by a chain of low hills dotted with indigenous villages. The serene heart of the city is Plaza 31 de Marzo where craft sellers, shoeshiners and lunch-breakers mill around in the sun. Commerce and industry have not left a strong architectural imprint: to this day the tallest structures are the lovely Spanish municipal buildings and centuries-old cathedrals. Combis go up Av Crescencio Rosas from the Pan-American Hwy to the town centre. You can also catch taxis within town.

PEOPLE

Due to their custom of wearing their hair in pony tails, the men of the early Spanish colonial town of San Cristóbal earned the nickname *coletos* (from the Spanish world *cola* or 'tail'). The word is still used to refer to a resident of the city although most citizens are mestizo (of mixed Spanish and indigenous ancestry). From its beginnings the town has been a regular meeting point for communities of Tzotzil and Tzeltal peoples, who continue to define the soul of the city.

TYPICAL COLETO

San Cristóbal is a city that wears its history on its sleeve, and residents have a strong sense of both their ancestral legacy and their place in the unfolding narrative. Largely untouched by the revolutionary land reforms of 1917, the inhabitants of the region continued to suffer under a punishing colonial structure until relatively recently. Indigenous pride is strong in the area and it's not unusual to see locals in their traditional dress going about their daily activities in the heart of the city. *Coletos* are confident but wary – cheerful faces veil simmering social tensions.

DEFINING EXPERIENCE

Getting up early to enjoy the freshest coffee from the city's own Museo Café (Coffee Museum), heading to the hills on a caffeine high to observe the unique lifestyles of San Cristóbal's neighbours, making it back to the market for an open-air lunch in the middle of the madness then winding down in the late afternoon sun at Plaza 31 de Marzo.

STRENGTHS

◣ Bartolomé de las Casas (early defender of indigenous rights; the city is partially named in his honour)
◣ Zapatista iconography
◣ Cobbled streets
◣ Clear highland light
◣ Plaza 31 de Marzo
◣ Mercado Municipal – the wonderfully chaotic city market
◣ Organic coffee
◣ Templo de Santo Domingo

WEAKNESSES

◣ Foreign missionaries
◣ Heavily armed soldiers
◣ Political tensions
◣ Intransigent councils
◣ Religious intolerance
◣ Culturally insensitive tourists

GOLD STAR

Weaving – Tzotzil weavers are some of the most skilled in Mexico and their distinctive needlework can be seen everywhere you wander.

STARRING ROLE IN...

◣ *A Place Called Chiapas* (1998)

IMPORT

◣ US-manufactured goods
◣ Crafts and textiles from neighbouring townships
◣ Tourists

EXPORT

◣ Amber
◣ Toy slingshots
◣ Marcos dolls
◣ *Huipiles* (traditional blouses)
◣ Zapatista ideology
◣ Coffee

SEE the charming Templo de Santo Domingo, a fine example of Spanish colonial architecture.

EAT rustic tortillas containing microscopic amounts of ground limestone.

DRINK organic coffee from locally harvested beans.

DO an excursion to the nearby indigenous villages.

WATCH a political demonstration in Plaza 31 de Marzo.

BUY expertly woven indigenous garments.

AFTER DARK check out the awesome live music at Creación, San Cristóbal's hippest nightspot.

URBAN MYTH

At midnight on 1 January 1994, a previously unknown leftist guerrilla army, the Zapatistas, emerged from the woods to occupy San Cristóbal de las Casas and other towns in Chiapas. Linking antiglobalisation rhetoric with Mexican revolutionary sloganism, their declared goal was to overturn a wealthy local oligarchy's centuries-old hold on land, resources and power and to fight to improve the wretched living standards of Mexico's indigenous people. The Zapatistas' charismatic pipe-puffing Subcomandante Marcos rapidly became a cult figure. His articulate dispatches – delivered in mocking, humorous and often self-deprecating tones – demanded justice and reform. Tensions continue to flare up between competing interest groups, and dialogue between the Zapatistas and the Mexican government is strained. A wry statement from the Zapatista leadership sums up the patient resilience of the people: 'For 500 years the authorities have failed to listen to us. We have time on our side.'

A WOMAN HAULS HER LOAD UP A STEEP HILLSIDE LANE.
Photographer: Macduff Everton / Corbis

A PUPPETEER IN A CROW COSTUME ACTS OUT A DRAMATIC SCENE FROM ONE OF THE ANCIENT MAYAN MYTHS.
Photographer: Macduff Everton / Corbis

SMILES ALL ROUND AT THE TIENDA DOÑA PANCHITA, A LOCALLY OWNED STORE ON CALLE DIEGO DUGELAY.
Photographer: Christian Heeb / Aurora

THE CROSS CASTS A LARGE SHADOW ON SAN CRISTÓBAL'S CATHEDRAL.
Photographer: Louis Grandadam / Getty Images

San Francisco

VITAL STATISTICS

NAME: SAN FRANCISCO

NICKNAME: FRISCO (ALTHOUGH NOBODY FROM SAN FRANCISCO WOULD EVER SAY THIS); CITY BY THE BAY

DATE OF BIRTH: 1776; WHEN A MILITARY POST WAS ESTABLISHED BY SPANISH MISSIONARIES FROM MEXICO

ADDRESS: USA (MAP 1, G10)

HEIGHT: 16M

SIZE: 121 SQ KM

POPULATION: 799,000 (CITY); 4.2 MILLION (METRO AREA)

LONELY PLANET RANKING: 107

Post dot-gone, the City by the Bay sparkles on with literary luminaries, artsy stars and a blinding array of cultures.

ANATOMY

The city is on the tightly packed tip of a peninsula bordered by the Pacific Ocean and San Francisco Bay. The central part resembles a generous slice of pie, with Van Ness Ave and Market St marking the two sides and the Embarcadero bend serving as the outer crust. Squeezed into this compact area are Union Sq, the Financial District, Civic Center, Chinatown, North Beach, Nob Hill, Russian Hill and Fisherman's Wharf. San Francisco's principal public transport system is Muni (San Francisco Municipal Railway), which operates nearly 100 bus lines (many of them electric trolleybuses), streetcars and the famous cable cars. BART (Bay Area Rapid Transit) is the limited subway system.

PEOPLE

Long ago an Anglo-Celtic town, the face of San Francisco has changed significantly since the early days. Though still predominantly a white population, the Asian community follows at a close second, as evidenced by the world's largest Chinatown outside Asia. The balance of the city's residents are Latino, the majority being Mexican, and black, with a significant 10% who classify themselves as 'other'. Best estimates say about 15% of city residents – some 110,000 people – are gays or lesbians. San Francisco also ranks as fairly young, with a median age of 36.5 years old.

TYPICAL SAN FRANCISCAN

Native San Franciscans are few and far between. San Francisco is a city of transplants, and the diversity of the city attracts eccentrics, individualists, free spirits and nature lovers. Everyone you meet will be writing a novel, producing a short film or performing their interpretive dance. They usually do it in between wine tasting in Sonoma Valley, being dazzled by the bay and bracing themselves for the next big one.

DEFINING EXPERIENCE

Hanging out in Haight Ashbury and getting a piercing or tat, browsing the latest wordy *wunderkind* works at the 826 Valencia bookstore, grabbing a boa constrictor of a burrito on Mission St, making new friends with leather chaps and handle-bar moustaches at Harvey's, chowing down on dim sum in Chinatown and then spotting the Golden Gate through a curtain of fog.

STRENGTHS

- Golden Gate Bridge
- The Presidio
- Mexican food
- Diverse sexuality
- World-class restaurants
- Eccentricity
- The Giants
- Alcatraz
- Beat poetry
- Carlos Santana
- The Ferry Plaza Farmers Market
- San Francisco 49ers
- City Lights bookstore
- Haight Ashbury
- Grateful Dead

WEAKNESSES

- Haight Ashbury
- Panhandlers
- Fog
- The Tenderloin
- San Andreas Fault
- Real-estate prices

GOLD STAR

Hanging out – Kerouac came here to learn how to do nothing and the city is still a great place to people-watch or just tune into the universe, man.

STARRING ROLE IN...

- *The Golden Gate* by Vikram Seth
- *On the Road* by Jack Kerouac
- *Tales of the City* by Armistead Maupin
- *Memento* (2000)
- *Basic Instinct* (1992)
- *Dirty Harry* (1971)
- *American Graffiti* (1973)
- *Birdman of Alcatraz* (1962)
- *Guess Who's Coming to Dinner* (1967)
- *The Joy Luck Club* (1993)

IMPORT

- Alice Walker
- Tom Waits
- Miles Davis
- Isabel Allende
- Amy Tan
- Jack Kerouac
- Mark Twain
- Hippies
- Allen Ginsberg
- Lawrence Ferlinghetti
- Robin Williams
- Dave Eggers

EXPORT

- Birkenstocks
- George Lucas
- Carlos Santana
- Web developers
- Grateful Dead
- Dead Kennedys
- William Randolph Hearst
- Martinis
- Performance poetry
- Jack London
- Levi's jeans
- Harvey Milk
- Gertrude Stein
- Gordon Getty
- OJ Simpson
- Joe DiMaggio
- Sam Spade
- Granola
- Thomas Pynchon

SEE the almost inescapable Alcatraz, which hosted Al Capone and a bird fancier or two.

EAT a juicy burrito at La Taquería on Mission St.

DRINK an English beer pumped straight from the cellar at Magnolia Pub Brewery.

DO the cycle around the Presidio as a warm-up for mountain biking in Marin County.

WATCH and heckle a spoken word performance (that's poetry reading to you and me) at Café Du Nord.

BUY an old vinyl copy of the Grateful Dead at Amoeba Records on Haight St.

AFTER DARK grab a brew and rock to the blues played at the Boom Boom Room.

URBAN MYTH

Emperor Norton I came to San Francisco as a young man and made a fortune from the city's boomtown economy, but lost everything in a business gamble in 1852 and never recovered. After eight years of increasing poverty, he snapped, at least in one key respect: he declared himself the Emperor of the United States, and within a month he added the title Protector of Mexico. Norton never appeared without his uniform, including a plumed hat and sword. He issued his own money, which was good-naturedly accepted by many shopkeepers. Norton also made an injunction against the word 'Frisco' with a princely penalty of $25. In 1880, thousands of people attended Norton's royal funeral. He now rests in Colma Cemetery under a headstone proclaiming him 'Emperor of the United States & Protector of Mexico'.

SALUTING THE SAN, ARTIST PETER RABBIT PAYS HOMAGE TO HIS HOME TOWN.
Photographer: Anthony Pidgeon / LPI

DANCERS SWITCH ON THE COLOURFAST SPIN CYCLE AT CARNIVAL ON MEMORIAL DAY WEEKEND.
Photographer: Rick Gerharter / LPI

THE NEON WONDERLAND OF CHINATOWN BY NIGHT.
Photographer: John Elk III / LPI

I'M PLASTIC AND I'M BEAUTIFUL! – A DOLL-FACED ACTIVIST AT THE GAY PRIDE PARADE.
Photographer: Rick Gerharter / LPI

WHISPERED PRAYERS RISE UP TO GREET THE BEAUTIFUL INTERIOR OF IGLESIA LA CIBA DE GUADALUPE.
Photographer: Anthony Plummer / LPI

San Salvador

VITAL STATISTICS

NAME: SAN SALVADOR

NICKNAME: SAN SAL

DATE OF BIRTH: 1525; WHEN IT WAS FOUNDED BY SPANISH CONQUISTADOR PEDRO DE ALVARADO

ADDRESS: EL SALVADOR (MAP 4, F6)

HEIGHT: 682M

SIZE: 75 SQ KM

POPULATION: 1.6 MILLION

LONELY PLANET RANKING: 170

You can come to be one of the few tourists to see San Salvador's spectacular natural sights, or to watch Salvadoran society reconstruct itself after the ravages of civil war, but really, just come for the people – San Salvadorans are friendly, helpful, curious and generous, the best reason to visit the city.

ANATOMY

Built on a volcanic slope that parallels the Pacific coast and located beneath the San Salvador volcano, the city of San Salvador is El Salvador's largest, and its principal crossroads. It functions as the transportation and economic hub of the nation, and is home to one-third of the population and half of the nation's wealth. Crossed by the Pan American Hwy, the city's modern downtown area has many high-rise buildings, but sadly earthquakes have destroyed the majority of historic landmarks. San Salvador's extensive bus network, from large smoke-spewing monsters to zippy microbuses, can get you just about anywhere you need.

PEOPLE

San Salvadorans are among the more European-looking Central Americans – the vast majority is undoubtedly mestizo (of mixed Spanish and indigenous ancestry), but fair skin and green and blue eyes are not uncommon. Around 10% of San Salvadorans are considered of full European ancestry, while only 1% are indigenous. Spanish is the official language.

TYPICAL SAN SALVADORAN

San Salvadorans are straight-talking, strong-minded and hard-working. They're extremely helpful and almost universally friendly, with a powerful sense of justice; few are shy about expressing their opinion. The civil war still looms large for many, but they're genuinely dismayed to learn that foreigners know little about their country *other* than war, and will talk with pride about El Salvador's natural virtues.

DEFINING EXPERIENCE

Beginning the day with bread and *cafecito* (short black coffee), stocking up on food in the Mercado Central, cooking a beans-and-rice lunch then snoozing away the siesta, drinking Pilsener and getting down to some *cumbia* (Colombian dance tunes) and salsa.

STRENGTHS

⊿ San Salvadorans
⊿ Few foreign tourists
⊿ The Mayan community
⊿ Creative street vendors
⊿ The Festival of El Salvador del Mundo (the Saviour of the World)
⊿ Lake of Ilopango
⊿ Museo de Arte de El Salvador (MARTE)
⊿ San Salvadorans' unity post–civil war
⊿ Adventure of travelling a relatively unvisited city
⊿ Great literary history
⊿ Year-round summer climate
⊿ Positive attitudes to the future

WEAKNESSES

⊿ Petty theft
⊿ High population growth
⊿ Poverty
⊿ Guns everywhere
⊿ Shanty towns
⊿ Pollution
⊿ Earthquakes
⊿ Bitter political history
⊿ Crossing the street
⊿ Environmental destruction
⊿ Traffic

GOLD STAR

Most improved – San Salvadorans have a strong work ethic and have quickly raised their country from the wreckage of civil war to close to the top of Central America's economic ladder.

STARRING ROLE IN...

⊿ *Salvador* (1986)
⊿ *Romero* (1988)
⊿ *One Day of Life* by Manlio Argueta
⊿ *Salvador* by Joan Didion
⊿ *San Salvador* by Roque Dalton

IMPORT

⊿ Conquistadors
⊿ Guerrilla warfare
⊿ Baseball
⊿ Football
⊿ Foreign aid

EXPORT

⊿ Liberation theology
⊿ Pilsener and Suprema beers
⊿ Tobacco products
⊿ Textiles
⊿ Soaps
⊿ Political activists worldwide
⊿ Coffee

SEE the view of the city from the rim of Boquerón volcano.

EAT *pupusas* (meat or cheese pastries) from a street stall.

DRINK Pilsener beer at a bar with the locals.

DO check out the MARTE.

WATCH the maelstrom of crowds scurrying through sprawling markets, music blaring from every direction and buses zipping around at breakneck pace.

BUY handicrafts, hand-woven textiles and ceramics at the Mercado Ex-Cuartel.

AFTER DARK see live jazz and salsa at La Luna Casa y Arte.

URBAN MYTH

The much-loved Archbishop Oscar Romero was an outspoken supporter of the poor and in public opposition to the government. As he gave mass in the chapel of the Hospital La Divina Providencia one day in March 1980, Romero was assassinated by government agents. The chapel is still used, and exhibitions in his former living quarters in the hospital display his blood-soaked robes and the typewriter he used to type his famously stirring homilies. The Centro Monseñor Romeros at the Universidad Centroamericana José Simeón Cañas also pays homage to his memory.

A LIFE OF POVERTY HAS NOT TARNISHED THE BEAUTY OF THIS SAN SALVADORAN WOMAN'S FACE.
Photographer: Anthony Plummer / LPI

THE SPIRIT OF THE REVOLUTION LIVES ON IN THE HEARTS OF SAN SALVADORANS.
Photographer: Anthony Plummer / LPI

IN FULL VOICE – WASHED DOWN WITH RUM, LIME AND COKE AT ONE OF THE CITY BARS.
Photographer: Anthony Plummer / LPI

San Sebastián

VITAL STATISTICS

NAME: SAN SEBASTIÁN (BASQUE NAME: DONOSTIA)

DATE OF BIRTH: 1174; SAN SEBASTIÁN WAS GRANTED SELF-GOVERNING STATUS BY THE KINGDOM OF NAVARRA, FOR WHOM THE BAY WAS THE PRINCIPAL OUTLET TO THE SEA

ADDRESS: SPAIN (MAP 3, E13)

HEIGHT: 7M

POPULATION: 183,000

LONELY PLANET RANKING: 111

A SURFER WAITS TO SPREAD HIS WINGS ON PLAYA DE LA ZURRIOLA.
Photographer: Dallas Stribley / LPI

BASQUE *PINTXOS*, WIDELY REGARDED AS THE BEST FOOD IN SPAIN.
Photographer: Dallas Stribley / LPI

PAINT SPLATTERED ON THE WALL OF THE SPANISH COMANDANCIA NAVAL BY BASQUE SEPARATISTS.
Photographer: Dallas Stribley / LPI

FAST-PACED *JAI-ALAI* ACTION IN PLAZA DE LA TRINIDAD.
Photographer: Dallas Stribley / LPI

One of the oldest and most famous beach resorts in the world, San Sebastián's breathtaking natural beauty, warm inhabitants and extraordinary cuisine ensure that the gloss never wears off this quintessential haunt of the bronzed and beautiful.

ANATOMY

San Sebastián has three main centres of activity. The busy and modern centre surrounds the Catedral del Buen Pastor, while the heart of San Sebastián beats in the Parte Vieja (Old Town), squeezed below Monte Urgull Parque on the eastern spur of the superb Bahía de la Concha. The third area is Gros, east across the Río Urumea, which also has a good beach, and is home to the Renfe train station. The main bus station is about 1km south of the cathedral.

PEOPLE

The Basque people have become one of Europe's most prominent yet least-understood minorities. The Basques have retained a language, and with it a separate identity, whose origin still puzzles linguists.

TYPICAL SAN SEBASTIÁN CITIZEN

Chic, hard-working and fond of food and drink, the typical citizen of San Sebastián speaks both Castilian (Spanish) and Euskara (the Basque language) and keeps a pragmatic but proud grip on local traditions. Older men will often be members of a *txoko* (all-male eating societies) and capable of wearing berets with much style. Younger men will often be keen surfers of the nearby beaches.

DEFINING EXPERIENCE

Starting the day with a refreshing dip at the beach to get the blood pumping after the night before, which saw you tripping between *pintxos* (Basque tapas) bars until the wee hours, then spending the morning sussing out some of the edgy graphic arts on display around the city, followed by a very, very satisfying Michelin-starred lunch.

STRENGTHS

- Burying of the Sardine ritual at the end of *carnaval*
- Great local beaches
- Stylish places to stay
- San Sebastián Film Festival
- Innovative nouvelle cuisine
- International Jazz Festival
- Views from Monte Igueldo
- Eduardo Chillida's *Peine de Vientos* sculpture
- Mesmerising Euskara

WEAKNESSES

- Crowds in summer
- Trying to get a good night's sleep in the Parte Vieja
- Angry young drunks around closing time on some of the Parte Vieja streets
- Unmentionable politics
- Impenetrable Euskara

GOLD STAR

Food – Basque *pintxos* are the greatest snacks in the world and San Sebastián's are the best of the lot.

STARRING ROLE IN...

- *The Sun Also Rises* (1926)
- *The Red Squirrel* (1993)
- *A Social Parade* (2004)

IMPORT

- Other Basques
- Surfboards
- Castellano (Castilian)
- Fireworks
- Jazz
- Cod (now)

EXPORT

- Loreak Mendian clothes
- *Pintxos*
- Beach chic
- Cod (then)
- Red berets
- Jai-alai (a Basque form of handball)
- Cider

SEE the world's prettiest city beach at Playa de la Concha.

EAT at Juan Mari Arzak's triple Michelin-starred Arzak.

DRINK red wine from nearby La Rioja.

DO a walk to the top of Monte Urgull by taking a path from Plaza de Zuloaga or from behind the aquarium.

WATCH hot cinema at the San Sebastián Film Festival.

BUY cutting-edge Basque fashion from the Loreak Mendian label.

AFTER DARK go bar-hopping in the Parte Vieja.

URBAN MYTH

Each Christmas Eve, locals will climb up Mt Igueldo with an effigy of a sea bream – a pre-Christian ritual to ward off the character of Olentzaro, a charcoal burner who slithers down chimneys on that day and wreaks havoc. Locals keep their fireplaces well stocked with burning wood on the day to keep him at bay. A pastry shaped like a sea bream is also eaten on Christmas Eve, as the fish is strongly associated with Olentzaro.

San'a

VITAL STATISTICS

NAME: SAN'A

NICKNAME: SAM CITY

DATE OF BIRTH: BIBLICAL TIMES; LEGEND SAYS IT WAS FOUNDED BY NOAH'S SON SHEM

ADDRESS: YEMEN (MAP 2, O9)

HEIGHT: 2250M

POPULATION: 1.7 MILLION

LONELY PLANET RANKING: 160

SAN'ANIS WEAR THEIR CULTURE WITH PRIDE.
Photographer: Chris Stowers / Panos Pictures

THE GRACIOUS SMILE OF AN OLDER SAN'ANI LOCAL.
Photographer: Bethune Carmichael / LPI

DISTINCT ARCHITECTURE MAKES THIS ONE OF THE WORLD'S MOST BEAUTIFUL CITIES.
Photographer: Noboru Komine / LPI

ANCIENT STREETS PAVE THE WAY FOR MODERN SAN'A.
Photographer: Chris Stowers / Panos Pictures

San'a is the capital of one of the last untouched corners of Arabia; the Old City is a perfectly preserved realm of traditional architecture with the stone foundations of some houses thought to date back 1000 years.

ANATOMY

San'a expands vigorously in all directions from its original heart, the walled Old City. The clamorous Midan at-Tahrir sits at the western edge of the Old City, while Az-Zubayri St defines its southern limits. Bab al-Yaman leads into the vibrant Souq al-Milh. Traffic is frantic and anarchic – to enter the fray your best options are taxis and motorbike taxis.

PEOPLE

The population of San'a is almost exclusively Arab – residents are said to have descended from different stock from the tribes that live in the rest of Yemen. The city's once-notable Jewish community has departed for Israel. There is a small and eclectic population of expats who call San'a home.

TYPICAL SAN'ANI

As a rule, San'anis are welcoming, spontaneous and gregarious to a fault. They are noted throughout the Middle East for their quick sense of humour. Tribe still plays an important role in the consciousness of Yemenis, although less so in San'a, but all Yemenis are proud of their distinctive culture.

DEFINING EXPERIENCE

Starting the day with a strong coffee at a Turkish coffee house near the Bab al-Yaman; pondering the exhibits, including examples of San'ani building styles, at the Museum of Traditional Arts and Crafts; diving in and getting lost in the labyrinth of the Souq al-Milh; chewing *qat* (a mild stimulant) with the locals in the afternoon; getting soapy and washing away the grit of the desert in a *hammam* (bathhouse).

STRENGTHS

- History around every corner
- Very safe for visitors and locals alike
- Free of touts and other tourism-related hassles
- Easy-going traders in the souqs (markets) – no hard sell

WEAKNESSES

- Dust
- Traffic and exhaust fumes
- Monsoon rains
- Kidnappings (only occasional!)
- Stray dogs
- Everything closing down every afternoon for the daily *qat*-chewing session

GOLD STAR

Architecture – San'a is home to prototypical skyscrapers built of mud and stone; the entire Old City has been declared a Unesco World Heritage Site.

STARRING ROLE IN...

- *Arabian Nights* (1974)
- *A New Day in San'a* (2003)
- *Travels in Dictionary Land* by Tim Mackintosh Smith
- *Eating the Flowers of Paradise* by Kevin Rushby
- *The Southern Gates of Arabia* by Freya Stark
- *Motoring with Mohammed* by Eric Hansen

IMPORT

- 'Authentic' Bedouin silver jewellery
- Rhino horn – for ceremonial *jambiyah* (daggers)
- Qat from the provinces

EXPORT

- Frankincense
- Labourers to work in the Saudi oil business
- Yemenite Jews
- Oil
- Coffee

SEE the Museum of Traditional Arts and Crafts.

EAT *shwarma*, or *salta*, a fiery stew of lamb, peppers and coriander.

DRINK coffee flavoured with cardamom, but don't come here for an alcoholic tipple.

DO a course in the Arabic language or Islamic culture at the San'a Institute for Arabic language.

WATCH the sun set over the domes and towers of the Old City.

BUY spices, fabrics, incense or coffee in the Souq al-Milh.

AFTER DARK wander the Old City – the stained-glass windows of the traditional buildings illuminate the city like a mass of coloured lanterns.

URBAN MYTH

In 2003 parliamentary sessions were disrupted by the intercession of a raging bull. The beast, intended for slaughter in a public display of protest outside the Parliament, broke free and crashed through the Parliament. It gored an official and knocked down a child, all the while being chased by disgruntled tribesmen, whose protest perhaps took on a more slapstick aspect than originally intended.

Santiago de Chile

VITAL STATISTICS

NAME: SANTIAGO DE CHILE

NICKNAME: SANTIAGO

DATE OF BIRTH: 1541; FOUNDED BY CONQUISTADOR PEDRO DE VALDIVIA

ADDRESS: CHILE (MAP 1, M20)

HEIGHT: 520M

SIZE: 140 SQ KM

POPULATION: 5.1 MILLION (CITY); 7 MILLION (METRO AREA)

LONELY PLANET RANKING: 066

Santiago de Chile is a modern metropolis with a shiny face, but at the same time, struggling street vendors board city buses to hawk everything from pins to ice cream, and housemaids commute for hours to scrub floors and change nappies in exclusive suburbs.

ANATOMY

Greater Santiago is an immense bowl-shaped city jammed in between the Andes and the coastal cordillera. The most important axis is the east–west thoroughfare Av O'Higgins (popularly known as the Alameda), which in the east becomes Av Providencia and, further east, Av Apoquindo and Av Las Condes. The metro's Línea 1 also follows this main axis, leading 'up' to the residential areas at the foot of the mountains and 'down' in the direction of the coast.

PEOPLE

Santiago's people are mainly of Spanish ancestry, but the Irish and English also made a mark. Other immigrants came from Germany, France, Italy, Croatia and Palestine. Spanish is the official language.

TYPICAL SANTIAGUINO

Santiaguinos tend to be polite, well-dressed and somewhat restrained, despite their predilection for staying out late. They are hard-working, prosperous and business-minded. Divorce has not been made legal, but this hasn't kept families together as much as it has increased the acceptance of couples living together and having children out of wedlock. While most Chileans are quite proud of their heritage, there's an obvious lack of patriotism and an increasing level of individualism.

DEFINING EXPERIENCE

Meandering in the city's historic centre, Plaza de Armas, a bustling square flanked by a clutch of colonial and neoclassical buildings, and stopping off in one of the busy little arcades flanking the square for an *empanada de queso* (cheese-filled turnover), then heading to Bino, the city's finest museum, or Parque de las Esculturas, an open-air sculpture garden on the banks of the Río Mapocho.

STRENGTHS

- Bellavista's hip, energetic restaurant and club scene
- Quirky architecture in the atmospheric Barrios París Londres, Concha y Toro and Brasil
- Barrio Santa Lucía's laid-back bars and cafés
- Renowned wineries
- Skiing at Portillo
- *The* place to buy Chilean handicrafts
- Proximity to the Andes
- High literacy rate
- Producing Nobel Prize-winning poets
- Cerro San Cristóbal, whose 863m summit is crowned by a dazzling white statue of the Virgin Mary

WEAKNESSES

- Pollution
- History of human-rights violations
- Poor environmental record
- Past dictatorships
- The growing number of pickpockets, especially in the Centro

GOLD STAR

There's something kind of great about being smack in the middle of a metropolis and then looking up and seeing, to your surprise, the second-highest mountain range in the world just a few kilometres away.

STARRING ROLE IN...

- *Johnny 100 Pesos* (1994)
- *El Chacotero Sentimental* (The Sentimental Teaser, 1999)
- *Taxi Para Tres* (A Cab for Three, 2001)
- *House of the Spirits* by Isabel Allende
- *Passions and Impressions* by Pablo Neruda

IMPORT

- Roman Catholicism
- Deforestation
- Obligatory military service (for all citizens aged 18 to 45)
- Guns
- Spaniards
- Neoclassical architecture
- Fast-food chains
- Ski resorts
- Tree-lined streets
- Bourgeois houses

EXPORT

- Pablo Neruda's poetry
- Copper
- Augusto Pinochet
- Novelist Isabel Allende
- Magic realism (literary genre)
- Wood chips

SEE the Barrio Brasil, a well-preserved traditional neighbourhood whose centrepiece is the relandscaped Plaza Brasil and its quake-damaged, neo-Gothic Basílica del Salvador.

EAT a hearty Chilean lunch at Galindo, a traditional, bohemian place that was one of Neruda's favourites.

DRINK a *pisco* sour while taking in some local theatre, poetry or live music at La Casa en el Aire.

DO catch the glass *ascensor* (lift) up the steep hillside to the beautiful gardens, footpaths and fountains of Cerro Santa Lucía.

WATCH a Chilean-style rodeo at Club de Huasos Gil Letelier.

BUY handicrafts from all over the country, including hand-woven alpaca shawls, Mapuche silver jewellery, lapis lazuli, black pottery and copperware at the artisans' village Centro Artesanal de Los Dominicos.

AFTER DARK head to the Tantra Lounge, where the cool folk go after drinks at Etniko.

URBAN MYTH

Café con piernas (café with legs) attract a male clientele by requiring its young female staff to dress in tight, revealing minidresses. While usually very tame, there does seem to be an ascending scale of risqué-ness; the serious stuff takes place in the cafés with mirror-glass windows (often in arcades), which are pretty much male-only venues. The only things customers can buy are nonalcoholic beer and hot, strong espresso (at least, that's the official story).

IN THE WAR AGAINST AIR POLLUTION, THE PEAK-HOUR SUBWAY SCRAMBLE PROVES TO BE A REAL BATTLE.
Photographer: Enrique Siqués / Getty Images

A RELAXED PACE ON THE COBBLED STREETS OF DOWNTOWN PARÍS LONDRES.
Photographer: Enrique Siqués / Getty Images

A MIDMORNING LULL AT A DESIGNER FURNITURE STORE/CAFÉ IN THE SANTA LUCÍA NEIGHBOURHOOD.
Photographer: Enrique Siqués / Getty Images

THE SKYSCRAPERS OF THE VITACURA NEIGHBOURHOOD ARE DWARFED BY THE CITY'S NATURAL BOUNDARY, THE ANDES.
Photographer: Enrique Siqués / Getty Images

Santo Domingo

VITAL STATISTICS

NAME: SANTO DOMINGO

DATE OF BIRTH: 1498; WHEN IT WAS FOUNDED BY BARTOLOMÉ COLOMBUS, BROTHER OF CHRISTOPHER

ADDRESS: DOMINICAN REPUBLIC (MAP 4, M4)

HEIGHT: 17M

POPULATION: 2 MILLION (CITY); 2.3 MILLION (METRO AREA)

LONELY PLANET RANKING: 185

The oldest Spanish city in the Americas has luscious natural surroundings, is profoundly festive and full of joyous, welcoming souls.

ANATOMY

Santo Domingo began as the birthplace of European colonies in the New World, and is now the political, economic and social centre of the Dominican Republic, which occupies the eastern side of the island of Hispaniola (Haiti occupies the western side). It's packed with gorgeous green-blue waters crashing against its cliff-lined coast, couples overlooking the surf, whispering sweet everythings to each other, and buses belching long trails of spent diesel. It's an urban city with a vast cave system beneath it, a huge old fort and a park that fills daily with hundreds of joggers and cyclists.

PEOPLE

Santo Domingans may have adopted the Spanish language and the Catholic religion of their founders, but racially they're predominantly mulattos (with one white and one black parent), with the rest of the population comprised of those of African and European descent.

TYPICAL SANTO DOMINGAN

Maintaining close family ties and cultivating friendships are top priorities to Santo Domingans, and the quintessential merengue (folkloric dance of the Dominican Republic) is more like a tool for fostering relationships than music. Santo Domingans are flexible enough to live with profound contrasts, such as the immensely wealthy coexisting with those caught in grinding poverty. They maintain many traditions and revere their rich history, yet most watch American TV with awe and readily adopt the latest US trends. It's a city of Catholics with no shortage of brothels, five-star hotels that function despite frequent power outages and heat that can be downright oppressive, but Santo Domingans remain optimistic and patient.

DEFINING EXPERIENCE

Strolling and dining on savoury Dominican food on the *malecón* (waterfront promenade), watching Licey play at Quisqueya Stadium, then dancing merengue at Guacara Taina until dawn.

STRENGTHS

- Not one, but two crazy carnivals a year – in February and August
- Latin Music Festival
- Two merengue festivals
- Historic buildings
- Baseball games
- Obelisco del Malecón
- Generous, smiling locals
- Calle de las Damas (Ladies' Street)
- All-night, or anytime, dancing
- Fantastic views over the cliffs
- Roba La Gallina (enormous chicken character in the carnivals)

WEAKNESSES

- Petty crime
- Hurricanes
- Cockfighting
- Exterminated Arawak Indians
- Violent political history
- Aggressive police
- One third of the country below the poverty line
- Racism against Haitians

GOLD STAR

Most mobile 'founding city' – Santo Domingo was originally located in La Villa de Navidad in Haiti, moved 100km east to La Isabela, then onto the east bank of the Río Ozama, and finally settled itself on the Ozama's west bank.

STARRING ROLE IN...

- *Santo Domingo Blues* (2004)
- *In the Time of the Butterflies* by Julia Álvarez
- *Sucre amer* (Bitter Sugar) by Maurice Lemoine
- *Santo Domingo, Past and Present* by Samuel Hazard

IMPORT

- Spanish and French culture
- US-trained dictators
- Slaves
- Baseball
- Poorly paid Haitian labourers
- Toussaint L'Ouverture (when he took the city in 1801)

EXPORT

- Rum
- Gold
- Hernando Cortés (before setting off to Mexico)
- Francisco Pizarro (before leaving for Peru)
- Julia Álvarez
- Cigars
- Merengue
- Baseball players to the US leagues

SEE *tabacos* (cigars) being rolled at the Boutique del Fumador or the Museo del Tabaco.

EAT *empanadas* (Chilean-style turnover stuffed with meat or cheese and raisins) and *pastelitos* (meat- and cheese-filled pastries) from street stalls.

DRINK rum at sunset at Plaza de Hispanidad.

DO bargain at the Pulga de Antigüedades (Antique Market) on Sunday.

WATCH a baseball game played by either Licey or Escojido at Quisqueya Stadium.

BUY amber or *larimar* (an opaque blue stone found only in the Dominican Republic) jewellery in the Zona Colonial.

AFTER DARK dance to music ranging from African drumming to French rock and Dominican dance music at Nowhere.

URBAN MYTH

To celebrate the 500th anniversary of Columbus' arrival in the Americas, President Belaguer planned to construct a lighthouse (the Faro a Colón). The plan was pilloried as ridiculously expensive and a show of megalomania; protests intensified, demonstrators were killed and foreign powers quietly withdrew their support. Two days before the inauguration, the president's 73-year-old sister, Doña Emma, had one last inspection, only to die mysteriously a few hours later. Belaguer refused to attend the inauguration, and Santo Domingans whispered of a *fukú* (curse) and reminded themselves that Columbus' name was always known to bring bad luck.

FRIENDSHIP IS ONE OF LIFE'S TRUE RICHES: A MOTORCYCLIST CHATS WITH NEIGHBOURS ON THEIR PORCH.
Photographer: Jeremy Horner / Corbis

LIFE ON DUARTE AVE SHOWS SIGNS OF CHAOS.
Photographer: Alfredo Maiquez / LPI

BE ENCHANTED BY SANTO DOMINGO'S OLD-WORLD CHARM AND LATIN CHARISMA.
Photographer: Kevin O'Hara / Photolibrary

BLENDING IN AS ONLY A LOCAL CAN.
Photographer: Jeremy Horner / Corbis

The crossroads of east and west since antiquity, Sarajevo nestles by the Miljacka River, surrounded by hills and mountains, and encompasses the essence of Bosnia's cultural diversity – a powerful merge of dance, music, food and hope for the future after centuries of war.

ANATOMY

Sarajevo lies in a wide valley created by the Miljacka River. The distant mountains of Jahorina and Bjelašnica (host to the 1984 Winter Olympics) flank the city to the south. From the airport, 6.5km to the southwest, the main road runs up to the suburb of Ilidža, then swings east through Novo Sarajevo. The bus and train stations are to the north. Near the town centre the road runs alongside the Miljacka River, before leaving it at Baščaršija (the bustling old Turkish Quarter), which occupies the eastern end of town.

PEOPLE

Serbs, Croats and Bosnian Muslims are all Southern Slavs of the same ethnic stock. Physically they are indistinguishable. The prewar population was incredibly mixed and intermarriage was common. Ethnic cleansing has concentrated Muslims in Sarajevo, but there are also high numbers of people who are Orthodox and Roman Catholic. Inhabitants are known as Bosnian Serbs, Bosnian Croats or Bosniaks (Muslims). Across Bosnia and Hercegovina, churches and mosques are being built (or rebuilt) at lightning speed. This is more symptomatic of strong nationalism than religion, as most people are fairly secular.

TYPICAL SARAJEVAN

For any city it's a stretch to summarise the general character of its denizens, and that goes for Sarajevo tenfold. Their differences are both their greatest challenge and greatest strength. What is certain is that they are proud, patriotic and traditionally minded but also very cosmopolitan and friendly. Given the speed and diligence with which they are rebuilding their city, to say that they were hard-working and determined would be an understatement.

Sarajevo

VITAL STATISTICS

NAME: SARAJEVO

DATE OF BIRTH: 1461; TURKISH SARAJEVO WAS FOUNDED BY ISA-BEY ISAKOVIC AND LATER BECAME A MILITARY, ADMINISTRATIVE, AND COMMERCIAL CENTRE

ADDRESS: BOSNIA & HERCEGOVINA (MAP 3, N12)

HEIGHT: 630M

SIZE: 142 SQ KM

POPULATION: 421,000

LONELY PLANET RANKING: 043

THE CROWDED SKYLINE TELLS OF THE CITY'S RICH CULTURAL PAST AND ITS ASPIRATIONS FOR THE FUTURE.
Photographer: Doug McKinlay / LPI

DEFINING EXPERIENCE

Exploring the polished-cobble laneways of Baščaršija, shopping for a handmade watch, then spending the afternoon cycling the old road that leads alongside the Miljacka River towards the Turkish bridge (Goat Bridge).

STRENGTHS

- Fresh *burek* (small round filo-pastry balls stuffed with minced beef or spinach and feta)
- Gazi-Husrevbey Mosque
- Baščaršija
- Multiculturalism
- National Museum
- The indoor and outdoor markets
- 20km ski run at Mt Jahorina
- The Sebilj fountain
- Latin Bridge
- Morića Han

WEAKNESSES

- Land mines
- Nationalism
- Confusing street-numbering system
- Limited vegetarian options
- War damage

GOLD STAR

Survival – for enduring a war that took it to the cusp of destruction and remaining a strong and enigmatic mix of cultures.

STARRING ROLE IN...

- *No Mans Land* (2002)
- *The Perfect Circle* (1997)
- *Welcome to Sarajevo* (1997)

IMPORT

- Turkish food and culture
- Foreign aid for reconstruction
- Islam
- International investment
- Western political influence

EXPORT

- Textiles
- Director Emir Kusturica
- Cigarettes
- Metalwork
- Handmade watches

SEE the Sarajevo roses (skeletal handlike indentations where a shell has exploded) on the pavements – some are symbolically filled in with red cement, often accompanied by a series of brass plaques giving the names of those killed by that shell.

EAT Turkish *ćevapčići* (grilled minced lamb or beef), usually accompanied by a half-loaf of spongy *somun* bread, in one of the many restaurants in Baščaršija.

DRINK shots of *šljivovica* (plum brandy) or *loza* (grape brandy) savoured with a meal at the Bosanska Kuća.

DO take in some of the rich local art and culture at the art gallery and National Museum.

WATCH the dance, music and street theatre of Baščaršija Noći (Nights of Baščaršija) – an annual festival in July.

BUY colourful woven items from Bosnian Handicrafts in Baščaršija – a nonprofit organisation working with refugees to produce these wonderful pieces.

AFTER DARK indulge in a local beer at the cavernous bar of the Sarajevo Brewery.

URBAN MYTH

During the recent conflict, Sarajevo's heritage of six centuries was pounded into rubble and its only access to the outside world was via a tunnel, which saved it. Most of the tunnel's 800m stretch under the airport has collapsed, but the Tunnel Museum, on the far (southwestern) side of the airport, gives visitors a glimpse of what it must have been like. The house that provided the tunnel's cover holds a small museum of digging equipment and photos from the days when the tunnel was in use.

A YOUNG MUSLIM WOMAN PLANS HER DAY FROM THE STEPS OF GAZI-HUSREVBEY MOSQUE.
Photographer: Doug McKinlay / LPI

MAKING HIS OWN FUN, A YOUNG BOY PLAYS AMONG THE PESKY PIGEONS IN THE MAIN SQUARE OF BAŠČARŠIJA.
Photographer: Doug McKinlay / LPI

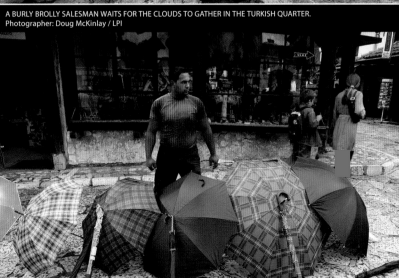

A BURLY BROLLY SALESMAN WAITS FOR THE CLOUDS TO GATHER IN THE TURKISH QUARTER.
Photographer: Doug McKinlay / LPI

THE COLOUR OF LIFE IN THE VIVID HEART OF THE SOUTH.
Photographer: Ray Laskowitz / LPI

Savannah

VITAL STATISTICS

NAME: SAVANNAH

DATE OF BIRTH: 1733; AS A BUFFER
AGAINST SPANISH INTERESTS IN FLORIDA

ADDRESS: USA (MAP 1, L11)

HEIGHT: 14M

SIZE: 388 SQ KM

POPULATION: 131,000 (CITY); 329,000 (METRO AREA)

LONELY PLANET RANKING: 164

Savannah is a city rich in history, charm and Southern hospitality with one of the largest historic districts in the USA. It features thousands of beautiful buildings, including classic examples of Federal, Italianate and Victorian architecture.

ANATOMY

The city lies on the Savannah River, 29km from the Atlantic Coast amid moors and mammoth oak trees dripping with Spanish moss. Careful urban design, both widely studied and admired, makes for a livable, beautiful and expandable city, with a gridlike pattern of streets, and houses and public buildings built around tree-filled squares. The city is pedestrian-friendly and there are also plenty of buses.

PEOPLE

This is the South, so about 30% of the population is African-American. Demographic changes across the continent are felt here too, with Latino and Asian-Americans becoming a growing force in Savannah. Disease, war and forcible removal have meant that Native Americans form only 1% of modern-day Savannah's populace.

TYPICAL SAVANNAH CITIZEN

The majority of voters are right-leaning conservatives, although in the early 1960s the city drew on its liberal traditions and became perhaps the first fully integrated city in the South. These contradictions are evidenced in a city culture where tradition battles with debauchery – pleasure and its indulgence are as much a part of tradition as the glorious façades of yesteryear. And while the city is now almost as cosmopolitan as Martha's Vineyard, Miami Beach or San Francisco, the legendary hospitality remains, as does a certain formality and politeness – opening doors for women is expected and the locals do like to dress up for special events.

DEFINING EXPERIENCE

Starting the day with a leisurely breakfast in the Historic District at Clary's Café then visiting the Savannah History Museum and taking a walking tour before the day heats up too much, catching lunch at an outdoor café then beating the heat by heading out onto the river aboard a paddle wheeler.

STRENGTHS

⊿ Historic District
⊿ Riverfront
⊿ Paddle-wheeler trips on the river
⊿ Cobblestone streets
⊿ Carriage rides around town
⊿ City Market
⊿ History Museum
⊿ Mercer House
⊿ Wonderful African Baptist churches and the oldest Reform Judaism temple in the USA (dating from 1733)
⊿ The sea islands
⊿ Great tours at all times of day and night
⊿ Telfair Art Museum

WEAKNESSES

⊿ The sticky height of summer
⊿ Petty crime

GOLD STAR

Savannah's vast historic districts show off extraordinary collections of 18th- and 19th-century buildings and a collection of immense Victorian townhouses.

STARRING ROLE IN...

⊿ *The Gift* (2000)
⊿ *The Legend of Bagger Vance* (1999)
⊿ *Forces of Nature* (1998)
⊿ *The General's Daughter* (1998)
⊿ *Midnight in the Garden of Good and Evil* by John Berendt (film 1997)
⊿ *Forrest Gump* (1993)
⊿ *Glory* (1989)
⊿ *The Return of Swamp Thing* (1988)
⊿ *Roots* (1976)

IMPORT

⊿ Damn Yankees
⊿ Five million tourists a year

EXPORT

⊿ Johnny Mercer
⊿ 'Moon River'
⊿ Poet Conrad Aiken
⊿ Flannery O'Connor

SEE the city, river and nearby Tybee Island from one of the replica riverboats plying the waters from River St.

EAT Southern cuisine (black-eyed peas, turnips, fried chicken, sweet potatoes, green beans and rice) at Mrs Wilkes' Dining Room.

DRINK with pleasing ease – drinking alcohol outdoors is OK on city streets, unlike other cities in the South.

DO take a tour of the houses and gardens to see legendary mansions and secret gardens.

WATCH great drama at the Savannah Shakespeare Festival or listen to musicians at the Savannah Jazz Festival.

BUY antiques from more than 100 registered dealers, or Civil War artefacts from True Grits.

AFTER DARK enjoy the sumptuous nightlife, go clubbing at City Market and the Riverfront or catch a drag show at Club One Jefferson.

URBAN MYTH

Books and films have glamorised Savannah as a surreal remnant of the old South, where tradition beds down with sweet decadence. Now most of the world knows Savannah through its roles in *Forrest Gump*, John Berendt's hugely successful 1994 murder-mystery travelogue *Midnight in the Garden of Good and Evil*, and the subsequent film directed by Clint Eastwood. Books such as *Wise Blood* by Savannah-born Flannery O'Connor, songs like 'Moon River' by native-son composer Johnny Mercer and the 2002 hit movie the *Legend of Bagger Vance* have added to the city's mythology. These days, hardly a year goes by without another feature film being made in Savannah with a gaggle of stars moving about incognito in the city's bars, clubs and restaurants and dipping into the local real-estate market to buy a little piece of this garden of good and evil.

THE HAUNTING BEAUTY OF BONAVENTURE CEMETERY – A JEWEL IN SAVANNAH'S GLITTERING CROWN.
Photographer: Ray Laskowitz / LPI

SAVANNAH'S GRACIOUS SPIRIT FLOWS INTO HER BUILDINGS AND WELL PLANNED STREETS.
Photographer: Ray Laskowitz / LPI

ENJOYING SOME OF THAT SOUTHERN HOSPITALITY.
Photographer: Ray Laskowitz / LPI

Seattle

VITAL STATISTICS

NAME: SEATTLE

NICKNAME: THE PACIFIC NORTHWEST'S EMERALD CITY

DATE OF BIRTH: 1851; WHEN NEW YORKERS ARTHUR AND DAVID DENNY LED A GROUP OF SETTLERS HERE

ADDRESS: USA (MAP 1, G8)

HEIGHT: 38M

SIZE: 85 SQ KM

POPULATION: 592,000 (CITY);3.3 MILLION (METRO AREA)

LONELY PLANET RANKING: 055

SUITED UP, A KAYAKER PREPARES FOR A PADDLE ON PORTAGE BAY.
Photographer: Lawrence Worcester / LPI

Mother of Microsoft, Nirvana and Starbucks, Seattle has stepped out of the limelight since the dot-com boom to enjoy a cornucopia of outdoor activities and a varied cultural scene.

ANATOMY

Seattle is stunningly sandwiched between the snowcapped Olympic Range to the west and the Cascade volcanoes, including towering Mt Rainier, to the south and east. The city is surrounded by water with Lake Washington to the east, Puget Sound to the west, and Lake Union and the Lake Washington Ship Canal slicing through the city. Downtown Seattle is fairly compact and contains Pike Place Market, Pioneer Sq and the Waterfront. The Space Needle is in Seattle Center, just north of downtown. Adjoining Seattle Center is the attractive, red-brick, residential Queen Anne area. The U district, home to the University of Washington, is on the northern side of Lake Union. Metro Transit buses blanket the metropolitan area.

PEOPLE

Almost three-quarters of Seattle's population are white. The rest are Asian-American, African-American, Hispanic and Native American. Seattle has one of the smallest percentages of children in an American city.

TYPICAL SEATTLEITE

Seattleites are laid-back and dress casually, even for the office. However, long hours and high pressure are the norm and people tapping on their Wifi-enabled laptops in coffee shops are a common sight. They like to party and bars are full pretty much all of the time. As well as drinking, book readings are popular. Seattleites are politically engaged and care about their environment. Outdoor activities are big news and it's not unusual for people to leave work early to head to the mountains for some skiing or hiking. Even if it's raining (and Seattleites swear it's more of a drizzle), you're bound to see them outside.

DEFINING EXPERIENCE

Zooming up to the top of the Space Needle for views of the Olympic and Cascade Mountains, the water and the city, then grabbing a tall, skinny, hazelnut latte in Pioneer Sq, before taking a walk in Discovery Park.

STRENGTHS

- Outdoor activities on tap
- Discovery Park
- Lakeside mega homes
- Opening Day of Yacht Season
- Pike Place Market
- Pioneer Sq
- The Waterfront
- Dim sum in the International District
- High salaries for tech types
- Profusion of vegan and vegetarian restaurants
- Easy recycling
- The Seattle Men's Chorus (180 gay members)
- Public art in Fremont
- Pacific Northwest Ballet
- The Space Needle
- Brewpubs
- Strong, tasty, ubiquitous coffee
- Skiing at nearby Whistler

WEAKNESSES

- Rain – and lots of it
- Traffic snarls
- Racial segregation
- Climbing house prices
- Struggling public transport

GOLD STAR

Coffee – Starbucks takes over the world but the coffee is good.

STARRING ROLE IN...

- *Sleepless in Seattle* (1993)
- *Singles* (1992)
- *Say Anything* (1989)
- *Snow Falling on Cedars* by David Guterson
- *Frasier* (1993–2004)

IMPORT

- Tech-savvy entrepreneurs (during the dot-com heyday)
- Software engineers
- Gary Larson, creator of *Far Side*
- Late-19th-century gold prospectors
- Novelist Tom Robbins

EXPORT

- Starbucks
- Nirvana
- Bill Gates, Paul Allen and Microsoft
- Amazon.com
- Boeing
- Adobe
- Savage Love sex-advice column
- Biotechnology
- Timber
- Jimi Hendrix
- Grunge (in the '80s and '90s)
- Pearl Jam
- Sherman Alexie
- Blown-glass sculptures

SEE market traders playing catch with live fish at Pike Place Market.

EAT scrumptious seafood at Belltown neighbourhood favourite Queen City Grill.

DRINK seasonal beers at the spacious Elysian Brewing Company on Capitol Hill.

DO take advantage of all that water and try windsurfing on Lake Washington.

WATCH hydroplane races, an airshow, a carnival and the arrival of a naval fleet at Seafair.

BUY weird and wonderful music from the knowledgable owners at Wall of Sound.

AFTER DARK attend a reading at Seattle's favourite bookstore, Eliot Book Company.

URBAN MYTH

The city that gave birth to Starbucks is understandably obsessed with coffee. But ordering a cup of the black stuff in Seattle can be a minefield. If you just want a cup of regular coffee, ignore the surprised look of the barista and ask for a 'large drip'. When ordering your cappuccino consider whether you like more foam than liquid ('dry') or the reverse ('wet'). Feel free to request the temperature of your coffee (though not in actual degrees). If the server queries 'room?' when you order, he's asking if you would like to add cream to your cup (we're still talking about coffee). Other terms should be familiar to the millions of regular Starbucks customers.

THE SUN SETS BEHIND THE MONUMENTAL MARKET SIGN AT PIKE PLACE.
Photographer: Lawrence Worcester / LPI

CARNIVAL RIDES WHIRLING AND SWOOPING BENEATH THE SPACE NEEDLE, SEATTLE'S SIGNATURE ICON.
Photographer: Richard Cummins / LPI

SHOPFRONT DETAIL OF ONE OF SEATTLE'S MANY GROOVY CAFÉS.
Photographer: Lawrence Worcester / LPI

A WOMAN IN A TRADITIONAL GOWN ACCESSORISES WITH FUR STOLE AND HANDBAG.
Photographer: Paul Chesley / National Geographic Image Collection

Seoul

VITAL STATISTICS

NAME: SEOUL

DATE OF BIRTH: 57 BC; DURING THE THREE KINGDOMS PERIOD, WHEN IT WAS RULED BY THE BAEKJE AND SILLA DYNASTIES

ADDRESS: SOUTH KOREA (MAP 1, JJ10)

HEIGHT: 87M

SIZE: 65 SQ KM

POPULATION: 10.7 MILLION (CITY); 24.5 MILLION (METRO AREA)

LONELY PLANET RANKING: 085

Seoul is the 600-year-old capital of a world-class economic powerhouse and a representation of a true rags-to-riches story – in every aspect of life and culture it is a fascinating melting pot of old and new, East and West.

ANATOMY

Bisected by the Hangang River, Seoul is surrounded by eight mountain peaks. The main historical, sightseeing and accommodation part of Seoul is the downtown area, with Namsan and Seoul Tower forming the southern perimeter. The touristy shopping and entertainment area of Itaewon is on the south side of Namsan. South of Itaewon, the Hangang River winds its way through the city. Within the river, to the west, is the small island of Yeouido, an important administrative centre. The Gangnam district, south of the river, is where upwardly mobile citizens aspire to live. To the east is Jamsil, home to the giant COEX Mall, Lotte World and Olympic Park. Seoul's subway system is modern, fast, frequent, clean, safe and cheap. There are also buses around the city.

PEOPLE

Birth rates are low, the population is getting older and there is a shortage of young females. Korea is ethnically and linguistically homogeneous and, although the number of foreigners visiting and working in Seoul is increasing, expats still comprise a very small percentage of the population.

TYPICAL SEOULITE

Seoulites work long hours, but also enjoy socialising and are generally more than kind to foreign visitors. Korean relationships are complicated by social hierarchy, and social status is very important. The concept of losing face is integral to Korean society. As a result Koreans are seemingly overly agreeable and pleasant, doing anything to smooth over potential disagreements or arguments that could lead to losing face. Seoulites are always very respectful and will greet each other with a short bow or nod. Seoul has over 40 top universities, and the Koreans' inexhaustible obsession with education and the social status it brings is nowhere more prevalent than here.

DEFINING EXPERIENCE

Exploring the royal palaces and War Memorial Museum and Seodaemun Prison for an introduction to Seoul's complex and tragic history, then sipping on ginseng tea in a tiny stall at Dongdaemun Market before adding the finishing touches to your wardrobe, and then climbing Inwangsan to the shamanist shrine at dusk to contemplate the lights of the city unfolding before you.

STRENGTHS

- Safe and friendly city
- Low crime rate
- High standard of living and clean streets
- Buzzing and modern Asian city
- Korean cuisine
- Ancient sculpture and architecture
- Leather goods
- Millions of trees (planted to try to improve the city's environment)
- Well-developed bicycle paths and sports facilities

WEAKNESSES

- Seoul is one of the world's most expensive cities
- Summer monsoon season
- Sometimes conservative outlook on women in society
- Sometimes conservative approach to Western and Korean relationships

GOLD STAR

Seoul is a fascinating melting pot of old and new, East and West.

STARRING ROLE IN...

- *Chihwasun* (2002)
- *Taegukgi* (2003)
- *Eunuch* (1968)
- *Nowhere to Hide* (1999)
- *The President's Last Bang* (2005)
- *Sunday Seoul* (2005)

IMPORT

- All things European: food, wine, books, movies…
- Japanese popular culture (the importation ban was recently lifted)
- Australian indigenous art (Aboriginal art) – the latest hot commodity
- Christianity
- Confucianism
- Buddhism

EXPORT

- North Korean missile technology
- Technology for cloning human embryos
- Hyundai and Daewoo automobiles
- Korean exchange students
- Leather jackets, belts, wallets, purses…anything leather
- Rice wines and Korean cuisine
- Cheap electronic goods
- Chemicals
- Textiles
- Machinery
- Lacquerware, made using a black paint that comes from the sap of the lacquer tree
- Reproduction Joseon Dynasty furniture

SEE the palaces of Gyeongbokgung and Deoksugung to soak up the atmosphere of the feudal royal court.

EAT temple food and take part in a tea ceremony with Buddhist monks at Jogyesa or Bongeunsa.

DRINK Geumsan Insamju, a rice wine made from a 600-year-old recipe.

DO a hike around the huge fortresses of Bukhansanseong and Namhansanseong that were built in the forest-covered mountains around Seoul.

WATCH the royal ancestral rites festival at Jongmyo, as well as other historical re-enactments that reveal an Asian society with its own very distinctive style.

BUY anything made of leather: jackets, belts, wallets, purses, bags and shoes are all Seoul specialities.

AFTER DARK head to one of the many tiny underground venues in Hongkik, Seoul's live indie-music hot spot.

URBAN MYTH

Every summer, Korean newspapers carry reports of people dying after sleeping in a room with the electric fan on and the doors and windows closed. It is widely believed that fans create an air current that seals the room, driving oxygen to the ceiling and carbon dioxide towards the floor, suffocating the person inside.

YOUNG BUDDHIST MONKS PUT THEIR HANDS TOGETHER TO COMMEMORATE BUDDHA'S BIRTHDAY AT THE CHOGYE TEMPLE.
Photographer: Chung Sung-Jun / Getty Images

LIKE MINIATURE HOT-AIR BALLOONS, PAPER LANTERNS FLOAT IN THE BRANCHES OF A TREE AT THE CHOGYE TEMPLE.
Photographer: Craig Brown / Getty Images

A CYCLIST SILHOUETTED AGAINST THE SUNRISE WITH THE SOARING DLI 63 BUILDING IN THE BACKGROUND.
Photographer: SETBOUN / Corbis

Shanghai

VITAL STATISTICS
NAME: SHANGHAI

NICKNAME: PEARL OF THE ORIENT; PARIS OF THE EAST

DATE OF BIRTH: 3900 BC; WHEN THE FIRST SETTLEMENTS APPEARED

ADDRESS: CHINA (MAP 5, R1)

HEIGHT: 7M

SIZE: 6341 SQ KM

POPULATION: 19 MILLION

LONELY PLANET RANKING: 048

THE SCIENCE FICTION CITYSCAPE OF NANJING LU SHOPPING PRECINCT.
Photographer: Walter Bibikow / Getty Images

China's most chichi city wows with its sharp fashion and dazzling architecture but still manages to keep it traditional.

ANATOMY
Central Shanghai is divided into Pudong (east of the Huangpu River) and Puxi (west of the Huangpu River), though there is no single focus to the city. Most attractions are in Puxi, including the Bund – the tourist centrepiece. West of the Bund is the former international settlement and one of Shanghai's main shopping streets, Nanjing Lu. South of the Bund is the Chinese city, a maze of narrow lanes. West of the old town and hidden in the backstreets north and south of Huaihai Lu (Shanghai's premiere shopping street) is the former French Town, with a major collection of Western-style restaurants and bars. Western Shanghai is dominated by Hongqiao, a hotel/conference centre/office zone with the expat area of Gubei further out. East of the Huanpu, Pudong is a 'special economic' zone of banks, skyscrapers and new residential complexes. Walking and catching buses can be a nightmare, but the metro and light railway system work like a dream.

PEOPLE
Most Shanghainese residents are the descendants of poor migrants who came to the city from the two adjacent provinces of Northern Jiangsu and Zhejiang, where Wu Chinese is the favoured dialect. Recent immigration from other parts of China has meant that Mandarin is more commonly spoken, but other languages are rare. To make Shanghai an 'international city' the government has a target of 5% foreign residents, so Shanghainese are welcoming of foreigners even if they can't speak their language.

TYPICAL SHANGHAINESE
The rest of China may view Shanghai as being in the thrall of the West with their interest in plastic surgery, fashion and progress, but the Shanghainese know they're just jealous. Shanghai's women are said to be the most beautiful in China and even the men are known for being fashionable, even if it just means having the latest mobile or knowing the hippest bar. There's a strong pride in the city, with other Chinese seen as *waidìrén* (outlanders) and the Taiwanese sniggered at as *táibazi* (Taiwanese hicks).

DEFINING EXPERIENCE
Snapping up fashion firsts along Huaihai Lu, queuing for *xiǎlóngbaō* (dragon balls) outside Nanxiang Steamed Bun Restaurant, people-watching on Nanjing Lu, and browsing the pirated CDs at Wushan Night Market.

STRENGTHS
- French Town
- The Bund
- Volkswagen taxis
- Jinmao Tower
- Nanjing Lu
- *Nòngtángs* (back-alley communities)
- Yuyuan Gardens and Bazaar
- Huzhou Pagoda

WEAKNESSES
- Bad public transport
- Pollution haze
- Little personal space
- Spitting

GOLD STAR
Architecture – from whopping Jinmao Tower to the disco-ball of the Oriental Pearl Tower, there's plenty to dazzle.

STARRING ROLE IN...
- *Shanghai Express* (1932)
- *Empire of the Sun* (1986)
- *Purple Butterfly* (2003)
- *The Red Violin* (1998)
- *The Blue Lotus* by Hergé
- *When We Were Orphans* by Kazuo Ishiguro

IMPORT
- Emily Hahn
- *Baiwēi* (Budweiser)
- Western influence
- Formula One Grand Prix
- *Màidāngláo* (McDonald's)
- Kooky architecture
- Mobile phones
- JG Ballard

EXPORT
- Clothing and textiles
- Zhou Xuan
- Movies
- Snakehead gangsters
- Ruan Lingyu, 'China's Garbo' of the 1930s
- Liao Changyong

SEE the daunting Jinmao Tower after a stroll along the ritzy Bund.

EAT the authentically Uygur *dapánjī* (fried chicken and potatoes) for a taste of China's colonies at Afanti Restaurant.

DRINK martinis in the Glamour Bar at M while enjoying evening views of the Bund.

DO a Chinese martial-arts course at the kick-arse Longwu International Kung Fu Centre.

WATCH the gymnastic genius of the Shanghai Acrobatics Troupe, bending most nights at Shanghai Centre Theatre.

BUY a *qipao* (cheongsam) tailored to any figure at Dongjiadu Cloth Market.

AFTER DARK head for Loft, a converted cinema with the chance to dance, drink and dine.

URBAN MYTH
The godfather of Shanghai's underworld, which covertly ran the city during the 1930s, was Du Yuesheng, or 'Big-Eared' Du, as he was called out of earshot. By 1927 he led the Green Gang, controlling the city's prostitution, drug-running and protection rackets. His favourite scheme was to kidnap the wealthy and then negotiate their release, pocketing half the ransom as commission. Du prowled town in a bulletproof sedan with armed bodyguards crouched on the running boards, styling himself as the Chinese Al Capone. In 1931 – after playing a part in Chiang Kaishek's anti-Communist massacre – he was elected to the municipal council and reigned as unofficial mayor until the Japanese invasion, when he fled to Chongqing, and then Hong Kong, where he died a billionaire in 1951.

FANS OF T'AI CHI EXPRESS GRACE AND POISE DURING MORNING EXERCISES ON THE BUND.
Photographer: Ray Laskowitz / LPI

SOME PEOPLE CALL IT AN EXTREME SPORT, BUT TO THESE SHANGHAINESE WINDOW WASHERS, IT'S JUST PART OF THE JOB. Photographer: Bradley Mayhew / LPI

EXPRESS TO THE FUTURE – A GLITTERY RIDE THROUGH THE ELECTRO-PSYCHEDELIC BUND TUNNEL.
Photographer: John Borthwick / LPI

Siena

VITAL STATISTICS

NAME: SIENA

DATE OF BIRTH: 1ST CENTURY BC; WHEN THE ROMANS ESTABLISHED A MILITARY SETTLEMENT HERE CALLED SENA JULIA

ADDRESS: ITALY (MAP 3, K13)

HEIGHT: 322M

POPULATION: 54,000

LONELY PLANET RANKING: 081

Stunning Gothic architecture, medieval city walls, the charmingly winding streets and that famous piazza (Il Campo) make peaceful Siena a Tuscan joy.

ANATOMY

At the heart of Siena is the large sloping Piazza del Campo, from which fan out the streets of the medieval town. Two of its main streets reveal Siena's history as a banking town – Banchi di Sopra and Banchi di Sotto. They form part of the Via Francigena pilgrims' route to Rome. Via di Città, another important thoroughfare, joins the other two behind Piazza del Campo. The town is enclosed by its original walls, which are punctured by eight city gates. There are no cars or motorbikes in Siena's city centre, which makes wandering through the streets a rare pleasure. Your only other option is to jump on a bus.

PEOPLE

Italy has one of the lowest birth rates in Europe and Siena's population is slowly dwindling. The majority of its citizens are Roman Catholic, with a small percentage made up of Jewish, Muslim and Protestant communities.

TYPICAL SIENESE

Siena is one of Tuscany's main university towns, and the Sienese are a well-educated, hard-working bunch. Family is very important to them and small family-run businesses are common. Loyal to their neighbourhood, they are more likely to fly the flag of their *contrada* (town district) than the Italian colours. They are gastronomes and very proud of Tuscan wine and cuisine. Politically, they tend towards the left, and finally, like all Italians, they like to look good.

DEFINING EXPERIENCE

Tucking into a dish of *pici* (thick Sienese spaghetti) at Il Carroccio before getting lost in the snaking streets of the town and miraculously ending up at a recognisable landmark, the Palazzo Communale.

STRENGTHS

- Sienese-Gothic architecture eg Il Campo, Palazzo Communale, the cathedral
- Il Palio (Siena's famous horse race)
- The Sienese school of painting
- First European city to ban motorised traffic in its centre
- Rivalry with Florence
- The Council of Nine
- Monte dei Paschi di Siena bank, a big employer in Siena
- Slow Food movement
- Marble font by Jacopo della Quercia in the Battistero (baptistry)
- Museo dell'Opera Metropolitana
- Sienese art in the Pinacoteca Nazionale
- Frescoes depicting Santa Caterina's life in the Chiesa di San Domenico
- Settimana Musicale Senese (July)
- Stunning Tuscan countryside
- Nannini, the best place to buy cakes and ice cream
- *Cantucci* and *biscottini di Prato* (almond-based biscuits)

WEAKNESSES

- Accommodation is elusive in summer, particularly during Il Palio
- It's easy to get lost in the medieval town
- The plague in 1348 (it killed 100,000 people)

GOLD STAR

Gothic architecture.

STARRING ROLE IN...

- *The English Patient* (1996)
- *Stealing Beauty* (1996)
- *Prince of Foxes* (1949)

IMPORT

- Students attending the Università per Stranieri
- Visitors on a tour of Tuscany

EXPORT

- Santa Caterina (one of Italy's most famous saints)
- Sienese school of painting: Guido da Siena, Duccio di Buoninsegna, Ambrogio Lorenzetti, Simone Martini, Taddeo di Bartolo
- Embroidery
- Brunello di Montalcino (wine)
- *Panforte* (a rich fruit cake originally cooked for the crusaders)
- Textiles
- Leather goods
- Porcini mushrooms

SEE the marble- and mosaic-clad cathedral, one of Italy's great Gothic churches.

EAT what you fancy from the *menu degustazione* (a seven-course tasting menu) at Cane e Gatto.

DRINK a pricey glass of Brunello di Montalcino at a bar on Il Campo – you're paying for the view but it's worth it.

DO a jazz course at the prestigious Associazione Siena Jazz.

WATCH 10 horses fiercely hauling their riders around Il Campo and see who wins the *Palio* (silk banner).

BUY cheese, sausages and porcini mushrooms from Pizzicheria de Miccoli.

AFTER DARK watch a concert at the Settimana Musicale Senese.

URBAN MYTH

Twice a year jockeys and riders compete in the world's shortest horse race, Il Palio. It is so famous in Italy that it has become legendary. Each of the 10 riders represents one of the 17 *contrade* (not all 17 take part), and compete for the *Palio* (silk banner), and the glory, of course. Each *contrada* has its own costume, flag and *Palio* museum – yes, they mean business. The riders thunder around for approximately 80 seconds on a dirt track, which is laid around Il Campo. Horses can win without their riders (the jockeys ride bareback), but it is a noncontact sport – so no pulling at the reins of competing horses, please!

WINNING SMILE – GIRLS IN ROMAN GOWNS JOIN CELEBRATIONS IN HONOUR OF IL PALIO.
Photographer: Paolo Sacchi / Getty Images

FRIENDS GATHER FOR A MORNING CHAT AT SUNRISE ON PIAZZA DEL CAMPO.
Photographer: Paolo Sacchi / Getty Images

WARM LIGHTS LURE OUTSIDERS INTO THE POPULAR GRATTACIELO TAVERN.
Photographer: Paolo Sacchi / Getty Images

PIAZZA DEL CAMPO FRINGED BY THE CREEPING SHADOW OF THE PALAZZO PUBBLICO AND THE TORRE DEL MANGIA.
Photographer: Paolo Sacchi / Getty Images

An island city that's a country unto itself all tricked-out with Southeast Asia's latest tech toys, Singapore is at a cultural crossroads that includes Indian, Malay and Chinese communities best served up at a hawker stall.

ANATOMY

The Singapore River weaves through the city centre, with the hippest dining and club spots lining the riverbanks at Boat, Clarke and Robertson Quays. Change into a suit to head south of the river to the central business district, or switch to a sari further north for Little India and Kampung Glam, the Muslim quarter. The southern island is the plastic theme park of Sentosa, while the eastern stretch of coast hosts the airport. The far north offers Bukit Timur, the last chunk of surviving wilderness. The west keeps it wild with Jurong's bird sanctuary but is largely industrial. Singapore's public transport is plentiful and varied.

PEOPLE

Predominantly Chinese (77% of the population), Singapore's population follows many traditional customs of mainland China, including speaking Mandarin or dialect languages. Neighbouring Malaysia has contributed 14% of the population, bringing an Islamic influence, while India has bought 8% of the population, many from the south, particularly Madras. The loud minority (1.7%) are expats who have made English the most spoken language.

TYPICAL SINGAPOREAN

Singaporeans love gadgetry and their traditional cultures so a Mass Rapid Transit (MRT) ride will usually feature images of kids listening to Goan hip-hop on the latest MP3 players while texting on their mobile for the latest Chinese horoscopes. The stomach of the Lion City roars for the best food and everyone has an opinion on the best hawker stalls. Privately, Singaporeans might hold opinions on the government and its tough policies, but publicly they're too busy filling their mouths with excellent cuisine to speak out. Shopping rivals eating as a national passion, with many Singaporeans jetting over to China or Indonesia on low-cost flights for bargains. The Hokkien word *kiasu* (afraid to lose) is a guiding philosophy along Orchard Rd around sale times, when bargain frenzies dismiss any notion of reserve.

Singapore

VITAL STATISTICS

NAME: SINGAPORE

NICKNAME: THE LION CITY

DATE OF BIRTH: MID-13TH CENTURY; WHEN THE REGION WAS ESTABLISHED AS A MINOR TRADING POST FOR THE POWERFUL SUMATRAN SRIVIJAYA EMPIRE

ADDRESS: SINGAPORE (MAP 5, L13)

HEIGHT: 10M

SIZE: 682.3 SQ KM

POPULATION: 4.6 MILLION

LONELY PLANET RANKING: 025

A TYPICALLY CONSERVATIVE SINGAPOREAN REVS UP THE CHINESE NEW YEAR PARADE.
Photographer: Alain Evrard / LPI

DEFINING EXPERIENCE

Breakfasting on *roti paratha* (grilled stuffed flat bread) in Little India and grabbing a discounted sari before heading over for some serious shopping in Orchard Rd, chilling out in the Botanic Gardens, then working up an appetite by strolling along the river to Boat Quay, where you'll find tasty Malay satays.

STRENGTHS

- Newly redeveloped Clarke Quay
- Hyper-efficient MRT
- Asian Civilisations Museum
- Orchard Rd shopping
- Hawker food at budget prices
- Cable-car ride from Mt Faber to Sentosa
- Club St
- World-class Changi Airport
- Cheap, abundant hawker cuisine
- Hi-tech gadgetry at Sim Lim Sq and the Tekka Centre
- Bargain flights to China, India and Southeast Asia
- Limited traffic
- Little India

WEAKNESSES

- Censorship
- Fines for jaywalking, eating on the MRT and chewing gum
- Freezing air-con
- High-priced booze
- Sentosa's overpriced, overhyped rides
- Touts hounding you along Temple St

GOLD STAR

Changi Airport – it has churches of every denomination, cinemas, restaurants and free internet, plus it's got zippy public transport straight to the city centre.

STARRING ROLE IN...

- *Army Daze* (1996)
- *Rogue Trader* (1999)
- *King Rat* by James Clavell
- *Saint Jack* by Paul Theroux

IMPORT

- Chicken rice
- Sir Thomas Stamford Raffles
- *Dosa* (an Indian pancake stuffed with potato)
- Stockbroking swindler Nick Leeson
- *Roti paratha*
- Coffee Bean & Tea Leaf outlets
- Satay
- Water from Malaysia

EXPORT

- Tiger balm
- Singapore Sling
- Lee Kuan Yew
- Chilli crab
- Self-proclaimed Makan food guru KF Seetoh
- Garbage to the nearby island of Pulau Semakau

SEE Clarke Quay lit with red lanterns on a romantic evening cruise.

EAT garlic stingray from a hectic Newtown Circus hawker stall.

DRINK a Singapore Sling at the Long Bar at the Raffles Hotel – a compulsory cliché.

DO a wet and weird Duck Tour on the river and through the colonial district.

WATCH a dazzling lion dance in front of Ngee Ann City on the lunar New Year.

BUY a Slurping Ape T-shirt from the hippest outlets along Orchard Rd.

AFTER DARK dance the night away at the multilevel institutional club, Zouk.

URBAN MYTH

The laws are the quirkiest part of Singapore and while you can find yourself wearing a fine for drinking water on the MRT there are good reasons behind some of the laws. Chewing gum was reputedly banned after an accident involving the doors of the MRT being wedged open using a humble piece of gum. You can now carry gum (for personal use) and buy it through a prescriptionlike system. Spitting and littering have always been cracked down on, but as a response to SARS the city took public hygiene to a new level, with fines, public education and a group of concerned volunteers who regularly patrol public toilets, awarding prizes for the cleanest.

GLITTERING WITH LIGHT, BUILDINGS ABOVE SINGAPORE RIVER BRIGHTEN UP THE NIGHT SKYLINE.
Photographer: Alain Evrard / LPI

STUDENTS FOR PEACE! PUPILS AT AN ELEMENTERY SCHOOL THROW THEIR HANDS IN THE AIR LIKE THEY JUST DON'T CARE. Photographer: Alain Evrard / LPI

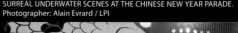

SURREAL UNDERWATER SCENES AT THE CHINESE NEW YEAR PARADE.
Photographer: Alain Evrard / LPI

STUNNINGLY BEAUTIFUL, TBILISI IS A CITY OF MYSTERY AND ENCHANTMENT.
Photographer: Stephane Victor / LPI

Hands down the most beautiful city in the Caucasus, the mysterious and historic Georgian capital enchants with its beautiful old town, dramatic cliff-side setting and wealth of historic churches.

ANATOMY

A long, slim city built into the gorge of the Mtkvari River, Tbilisi is eminently manageable on foot. The right bank of the river is home to the charming old town, the sulphur baths and the dramatic *Mother Georgia* monument, while the more modern left bank is perched on a clifftop giving stunning views of the old town. An efficient Soviet-built metro system connects the city to the suburbs.

PEOPLE

The cultural centre of Georgia, Tbilisi is excessively cosmopolitan, with large Russian, Armenian, Azeri and Jewish minorities all living peacefully side by side. Most people speak both Russian and Georgian, and often more languages on top of that.

TYPICAL TBILISIAN

Just as likely to speak Russian as Georgian, your typical resident of this city is a hardened cynic, having lived through a turbulent two decades and seen pretty much everything in that time, from food shortages and starvation to civil war and mass protest. Used to days without electricity, running water and gas, they never lose their sense of humour about the post-Communist chaos into which Georgia was plunged under former president Eduard Shevardnadze. Things might be looking better today under pro-US President Mikhail Saakashvili, but locals still need to be convinced.

Tbilisi

VITAL STATISTICS

NAME: TBILISI

DATE OF BIRTH: NEOLITHIC PERIOD; ALTHOUGH LOCALS LIKE TO BELIEVE IT WAS FOUNDED IN THE 5TH CENTURY, ACCORDING TO A MUCH-LOVED LOCAL LEGEND

ADDRESS: GEORGIA (MAP 3, Y14)

HEIGHT: 490M

SIZE: 140 SQ KM

POPULATION: 1.5 MILLION

LONELY PLANET RANKING: 151

BUILDING A BETTER FUTURE – TBLISIANS HAVE LIVED THROUGH A TURBULENT PAST.
Photographer: Stephane Victor / LPI

FOOD FOR THOUGHT – WELL, THE BREAD'S GOT TO GET THERE SOMEHOW!
Photographer: Stephane Victor / LPI

KEEPING THE FAITH AT ST MARY'S DAY PRAYERS.
Photographer: Stephane Victor / LPI

DEFINING EXPERIENCE

Having an invigorating bath and massage at the famous Tbilisi sulphur baths (where Pushkin and Dumas both took the waters), then a bracing walk up to *Mother Georgia*, the vast metallic lady who overlooks the city, and the fascinating Narikala Fortress, before finding the way back down through the old town, checking out some of the beautiful churches and then settling on a traditional Georgian restaurant for the full Georgian culinary experience.

STRENGTHS

- Food, oh! the food…
- Decent wines
- Kind people
- Sioni Cathedral Church, dating from the 5th century
- Ancient Narikhala fortress
- Famous and long-established theatres
- Paliashvili Opera House
- Gorgeous architecture
- Fascinating history

WEAKNESSES

- Petty crime
- Unique alphabet that makes getting around rather tough
- Steep hills that make walking hard work
- Street muggings
- Potential instability

GOLD STAR

Dominating the city skyline (until the TV tower came along, anyway), the Narikala Fortress is an ancient symbol of Tbilisi's defensive brilliance. Its walls date from various periods, the earliest being the 4th-century Persian citadel. The tower foundations and much of the present walls were built on the orders of the Arab emirs in the 8th century.

STARRING ROLE IN…

- *Since Otar Left* (2003)

IMPORT

- Electricity
- Gas
- Mercedes Jeeps
- American-trained lawyers

EXPORT

- Wine
- Stalin
- Polyphonic singing
- Aubergines
- Kate Melua

SEE the astonishing collection at the Treasury of the Janashia State Museum of Georgia.

EAT as much as you can – try a full Georgian feast at Dzveli Sakhli.

DRINK some of the country's wine – Saperavi tends to get the best reaction from visitors with a Western palate.

DO take a day trip to nearby religious centre Mtskheta.

WATCH a show at the beautifully ornate Paliashvili Opera House, founded in 1851.

BUY cha cha (Georgian firewater) from the market if you want a memorable introduction to Tbilisi.

AFTER DARK head down to Akhvlediani kucha for the late-night bars.

URBAN MYTH

Despite a history of settlement in the area stretching back to Neolithic times, Georgians prefer the legend of King Gorgasali, who remains honoured as a saintlike figure today, and is said to have founded Tbilisi in the 5th century. The legend runs that the king was hunting (either for deer or pheasant, depending on whom you believe) and that either the pheasant fell into a hot sulphur spring and was conveniently cooked for dinner, or that the wounded deer fell into the hot sulphur spring and was miraculously healed. Either way, the name 'Tbilisi' derives from the Georgian word *tbili* (warm), and there seems to be little doubt that it was the magnificent hot springs, which still lure visitors today, that attracted the king.

MODERN AND FUNKY, TEL AVIV IS A CITY KNOWN FOR ITS OPENNESS AND TOLERANCE.
Photographer: Stephane Victor / LPI

Tel Aviv

VITAL STATISTICS

NAME: TEL AVIV

NICKNAME: THE WHITE CITY; THE BIG ORANGE

DATE OF BIRTH: 1909; WHEN IT WAS FOUNDED BY 60 FAMILIES AS A JEWISH NEIGHBOURHOOD NEAR JAFFA

ADDRESS: ISRAEL (MAP 2, L2)

HEIGHT: 34M

SIZE: 52 SQ KM

POPULATION: 390,000 (CITY); 3.2 MILLION (METRO AREA)

LONELY PLANET RANKING: 132

While Jerusalem is considered the spiritual centre of Israel, Tel Aviv, conversely, is the pop-cultural centre, with its cafés, Mediterranean beaches and Israeli trance music, which is loud and unavoidable.

ANATOMY

Hayarkon St, Herbert Samuel Rd and Ibn Gvirol St are the main streets of Tel Aviv, running north–south and parallel to the seafront. Dizengoff Sq, Rabin Sq and Hamedina Sq are critical reference points. The New Central Bus Station is officially the world's biggest bus station and buses will take you practically everywhere in Israel.

PEOPLE

Around a third of Israel's population lives in Tel Aviv. It is a predominantly Jewish city.

TYPICAL TEL AVIVIAN

Tel Avivians are youthful and brash and totally unlike their neighbours in Jerusalem, which is only around 45 minutes away but may as well be on another continent. As a Tel Aviv shopkeeper once said, 'In Jerusalem they like their religion, in Tel Aviv we like our drugs'. It may not ring true for the entire city, but it certainly provides an insight.

DEFINING EXPERIENCE

After you've taken in the spiritual teachings of the kabbalah and eaten an icy pole (ice lolly) on the beach, head over to Nachalat Binyamin (street of artists) for a look at the work of the city's artisans and street performers.

STRENGTHS

- Weather
- Beaches
- Proximity to the country's amazing sights and relics
- Museum of the Diaspora
- Cafés spilling out onto the streets and beaches

WEAKNESSES

- Young soldiers carrying machine guns
- Drivers on mobile phones
- The occasional market-place bombing

GOLD STAR

Behind some drab façades is an incredible collection of Bauhaus buildings along Rothschild Blvd, Ahad Ha'am St, Engel St, Nachmani St, Melchett St and Balfour St, making it the Bauhaus capital of the world.

STARRING ROLE IN...

- 'Tel Aviv' by Duran Duran
- *Tel Aviv-Berlin* (1987)
- *Walk on Water* (2004)
- *The Flower of Anarchy* by Meir Wieseltier

IMPORT

- New York bagels
- T'ai chi in Yarkon Park
- Italian *gelati*
- The usual fast-food suspects (but with inflated prices)
- Cable TV
- US culture
- Mobile phones
- Bauhaus architecture
- Poet Meir Wieseltier
- Tim Tam biscuits (around 700,000 packets a year)

EXPORT

- Kabbalah
- Diamonds
- Jaffa oranges
- Israeli trance music
- Tomato-growing technology
- Jazz musician Avi Leibovitz
- Fertilisers

SEE fresh-faced soldiers, lads and lasses in shopping malls and nightclubs bandying about their machine guns.

EAT halva ice cream down along Ibn Givrol and Frishman Sts.

DRINK home-brewed ale at the Tel Aviv Brewhouse.

DO walk along powder-fine sand beaches – you'll find sand in every nook and cranny for days to come.

WATCH avant-garde and new wave films at the Cinematheque.

BUY secondhand goods at Shuk Hapishpeshim, Jaffa's flea market.

AFTER DARK take your *darbuka* (drum) and pound the night away on drum beach.

URBAN MYTH

According to the Bible, Jonah departed from Jaffa on that fateful day in an attempt to escape from God. But then he was swallowed by a whale, where he spent three days and nights. Let that be a lesson. And if you have any doubts about the legend, a statue of the whale in Jaffa serves as a portentous reminder.

COEXISTENCE – THE OLD AND NEW CONVERGE IN THE BUILDINGS OF TEL AVIV.
Photographer: Stephane Victor / LPI

TAKING IT TO THE STREETS – A YOUNG RABBI SPREADS THE WORD.
Photographer: Stephane Victor / LPI

HAVE YOUR CAKE AND EAT IT TOO AT THE FAMOUS SAID ABU ELAFIA & SONS BAKERY.
Photographer: Stephane Victor / LPI

Thimphu

VITAL STATISTICS

NAME: THIMPHU

NICKNAME: SHANGRI-LA

DATE OF BIRTH: 13TH CENTURY; WHEN A HUGE FORTRESS WAS BUILT, BUT THE SMALL TOWN ONLY BECAME THE NATIONAL CAPITAL IN 1961

ADDRESS: BHUTAN (MAP 5, H3)

HEIGHT: 2300M

POPULATION: 99,000

LONELY PLANET RANKING: 173

WEIGHING UP THE COSTS – WEEKEND MARKETS ARE GREAT PLACE FOR LOCAL PRODUCE.
Photographer: Richard I'Anson / LPI

With one foot in the past and one in the future, the last Buddhist Himalayan kingdom strolls confidently towards modernisation on its own terms.

ANATOMY

Thimphu lies in a beautiful, wooded valley, sprawling up a hillside on the bank of the Thimphu Chhu River. Several north–south streets run through the town, and numerous smaller streets weave their way uphill to government offices and the posh suburb of Motithang at the top of the town. In the central district, numerous lanes and alleys lead off the north–south streets to provide access to the new shopping centres as well as shops, bars and small restaurants. For those on a normal tourist visa, you will have a car, driver and guide available throughout your stay in Bhutan; and it's easy to pop out for a drink or a round of shopping on foot.

PEOPLE

Thimphu's people, like that of the country, are fairly homogeneous, comprising Drukpas (Ngalops and Sharchops) and indigenous or migrant tribes. The main language is Dzongkha, but Tibetan and Nepali are also spoken. The religious divide is nominally Buddhist (75%) and Hindu (25%).

TYPICAL THIMPHUITE

Bhutanese people are very friendly, open and polite. Despite the fact that Bhutan is not a rich country, the Bhutanese people seem to be content – full of inner and outer beauty, dignity and power. Thimphu, as the capital and only real city, also has the lion's share of bureaucrats, diplomats, politicians and non-governmental organisations (NGOs).

DEFINING EXPERIENCE

Wandering Norzin Lam, lined with shops, restaurants and retail arcades, taking in the view of the river and climbing the Telecom tower to see the valley below before letting your guide choose a restaurant and bar followed by a good night's sleep.

STRENGTHS

- Weekend market
- Tourism as a low-volume, high-cost affair
- Trashi Chhoe Dzong (Fortress of the Glorious Religion)
- Pristine mountain air
- No advertising
- Mobile phones have arrived, but are blissfully rare – the mountainous terrain renders them generally useless
- Rugged mountains
- Enchanting valleys
- Meandering rivers
- Crystal lakes
- Dense forests

WEAKNESSES

- The cost of getting there
- The cost of being there

GOLD STAR

The weekend market – village people jostle with well-heeled Thimphu residents, Bhutanese housewives and monks from nearby monasteries. In one section of the market is an odoriferous collection of dried fish, beef and balls of *datse* (homemade soft cheese that is used to make sauces). During the winter you can even pick up a leg of yak (with the hoof still attached). At the northern end of the market is a collection of indigenous goods and handicrafts. Here you will find locally produced goods, including religious objects, cloth, baskets and strange hats from various minority groups.

STARRING ROLE IN...

- *Travellers and Magicians* (2003)
- *The Other Final* (2002)
- *Dreams of the Peaceful Dragon* by Katie Hickman and Tom Owen Edmonds

IMPORT

- TV – finally, in the 21st century
- NGOs
- Very wealthy tourists
- Mobile phones, but few

EXPORT

- Philately
- Feature films directed by high-ranking Buddhist lama Khyentse Norbu

SEE the spectacular view of Thimphu Valley from the Telecom tower.

EAT green chilli for breakfast – or maybe not.

DRINK Tsheringma, a safflower-based herbal tea.

DO take a day walk up to either Tango Goemba or Cheri Goemba monastery.

WATCH a *tsechu* (festival) at a *dzong* (monastery) in honour of Guru Rinpoche, who brought Buddhism to Bhutan.

BUY contemporary paintings and handmade paper at the Jungshi Handmade Paper Factory or Mangala Paper House.

AFTER DARK stay up late and sample Bhutanese nightlife in Thimphu's friendly discos and bars.

URBAN MYTH

It is often said that Thimphu is the only world capital without traffic lights. One was installed several years ago, but the residents complained that it was impersonal and ugly and it was removed within days. Traffic continues to be directed by policemen stationed at two traffic circles, one at the north end and another near the south end of Norzin Lam, Thimphu's wide, tree-lined main street. They keep Thimphu's traffic flowing throughout the day using elegant, exaggerated gestures. They disappear at night and leave drivers to sort things out for themselves.

HOPES AND DREAMS SPIN IN A RIOT OF COLOUR ON GIANT PRAYER WHEELS.
Photographer: Izzet Keribar / LPI

TIME IS SLOW TO CATCH UP WITH THE PAST IN THIS BEAUTIFUL CITY.
Photographer: Richard I'Anson / LPI

THE PHALLUS, PAINTED ON THE WALL OF THIS HOUSE, BRINGS FERTILITY AND PROTECTION TO THE OCCUPANTS.
Photographer: Alison Wright / LPI

Tirana

VITAL STATISTICS

NAME: TIRANA

DATE OF BIRTH: 1614; WHEN THE CITY WAS FOUNDED BY A TURKISH PASHA

ADDRESS: ALBANIA (MAP 3, N14)

HEIGHT: 89M

SIZE: 41 SQ KM

POPULATION: 616,000

LONELY PLANET RANKING: 149

ENJOYING SUNSHINE AND GOSSIP IN THE BLLOKU AREA, FORMERLY THE DOMAIN OF THE COMMUNIST ELITE BUT NOW A PLAYGROUND FOR THE URBAN HIP.
Photographer: Doug McKinlay / LPI

BRIGHT, NEWLY CONSTRUCTED BUILDINGS ARE BEGINNING TO PUSH STALINIST GREY OUT OF THE CAPITAL.
Photographer: Doug McKinlay / LPI

THE INSPIRING ET'HEM BEY MOSQUE, SHESHI SKËNDERBEG.
Photographer: Doug McKinlay / LPI

LACK OF URBAN INFRASTRUCTURE MEANS THAT SOME PEOPLE STILL RELY ON COMMUNAL WATER SUPPLIES.
Photographer: Doug McKinlay / LPI

The proud and plucky capital of Albania is charming and surprising, with colonial Italian villas interspersed with monolithic Communist-era structures and traditional Turkish mosques.

ANATOMY

The tiny Lana River is little more than a stream that runs unobtrusively through the city, barely noticed by most people. The central square is the busy Sheshi Skënderbeg (Skënderbeg Sq) from where streets radiate like spokes on a wheel. The city's main street, Bulveardi Dëshmorët e Kombit (Blvd of Heroes and Martyrs) runs from here to Tirana University, hiding ministries and hotels behind its plentiful trees. Near here is the Blloku – once the closed-off residential area of Tirana's Communist elite and now the trendy bar and nightclub quarter. Crowded city buses operate in Tirana.

PEOPLE

Traditionally Tirana has been almost entirely Albanian, particularly as foreigners were almost barred from even visiting until the end of communism in 1990. Since then, though, Tirana has been swamped by a succession of outsiders. First came ethnic Albanian refugees from the conflict in Kosovo and second the waves of aid workers and military peacekeepers who used Tirana as a base in the aftermath of the crisis created. Both have had a large influence on what was in many ways a total backwater and – for better or worse – have contributed to the rapid modernisation and Westernisation of Tirana.

TYPICAL TIRANA CITIZEN

Tirana continues to breed surprisingly conservative people – although this is doubtlessly changing. The influence of both Muslim and Christian mores and the later wave of extremist Stalinism since the end of WWII has had an effect, and while being exceptionally kind and friendly, Tirana's residents are far more easily shocked than their cousins in other European capitals.

DEFINING EXPERIENCE

Wandering the pleasant tree-lined avenues on a summer evening when everyone's out for their evening stroll, and soaking up the charming atmosphere of this friendliest of European capitals.

STRENGTHS

- ◢ Compact city
- ◢ Undiscovered by the tourist hoards
- ◢ A great base for exploring this totally overlooked European country

WEAKNESSES

- ◢ Still a large amount of poverty despite the progress
- ◢ Litter is a huge problem – civic pride is still something that very few people attach importance to
- ◢ Plenty of petty crime
- ◢ Gaping potholes in the streets to twist ankles

GOLD STAR

Mt Dajti, the mountain overlooking the city, has some beautiful walking and great spots for weekenders leaving the heat of the capital for more alpine climes.

STARRING ROLE IN...

- ◢ *Slogans* (2001)

IMPORT

- ◢ Foreign aid workers
- ◢ Refugees from Kosovo

EXPORT

- ◢ Fruit and vegetables
- ◢ Natural gas
- ◢ Oil

SEE the impressive Et'hem Bey Mosque – one of the few religious buildings in the city to survive the Hoxha dictatorship.

EAT pretty much anything you want in Tirana's ever-evolving restaurant scene.

DRINK Albanian *rakia* (similar to cognac) if you want a truly rough hangover.

DO make an effort to visit Kruja, the pleasant mountain town a short trip out of Tirana, for an insight into the Albanian struggle for independence.

WATCH the nightly processions of Skënderbeg Sq as the entire city takes an evening stroll during the summer months.

BUY anything and everything emblazoned with the impressive Albanian flag – this is one proud country.

AFTER DARK head to the Blloku area for bar-hopping, outdoor cocktails or a boogie at the latest nightspot.

URBAN MYTH

So paranoid was former dictator Enver Hoxha that he found a man who looked just like him and sent him regularly to stand in for him at public events, convinced that he was going to be assassinated at any moment. When Hoxha finally died and communism was overthrown a few years later, the doppelgänger was greeted by such terror from everyone he met who thought the dictator had come back to life, that he went mad and cut off his own face. Nice.

Tokyo

VITAL STATISTICS

NAME: TOKYO (FORMERLY EDO)

NICKNAME: EASTERN CAPITAL

DATE OF BIRTH: 10,000–300 BC; DURING THE JŌMON PERIOD, WHEN PEOPLE ENJOYED GOOD HUNTING IN THE MARSHY REGION

ADDRESS: JAPAN (MAP 1, KK10)

HEIGHT: 6M

SIZE: 616 SQ KM

POPULATION: 12.7 MILLION

LONELY PLANET RANKING: 026

TRENDY VENDORS IN HARAJUKU DEMONSTRATE THE ART OF AIR ORIGAMI.
Photographer: Simon Charles Rowe / LPI

Japan's mighty metropolis rises manga-style from economic ashes and earthquake fears to take on the world by transforming from business-as-usual salaryman to gadget-wielding monster and protector of Edo's tradition.

ANATOMY

Tokyo's massive size is only understandable in terms of the spaghetti-tangle rail map that includes three different train systems. Tourists stick to the Japan Railway's (JR) Yamanote line, which takes in the Imperial Palace with Ginza and Marunouchi (business district) in the east. To the west lies club-paradise Roppongi and then more nightlife in Shibuya and Shinjuku. Addresses are determined not by street name (few have actual names) but by indicating the *ku* (ward), then the *chō* or *machi* (like suburbs) and then *chōme* (roughly a couple of blocks). It's no wonder even taxi drivers ask for directions.

PEOPLE

Japan's famous homogeneity is disturbed by cosmopolitan Tokyo, but only slightly. Non-Japanese number less than 400,000 and form a *gaijin* (foreigner) population of business visitors, English-language teachers and Korean communities. Broadly, the population is Japanese, some of whom have a grasp of English, but many know only their native tongue.

TYPICAL TOKYOITE

In a city where there's half a vending machine for every citizen, you can expect a consumer culture to be important, with an obsession for owning the latest. Foreigners often snap up bargains of last-season electronics or clothing. And the bursting of the economic bubble means real estate is finally becoming more affordable. Expressing *honne* (personal views) is frowned upon socially with a need for *tatamae* (or safer views)…unless the sake is flowing, when even karaoke seems like a good idea.

DEFINING EXPERIENCE

Breakfasting on sushi in gumboots with the fisherfolk at Tsukiji Central Fish Market, striking a pose with the *Cos-play-zoku* (dress-up gangs) near Meiji Shrine, getting spiritual at the shrines of Sensō-ji, then polishing off the night with beer and snacks at an *izakaya* (pub/eatery).

STRENGTHS

- *Cos-play-zoku*
- Ginza
- Ueno Park
- 'Bullet' trains
- Tokyo National Museum
- Bonsai Park
- Shinjuku
- Mt Fuji
- *Kaijū* (monster movie)
- Imperial Palace
- Meiji Shrine and surrounding Harajuku and Aoyama areas
- Kabuki-za Theatre
- *Hanami* (cherry-blossom viewing) in spring
- Kite Museum

WEAKNESSES

- Eating *unagi* (eel)
- Impossible traffic
- Distant Nairita airport
- Yakuza (Japanese mafia)
- Earthquakes

GOLD STAR

Low crime – three people will stoop to help if you drop your wallet, and the streets are safe at all hours.

STARRING ROLE IN...

- *Lost in Translation* (2003)
- *Kill Bill: Vol 1* (2003)
- *Shinjuku Boys* (1995)
- *Tora! Tora! Tora!* (1970)

IMPORT

- Tokyo Disneyland
- Coffee
- *Gaijin* (foreigners)
- Whisky
- Korean labourers
- The Beatles

EXPORT

- Sony
- 17th-century haiku poet Bashō
- 'Bullet' trains
- Yohji Yamamoto
- Hayao Miyazaki
- Issey Miyake
- Asahi beer
- *Yu-Gi-Oh!* trading cards and TV series
- Manga
- *Sailor Moon* animated TV series
- Dragon Ball
- Nikon
- J-pop
- *Denki* (electronic music)
- Banana Yoshimoto
- *Iron Chef* TV series
- Haruki Murakami

SEE the Meiji Shrine, a tranquil Shinto sanctuary.

EAT the after-work favourite, *yakitori* (grilled skewers of chicken or vegetables), at the ever-busy Akiyoshi

DRINK *shōchū* – distilled liquor used as a disinfectant during the Edo period – at any trendy Shinjuku bar.

DO soak and scrub your cares away at Jakotsu-yu, an Edo-era *onsen* (traditional bathhouse).

WATCH sumo at the Ryōgoku Kokugikan Stadium, though you'd have to join the *yakuza* to get a seat.

BUY cold Big Boss coffee from a vending machine, undrinkable but *very* Tokyo.

AFTER DARK pack your fangs for a night out at the vampy campy movie-tribute bar Dusk Till Dawn.

URBAN MYTH

Tokyo's apparent political conformity is often disturbed by mysterious black vans that prowl the streets blasting out right-wing patriotic songs, which bear an uncanny resemblance to children's *manga* theme songs. This is the propaganda arm of the *uyoku* – a collection of seriously far-right political parties. Most Tokyoites studiously ignore them, but the *uyoku* have been known to police criticism of the emperor either through threats and, occasionally, violence.

TRAINEE WRESTLERS POSE FOR A 'BEFORE' PHOTO AT A SUMO ACADEMY.
Photographer: Martin Moos / LPI

BASEBALL FANS WAVE THEIR SCARVES IN TRIBUTE TO THE YOMIURI GIANTS AT TOKYO DOME.
Photographer: Greg Elms / LPI

FUSSY BUYERS INSPECT ROWS OF TUNA AT TSUKIJI FISH MARKET.
Photographer: Paul Dymond / LPI

Ulaanbaatar

VITAL STATISTICS

NAME: ULAANBAATAR

NICKNAME: UB

DATE OF BIRTH: 1693; ALTHOUGH THE CITY WAS LARGELY NOMADIC, SO IT ACTUALLY CHANGED LOCATIONS REGULARLY UNTIL THE 20TH CENTURY

ADDRESS: MONGOLIA (MAP 1, HH8)

HEIGHT: 1325M

SIZE: 1368 SQ KM

POPULATION: 1 MILLION

LONELY PLANET RANKING: 157

Definitely one of the world's most unusual capitals, UB is the furthest capital city in the world from the sea; it's the decidedly rough-and-ready capital of a seminomadic country, at a vast remove from the rest of the world.

ANATOMY

The city is a sprawl without much natural definition. It's centred around the vast Sükhbaatar Sq, named after Mongolia's Stalinist leader during early Communist times. The Trans-Mongolian railway runs right through the city too, and provides a useful landmark, running parallel to the Dund River. Local public transport is reliable and departures are frequent, but buses can get crowded. Green minivans run along a similar route to the buses, and for short trips it's just as cheap to take a taxi.

PEOPLE

UB is bursting at the seams these days, with more and more people from the countryside coming in to find work in the overstretched capital. Almost half of the country's population lives here, which, given the country is twice the size of France, is quite indicative of just how empty the Mongol plains really are. The capital's population is almost entirely Mongolian.

TYPICAL ULAANBAATAR CITIZEN

This sprawling city's residents are different from most other city dwellers in every way. On the city's outskirts are *ger* (tent) suburbs, where mangy mongrels patrol the unpaved lanes and most residents still live in traditional circular felt tents. Some districts still serve their traditional role as the protective ring around a monastery. Of great contrast are the narrow lanes off Sükhbaatar Sq that are undergoing a renaissance of ultra-progressive fashion shops and trendy cafés. The city is still spirited, with a heady cross section of society – crimson-robed monks rub shoulders with sombre-suited politicians and businesspeople, while mobile-phone–toting teenagers skip past bewildered nomads fresh off the steppes.

DEFINING EXPERIENCE

Visiting the market to see the colours and the excited bartering, wandering the unusual streets of this extraordinary city as the houses give way to *ger*, where you'll as likely as not be invited in by one of the families living there, then checking out some Mongolian throat singing or the circus in the evening after some hearty fare in a traditional Mongolian restaurant.

STRENGTHS

- Extremely friendly local population
- Very well set up for tourism
- You really do feel like you've reached the end of the earth
- Superb trips to the surrounding stunning countryside

WEAKNESSES

- Unbelievable litter – Mongolians aren't used to nonbiodegradable materials and still simply throw everything onto the floor once they've done with it
- UB has become such a huge tourist draw that sometimes you feel you're in India or Thailand come the summer months

GOLD STAR

The monasteries here are spectacular. Visiting the Gandantegchinlen Khiid is a humbling and memorable experience, as is seeing the interior of the Winter Palace of the Bogd Khaan.

STARRING ROLE IN...

- There have been several very successful films shot in Mongolia including *Urga* (1991) and *The Weeping Camel* (2003), but they tend to focus on rural life and as such have not been shot in Ulaanbaatar.

IMPORT

- Korean cars
- Processed and consumer goods
- Oil

EXPORT

- Copper
- Cashmere
- Leather
- Gold

SEE wrestling and other traditional sports during the Nadaam Festival in July.

EAT *buuz* (steamed mutton dumplings) and *khuushuur* (fried mutton pancakes) for a taste of Mongolia.

DRINK the ubiquitous local brew, Chinggis Beer.

DO not miss the staggering exhibits of dinosaurs at the National History Museum.

WATCH extraordinary performances of unique Mongolian throat singing.

BUY traditional Buddhist good-luck trinkets at the shops around any monastery or religious building.

AFTER DARK be aware that much of the city isn't lit at night!

URBAN MYTH

Unfortunately this is not so much a myth as a terrible reality, which has attained its own morbid fame. Thousands of Mongolian children – orphans or those abandoned by families unable to feed them – live beneath the city in underground slums, congregating around heating pipes to keep themselves alive during the extremely harsh Mongolian winter, when it regularly goes below minus 20°C. Despite the best efforts of local aid workers, the problem doesn't seem to be going away and child beggars are still extremely common on the streets.

WRESTLING FOR INDEPENDENCE – IT'S ALL ABOUT THE SHOWMANSHIP.
Photographer: Bradley Mayhew / LPI

RIDING, WRESTLING, ARCHERY – THE THREE MANLY SPORTS OF THE ANNUAL NADAAM FESTIVAL.
Photographer: Felicity Volk / LPI

TRADITIONAL YURTS FORM THIS SUBURB WITH A DIFFERENCE.
Photographer: Olivier Cirendini / LPI

A SLOW GAME OF DRAUGHTS OR CHESS PASSES TIME.
Photographer: Scott Darsney / LPI

Valletta

VITAL STATISTICS

NAME: VALLETTA

DATE OF BIRTH: 1566; VALETTA WAS BUILT BY THE KNIGHTS OF THE ORDER OF ST JOHN

ADDRESS: MALTA (MAP 3, L16)

HEIGHT: 70M

SIZE: 0.6 SQ KM

POPULATION: 6500

LONELY PLANET RANKING: 192

The capital of Malta is a World Heritage site whose neat streets are crammed with signs of its history, including enlightening museums; forts, fortifications and monuments testifying to a valiant past; and remnants of British rule, such as red telephone- and postboxes.

ANATOMY

Perched on the tip of the Sceberras Peninsula, Valetta's gridlike pattern of streets makes it easy to navigate. Entering through City Gate, where you'll find the bus terminus, the main street, Triq ir-Repubblika (Republic St) runs northeast to Fort St Elmo. Parallel with Repubblika run Triq ir-Merkanti (Merchant St) to the southeast and Triq ir-Ifran (Old Bakery St) to the northwest. Triq ir-Repubblika and Triq ir-Merkanti are on the highest point of Valetta and the side streets run downhill. The main landmarks, St John's Co-Cathedral and the Grand Master's Palace, are on Triq ir-Repubblika. Valletta is easily explored on foot, although there is a bus service if you're feeling lazy.

PEOPLE

Over 95% of Malta's population was born on the island. The majority of the foreign community is British but there is a growing North African Muslim community.

TYPICAL VALETTA CITIZEN

The Maltese are proud of their country's rich history. Since their independence from Britain in 1964, they have shown themselves to be politically engaged (around 90% of people vote). The Roman Catholic Church still has a large influence, although this is decreasing, and family values are very strong. Unemployment is low and there is free education for under-16s. Most people are friendly towards tourists and speak English; the native language is Malti. Football, horse racing and water polo are popular spectator sports.

DEFINING EXPERIENCE

Remembering Malta's WWII experiences in the National War Museum and spying that George Cross medal, before walking around the fortifications past the Siege Bell Memorial then into town for a coffee at Caffè Cordina and a trip around the Grand Master's Palace.

STRENGTHS

- Grand Harbour
- St John's Co-Cathedral
- The Malta experience
- 300 days of sunshine per year
- Mediterranean film studios – Europe's biggest film-production water tanks
- The city's fortifications
- The Grand Master's Palace
- National War Museum
- Ghana nights (Maltese folk music) at the St James Cavalier Centre for Creativity
- Church of St Paul's Shipwreck
- Excellent scuba-diving eg HMS *Maori*
- Rich marine life, such as sea horses and bottlenose dolphins
- Warm sea (over 20°C in summer)
- Kinnie orange-and-herb soft drink
- Cisk lager
- Hopleaf beer
- Agius Pastizzerija for pastries
- Carnival (February/March)
- National Museum of Archaeology

WEAKNESSES

- The Maltese Falcon – not spotted since the 1980s
- Rubbish in landfill sites

GOLD STAR

History.

STARRING ROLE IN...

- *Troy* (2004)
- *Gladiator* (2000)
- *The Spy Who Loved Me* (1977)

IMPORT

- Mattia Preti
- Caravaggio
- Jean Parisot de la Vallette (hero of the 1565 Great Siege and founder of Valletta)
- The Knights of the Order of St John

EXPORT

- Oliver Friġġieri
- Edward de Bono, inventor of 'lateral thinking'
- Handmade lace
- Silver filigree
- Glassware

SEE where the knights used to worship, St John's Co-Cathedral, and admire Caravaggio's paintings in the Cathedral Museum.

EAT seasonal Maltese cuisine at local favourite Rubino.

DRINK and taste local wines in the Castille Wine Vaults underneath the stock exchange.

DO walk around the city's fortifications for views of the Grand Harbour and the Three Cities.

WATCH historical pageants and re-enactments at Fort St Elmo.

BUY locally produced glassware, lace and ceramics at the Malta Crafts Centre.

AFTER DARK see concerts, plays and art-house films in the St James Cavalier Centre for Creativity.

URBAN MYTH

Malta has been under siege more than once. Indeed it was a siege that prompted Valetta to be built in the first place (the Great Siege of 1565). But possibly the worst battle experienced by the island was in 1942, when they were bombed for 154 consecutive days and nights (when London's Blitz was at its worst, there were 57 days of continuous bombardment). Operation Pedestal was launched to rescue the island. Under heavy attack only five supply ships made it through, but this was enough for Malta to be saved. On 15 April 1942 King George VI awarded the George Cross to the population of Malta, for their bravery.

GETTING AROUND THE CITY IS EASY BY BUS OR ON FOOT.
Photographer: Bethune Carmichael / LPI

THE CULTURAL AND COMMERCIAL HEART OF MALTA, VALLETTA IS A CITY OF INTRICATE CHARM.
Photographer: Doug Scott / Photolibrary

THE MAJORITY OF CITIZENS WERE BORN ON MALTA AND REMAIN FIERCELY PROUD OF THEIR HERITAGE.
Photographer: Network Photographers / Alamy

VALLETTA IS A FASCINATING MASTERPIECE OF BAROQUE ARCHITECTURE.
Photographer: Doug Scott / Photolibrary

A BIRD'S-EYE VIEW OF THE WINDING STAIRWAY OF THE MERCADO CENTRAL.
Photographer: Brent Winebrenner / LPI

Valparaíso

VITAL STATISTICS

NAME: VALPARAÍSO

NICKNAME: VALPO, LA PERLA DEL PACÍFICO
(THE PEARL OF THE PACIFIC)

DATE OF BIRTH: 1536; WHEN IT WAS FOUNDED BY
THE SPANISH CONQUISTADOR JUAN DE SAAVEDRA,
THEN PERMANENTLY ESTABLISHED IN 1544 WHEN
PEDRO DE VALDIVIA MADE IT HIS OFFICIAL PORT

ADDRESS: CHILE (MAP 1, M20)

HEIGHT: 40M

POPULATION: 276,000

LONELY PLANET RANKING: 096

Valparaíso is a city of dramatic nature – narrow wave-cut terraces with steep, labyrinthine roads and crumbling mansions, precipitous cliffs and a rugged Pacific coastline.

ANATOMY

Chile's principal port and second-largest city, Valparaíso occupies a narrow strip of land between the waterfront and nearby hills. Its convoluted centre (known as El Plan) has distinctive, sinuous cobblestone streets and is overlooked by precipitous cliffs and hilltop suburbs, which are accessed by funicular railways and stairway footpaths. It is conducive to mazelike strolls and rides on the funicular, and its natural history, fine arts and maritime museums are justly famed. Muelle Prat, the redeveloped pier, is a lively market area.

PEOPLE

The lineage of Valpo residents is strongly European, particularly Spanish, English and German. The Catholic Church has a great deal of political power, and as a consequence many *porteños*, as locals are known, are quite conservative in their views.

TYPICAL PORTEÑO

Porteños are laid-back and cultured. They are known for their fine taste in seafood and wine, their prolific cultural output in films and literature, and their pride in their port city. They boast of their individuality but are as conservative as most other Chileans. Their parties are as raucous as their family feuds, and they love them both. They explore their own town and take the time to share it with visitors.

DEFINING EXPERIENCE

Having a *cafecito* (short black coffee) for breakfast, then a *paseo* (walk) through the winding streets and parks, shopping at the fresh fish market on the port and cooking up a *caldillo* (seafood soup), having a siesta in the afternoon and dancing until the wee hours on the waterfront.

STRENGTHS

◿ *Ascensores* (funicular lifts) and the quirky individuals who operate them
◿ Generally mild climate
◿ Views from the *cerros* (hills)
◿ Tangled, cobbled backstreets
◿ Spectacular Pacific coastline
◿ Excellent seafood
◿ Rich literary history
◿ Brightly coloured *barrios* (neighbourhoods) on the hillsides
◿ *Porteños* and their pride in their city's history
◿ The murals at the Museo a Cielo Abierto (Open-Sky Museum)
◿ *El Mercurio de Valparaíso* – the world's oldest Spanish-language newspaper

WEAKNESSES

◿ Social conservatism following the Pinochet years
◿ Earthquakes
◿ Shantytowns
◿ Machismo
◿ Petty theft
◿ Northern gales in winter

GOLD STAR

Often described as Chile's most distinctive city with its unique, faded grandeur and spontaneous, bohemian charm, the entire city has been named a Unesco World Heritage site.

STARRING ROLE IN...

◿ *El Wanderers de Valparaíso* (2003)
◿ *Valparaíso* (1994)
◿ *Valparaiso, Valparaiso* (1971)
◿ *Canto General* and *Confieso que he vivido* (I Confess That I Have Lived) by Pablo Neruda
◿ *Azul* by Rubén Darío

IMPORT

◿ Spanish colonists
◿ *Fútbol* (football)
◿ Rubén Darío
◿ British and German immigrants
◿ Chile's National Congress
◿ Nearly everything that comes to Chile via the sea

EXPORT

◿ Augusto Pinochet
◿ Salvador Allende
◿ Nobel prize–winning poetry by Pablo Neruda and Gabriela Mistral
◿ Experimental cinema
◿ Chilean folk musicians
◿ Wine
◿ Most of Chile's produce

SEE the final steps of 500,000 pilgrims walking the Virgen de lo Vasquez Pilgrimage in December each year.

EAT *curanto* – a hearty stew of fish, shellfish, chicken, pork, lamb, beef and potato.

DRINK good Chilean wines with the locals at Café Vinilo.

DO ride the *ascensores* to Cerro Concepción, both for the view and the neighbourhood.

WATCH the spectacular fireworks over the harbour on Año Nuevo (New Year).

BUY antiques in the market at Plaza O'Higgins.

AFTER DARK check out the live music at Valparaíso Eterno.

URBAN MYTH

The town of Valparaíso has certainly mythologised its most famous poet. Pablo Neruda maintained one of his three Chilean homes here in Valparaíso, known as La Sebastiana. Although it was his least-visited house, Neruda made it a point to watch Valparaíso's annual New Year's fireworks from his lookout on Cerro Bellavista. He heaped praise on Valpo in his works *Canto General* and *I Confess That I Have Lived*, and *porteños* have not forgotten his tribute. On the 100th anniversary of the birth of Pablo Neruda, *porteños* composed the world's largest poem in his honour. It was printed on a roll of paper 20m long and 1m wide, and included contributions from throughout Chile.

ESCAPING THE URBAN MADNESS AT THE PORT OF VALPARAÍSO.
Photographer: Brent Winebrenner / LPI

COLOURFUL BUILDINGS CLUSTER ON THE HILLS ABUTTING TOWN.
Photographer: Brent Winebrenner / LPI

PROTESTORS STILL INCENSED OVER THE NAVY'S REPRESSIVE ROLE DURING THE PINOCHET ERA.
Photographer: Brent Winebrenner / LPI

A BRUNCH WITH A VIEW – LAID-BACK DINING AT ONE OF THE RESTAURANTS ON GRANVILLE ISLAND.
Photographer: Chris Cheadle / Getty Images

Casual but cosmopolitan, freewheeling offbeat Vancouver is framed by a mountain backdrop with the sea kissing its edges.

ANATOMY

Straddling the lowlands of the Fraser River and the Coast Mountains of southwest British Columbia, Vancouver sits atop the most active earthquake zone in Canada. There are many bays, inlets and river branches shaping the city and coastline. Skyscrapers, big business and high finance sit just blocks from Stanley Park's thick rainforest. The city spreads east and north, and is well served by an elevated skytrain, buses, trains and the sea-bus crossing to North Vancouver.

PEOPLE

Vancouver's population comes from all over the world. By the end of the 20th century it had the largest Asian population in North America with an influx of Hong Kong Chinese. Forty percent of Vancouver residents are foreign-born.

TYPICAL VANCOUVERITE

With the knowledge that they live in an all-round 'top foreign city' known for its 'best quality of life', Vancouverites have a laid-back mind-set, happy to be part of a pioneering Pacific Rim city where marijuana is tolerated and the foodie scene has exploded. Vancouverites are aggressively outdoors oriented (they don't wear all that Gore-Tex for nothing), skiing in the winter but also cycling, blading, paddling on False Creek and sailing on English Bay.

DEFINING EXPERIENCE

Strolling through Stanley Park, lunching on the terrace at the Vancouver Art Gallery (having wandered through the permanent collection of local artists and caught the latest temporary exhibition), taking the sea bus across to North Van and watching for seals in the harbour before heading out to the university campus and the huge collection of First Nation artefacts at the Museum of Anthropology then finishing the day by dining on Pacific Northwest cuisine on Granville Island.

Vancouver

VITAL STATISTICS

NAME: VANCOUVER

NICKNAME: HOLLYWOOD NORTH; HONGKOUVER; CITY OF GLASS

DATE OF BIRTH: 1867; FIRST NAMED GASTOWN, A SALOON WAS OPENED NEXT TO A SAWMILL AND A TOWN SPRANG UP AROUND IT

ADDRESS: CANADA (MAP 1, G8)

HEIGHT: 14M

SIZE: 107 SQ KM

POPULATION: 2.4 MILLION

LONELY PLANET RANKING: 015

CANADA'S LONGEST POOL, KITSILANO SALT POOL (137M), IS OFFSET BY THE NATURAL BEAUTY OF THE NORTH SHORE MOUNTAINS. Photographer: Chris Cheadle / Getty Images

DAWN'S SOFT LIGHT MUTES THE GLITTERING GLASS FAÇADE OF THE EVENTS VENUE 'PLAZA OF NATIONS' AND ITS ATTENDANT PLEASURE BOATS. Photographer: Chris Cheadle / Getty Images

A MERCHANT DISPLAYS HIS WARES AT THE 'CLOTHING OPTIONAL' WRECK BEACH. Photographer: Chris Cheadle / Getty Images

STRENGTHS

- Vancouver Art Gallery
- Wreck Beach
- Stanley Park
- Museum of Anthropology
- The startling Coast Mountains north of the city
- Coal Harbour Seawalk
- Marijuana cafés
- Eating outside all year round
- Star-spotting on film sets
- Dr Sun-Yat Sen Garden
- Illuminares Lantern Festival
- Bare Buns Fun Run
- 200-plus ice-cream flavours at La Casa Gelato – wasabi or balsamic anyone?
- The tiny ferries across to Granville Island

WEAKNESSES

- The rain – 170 days a year
- Rapidly gentrifying neighbourhoods
- Eating out year-round – 'Can we please go inside, now?'
- Fleece/Gore-Tex – does everyone have to wear it?
- Blocked-off streets for film sets
- Always substituting for somewhere else

GOLD STAR

Granville Island – not really an island but an enclave of artists, artisans, theatre companies and restaurants with great views over the city any time of the day.

URBAN MYTH

There is a haunted house on the southeast corner of King Edward and Cambie Sts. A doctor killed his wife there in the 1930s…or maybe someone else was murdered and now Chinese monks that summon the dead live there and things fly around in the house. Or the house was bought by a group of nuns from Taiwan, who later sold the house. Or the house that stands there now is a newer dwelling but the ground that the house sits on is still cursed and the spirits of the dead have not left. Exorcisms have failed – in one case, a priest, or some other holy person, went to sleep inside the house and woke up in the middle of the night somewhere outside the house. Or maybe, just maybe, locals are getting themselves worked up over nothing.

STARRING ROLE IN...

- *The X Files* (1993–98)
- *Double Jeopardy* (1999)
- Douglas Coupland novels

IMPORT

- Hong Kong Chinese citizens
- Hong Kong Chinese money
- Hollywood productions
- South Asian communities
- William Gibson

EXPORT

- Greenpeace
- Generation X
- kd lang
- Michael J Fox
- Pamela Anderson
- Jason Priestley
- Carrie-Ann Moss
- Hayden Christensen
- Diana Krall
- Bryan Adams
- Michael Bublé
- Smoked salmon
- Maple syrup
- Salmon jerky

SEE the steam-powered clock in Gastown.

EAT Pacific Northwest food – salmon with a hazelnut and maple crust?

DRINK Maple Cream Ale at Granville Island Brewery.

DO explore Dr Sun Yat-Sen Park, a tranquil oasis where every pebble and brook has its place.

WATCH First Nations carvers working at the Museum of Anthropology.

BUY up-and-coming local fashion on the decidedly inappropriately named Main St.

AFTER DARK catch some jazz or blues at Café Deux Soleil or Bukowski's on Commercial Drive.

A DEVOUT PILGRIM WADES INTO THE RIVER TO PRAY AT SUNRISE.
Photographer: Chris Beall / LPI

India's holiest city attracts masses of Hindu pilgrims and visitors to the mighty Ganges to bathe, offer blessings, do yoga, wash clothes, get a massage, play cricket and witness cremations; and to drink in the spectacle of life's vibrancy on the riverbanks.

ANATOMY

The old city of Varanasi is situated along the western bank of the Ganges and extends back from the riverbank ghats in a labyrinth of alleys called *galis* that are too narrow for traffic. The *galis* can be disorienting but the hotels are usually well-signposted and however lost you become, you will eventually land up at a ghat where you can get your bearings. Catch crowed buses or a cycle-rickshaw or autorickshaw.

PEOPLE

As you'd expect, the majority of Varanasi's inhabitants are Hindu. Uttar Pradesh is an important political state and has produced half the country's prime ministers.

TYPICAL VARANASI CITIZEN

Despite Uttar Pradesh's prominent political position, poor governance has not made the citizens of Varanasi's life easy. Economic progress is slight, the erratic electricity supply causes problems and the state's overall literacy rate is low. Varanasi, however, has an excellent university and is a well-respected centre of learning attracting scholars from all over India. Family is important for Indian society and the birth rate is high – it is rare for people in their thirties to be unmarried or childless. Most Hindu marriages are arranged and although dowries are illegal, they are often still supplied, straining finances for the family concerned.

Varanasi

VITAL STATISTICS

NAME: VARANASI

NICKNAME: THE ETERNAL CITY; THE CITY OF SHIVA

DATE OF BIRTH: 1400 BC; VARANASI HAS BEEN A CENTRE OF LEARNING AND CIVILISATION SINCE THIS TIME

ADDRESS: INDIA (MAP 5, F4)

HEIGHT: 81M

SIZE: 74 SQ KM

POPULATION: 1.2 MILLION

LONELY PLANET RANKING: 072

BEFORE DESCENDING INTO THE WATERS OF THE GANGES A MAN HAS HIS HEAD SHAVED BY A RIVERSIDE BARBER.
Photographer: Chris Mellor / LPI

LIKE NOTES ON A STAVE, WEARY GOATS RECLINE ON THE MULTI-COLOURED TULSI GHATS.
Photographer: Anders Blomqvist / LPI

HINDU PILGRIMS IN GORGEOUSLY VIVID SARIS ON DARBHANGA GHAT.
Photographer: Richard I'Anson / LPI

DEFINING EXPERIENCE

Watching pilgrims perform *puja* (prayer) at dawn on the ghats, before buying some *paan* (betel nut and leaves concoction) and heading to the International Yoga Clinic & Meditation Centre for a hatha lesson.

STRENGTHS

- ◢ The Ganges
- ◢ People-watching at Dasaswamedh Ghat
- ◢ Manikarnika Ghat – the most auspicious place for a Hindu to be cremated
- ◢ The Ganges *susu* (dolphin)
- ◢ The particularly holy water between the turrets of Trilochan Ghat
- ◢ Vishwanath Temple
- ◢ Benares Hindu University
- ◢ Ramnagar Fort & Museum
- ◢ Steam baths and massages
- ◢ Silk
- ◢ Noise and colour
- ◢ Hindi courses at Bhasha Bharati Language Institute
- ◢ International Music Centre Ashram
- ◢ International Yoga Clinic & Meditation Centre
- ◢ Hotel Ganges View
- ◢ Ram Lila (September/October)

WEAKNESSES

- ◢ Pollution of the Ganges
- ◢ Blackouts caused by the power-hungry sewage treatment plants
- ◢ Rickshaw-wallahs and touts
- ◢ Street crime after dark
- ◢ Fishing the Ganges *susu*

GOLD STAR

Religious tradition.

STARRING ROLE IN...

- ◢ *Ganges Dreaming* (2004)
- ◢ *Ganges: River to Heaven* (2003)

IMPORT

- ◢ Foreign students at the university
- ◢ Hindu pilgrims
- ◢ Tulsi Das
- ◢ Mark Twain

EXPORT

- ◢ *Langda aam* (mangoes)
- ◢ *Sitafal* (custard apples)
- ◢ Silk brocades
- ◢ Benares saris
- ◢ Bhadohi carpets
- ◢ Ravi Shankar
- ◢ Rajul Mehta

SEE the incredible gold dome and tower of Vishwanath Temple – from the shop over the road if you're not Hindu, or from inside the temple if you are.

EAT local specialities at one of the city's best restaurants, Varuna Restaurant, and enjoy live sitar and tabla music.

DRINK a glass of history at Princep Bar, named after James Princep, illustrator of Varanasi's temples and ghats.

DO an uplifting boat trip down the Ganges from Dasaswamedh Ghat to Harishchandra Ghat at dawn.

WATCH cremations at Manikarnika Ghat.

BUY different types of beautiful silk at Ganga Silk.

AFTER DARK watch a sitar concert at the International Music Centre Ashram, and take lessons there if you feel inspired.

URBAN MYTH

Varanasi is the centre of the Hindu world, a crossing place between the physical and the spiritual, and the River Ganges is thought to offer salvation. Hindus believe that washing in the river will cleanse their bodies of sin. Varanasi is a popular place for Hindu cremations as the city is credited with a direct route to heaven. If a Hindu dies here they receive *moksha*, which is liberation from the cycle of life and death.

Venice

VITAL STATISTICS

NAME: VENICE

NICKNAME: LA SERENISSIMA; THE QUEEN OF THE ADRIATIC

DATE OF BIRTH: 5TH AND 6TH CENTURIES; WHEN THE ISLANDS OF THE VENETIAN LAGOON WERE FIRST SETTLED DURING THE BARBARIAN INVASIONS

ADDRESS: ITALY (MAP 3, K11)

HEIGHT: 1M

SIZE: 458 SQ KM

POPULATION: 62,000 (CITY); 269,000 (INCLUDING MAINLAND)

LONELY PLANET RANKING: 022

There's no city on earth whose visual impact has the same power as Venice – the Adriatic island republic is reluctantly part of Italy, but in reality belongs to the entire world as one of the great cultural treasures anywhere on the planet.

ANATOMY

Spread over an incredible 117 islands, connected by over 400 bridges and divided by some 150 canals, Venice is in many places a cramped and dark city whose astonishing colours and vibrancy suddenly become apparent in the plentiful open spaces and along the magnificent Grand Canal, the main artery of the city, which hums with traffic day and night. Few cities reward walkers so generously as Venice. A vaporetto is the other essential method of getting around, and it can be equally rewarding: you won't find too many public transport routes as unforgettable as vaporetto No 1's trip along the Grand Canal. Taking a ride in a gondola is corny, expensive, embarrassing and…well, if you really want to, why not? Water taxis are almost as expensive as gondolas, but their pilots don't wear stripy shirts or sing 'O Sole Mio'.

PEOPLE

Venetians are sadly a declining breed, if not necessarily a dying one. The lack of jobs outside the tourist industry has led to many young people leaving the city for the mainland at the earliest opportunity, and as such the native population is in sharp decline. House prices – high enough already – are forced higher by large numbers of non-Venetians purchasing second homes here.

TYPICAL VENETIAN

Defined by their own dialect of Italian, a separate history and an island mentality, Venetians are somewhat reluctant Italians and define themselves far more in terms of their city than in terms of their country. There's a love-hate relationship going on here though – Venetians will tell you the disadvantages of living in their unique overpriced and sinking city, but will expect nothing but praise from you as a visitor!

DEFINING EXPERIENCE

Taking a trip across the lagoon at dawn to see San Marco before the crowds, stopping off at a café to sip coffee, getting lost in the back alleys, discovering a magnificent church, vaporetto-hopping up and down the Grand Canal and munching some top-notch seafood for dinner.

STRENGTHS

- Discovering that despite the crowds, the smells and the high prices there's absolutely nowhere like this remarkable city
- The Giardini – Venice's green lung beyond San Marco
- The Lido – roads! And a beach!
- The annual film festival, which sees Hollywood royalty rubbing shoulders with the locals
- The Venice Biennale, one of the greatest art shows on earth.

WEAKNESSES

- The crowds
- The smelly canals (particularly foul when they are being dredged)
- The high prices

GOLD STAR

The Venice Carnival is a once-in-a-lifetime experience that will thrill and exhaust in equal measure. Held in February or March, the city parties nonstop, although you'll feel out of place if you haven't spent a lot of time and money on your costume.

STARRING IN…

- *Death in Venice* (1971)
- *Don't Look Now* (1973)
- *The Merchant of Venice* by Shakespeare
- *Everyone Says I Love You* (1996)
- *The Talented Mr Ripley* (1999)
- *The Aspern Papers* by Henry James

IMPORT

- Tourists, tourists and more tourists
- Hollywood royalty (annually)
- Artistic royalty (biennially)

EXPORT

- Murano glass
- Marco Polo
- Titian
- Giacomo Casanova
- Dramatist Carlo Goldoni
- Vivaldi

SEE the extraordinary interior of the Basilica di San Marco early in the morning before the crowds arrive.

EAT superb seafood, but avoid anywhere with a *menu turistico*.

DRINK the world's most expensive espresso on Piazza San Marco.

DO try to get there for the Carnival, or one of Venice's other big municipal celebrations.

WATCH opera at the stunningly rebuilt La Fenice opera house.

BUY Murano glass (admittedly an acquired taste) at bargain prices.

AFTER DARK enjoy a world-famous Bellini (Venice's native cocktail, made with champagne and peaches) at Harry's Bar.

URBAN MYTH

Many are now arguing that Venice is no longer sinking, although the jury's out until conclusive proof is produced. The major sinking of the city occurred in the first half of the 20th century, when artesian wells were dug into the periphery of the lagoon to draw water for local industry. This caused subsidence, which has been enormously reduced by the banning of the wells in the 1960s. However, the city is not out of danger – as a result of the subsidence it is at constant risk from the *acqua alta* – the high tides that come in regularly from the Adriatic.

PEAK HOUR ON THE GRAND CANAL WHERE GONDOLAS LINE UP BEFORE LAUNCHING OFF.
Photographer: Jon Davison / LPI

WASHING DAY NEAR CATHEDRAL SAN PIETRO DI CASTELLO.
Photographer: Juliet Coombe / LPI

SIBLINGS TAKE TIME OUT TO SKETCH AND RELAX AT SIESTA TIME.
Photographer: Roberto Soncin Gerometta / LPI

EERILY EMPTY, THE FAMOUS PIAZZA SAN MARCO GLISTENS AFTER A STORM.
Photographer: Juliet Coombe / LPI

Vienna

VITAL STATISTICS

NAME: VIENNA

DATE OF BIRTH: AD 8; WHEN VINDOBONA WAS FOUNDED BY THE ROMANS

ADDRESS: AUSTRIA (MAP 3, M10)

HEIGHT: 203M

SIZE: 415 SQ KM

POPULATION: 1.7 MILLION (CITY); 2.3 MILLION (METRO AREA)

LONELY PLANET RANKING: 040

THE FAÇADE OF THE SCHLOSS BELVEDERE ROYAL PUTS IN A BID FOR BEST POSTCARD VIEW IN VIENNA.
Photographer: Martin Brent / Getty Images

Once the most sparkling gem in the Hapsburg crown, Vienna remains a city of culture, class and beauty, famous for its opera and classical music; but peer beneath this tradition and you'll see experimental arts, world food and green living.

ANATOMY

The blue Danube runs through Vienna, nudging the old city and most tourist attractions to the west. Heading south from the river, the Danube Canal creates one rim of the historic centre (Innere Stadt). In the middle of the Danube River, the long Donauinsel promises fun with many beaches and playgrounds. The beloved Wienerwald (Vienna Woods) undulates appealingly to the west and north of the city. The greenery doesn't stop there – almost half the city comprises green spaces, more than any other European capital. Trams trundle through the city, while the U-Bahn whizzes around below ground.

PEOPLE

Almost a quarter of today's population hails from outside Austria, with the largest ethnic communities being from Eastern Europe and the Balkans. The majority of the population is Roman Catholic and there are also significant groups of Protestants and Muslims.

TYPICAL VIENNESE

Despite their reputation for being grumpy, the Viennese are consistently inconsistent, being cheery one day and dour the next. Their dark sense of humour is often self-deprecating and utterly beguiling, and they have a strange fascination with death – fancy visiting a museum devoted to funerals and undertakers (Bestattungs-museum)? Politeness is important – look your co-drinker in the eye when clinking glasses, to avoid appearing insincere. Employees receive extra salary payments for the summer and Christmas holidays, and rents are low. Around 8.3% of households own a dog, which approximates to 65,000 dogs. The Viennese are politically engaged and Austria's strongest advocates of socialism. Not surprisingly, they are also cultural, enjoying their theatre, music, opera, art, food and wine.

DEFINING EXPERIENCE

Gazing at Schiele's work in the Leopold Museum, before lapping up some sun and coffee in the MuseumsQuartier's courtyard, then heading to the Old Danube for a leisurely swim and refuelling at a *Heuriger* (wine tavern) in Stammersdorf.

URBAN MYTH

Disputes over the origin of the rich chocolate *Sacher Torte* cake raged between Hotel Sacher and Demel café in 1938 and 1953, with the crucial debate centring on whether the apricot jam should go under the icing or in the middle of the cake. The Hotel Sacher bakes 500 to 600 *Sacher Torte* a day and up to 3000 during Christmas – no wonder the recipe is fiercely protected. The Hotel Sacher claims that Japanese spies have infiltrated their kitchen in an attempt to discover the mysteries of the cake (and stage a cake coup?). But the hotel is determined that the ingredients should remain secret.

STRENGTHS

- Magnificent imperial palaces eg Schönbrunn
- Gothic Stephansdom (St Stephen's Cathedral)
- Secessionism and Secession Hall
- Otto Wagner's metro stations
- *Beisln* (pubs/bistros)
- *Heuriger*
- *Würstelstände* (sausage stands)
- The Danube
- The Wienerwald
- Vineyard day trips
- Christmas markets
- Vienna Boys' Choir
- The Spanish Riding School and its Lipizzaner stallions
- Staatsoper (the opera house)
- *Sacher Torte* (a rich chocolate cake)
- Hapsburg history
- The *Wiener Zeitung* (the oldest newspaper in the world, first published in 1703)
- Compulsory recycling
- Abundant cycle lanes
- The Vienna Philharmonic
- Avant-garde art eg Viennese Actionism
- Low crime
- Efficient trams
- The Naschmarkt (a market dating back to the 16th century)

WEAKNESSES

- Home-grown fashion (except Helmut Lang)
- Occasional xenophobia
- Bureaucratic hoops for budding entrepreneurs
- Labyrinthine one-way system
- Confusing or nonexistent WC labels
- Ubiquitous dog turds
- Grumpy waiters

GOLD STAR

Opera and classical music.

STARRING ROLE IN...

- *The Piano Teacher* (2001)
- *Before Sunrise* (1995)
- *The man with Two Brains* (1983)
- *The Third Man* (1949)

IMPORT

- High-street fashion shops
- Wolfgang Amadeus Mozart
- Wiener schnitzel (this originated in Milan)
- World food
- Music fans

EXPORT

- Helmut Lang
- Josef Haydn
- Franz Schubert
- The waltz
- Egon Schiele
- Gustav Klimt
- Ludwig Wittgenstein
- Novelist and playwright Peter Handke
- Sigmund Freud
- Container transloading
- Riesling and Veltliner wines

SEE as many museums as you can on the evening of 20 September, Lange Nacht der Museen.

EAT *Kaffee und Kuchen* (coffee and cake) in Konditorei Oberlaa Stadthaus.

DRINK in the Palmenhaus, a beautifully renovated Palm house, complete with high, arched ceilings, glass walls and steel beams.

DO a gentle but illuminating bicycle tour of Vienna's parks and waterways.

WATCH the Vienna Boys' Choir doing their sensational stuff in the Hofburg's Royal Chapel.

BUY a very traditional but exquisite porcelain ornament from the Wiener Porzellanmanufaktur Augarten.

AFTER DARK throw some shapes on the dance floor at Flex to the soundtrack of Viennese and international DJs.

WHAT'RE YOU LOOKIN' AT?' A PUNK COMPETES WITH A MOZART IMPOSTOR FOR MOST INTERESTING HAIRSTYLE.
Photographer: Martin Brent / Getty Images

THE VIEW OF SOME CLASSIC VIENNESE TILING FROM STEPHANSDOM SOUTH TOWER.
Photographer: Martin Brent / Getty Images

A WAITER PEERS THROUGH SMOKE TO MAKE SURE ALL'S WELL WITH THE BILL IN CAFÉ HAWELKA.
Photographer: Martin Brent / Getty Images

LOCAL BOYS PRACTICE THEIR MOVES AGAINST THE BACKDROP OF VILNIUS CATHEDRAL.
Photographer: Bruce Yuan-Yue Bi / LPI

Vilnius is kooky, mysterious and spooky, a spectacular city with astonishing contrasts: eerie shadowy courtyards, a thriving bohemian community of artists, and beautiful baroque buildings (the Old Town is a World Heritage site).

ANATOMY

The centre of Vilnius is on the south side of the Neris River. Its heart is Katedros aikšatė (Cathedral Sq), with the cathedral on the north side and Gedimino kalnas (Gediminas Hill) rising behind. South of Katedros aikštė are the cobbled Old Town streets *(senamiestis)*; to the west, Gedimino prospektas cuts straight across the newer part of the centre to Parliament. The train and bus stations are beyond the Old Town's southern edge, 1.5km from Katedros aikštė. The city has tourist signs in English and Lithuanian pointing to sites around the Old Town, making it impossible to get lost!

PEOPLE

Lithuania has the most ethnically homogeneous population of the three Baltic countries, with Lithuanians accounting for about 80% of inhabitants – Russian, Polish and Jewish groups make up the rest. Lithuanian is the official language, though locals are willing to speak English, German and even Russian (in stark contrast to Latvia and Estonia).

TYPICAL VILNIUS CITIZEN

Living in a self-proclaimed (albeit unofficial) independent republic, the typical Vilnius citizen is spirited, artistic, bohemian, fiercely proud of their bizarre, beautiful and bewitching city, and, as well as being a purveyor of rockin' baroque, is also a committed custodian of the world's only bronze Frank Zappa statue.

DEFINING EXPERIENCE

Cruising the blue lagoon around Trakai Castle in a yacht before getting lost in the cobbled streets of the Old Town and hiking up Gedimino kalnas to the tower for a sublime sunset over the city spires.

Vilnius

VITAL STATISTICS

NAME: VILNIUS

DATE OF BIRTH: 1323; WHEN IT WAS FOUNDED BY THE LITHUANIAN DUKE GEDIMINAS

ADDRESS: LITHUANIA (MAP 3, P6)

HEIGHT: 189M

SIZE: 401 SQ KM

POPULATION: 544,000

LONELY PLANET RANKING: 137

UNESCO WORLD HERITAGE–LISTED VILNIUS OLD TOWN IS ADMIRED FOR ITS STUNNING GOTHIC ARCHITECTURE.
Photographer: Bruce Yuan-Yue Bi / LPI

HUMOUR SIGNALS THE WAY FOR ARTISTS, DRUNKS AND DREAMERS AT THE BORDER OF UZUPIO REPUBLIC.
Photographer: Bruce Yuan-Yue Bi / LPI

THE PEOPLE OF VILNIUS ARE PROUD OF THEIR LITHUANIAN HERITAGE.
Photographer: Bruce Yuan-Yue Bi / LPI

STRENGTHS

- Baroque Old Town
- World Heritage site status
- Spires of Orthodox and Catholic churches
- Bohemian locals
- Strange bars in dim courtyards
- Narrow cobbled streets
- Gates of Dawn
- Pilies gatvė (Castle St)
- Applied Art Museum
- World's only Frank Zappa statue
- New rail links
- English signage (easy to navigate)
- The artists' Republic of Užupis, the Montmartre of Vilnius
- Ausros Vartu gatvė
- Great sense of humour
- Settling disputes with former neighbours

WEAKNESSES

- Some undercurrents of anti-Semitism
- Accusations of 'cashing in' on dark past eg the Soviet Sculpture theme park at Grūtas
- Uncomfortable KGB jokes
- The older generation's antiquated views of gays and ethnic/minority groups
- Western excesses – burgeoning strip clubs and casinos

GOLD STAR

Chocolate-box baroque – decadent and fragile, bohemian and tough, devilishly attractive Vilnius seduces visitors with its Old Town charm and a warm, wizened soul.

STARRING ROLE IN...

- *Koridorius* (The Corridor, 1995)
- *The Necklace of Wolf's Teeth* (1998)
- *The Book of Sorrow* by Josif Levinson
- *Forest of the Gods* by Balys Sruoga
- *Bohin Manor* by Tadeusz Konwicki
- *The Theology of Rain* by Alfonsas Nyka-Niliūnas

IMPORT

- The ill-fated concept of 'community' bicycles
- Remnants of Soviet-era architecture
- Casinos
- Strip bars
- Entrepreneurial outlook
- Frank Zappa (well, his statue), as a prodigal son
- Tourists
- Other bohemians

EXPORT

- Folk art (particularly carved wooden crosses)
- Jazz
- Pianist Gintautas Abarius
- Saxophonist Petras Vysniauskas
- The Ganelin Trio
- Amber
- Crosses

SEE the treasure-trove of religious jewels on display at the Applied Art Museum.

EAT smoked pigs' ears at Rotis Smuklė while the spit roast turns, no Coca-Cola in sight.

DRINK a 'Neprisikashkopustelaujancho punch' at funky studenty hang-out Mano Kavinė, then try pronouncing it!

DO catch a free performance of the Vilnius String Quartet in the courtyard of Grybas House every Wednesday.

WATCH the sun set over Vilnius' Gothic-steepled skyline from the tower on Gediminas Hill.

BUY pottery bells, woven wicker baskets, wooden toys and painted eggs from the artisan stalls that line the length of Vilnius' Pilies gatvė.

AFTER DARK head to Bix, formed by the eponymous Lithuanian hard-rock band – with an avant-garde industrial décor, it remains a favourite among the city's youngsters and funsters.

URBAN MYTH

According to legend, Vilnius was founded in the 1320s, when Lithuanian grand duke Gediminas, while camping on a hunting trip, dreamt of an iron wolf that howled with the voices of 100 wolves. His interpretation was to build an impregnable city as mighty as their cry. In fact, the site had been occupied at least 1000 years before and may also have been a political and trade centre.

Washington DC

VITAL STATISTICS

NAME: WASHINGTON DC

NICKNAME: DC, CAPITAL CITY

DATE OF BIRTH: 1791; WHEN CONGRESS CHOSE THE SITE FOR THE NEW FEDERAL CAPITAL

ADDRESS: USA (MAP 1, L10)

HEIGHT: 22M

SIZE: 177 SQ KM

POPULATION: 592,000 (CITY); 5.3 MILLION (METRO AREA)

LONELY PLANET RANKING: 103

Washington DC is full of great monuments and museums but it's also one of North America's great culinary capitals.

ANATOMY

The city lies at the last navigable point on the Potomac River, where the coastal plain meets a higher, rockier plateau. The latter is the setting for DC's wealthy residents; monumental Washington sits on the coastal lowlands. It's a city of gridded streets and diagonal avenues radiating from ceremonial squares and elegant circles. The city proper is quite small, with much of the metropolitan population living in the Virginia and Maryland suburbs. The centre has wide sidewalks and few highways, ideal for walking to many destinations, and the subway is excellent, uncrowded and convenient.

PEOPLE

Washington is a predominantly black and fairly segregated city. The majority is of African-American descent; there are growing numbers of Asians and Hispanics. A high proportion of the residents are foreign-born.

TYPICAL WASHINGTONIAN

This being a company town, and the industry being politics, there isn't one typical Washingtonian, although about a third of all residents work in government. Whites and blacks don't mix much socially or professionally. Driven and secular (although less so of late), the largely white political class is in stark contrast to the majority. Poverty affects 20% of the population, which is way above the national average – and this in a town with the second-highest per-capita income in the USA.

DEFINING EXPERIENCE

Breakfasting at Jimmy T's diner on Capitol Hill, wandering down the mall past the Capitol, picking a museum to explore before blowing your mind in the National Sculpture Garden, strolling along the Potomac to lunch at Dean & Deluca in Georgetown, and then taking in blues at Madam's Organ.

STRENGTHS

- Smithsonian Institution
- Vietnam Veterans Memorial
- Lincoln Memorial
- National Gallery of Art
- International Spy Museum
- Capitol Hill
- The White House
- Library of Congress
- The buzz of Dupont Circle
- Union Station
- The subway – it's a pleasure to ride
- DC Blues Festival
- Arlington Cemetery
- Funky jazz bars in Adams-Morgan
- Townhouses and cafés of Georgetown
- Watergate complex
- National Cherry Blossom Festival
- National Arboretum
- Eastern Market
- Black Fashion Museum

WEAKNESSES

- Politicians
- The contrived grandeur of Graeco-Roman monuments
- Segregation
- The murder rate
- The government (white, conservative)/populace (black, liberal) divide
- The long ride in from Dulles airport
- The hot air – humidity in summer and from the politicians

GOLD STAR

The National Mall has monuments and museums to occupy visitors for days. It's a history lesson in sod and stone, with a wide expanse of green that stretches from the Potomac in the west to Capitol Hill in the east. It is the scene of protests and celebrations, lined with gravel paths and bordered by tree-shaded avenues.

STARRING ROLE IN...

- *All the President's Men* (1978)
- *Mr Smith Goes to Washington* (1939)
- *Wag the Dog* (1997)
- *The Pelican Brief* (1993)
- *Enemy of the State* (2003)
- *In the Line of Fire* (1993)
- *Patriot Games* (1992)
- *Primary Colors* (1998)
- *Thirteen Days* (2000)
- *Advice & Consent* (1962)
- *Dave* (1993)
- *Being There* (1979)
- *Legally Blonde 2* (2004)
- *The Contender* (2000)
- *The West Wing* (1999–2006)
- *Lost in the City* by Edward Jones
- *Far East Suite* by Duke Ellington
- *In this Land* by Sweet Honey in the Rock

IMPORT

- Woodward and Bernstein
- Ambitious politicians
- Wily bureaucrats
- Oleaginous lobbyists
- Eager interns
- Presidents of varying quality
- Journalists
- Mendacious diplomats
- Carpetbaggers of all types

EXPORT

- Portentous rhetoric
- CIA operatives
- The link between Saddam and Al Qaeda
- Operation Shock and Awe
- War in Iraq
- Novels of George Pelecanos
- Novels of Gore Vidal
- Polemic of Gore Vidal

SEE the suits arriving on Capitol Hill of a morning.

EAT adventurously – choose food from around the world at Dupont Circle or Adams-Morgan, or Southern cuisine at Georgia Brown's, a Clinton fave.

DRINK a fiery red Martini at trendy Degrees Bar & Lounge in Georgetown.

DO have your photograph taken under the Alexander Calder sculpture in the National Gallery of Art.

WATCH a game of football (it's a football town!) featuring the Washington Redskins.

BUY souvenirs, from rubber Nixon masks to shredded money, at the Bureau of Printing & Engraving.

AFTER DARK hit the sidewalks of Adams-Morgan and go clubbing: Heaven & Hell to tempt fate or vigorous Latino at Habana Village.

URBAN MYTH

Washington was torched by British troops in the War of 1812, and although the Capitol was eventually rebuilt, the city entered a slump from which it wouldn't recover for decades. A dispirited vote to abandon the capital lost by only nine votes.

PUTTING ON THE MOVES – HIGH SCHOOL FOOTBALLERS PLAY A FAST-PACED MATCH, CHEERED ON BY SUPPORTERS.
Photographer: Jeff Hutchens / Getty Images

THE BEST AND FRESHEST SEAFOOD FROM CHESAPEAKE BAY ON SALE AT WASHINGTON MARINA.
Photographer: Jeff Hutchens / Getty Images

AN EXHAUSTED SIGHTSEER FINDS THE BENCH CAN OFFER A MUCH WELCOMED NEW PERSPECTIVE ON THE WASHINGTON MONUMENT. Photographer: Jeff Hutchens / Getty Images

THE LIVELY STREETS OF GEORGETOWN MAKE CELEBRITIES AND POLITICIANS LOOK POSITIVELY TWO-DIMENSIONAL.
Photographer: Jeff Hutchens / Getty Images

WHILING AWAY A LAZY AFTERNOON AT CAFÉ L'AFFARE'S BAR.
Photographer: David Wall / LPI

Hosting the *Lord of the Rings* world premieres put New Zealand's beautiful and blustering capital on the international movie map, but you don't have to be a filmstar to enjoy 'Wellywood'– the bohemian vibe, great café scene and plentiful outdoor pursuits make it as attractive to civilians as it is to famous hobbits.

ANATOMY

Wellington's harbour sits between two peninsulas at the southern tip of New Zealand's North Island. Ferries regularly cross the Cook Strait from here to South Island. The main business street, Lambton Quay, used to sit on the waterfront but is now separated from the sea by reclaimed land. The city centre is bounded by the train station, at the northern end of Lambton Quay, and Cambridge and Kent Tce to the southeast. The historic and embassy area of Thornton lies just north of the centre. Wellington has an efficient local-bus system and suburban trains.

PEOPLE

New Zealand is a bicultural nation and Maori and English are the official languages. For most of Wellington's population at least one of these (probably English) is their mother tongue, but the number of Asian inhabitants in the city is on the increase.

TYPICAL WELLINGTONIAN

Wellingtonians enjoy a healthy rivalry with erstwhile capital Auckland. Like all Kiwis they are passionate about rugby and feel a great loyalty to New Zealand. Wellington is New Zealand's wealthiest region and Wellingtonians like outdoor activities and sports; they are also New Zealand's most culturally engaged people. The OE (overseas experience) is a rite of passage, although Australia is overtaking Britain as the most popular destination.

Wellington

VITAL STATISTICS

NAME: WELLINGTON

NICKNAME: WINDY WELLY

DATE OF BIRTH: 1840; EUROPEAN SETTLERS ARRIVED TO BUY LAND OFF THE MAORIS

ADDRESS: NEW ZEALAND (MAP 1, OO22)

HEIGHT: 127M

SIZE: 290 SQ KM

POPULATION: 381,000

LONELY PLANET RANKING: 083

INDUSTRIAL-STYLE SCULPTURES ON THE EDGE OF WELLINGTON HARBOUR.
Photographer: Sally Dillon / LPI

A SURFER HANGS TEN – OR AT LEAST THREE – AT LYALL BAY.
Photographer: Paul Kennedy / LPI

MAJESTIC VICTORIAN WEATHERBOARD HOUSES OVERLOOK ORIENTAL BAY.
Photographer: Peter Bennetts / LPI

DEFINING EXPERIENCE

Taking a stroll around the Botanic Gardens before riding the cable car down to town for a steaming cup of coffee, grabbing your sailboard for some windsurfing in the harbour and going drinking later on Courtenay Pl.

STRENGTHS

- Radio New Zealand, based in Wellington
- Te Papa (Museum of New Zealand)
- City Gallery Wellington
- Old St Paul's Cathedral
- Government Buildings – among the world's largest all-wooden buildings
- Museum of Wellington City and Sea
- National Cricket Museum
- Beehive – the architectural emblem of New Zealand
- Katharine Mansfield's birthplace
- Botanic Gardens
- Red cable car
- Bill Manhire's creative writing course at Victoria University
- Live music from Fat Freddy's Drop
- View of the city from Mt Victoria
- Mountain biking at Makarara Peak
- Windsurfing
- Great café scene (more cafés per capita than New York City)

WEAKNESSES

- Many houses are not insulated and have no central heating
- Wellington is on a fault line
- Windy weather
- Mad bus drivers

GOLD STAR

Cultural and physical activities on tap.

STARRING ROLE IN...

- *King Kong* (2005)
- *Lord of the Rings trilogy* (2001, 2002, 2003)

IMPORT

- Director Peter Jackson
- Architect Ian Athfield
- Rugby fans

EXPORT

- Jane Campion
- Katharine Mansfield
- Director Lee Tamahori
- Author Catherine Chidgey
- Lamb
- Rugby players

SEE exhibits revealing New Zealand's history, and experience an earthquake at the fabulous Te Papa museum.

EAT a slap-up breakfast at one of the city's many cafés.

DRINK Pinot Noir and Sauvignon Blanc at Toast Martinborough, a food, wine and music bonanza.

DO take a ride in Wellington's red cable car up to the Botanic Gardens.

WATCH rock, Latin and soul in Wellington's oldest live-music venue, Bodega.

BUY retro fashion and funky furniture on Cuba St.

AFTER DARK take your pick of the bars and clubs on Courtenay Pl.

URBAN MYTH

Katharine Mansfield is New Zealand's most eminent author and is often compared to Chekhov and Maupassant. She spent five years of her childhood living at 25 Tinakori Rd in Wellington and this house, which pops up in her stories the *Aloe* (which became *Prelude*) and *A Birthday*, is open to the public. After leaving Wellington at the age of 19, she spent much of her time in Europe hanging out with famous scribes such as DH Lawrence, TS Eliot and Virginia Woolf and marrying the literary critic and author John Middleton Murry. A vicious bout of tuberculosis ended her life in 1923 in Fontainebleau in France when she was just 34. At Tinakori Rd you can see excerpts of her writing alongside photographs of her time there.

WILD AND WET AT THE NEW YEAR WATER FESTIVAL.
Photographer: Alison Wright / LPI

Yangon

VITAL STATISTICS

NAME: YANGON (FORMERLY RANGOON)

NICKNAME: THE GARDEN CITY OF THE EAST

DATE OF BIRTH: 1755; WHEN KING ALAUNGPAYA CONQUERED CENTRAL MYANMAR AND BUILT A NEW CITY ON THE SITE OF YANGON, WHICH AT THAT TIME WAS KNOWN AS DAGON

ADDRESS: MYANMAR (BURMA)

HEIGHT: 6M

SIZE: 400 SQ KM

POPULATION: 4 MILLION

LONELY PLANET RANKING: 139

Situated in the fertile delta country of southern Myanmar on the Yangon River, Yangon is a city of golden pagodas, colonial edifices and wide boulevards that come alive at night with hordes of stalls selling delicious food and piles of huge cigars.

ANATOMY

Located in the Irrawaddy Delta, Yangon is a lush paradise in comparison to most of its Southeast Asian counterparts. Central Yangon is easy to navigate. The main streets are set in grids and the best way to plot a course is to flag down a trishaw, walk or catch one of the myriad, albeit unreliable, means of transport. Yangon's battered buses are crowded but colourful.

PEOPLE

By far the majority of Yangon's citizens are Bamar. A small portion of the population is of Shan and even fewer are Karen, Rakhine, Indian, Mon and Chinese. While Buddhists comprise most of the population, Muslims, animists and Christians make up the rest of its religions, along with a handful of other indigenous beliefs.

TYPICAL YANGONESE

Deprived of more than a few civil liberties, Yangon's citizens hope for a brighter future when their heroine, Aung San Suu Kyi, is released from a lengthy house arrest and will hopefully bring democracy. The Yangonese are optimistic and it shows in their questions and relaxed conversations.

DEFINING EXPERIENCE

Handling some of the finest lacquerware in the world at the Bogyoke Aung San Market followed by a moment's reflection inside a prayer hall of the Shwedagon Paya, then taking a class in Burmese kick boxing at Yangon University and winding down with a cup of syrupy tea and *mohinga* (a fish-based noodle soup) in the balmy afternoon at one of Yangon's famous teashops.

STRENGTHS

- Unspoilt by mass tourism
- Shrines to *nat* (animist spirits)
- British colonial architecture on leafy streets
- Shwedagon Paya
- Teashops and sickly sweets

WEAKNESSES

- The government
- A virtually nonexistent nightlife
- No ATMs, credit-card or travellers-cheque facilities
- Censorship of the democratic voice
- Ban on foreign films
- Betel nut–spit on the ground
- Soaring HIV rates
- Teak logging

GOLD STAR

Shwedagon Paya, the most sacred of Buddhist sites in Myanmar, is the highlight of a trip to Yangon. Kipling once called it 'a golden mystery…a beautiful winking wonder'. The glittering gold-leaf covered stupa is said to house eight of Buddha's hairs.

STARRING ROLE IN…

- *Beyond Rangoon* (1995)
- *Burmese Days* by George Orwell
- *Secret Histories: Finding George Orwell in a Burmese Tea Shop* by Emma Larkin
- *Letters from the East* by Rudyard Kipling
- *True Love* (2005)

IMPORT

- George Orwell
- Hip-hop
- Rudyard Kipling
- Chinese-style buildings
- Martin Sheen
- Cars

EXPORT

- Shan shoulder bags (seen on a Southeast Asian traveller near you)
- Poetry
- The father of modern Burmese art, Aung Myint
- The New Light of Myanmar, the government's English-language mouthpiece
- Gilded marionettes
- Rubies
- Opium

SEE t'ai chi practised at the crack of dawn at Mahabandoola Garden.

EAT *lethouq* – a spicy salad of raw vegetables dressed with lime juice, onions, peanuts, chillies and a variety of spices.

DRINK *lahpeq ye* (tea water) poured from the cup and drunk from the saucer at the Sei Taing Kya Teashop or any one of Yangon's renowned teashops.

DO have a go at rolling a *cheroot* (like a cigar) and, if you're up for it, try the 2cm-thick variety.

WATCH an impromptu game of *chinlon* (cane ball) on any street at any time of day and watch the players perform gravity-defying pirouettes.

BUY a *longyi* (the Bamar version of the sarong) from the sprawling Bogyoke (Scott) Market.

AFTER DARK wander barefoot along the cool stone floor of the Shwedagon Paya and watch the many-coloured jewels sparkle at its tip.

URBAN MYTH

During the New Year water festival, Thingyan, it's not uncommon to walk around Yangon soaked to the bone after a drenching by a local. The belief is that the water will purify the believer both spiritually and physically for the coming year. Taking it that one step further, the Yangonese may purchase live fish and cows and release them into rivers or sanctuaries on Thingyan Ah-Tet Day (the final day of the festival). For extra karmic points, kids like to wash an old person's hair – you get bonus points if you wash their body as well.

REACHING GREAT HEIGHTS ON THE SHWEDAGON PAYA.
Photographer: John McDermott / Getty Images

ANAW RA HTA PLAYS HOST TO THE EVENING MARKETS.
Photographer: Richard I'Anson / LPI

BUSINESS IS DEFINITELY PLEASURE FOR THIS SHOP OWNER.
Photographer: Network Photographers / Alamy

ARMENIANS ENJOY A HEIGHTENED SENSE OF CULTURE.
Photographer: Stephane Victor / LPI

Yerevan

VITAL STATISTICS

NAME: YEREVAN

DATE OF BIRTH: 782 BC; WHEN KING ARGISHTI BUILT THE TOWN FORTRESS OF EREBUNI ON THE ARARAT PLAIN

ADDRESS: ARMENIA (MAP 3, Y14)

HEIGHT: 990M

SIZE: 210 SQ KM

POPULATION: 1.2 MILLION

LONELY PLANET RANKING: 178

Yerevan is the cultural heart of the Armenian people, one of the surviving ancient peoples of the Near East; it is a proud, cultured and enterprising city stunningly situated in the mountainous realm of the Caucasus.

ANATOMY

The centre of Yerevan sits on the east bank of the Hrazdan River. Streets are arranged in a strict grid system, and the heavily trafficked Opera Sq where Mashtots, Marshall Baghramian and Sayat-Nova Aves meet is often patrolled by female traffic cops in high heels. The city itself is surrounded on three sides by mountains. To the southwest stands Mt Ararat, holy mountain of the Armenian people, in full view, yet poignantly sited just across the Turkish border. Yerevan has tonnes of public transport, including buses, minibuses, trolleybuses and a metro.

PEOPLE

Yerevan is populated almost entirely by Armenians; there are some Russians, Kurds (including the little-known Yezidis, a Gnostic sect sometimes mistakenly called devil-worshippers) and nationals from other Caucasian republics.

TYPICAL YEREVANI

The typical Yerevani is hospitable and eager to help visitors. They are likely to be adherents of the Armenian Apostolic Church (Armenia was the first nation to convert to Christianity – in AD 301). They are resourceful, industrious and resilient, if a little melancholy, in the face of hardship (to which Yerevan, and Armenia as a whole, is no stranger). Members of a nation of stonemasons, philosophers and poets, they are fiercely proud of their culture and artistic traditions. Yerevanis tend to linger over meals and have a relaxed attitude to work, happy to stay out late at night, turn up at work around 10.30am and then take a long lunch. In fact, attitudes to time are pretty relaxed. Punctuality isn't *de rigueur* in Yerevan.

DEFINING EXPERIENCE

Visiting Matenadaran, a repository of the country's culture and literature and home to tens of thousands of documents and manuscripts in the elaborate Armenian script; heading to Echmiadzin, the spiritual heart of the Armenian church, just a few kilometres out of Yerevan; pondering Armenia's traumatic past at the Genocide Memorial; climbing the Cascade to enjoy the view over the entire city; getting melancholy as you watch the sun set over Mt Ararat, tantalisingly close yet unreachable across the Turkish border; then following your nose and choosing a delicious and sizzling *khoravats* (barbecue) somewhere along Proshyan Poghots.

STRENGTHS

- Cafés at every turn
- Thriving heart of Armenian art and culture
- Hospitality and generosity of the locals
- Intriguing atmosphere – a city poised between East and West, Europe and Asia
- Proximity to all of Armenia's attractions – it's a small country!
- Long lunches and dinners

WEAKNESSES

- Vodka toasts – fine, until you realise it is poor form to reveal any sign of drunkenness
- Power shortages
- Bitterly cold winters
- Earthquakes
- Soviet-style customer service (or lack thereof)
- Stalinist architecture
- Corruption and local mafia

GOLD STAR

Art and culture – a city of museums and galleries in a nation of writers, poets and artists.

STARRING ROLE IN...

- *The Claws of the Crab* by Stephen Brook
- *The Crossing Place* by Philip Marsden
- *Among the Russians* by Colin Thubron
- *Imperium* by Ryszard Kapuscinski
- *Calendar* (1993)

IMPORT

- Armenians – children of the diaspora returning to discover and reinvigorate their homeland

EXPORT

- Armenians – the nation's traumatic past saw massive emigration (and flight) to Russia, Eastern Europe, America and elsewhere
- Notable people of Armenian extraction: Andre Agassi, Charles Aznavour, Cher and chess master Gary Kasparov

SEE the intermingled influences of East and West at the National Folk Art Museum of Armenia.

EAT *khoravats* (barbecued lamb or pork).

DRINK Armenian cognac – smooth and potent.

DO visit Sarian Park on the weekend to see the gatherings of contemporary artists who critique each other's work.

WATCH a performance of the Yerevan Ballet Company.

BUY local handicrafts and lacework at the market at Vernissage, or an Armenian carpet.

AFTER DARK check out the casinos at Argavand, slightly seedy and very garishly lit, or visit Astral, Yerevan's ground zero for dance music.

URBAN MYTH

The National Chamber Orchestra of Armenia was formed in 1997. At their first meeting (held in a public square) there weren't enough chairs for all members to sit down. By 1998 they had released their first CD; by 2003 they had toured three continents.

A PAUSE FOR REFLECTION – SURP GRIGOR LUSAVORICH CATHEDRAL RESTS IN THE SHADOW OF MT ARARAT.
Photographer: Stephane Victor / LPI

YEREVANIS TAKE PLEASURE IN THEIR CULTURAL TRADITIONS.
Photographer: Stephane Victor / LPI

THE STATELY PEAKS OF MT ARARAT OFFER A STRIKING BACKDROP TO THE CITY.
Photographer: Stephane Victor / LPI

Yogyakarta

VITAL STATISTICS

NAME: YOGYAKARTA

NICKNAME: YOGYA

DATE OF BIRTH: 1755; WHEN PRINCE (LATER SULTAN) MANGKUMBI BUILT THE KRATON OF YOGYAKARTA

ADDRESS: INDONESIA (MAP 1, HH17)

HEIGHT: 106M

SIZE: 33 SQ KM

POPULATION: 510,000

LONELY PLANET RANKING: 129

COLOURFUL KITES FLY OVER TAMAN SARI.
Photographer: Dimas Ardian

PICKING UP A NIGHTTIME SNACK OF *GUDEG*.
Photographer: Dimas Ardian

SHAKING TO THE BEAT OF THE NIGHTLIFE AT PURAWISATA AMUSEMENT PARK.
Photographer: Dimas Ardian

A DANCER PREPARES TO PERFORM THE RAMAYANA, A TRADITIONAL HINDU EPIC.
Photographer: Dimas Ardian

If Jakarta is Java's financial and industrial powerhouse, Yogyakarta is its soul: central to the island's artistic and intellectual heritage, Yogyakarta is where the Javanese language is at its purest, Javanese arts are at their brightest and Javanese traditions at their most visible.

ANATOMY

Jalan (Jl) Malioboro, named after the Duke of Marlborough, is Yogya's main road, running from the train station to the *kraton* (walled palace) at the far end. The road becomes Jl A Yani further south, but is generally referred to as Jalan Malioboro. The tourist office and many souvenir shops and stalls are along this street and most of the budget places to stay are west of it, in the Jl Sosrowijayan area near the railway line. The old, walled *kraton* is the centre of old Yogya, where you will also find the Taman Sari (Water Castle), Pasar Ngasem (Bird Market) and numerous batik galleries. While easy to navigate, it is impossible to go to any tourist areas without being greeted by *becak* (auto-rickshaw) drivers. Regular taxis are metered and efficient.

PEOPLE

With a mix of Javanese, Sundanese and Madurese peoples, the main languages spoken in Yogya are Javanese, Sundanese, Madurese and Bahasa Indonesian. While the predominant religion is Muslim, there are Hindu, Buddhist and Christian minorities.

TYPICAL YOGYAKARTA CITIZEN

Living in a cultural and intellectual centre crammed with prestigious universities and academies, the typical Yogya citizen is used to living in a city enduring a Westernised puberty. While the town swings moodily between fast-food joints, shopping malls and satellite TV, locals have a traditional focus, centred around the family, the 'village' and religious piety.

DEFINING EXPERIENCE

Scoffing down a street-stall *gudeg* (Yogya's signature dish: it's sweet and made with jack fruit, coconut and eggs among other ingredients), meandering the grounds of the *kraton*, then being enchanted by one of the many *wayang kulit* (shadow-puppet) plays at night.

STRENGTHS
- The *kraton*
- The Gerebeg festivals
- Pasar Ngasem
- Pasar Beringharjo (Yogya's main market)
- The Dutch-era fort Benteng Vredeburg
- First-class Javanese art
- Shadow-puppet plays
- Museum Kareta Kraton
- Sumptuous spices
- The Affandi Museum
- Purawisata amusement park
- Kota Gede
- Museum Sansana Wiratama

WEAKNESSES
- 'Last chance' batik scammers
- Copycat batik painting galleries
- Bag snatchers
- Bike bandits
- Pickpockets

GOLD STAR

Location – aside from being Java's premier tourist city, Yogya is an ideal base for exploring nearby attractions, including Indonesia's most important archaeological sites, Borobudur and Prambanan Temples.

STARRING ROLE IN...
- *Agung Gives Ivor a Haircut* (1991)
- *Becak driver – Superimposed* (1998)

IMPORT
- Tourism
- Rapid Westernisation
- Burger joints
- Bar girls
- Big hotels

EXPORT
- Affandi (Indonesia's best-known artist)
- Batik
- Silverwork
- Leather puppets and wooden masks
- Traditional and contemporary Javanese art

SEE hundreds of budgerigars, orioles, roosters, singing turtledoves and pigeons, all in ornamental cages at Pasar Ngasem on the edge of Taman Sari.

EAT anything from nasi goreng to greasy-spoon fry-ups at the FM Café on Jl Sosrowijayan, with stacks of atmosphere and an eclectic, well-priced menu.

DRINK draught Heineken with homesick Hollanders at the Dutch Café on Jl Tirtodipuran, a venerable traveller and expat haunt.

DO marvel at the restored 1760s bathing pools in the Taman Sari, and imagine the sultan and harem members relaxing in this one-time pleasure park.

WATCH the spectacular Ramayana ballet held in the open air at Prambanan in the dry season.

BUY exquisite leatherwork, batik bags, *topeng* (masks) and *wayang golek* (wooden puppets) from all over the archipelago in Jl Malioboro.

AFTER DARK *wayang kulit* performances can be seen at several places around Yogya every night.

URBAN MYTH

In the *kraton's* southern square are two similar banyan trees, which are said to bring great fortune if you walk through them without mishap while blindfolded. The *kraton* is closed on national holidays and for special *kraton* ceremonies, yet batik touts after a bonanza of their own will advise it's closed to lure you to Taman Sari and a batik gallery.

IN 1430 THIS MEDIEVAL HALL IN FOSSGATE BECAME THE HOME OF THE GUILD OF MERCHANT ADVENTURERS.
Photographer: Neil Setchfield / LPI

York is a magical kind of place that makes you wish – if only for an instant – that the Industrial Revolution had never happened.

ANATOMY

Compact and eminently walkable, York has five major landmarks: the wall enclosing the small city centre, the minster at the northern corner, Clifford's Tower at the southern end, the River Ouse that cuts the centre in two, and the train station to the west. Just to avoid the inevitable confusion, remember that round these parts *gate* means street and *bar* means gate. York is easily walked on foot – you're never more than 20 minutes from any of the major sights.

PEOPLE

Traditional York has a very traditional demographic: almost all of the locals are white Brits. Although the University of York (established in 1963) heralded a 'return of the young people', York has an ageing population, with a higher proportion of elderly folks than anywhere else in England.

TYPICAL YORKIE

Possibly employed in the tourist industry (as over 9000 Yorkies are), the typical York citizen is a proud expert on their city's heritage, unfazed by the four million tourists that trod the narrow *snickets* (alleyways) each year. However, the newer breed of Yorkie might well be a person of science, as York's R&D laboratories steam full-speed ahead in the city's reinvention as a 'Science City'.

DEFINING EXPERIENCE

Marvelling at the tennis court–sized stained-glass Great East Window at York Minster before enduring the claustrophobic climb of 275 steps to the awesome central tower (the heart of the minster), then following the city walls clockwise to Monk Bar, York's best-preserved medieval gate.

York

VITAL STATISTICS

NAME: YORK

DATE OF BIRTH: AD 71; PRIOR TO THE ARRIVAL OF THE ROMANS WERE THE BRIGANTES, A LOCAL TRIBE WHO MINDED THEIR OWN BUSINESS

ADDRESS: ENGLAND (MAP 3, E6)

HEIGHT: 17M

SIZE: 272 SQ KM

POPULATION: 193,000

LONELY PLANET RANKING: 076

SURVEYING THE SITES FROM A RESTFUL VIEWPOINT.
Photographer: Neil Setchfield / LPI

BUILT BETWEEN 1220 AND 1472, THE MINSTER IS STILL YORK'S TALLEST BUILDING.
Photographer: Neil Setchfield / LPI

CLIFFORD'S TOWER, THE KEEP OF THE OLD CASTLE BUILT IN 1245, IS NOW ALL THAT IS LEFT OF YORK CASTLE.
Photographer: Neil Setchfield / LPI

STRENGTHS

- ◢ Oodles of history
- ◢ York Castle Museum
- ◢ York Minster
- ◢ Museum Gardens
- ◢ The Shambles
- ◢ Clifford's Tower
- ◢ Narrow *snickets*
- ◢ Jorvik Viking Centre
- ◢ Castle Howard
- ◢ Easily negotiable on foot
- ◢ National Railway Museum
- ◢ Medieval churches

WEAKNESSES

- ◢ Summertime traffic congestion
- ◢ Severe flooding from the River Ouse
- ◢ Demented tourism in the high summer season
- ◢ Cold, dark and grim winters

GOLD STAR

Resilience – garrisoned by the Romans, rampaged by Vikings, besieged by Parliamentarian forces in the Civil War of 1644 and blitzed by the Nazis in 1942, at almost 2000 years old York stands strong as a living museum – a true gem in England's crown.

STARRING ROLE IN...

- ◢ *Elizabeth* (1998)
- ◢ *Harry Potter and the Philosopher's Stone* (2001)
- ◢ *All Creatures Great and Small* by James Herriot
- ◢ *Behind the Scenes at the Museum* by Kate Atkinson
- ◢ *Possession* by AS Byatt

IMPORT

- ◢ Romans
- ◢ Vikings
- ◢ William the Conqueror
- ◢ Four million tourists annually

EXPORT

- ◢ Kit Kats
- ◢ Smarties
- ◢ AS Byatt
- ◢ Terry's Chocolate Orange
- ◢ Dame Judi Dench
- ◢ The grand old Duke of York
- ◢ Yorkshire pudding
- ◢ Guy Fawkes

SEE Castle Howard, the palatially Palladian Vanbrugh/Hawksmoor creation surrounded by the rolling Howardian Hills, acres of terraced gardens, landscaped vistas and a scattering of monumental follies and obelisks.

EAT sandwiches and high tea, old-school style, at Betty's, a Yorkshire institution – a pianist tinkles Bett's ivories after 6pm (for added class).

DRINK an ale or few with the old blokes at Ackhorne on St Martin's Lane, a locals' inn that's as comfy as old slippers.

DO visit what is easily Yorkshire's most important historic building – the simply awesome York Minster.

WATCH well-regarded productions of theatre, opera and dance at the York Theatre Royal on St Leonard's Pl.

BUY unusual secondhand books from the Worm Holes Bookshop in Bootham, with a decent and far-reaching selection of old and new titles.

AFTER DARK join the 'ghost hunt' of York, an award-winning and highly entertaining 75-minute tour beginning at the Shambles.

URBAN MYTH

In AD 71, the Romans erected a walled garrison dubbed Eboracum (now York) at the strategically important confluence of the Rivers Ouse and Foss. The fort steadily increased in importance, becoming the Romans' British campaign headquarters and attracting visits by big-name emperors such as Hadrian, Septimius, Severus (who died there) and Constantine. It's thought that Constantine was proclaimed emperor on the future site of York Minster – spooky, because he went on to become the first Christian emperor.

Zagreb

VITAL STATISTICS

NAME: ZAGREB

DATE OF BIRTH: 9TH CENTURY; WHEN SLAVIC SETTLEMENTS WERE FOUNDED

ADDRESS: CROATIA (MAP 3, M11)

HEIGHT: 163M

SIZE: 631 SQ KM

POPULATION: 786,000 (CITY); 1.1 MILLION (METRO AREA)

LONELY PLANET RANKING: 125

A VIVID REMINDER OF THE CITY'S CHEQUERED HISTORY – THE TILED ROOF OF THE 13TH-CENTURY ST MARK'S CHURCH.
Photographer: Richard I'Anson / LPI

Vibrant, cultured and laid-back in equal measure, Zagreb is the gateway to the Balkans, an often overlooked melange of Slavic, Central European and Austro-Hungarian (understated) grandeur.

ANATOMY

Upper Zagreb sprawls across the hills of Gradec and Kaptol, the sites of the city's original settlements. Dolac Market is the hub of the upper city, just near the imposing Cathedral of the Assumption of the Blessed Virgin Mary with its distinctive twin spires. The central square of Trg Josip Jelačića is the heart of Lower Town. Crisscrossed by tramlines, this is where old men meet for morning coffee and where teenagers congregate on Friday evenings. The tram system is an effective, if overcrowded, way to get around, although the city is so compact you can probably walk anywhere you need to go.

PEOPLE

Zagreb's citizens are uniformly Croatian; the era of Yugoslavian multiculturalism is now sadly passed.

TYPICAL ZAGREBIAN

The typical Zagreb local is resolutely Western in outlook – they see themselves as distinct from their Slavic Balkan counterparts – and staunchly Catholic. They are elegant, but casually so – although Croatia was the birthplace of the necktie, no self-respecting Zagreb habitué would be seen in anything other than an open-neck shirt. Remaining well dressed at all times is paramount for Zagrebians. They will forgo other extravagances to ensure that they can be suitably dressed for all occasions. Relishing the culture, history and artistic heritage of their city, Zagreb locals are given to conviviality and amiable chatter and enjoy the outdoor café lifestyle (especially during the summer months).

DEFINING EXPERIENCE

Wandering through Dolac market and choosing grapes as big as plums and plums as big as your fist, watching the changing of the guard at the Banski Dvori, contemplating the airy interior of the Cathedral of the Assumption of the Blessed Virgin Mary, taking your time to ponder Zagreb's long and eventful history and lively arts scene at the city's museums and galleries, and then bar-hopping with the crowds along Tkalčićeva after dark.

STRENGTHS

- Cobbled streets
- Elegant squares and gardens
- Cafés and streetlife on spring afternoons
- Streets not fouled with traffic
- A compact and conveniently walkable city
- People-watching
- Few tourists – Zagreb is generally overlooked by travellers
- Meaty cuisine

WEAKNESSES

- Bad coffee
- Shortage of reasonably priced accommodation
- Pockets of Soviet-era architecture
- Steep streets in Upper Town
- Meaty cuisine
- Shortage of green vegetables in restaurant meals (some may consider this a strength!)

GOLD STAR

Central European elegance (if somewhat faded) and architecture, without the hype and crowds of Prague.

STARRING ROLE IN...

- *The Zahir* by Paulo Coelho
- *How We Survived Communism and Even Laughed* by Slavenka Drakulić
- *Black Lamb and Grey Falcon* by Rebecca West
- *Café Europa* by Slavenka Drakulić

IMPORT

- Fresh fish from the Dalmatian Coast
- European fashions
- A knack for making delicious pizzas (from near neighbours, the Italians)

EXPORT

- Neckties ('cravat' is a corruption of 'Croat')
- Ballpoint pens – invented by a Croat
- Basketball players (tall ones!)
- Electronics
- Machine tools
- Textiles

SEE the view from Lotršćak Tower, a 360-degree vista of the rooftops, spires and squares of Upper and Lower Towns.

EAT čevapčiči (meaty, garlicky Balkan sausages) with sliced onions or ayvar (capsicum paste) and flat bread.

DRINK slivovica (plum brandy) or locally brewed Ozujsko (beer).

DO visit Zagreb's museums and galleries for a view of a little-known, but surprisingly rich, culture.

WATCH any of the free, open-air performances of the Zagreb Summer Festival.

BUY embroidery in cheerful red-and-white geometric patterns.

AFTER DARK head for the bars on Tkalčićeva, or around Trg Petra Preradovića.

URBAN MYTH

When the all-conquering Ottoman Turks were approaching Zagreb in the 14th century, an inadvertently fired cannon shot smothered a rooster in full view of the Turkish camp. This was interpreted as an unusually bad omen by the hitherto fearless Turks, who immediately broke camp never to return, leaving Zagreb a bastion of Catholicism amid the Ottoman Empire.

TRG JOSIP JELAČIĆA, THE COLOURFUL HEART OF THE CITY, IS FILLED WITH FLOWER MARKETS, SHOPS, CAFÉS AND THEATRES.
Photographer: Richard I'Anson / LPI

COFFEE, CIGARETTES AND A GOOD BOOK – A LEISURELY AFTERNOON IN ONE OF THE CITY'S MANY CAFÉS.
Photographer: Richard I'Anson / LPI

THE NEO-GOTHIC BELL TOWERS OF THE CATHEDRAL OF THE ASSUMPTION OF THE BLESSED VIRGIN MARY WATCH OVER TKALČIĆEVA. Photographer: Richard I'Anson / LPI

Zanzibar Town

VITAL STATISTICS

NAME: ZANZIBAR

DATE OF BIRTH: 8TH CENTURY; WHEN SHIRAZI TRADERS FROM PERSIA ESTABLISHED A SETTLEMENT

ADDRESS: TANZANIA (MAP 2, M16)

HEIGHT: 15M

SIZE: 1574 SQ KM

POPULATION: 1 MILLION

LONELY PLANET RANKING: 074

Zanzibar's old quarter, Stone Town, could have been lifted directly out of a Persian fairy tale, bringing together a mesmerising and evocative mix of influences from the Indian Subcontinent, the Arabian Peninsula and mainland Africa, and all in a tropical setting.

ANATOMY

Stone Town juts into the Indian Ocean on the western side of Zanzibar Island. Mizingani Rd runs along the waterfront from the ferry terminal to Stone Town. Here is a magical jumble of cobbled alleyways where it's difficult to get your bearings. The best approach is to dive in and follow your nose – you'll either emerge on the waterfront or on Creek Rd on the eastern edge of Stone Town. There's no transport system in Stone Town (and no need for one). Crowded *dalla-dallas* (minivans) connect the town with the rest of Zanzibar Island.

PEOPLE

The residents of Zanzibar mirror the melting pot that is their Swahili culture: they trace a mix of Omani, Shirazi and African ancestors in their bloodlines. There are also sizable Asian (Indian) and Arabic communities. You may also encounter a few Maasai tribesmen, conspicuously clad in blue, unlike their red-robed Kenyan brethren.

TYPICAL ZANZIBARI

Zanzibar is the Swahili town par excellence, hence it retains a sedate Muslim atmosphere. Most Zanzibaris are relatively conservative, modest in dress and behaviour, yet friendly, welcoming and gregarious. The *baraza* on houses' outer walls exemplify the gregarious nature of Zanzibaris – these stone benches serve as focal points where people can sit, watch the world go by and catch up on gossip. Zanzibaris are given to long and elaborate greetings, love to discuss politics and take life at a languid, tropical pace.

DEFINING EXPERIENCE

Passing through the huge carved doors of the House of Wonders; pondering the horrors of the past at the Anglican Cathedral built on the old slave market; wandering the Darajani Market and inhaling the scents of spices and dried fish; strolling aimlessly and endlessly in Stone Town, getting deliciously lost in the maze of streets, discovering children chanting Koranic verses, or a beautiful mansion with overhanging balconies, or a coffee vendor with long-spouted pot clacking cups to drum up business; sampling the delights of the foodstalls in the Forodhani Gardens in the early evening.

STRENGTHS

- The scent of cloves
- The twisting, turning alleys of Stone Town
- Overhead lattice balconies, ornate doors and window frames
- Wandering barefoot on the cobbles
- Games of football on the beach
- Breakfasts of mango, pawpaw and chai
- Skipping ropes with local kids
- Lateen sails of dhows bobbing in the harbour
- Hearing the lap of the bay as you sleep
- Nearby beaches – azure waters and pristine white sand
- Diving the crystal seas
- Seafood, grilled or cooked with coconut milk

WEAKNESSES

- Humidity and monsoon rains
- Political tensions
- Security after dark (an issue in some parts of town)
- Street touts, known locally as *papasi* (ticks)

GOLD STAR

Tropical enchantment – it's hard to think of a more evocative place name than 'Zanzibar' and the reality doesn't disappoint.

STARRING ROLE IN...

- *Admiring Silence* and *By the Sea* by Abdulrazak Gurnah
- *Zanzibar* by Giles Foden
- *Revolution in Zanzibar: An American's Cold War Tale* by Don Petterson
- *Dhows & Colonial Economy In Zanzibar : 1860–1970* by Erik Gilbert
- *Zanzibar Stone Town: an Architectural Exploration* by Abdul Sheriff
- *Zanzibar Style* by Javed Jafferji and Gemma Pitcher

IMPORT

- Spices – originally from Asia
- Merchants from around the Indian Ocean
- Honeymooners from Europe
- Property developers lusting after idyllic beaches

EXPORT

- Slaves and ivory (in the bad old days)
- Cloves, cinnamon, cardamom
- Farokh Bulsara, better known as Freddie Mercury
- *Taarab* music – a fusion of African, Arabic and Indian rhythms
- Dr Livingstone, who set off to explore Africa's interior from his base in Zanzibar

SEE the Festival of the Dhow countries (every year in July), where participants come from around the Indian Ocean.

EAT savoury pilau at the Passing Show restaurant.

DRINK chai, milky and sweet.

DO a Spice Tour with Mr Mitu and learn all there is to know about the spice trade.

WATCH the moon rise over the dhow harbour and the House of Wonders.

BUY spices, silver jewellery or fabrics *(kangas and kikois)*.

AFTER DARK head for any of the bars overlooking the bay.

URBAN MYTH

The 11th (and last) Sultan of Zanzibar was granted asylum in England after the revolution in 1964. He lived modestly in Portsmouth – in marked contrast to his earlier life on Zanzibar – on an annual stipend from the British government.

ON THE PROWL FOR FEATHERED BARGAINS AT THE CHICKEN MARKET IN STONE TOWN.
Photographer: Bethune Carmichael / LPI

A SMILING WOMAN PEERS FROM A LAVISH WOODEN DOORWAY IN STONE TOWN.
Photographer: Ariadne Van Zandbergen / LPI

AD FOR A BEAUTY STORE – EVERYTHING FROM MANICURES TO…ERR…MAKING BRIDES?
Photographer: Mitch Reardon / LPI

A SCENE UNCHANGED THROUGH THE CENTURIES – ENCHANTING DHOWS MOORED AT SHANGANI POINT.
Photographer: David Else / LPI

THE CITIES BOOK
A Journey Through the Best Cities in the World
October 2009

Published by:
Lonely Planet Publications Pty Ltd
ABN 36 005 607 983
90 Maribyrnong St, Footscray,
Victoria 3011, Australia
www.lonelyplanet.com

10 9 8 7 6 5 4

Printed in China.

Photographs:
Many of the images in this book are available for licensing from Lonely Planet Images.
www.lonelyplanetimages.com

ISBN 978 1 74179 887 6

Lonely Planet Offices
Australia Locked Bag 1, Footscray, Victoria, 3011
Phone 03 8379 8000 Fax 03 8379 8111
Email talk2us@lonelyplanet.com.au

USA 150 Linden St, Oakland, CA 94607
Phone 510 250 6400 Toll free 800 275 8555 Fax 510 893 8572
Email info@lonelyplanet.com

UK Media Centre (GH0S), 201 Wood Lane, London, W12 7TQ
Phone (44) 20 8433 1333 Fax (44) 20 8702 0112
Email go@lonelyplanet.co.uk

PAPERBACK
Publisher: Chris Rennie
Associate Publisher: Ben Handicott
Project Managers: Jane Atkin, Kate Morgan
Print Production: Graham Imeson
Pre-press Production: Ryan Evans
Managing Layout Designer: Sally Darmody
Layout Designer: Nicholas Colicchia, Indra Kilfoyle, Clara Monitto
Editors: Trent Holden, Anna Metcalfe

Thanks to the team who worked on the hardback edition:
Roz Hopkins, Laetitia Clapton, Bridget Blair, Jenny Bilos, Daniel New, Brendan Dempsey, Kaitlin
Beckett, Vicki Beale, Rebecca Dandens, Glenn Beanland, Jane Pennells, Pepi Bluck, Martine
Lleonart, Adrienne Costanzo, Elizabeth Swan, Wayne Murphy

Text: The text in this book is partially based on Lonely Planet's guide books, trade and
reference books and website content, which is researched and written by a global team of
staff and authors. Content for this book was researched and compiled by: Holly Alexander,
Samone Bos, James Bridle, Laetitia Clapton, Karina Coates, George Dunford, Susannah Farfor,
Will Gourlay, Robert Harding, John Hinman, Niki Horin, Piers Kelly, Martine Lleonart, Ian
Malcolm, Jodie Martire, Tom Masters, Laura McKay, Sally O'Brien, Miriam Raphael, Craig Scutt,
Jo Vraca, Katrina Webb, Donna Wheeler, Sarah Wintle

Image captions: Tenar Dwyer, Niki Horin, Piers Kelly, Vivek Wagle
Cities Past, Present & Future: Craig Scutt

Cover photographs: Lonely Planet Images: front cover No 1, 5, 6, back cover No 3, 6
Getty Images: front cover No 2, 3, 4, 7, 8, back cover No 1, 2, 4, 5, 7, 8